Building English Skills

Blue Level
Revised Edition

Building English Skills

THE McDOUGAL, LITTELL ENGLISH PROGRAM

Building English Skills

Blue Level
Revised Edition

Joy Littell, EDITORIAL DIRECTOR

McDougal, Littell & Company
Evanston, Illinois
Sacramento, California

Prepared by the Staff of
THE WRITING IMPROVEMENT PROJECT

Joy Littell, Editorial Director, McDougal, Littell & Company

J. A. Christensen, East High School, Salt Lake City, Utah

Stephen G. Ham, New Trier Township High School East, Winnetka, Illinois

William H. Horst, Henrico County Schools, Virginia

Alice E. Johnson, Librarian, Evanston Township High School, Evanston, Illinois

Patricia Phelan, Chairman of the English Department, Hale Jr. High School, San Diego, California

Debbie Rosenberger, teacher and writer; formerly, Henrico County Schools, Virginia

Marcia Baldwin Whipps, East High School, Salt Lake City, Utah

The Staff wishes to thank the more than 1500 students who contributed samples of their writing for analysis.

Acknowledgments: See page 537.

ISBN: 0–88343–884–4

Chapters 1, 2, 4, and the Handbook contain, in revised form, some materials that appeared originally in *English Arts and Skills,* by Ronald J. Wilkins et al, copyright © 1965, 1961 by The Macmillan Company. Used by arrangement.

Contents

**The Table of Contents for the Handbook
begins on the next page.**

Handbook

12.0 The Semicolon, the Colon, the Dash, and Parentheses 474

13.0 The Apostrophe 483

14.0 Quotations 491

The Composition Chapters   (First half of text)

Vocabulary Development.   Chapter 1 emphasizes the study of *prefixes, suffixes,* and *roots and word families.* Chapter 2 analyzes each item of a dictionary entry as a basis for building word power. An adequate vocabulary, and the ability to use synonyms precisely, are prerequisites to good writing.

Sentence Combining.   Chapter 3 presents a basic course in sentence combining. Its purpose is to help students create mature sentences, and to help them become aware of the options open to them in combining ideas.

Sentence Improvement.   Chapter 4 provides an intensive program for sentence improvement based on a study of over 3000 student themes. The chapter is devoted to those sentences which, though grammatically correct, are nonetheless unsatisfactory. It deals with empty sentences, the circular sentences that say nothing; it also deals with overloaded sentences, the sentences that contain too many ideas.

The Process of Writing.   Chapter 5 analyzes the three major steps in writing: *pre-writing; writing the first draft;* and *rewriting, or revising,* which includes proofreading.

The Paragraph.   Chapters 6 and 7 comprise an intensive study of the paragraph. Chapter 6 emphasizes unity and coherence, and the importance of the topic sentence. Chapter 7 treats in detail the narrative paragraph, the descriptive paragraph, and the explanatory paragraph. Both chapters provide a wealth of first-rate models, along with helpful analysis.

The Composition.   Chapter 8 provides a clear, workable blueprint for an expository composition, or report. Chapter 9 deals with narrative, descriptive, and explanatory compositions.

Letters, Applications, and Résumés.   Chapter 10 presents the proper forms for business letters and discusses various types of business letters. It also provides help in filling out college and job applications and in writing résumés.

The Handbook   (Second half of text)

The Handbook is arranged in 18 numbered sections, as follows:

Grammar.   Sections 1–4 provide a thorough treatment of grammar in a contemporary setting.

Usage.   Sections 5–9 deal with problems of usage.

Capitalization, Punctuation, Spelling, and Manuscript Form.   Sections 10–18 deal with the mechanics of writing.

Special Features of the Handbook.   The Handbook has distinct advantages over other available handbooks:

1. The typographic arrangement is clear and attractive. Type and open space have been used to set off definitions and examples so as to make them easy to find and easy to read.

2 Within each topic, there is a full explanation of each concept, followed by examples, and where appropriate, by the definition or generalization printed in boldface type.

Chapter 1

Building Your Vocabulary

Vocabulary development is a lifelong process. It begins with a child's first utterance of "da-da" or "ma-ma." By the time they enter first grade, most children have vocabularies in excess of 10,000 words. Most well educated adults have vocabularies ranging upward from 50,000 words. The size of your vocabulary bears a close relationship to your success, not only in school, but also in your career. For this reason alone, it is important for you to adopt a system of vocabulary development.

This chapter sets forth an efficient method of developing your vocabulary. The method is based on a mastery of word parts and certain "families" of related English words. It involves a careful examination of *prefixes*, *suffixes*, and *roots*.

Part 1 Prefixes

One way to increase your vocabulary is to learn to recognize and to use prefixes. A **prefix** is one or more syllables placed in front of a root word to change the meaning of the root. Just as each root word in our language has one or more meanings, so does every prefix. By adding prefixes to roots, you can construct new words. For example:

PREFIX		ROOT		NEW WORD
dis	+	appear	=	disappear
re	+	appear	=	reappear
pre	+	arrange	=	prearrange

Some prefixes have a single, unchanging meaning. Other prefixes have more than one meaning. In this chapter you will study both groups of prefixes.

The following prefixes are useful to know because each one has a single, unchanging meaning.

Prefixes Having a Single Meaning

PREFIX	MEANING	EXAMPLE OF USE	MEANING
bene-	good	benefit	anything for the good of a person or thing
circum-	around	circumscribe	to draw a line around something
equi-	equal	equidistant	equally distant
extra-	outside	extracurricular	outside the curriculum
intra-	within	intrastate	within a state's boundaries
intro-	into	introspect	to look into one's own thoughts
mal-	bad	maltreat	to treat badly
mis-	wrong	misspell	to spell wrong
non-	not	nonworking	not working

| pre- | before | predawn | before dawn |
| sub- | under or below | subzero | below zero |

Some prefixes are useful in unlocking word meanings even though the prefixes have more than one meaning.

Prefixes Having More Than One Meaning

PREFIX	MEANING	EXAMPLE OF USE	MEANING
dis-	1. opposite of	distrust	the opposite of trust
	2. depriving of	dispirit	to deprive of cheerful spirits
	3. away	dispatch	to send off or away
in- ir- il- im-	1. not	incomplete impossible irregular	not complete not possible not regular
	2. in, into	investigate	to look into
	3. very	illustrious	shining brightly, famous
pro-	1. in favor of	procapitalism	in favor of capitalism
	2. forward, ahead	propel	to push forward
re-	1. again	replant	to plant again
	2. back	repay	to pay back
super-	1. over and above	superhuman	more than human, above human
	2. very large	supertanker	very large tanker
trans-	1. across	transatlantic	across the Atlantic
	2. beyond	transnational	beyond national boundaries
un-	1. not	unafraid	not afraid
	2. the opposite of	untie	the opposite of tie

Exercises **Prefixes**

A. Determine the meaning of the prefix in each word below. If necessary, refer to the list of prefixes on pages 2 and 3. Try to determine the meaning of each word by adding the meaning of the prefix to the meaning of the root.

1. preplan	6. submarine	11. benediction
2. extraordinary	7. nonpoisonous	12. miscalculate
3. prejudge	8. extrasensory	13. nonviolent
4. misjudge	9. intravenous	14. pretest
5. intramuscular	10. malfunction	15. circumnavigate

B. The prefix *in-* has three distinct meanings.

in- = not	Example:	incorrect
in- = in or into	Example:	input
in- = very	Example:	invaluable

The prefix *in-* often becomes

ir- before a word beginning with *r*	Example:	irregular
il- before *l*	Example:	illuminate
im- before *b, p,* or *m*	Example:	imbalance
		impatient
		immobile

Decide which of the three meanings of *in-* applies in each of the following words:

1. insert	5. immobile	9. irrelevant
2. incapable	6. illogical	10. imperfect
3. inhale	7. immigrate	11. illegal
4. insensitive	8. irresponsible	12. inactive

C. Replace each italicized phrase with a single word. Each word should contain one of the prefixes you have learned.

1. Stealing is *not legal*. Stealing is _____.

2. It is *not probable* that a lion will make a good pet. Lions are _____ pets.

3. My respect for her *is not measurable*. My respect for her is _____.

4. Paper is *very flammable*. Paper is _____.

5. Please *tell* that story *again*. Please _____ that story.

6. That ship sails *across the Pacific*. It is a _____ ship.

7. The explorers went on a search *outside the territorial* boundaries. It was an _____ search.

8. Her good nature was *wrongly used*. Her good nature was _____.

9. This area is *not residential*. It is a _____ area.

10. The check was *dated beforehand*. The check was _____.

D. The prefixes in the following words all have more than one meaning. Decide which meaning of the prefix applies in each case. Then give the meaning of the word.

1. retype
2. transoceanic
3. supersonic
4. unfasten
5. pro-American
6. unravel
7. proagreement
8. transcultural
9. restate
10. disembark
11. ingenius
12. superpower
13. impatient
14. inorganic
15. disregard

Part 2 Suffixes

Another way to increase your vocabulary is to use *suffixes*. A **suffix** is one or more syllables placed after a root word to form a new word. Like prefixes, each suffix has its own meaning or meanings. Once you know different suffixes and their meanings, you can attach them to roots to form new words. For example:

ROOT		SUFFIX		NEW WORD
appear	+	-ance	=	appearance
adjust	+	-ment	=	adjustment
arrange	+	-ment	=	arrangement
friend	+	-ship	=	friendship

Study the following groups of suffixes. Once you learn their meanings, you will further increase your ability to recognize the basic meanings of words.

Noun Suffixes

Noun Suffixes That Mean "One Who Does Something"

SUFFIX	EXAMPLE OF USE	MEANING
-ant	commandant	one who commands
-eer	auctioneer	one who auctions
-er	photographer	one who takes photographs
-ist	geologist	one who studies or is experienced in geology
-ician	magician	one who performs magic

Notice that all the words listed above refer to people who do something. The suffixes *-ant, -eer, -er, -ist,* and *-ician* tell you that the word describes a person who does something.

Noun Suffixes That Make Abstract Words

SUFFIX	EXAMPLES OF USE
-ance, -ence	vigilance, independence
-ation, -ition	imagination, condition
-dom	freedom
-hood	womanhood
-ice	cowardice
-ism	realism
-ment	encouragement
-ness	kindness
-ship	friendship
-tude	solitude
-ty, -ity	frailty, ability

All of the words listed are abstract words. They describe a state of being. For example, *heroism* is the state of being heroic. *Frailty* is the state of being frail. What abstract word would describe the state of being romantic?

Exercises Suffixes

A. From each of the words listed below, form another word by adding a noun suffix that means "one who does something."

1. electric	5. racket	9. manage
2. biology	6. engine	10. mathematics
3. novel	7. machine	11. profit
4. politics	8. beauty	12. ideal

B. The following words can be changed so that they function as abstract nouns. Add a suffix that will change each word so that it can function as a noun. (Be careful of spelling changes as you form the nouns. Check a dictionary if you are not sure of the spelling of a word.)

1. nonviolent	5. equal	9. add
2. wise	6. judge	10. limit
3. note	7. real	11. child
4. friendly	8. assign	12. resign

Adjective Suffixes

The following suffixes mean "full of." When you add these suffixes to a root, you change the root to an adjective. You also change the meaning of the root.

Adjective Suffixes That Mean "Full of"

SUFFIX	EXAMPLES OF USE	MEANING
-ous	furious	full of fury
-ose	verbose	wordy (full of words)
-acious	vivacious	full of vivacity
-ful	harmful	full of harm

The adjective suffixes listed below mean "relating to" or "pertaining to." When added to a root, they change the word to an adjective.

Adjective Suffixes That Mean "Relating to" or "Pertaining to"

SUFFIX	EXAMPLE OF USE	MEANING
-al	musical	relating to music
-ant	triumphant	relating to triumph
-ic	heroic	pertaining to a hero; like a hero
-ical	economical	pertaining to economy
-ative	talkative	relating to talk
-ish	childish	relating to a child; like a child
-ive	active	pertaining to action

The word *music* is a noun. When the adjective suffix *-al* is added to it, it becomes the adjective *musical*.

The following adjective suffixes mean exactly what they say. You can unlock the meanings of certain words by taking them apart. If you understand the meanings of both the suffix and the root, you will understand the meaning of the combination.

Adjective Suffixes That Mean What They Say

SUFFIX	EXAMPLE OF USE	MEANING
-able, -ible	readable convertible	able to be read able to be converted
-most	topmost	being at the very top
-less	senseless	without sense (less sense)
-like	lifelike	like life

Exercises **Adjective Suffixes**

A. What clues do the suffixes give you to the meaning of the following words? Try to determine the meaning of each word. Then check a dictionary.

1. bookish	6. additive	11. historical
2. cautious	7. peerless	12. reducible
3. grandiose	8. laudable	13. uppermost
4. wakeful	9. credible	14. communicative
5. angelic	10. biological	15. exultant

B. Most dictionaries list *irregardless* as "nonstandard or humorous." Why is *irregardless* considered improper usage? What is the correct word to express this idea?

C. What is the meaning of *inflammable?* Why could this word be misinterpreted?

D. Many of the words in the following list may be unfamiliar to you. However, you should be able to determine their meanings from what you have learned in this chapter. Use each word in a sentence that shows your understanding of the meaning of the word. Then check your use of the word with the dictionary definitions.

1. unabridged	6. interpreter	11. subterranean
2. impractical	7. pompous	12. incompetence
3. provocative	8. malformation	13. uninformative
4. melodious	9. maladjusted	14. imprecise
5. immobility	10. prohibitive	15. transaction

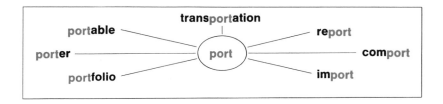

Part 3 Roots and Word Families

Another way to develop your vocabulary is to become familiar with roots. The **root** is the part of a word that contains its basic meaning. A great many roots used in our language originally came from Latin. Each of the following Latin roots is responsible for a whole family of English words. If you know the meanings of these roots, you will be able to unlock the basic meaning of many new English words.

Eight Useful Latin Roots

ROOT	MEANING	EXAMPLES OF ENGLISH WORDS
capt	take, hold, seize	capture, captive, captivate
cede, ceed, cess	go, yield, give away	recede, recession
dic, dict	speak, say, tell	dictate, diction, dictator
cred	believe	credit, creed, credible
duc, duct	lead	induce, conductor, conducive
fac, fec	do, make	factory, defector, fact
mit, miss	send	remit, missile, mission
pon, pos, posit	place, put	component, deposit, position

Exercises **Latin Roots**

A. Examine each of the following roots and give its meaning. Then use your knowledge of prefixes and suffixes to tell what each word means. Check a dictionary to see if your meanings are correct.

1. cap<u>tiv</u>ity
2. <u>port</u>able
3. <u>cred</u>ence
4. pro<u>ceed</u>
5. dis<u>pose</u>

6. <u>dic</u>tation
7. <u>fac</u>tual
8. in<u>duct</u>
9. pre<u>cede</u>
10. trans<u>mit</u>

11. bene<u>fac</u>tor
12. transpose
13. <u>cred</u>ible
14. dis<u>miss</u>al
15. e<u>duc</u>ate

B. Each of the following sentences contains a word or group of words that can be expressed by using one of the eight Latin roots listed on page 10. Decide which word is derived from a Latin root. Then add a prefix or a suffix to the root to form the proper word.

Example: That story is simply *not believable.*
That story is *incredible*

1. The army *seized* the fort. The army _____ the fort.

2. Please *send back* your payment. Please _____ your payment.

3. This is the part of the engine where air is *let in*. This is the _____ chamber.

4. A _____ is a place where things are *made*.

5. She told a very *believable* lie. She told a very _____ lie.

6. At low tide, the level of the ocean water *went back* down. The water _____.

7. The *placement* of the verb in the sentence is incorrect. The _____ of the verb in the sentence is incorrect.

8. We were *sent* to find water. Finding water was our _____.

9. A _____ is a book that *tells* us the meanings of words.

10. I *put* my entire pay check into my savings account last week, but this time I will _____ only half of it.

Eight More Useful Latin Roots

ROOT	MEANING	EXAMPLES OF ENGLISH WORDS
port	carry	porter, portable, export
scrib, script	write	inscribe, description, scripture
spec	look, see	spectacle, inspector, spectator
stat	stand, put in place	statue, stature, static
vers, vert	turn	versatile, convert, vertical
vid, vis	see	video, vision
voc, vok	call	invoke, revoke, vocation
vol	wish	volunteer, malevolent

Exercises Latin Roots

A. Examine each of the following roots and give its meaning. Then use your knowledge of prefixes and suffixes to tell what each word means. Check a dictionary to see if your meanings are correct.

1. inspector
2. volunteer
3. scribe
4. export
5. stature
6. invert
7. porter
8. video
9. static
10. transport
11. vocal
12. scripture
13. invoke
14. spectator
15. respect

B. The following sentences all contain a word or group of words that can be expressed by using one of the eight Latin roots listed above. Decide which word is derived from a Latin root. Then add a prefix or suffix to the root to form the proper word.

1. A person who *wishes good* for others is _____.
2. Teaching is my *calling* in life. Teaching is my _____.
3. Dr. Jekyll *turned back* into Mr. Hyde. He _____ to his other personality.

4. Coffee is *carried into* our country from Brazil. Coffee is
_____ into our country from Brazil.

5. The train *stood* at the _____.

6. If John watches, or *looks at*, the football game, he is a
_____.

7. The parts of an atom cannot be seen. They are _____.

8. Glasses are sometimes called _____ because they help
us to *see*.

Word Families

A **word family** is a group of words that have a common root. You
can develop your vocabulary by recognizing these roots and looking for them in difficult or unfamiliar words.

As you have learned, the Latin root *scrib, script* means "write."
Many English words contain this root:

scribe   script
scribble   scripture

Many additional words that contain this root have prefixes
added in front of the root.

subscribe   postscript
prescribe   transcript

Still other words that contain this root have both prefixes and
suffixes.

prescription   inscription
description   descriptive

All of the words listed above belong to the same word family.
All of them are derived from the Latin root *scrib, script*, meaning
"write."

Being able to identify the root in a longer word will help you
unlock its meaning. Also, seeing how words are grouped into word
families will give you a method of sorting out the new words you
read or hear.

Exercises Word Families

A. Listed below are several different word families. For each word family, identify the Latin root. Then add two other words to each family. Tell why each new word belongs to the family.

1. capture
   recapture
   caption

2. incredible
   credence
   creditor

3. remit
   commit
   mission

4. spectacle
   introspection
   specimen

5. vision
   television
   visual

6. import
   export
   portable

7. repose
   postpone
   position

8. recess
   procession
   secede

9. duct
   conduct
   reduce

B. For each of the following words, identify the word family. Make a chart and fill it in. Use your knowledge of prefixes, suffixes, roots, and word families. The first line has been completed for you.

	WORD	FAMILY	ROOT MEANING	WORD MEANING
1.	transmit	mit, miss	send	send across
2.	dictator			
3.	reverse			
4.	circumspect			
5.	vocal			
6.	benefactor			
7.	malevolent			
8.	substation			

C. Senator Verbosa Pomposity has given the following speech to her Committee on Intergalactic Affairs. It contains many difficult words. Use your knowledge of prefixes, suffixes, roots, and word families to "translate" the speech so that Verbosa's message is more effective and more easily understood by her committee.

Involuntarily, I must superimpose upon my otherwise benevolent visage a mood and tone of severity and impatience. You have been informed an inestimable number of times as to my extraordinary knowledge of extraterrestrial beings. Additionally, I have frequently speculated on the adverse effects of interplanetary transit by inhabitants of alien galaxies. Uppermost in my concerns are the distasteful Green Pooklas from the planet Gerbiga. Regardless of my informative speeches and provocative lectures as your chairperson, these unrelenting invaders have been allowed to disembark their excessively irregular space vehicles in suburban Zonar. Their preoccupancy of the Stellar Pad has greatly distressed the Zonar Startreks. I am absolutely positive that the situation is ominous.

Legislation, namely a statute encouraging transcultural disassociation with such horrific individuals as the Green Pooklas, must be introduced immediately. My more lenient opponents must be dissuaded from their equivocal stance. Do not allow them to circumvent the issue. The statute must be inalterable and unambiguous. The malevolent Green Pooklas, superhuman though they may appear, are disruptive and invasive. The intrepid Zonar Startreks must regain their vocational post. And as equitable, nonprejudiced realists, we as a committee must find an alternative destination for future Pookla teams seeking encampment facilities. However, Zonar must be rendered safe from further extraterrestrial intervention.

Chapter 2

Using the Dictionary To Build Word Power

Dr. Samuel Johnson, the author of one of the most famous English dictionaries, said:

> Dictionaries are like watches; the worst is better than none, and the best cannot be expected to go quite true.

Even though Dr. Johnson lived over 200 years ago, his statement is still true. Languages are constantly changing, and dictionaries must change to reflect the changes in the languages.

The dictionary is an invaluable aid to every educated person. When it is used to its fullest extent, the dictionary can provide a great deal of useful information. Unfortunately, many people do not know how to get the most out of a dictionary. This section is designed to help you use the dictionary more effectively.

Abridged and Unabridged Dictionaries

In the reference section of your school or public library, you have probably seen a huge dictionary placed on a special stand. This is an **unabridged dictionary.** This massive volume contains several hundred thousand detailed entries. Occasionally you will need to use an unabridged dictionary. For most of your work, however, you will find it much more convenient to use an **abridged dictionary.** The smaller size of the abridged dictionary makes it easier to use. There are many good abridged dictionaries that contain enough information to answer most of your questions.

Since dictionaries differ in their organization, symbols, and abbreviations, you will probably find it most helpful to use one dictionary consistently. Even if you don't have a dictionary of your own, you should become familiar with a dictionary in your classroom or library. A thorough understanding of one particular dictionary will prove more beneficial than an incomplete understanding of the organization of several dictionaries. As your skill in using the dictionary increases, you will, of course, want to learn to use other dictionaries.

Part 1 Finding Information in the Dictionary

What's on a Dictionary Page?

As you study the information given below, refer to the dictionary page reproduced on pages 22 and 23.

1. **Guide Words.** The two large words printed at the top of the page are **guide words.** These indicate the first and last words entered alphabetically on that page. You should check the introduction to the dictionary to see how words are alphabetized in that dictionary. (For example, Is *St. Louis* entered under *st-* or *sa-?*) The guide words should help speed up your process of locating a word.

2. **Entry.** All of the information about a word in the dictionary is called an **entry.** In the dictionary page reprinted here, each entry follows this general pattern:

    a. entry word
    b. pronunciation (or pronunciations)
    c. part of speech
    d. etymology
    e. definition (or definitions)
    f. synonymy
    g. words derived from the entry word
    h. cross reference

Not every item is included for every entry.

3. **Key.** In most dictionaries, the bottom right-hand page contains a **key** to the pronunciation symbols and other symbols used in the dictionary. There is usually a fuller set of symbols and abbreviations given at the front or back of the dictionary.

What's in a Dictionary Entry?

A closer look at the entry for the word *enmity* will help illustrate the entry items listed above.

Entry Words. Printed in dark type, the **entry word** is divided into syllables. Occasionally, when you are writing or typing a paper, it may be necessary to divide a long word, putting it on two separate lines. Custom dictates that such division occur only between syllables. You may need to check the syllabication of a word in order to divide the word correctly.

Pronunciation. Follow the entry words, the pronunciation is given in parentheses. Since different dictionaries use different pronunciation and accent symbols, it is important for you to understand the system your dictionary uses. By using the pronunciation key at the bottom of the page, you can determine the pronunciation of *enmity*. If a word has more than one acceptable pronunciation, or if the word is pronounced in different ways at different times (for example, *contract*), those differences will be explained at this point.

Part of Speech. The letter *n.* following the pronunciation indicates that *enmity* is a noun. If the plural of a noun is not formed by simply adding *-s* or *-es* to the singular form, most dictionaries give the correct spelling of the plural form at this point. The designation *pl.* -**ties** tells that the correct spelling of the plural form is *enmities*.

Etymology. The material printed within the dark brackets gives the etymology of the word *enmity*. **Etymology** is the tracing of a word back to its origins. The symbols <OFr<L. tell that the word comes from an Old French word which was derived from the Latin word *inimicus*. The word ENEMY printed in small capital letters is a cross reference. By turning to the entry for *enemy* on another page, you can learn that the Latin word *inimicus* is a compound of the prefix *in-*, meaning "not," and the word *amicus*, meaning "friend."

Definition. Following the etymology, you find the definition of the word *enmity*. Frequently, this may be your only reason for looking up a word, but as you can see from the preceding discussion, each dictionary entry gives much more than just the definition.

Synonymy. The abbreviation *SYN.* after the definition indicates the **synonymy.** Here you find a discussion of words that are similar in meaning to *enmity*. This synonymy points out the slight differences in the meanings of *enmity*, *hostility*, *animosity*, and *antagonism*.

Derived Words. Following some of the entries on this page (for example, *enlist* and *ensign*), you will notice additional words, printed in bold type and divided into syllables. These are words that are derived from the entry word. These words are so closely related to the entry word that the editors of the dictionary did not feel it necessary to list them as separate entries.

Cross Reference. In the discussion of the etymology of *enmity,* you saw an example of **cross reference.** The word ENEMY printed in small capital letters tells you to turn to another entry for additional information about the etymology of this word. Note also the cross reference at the end of the entry for *ensue.* If you look closely, you will find additional cross references on this page.

Exercise Learning How To Use the Dictionary

The questions below are designed to ensure your understanding of how to get information from a dictionary. In answering the questions, refer to the sample dictionary page reproduced on pages 22 and 23.

1. What is an etymology?

2. Where could you find more information about the origin of the word *entail?*

3. Where could you find more information about the origin of the word *ensign?*

4. What is a synonymy?

5. Where would you find a synonymy of words similar in meaning to *ensue?*

6. The abbreviations *vt.* and *vi.,* as in the entry for *enlist,* often give students problems. The abbreviation *vt.* indicates that in this sense the verb is *transitive,* one that takes a direct object. **Vi.** means that the verb is *intransitive,* one that does not take a direct object. Study carefully the entry for *enlist* and write one sentence using *enlist* as a transitive verb and one sentence using it as an intransitive verb.

7. What does the double dagger symbol (‡) before the entry *en rapport* indicate? Why is there no such symbol before *en masse, ennui,* and *entente?*

8. What does the symbol ☆ indicate before the second definition of *enlistment?*

9. What does the symbol < mean?

10. What does the hyphen indicate before the entry *-ent?*

11. Study carefully the synonymy following the entry for *enmity.* Use each of the synonyms listed there in a separate sentence. Write your sentences in such a way that the differences in the meanings become clearer.

en·list (in list′) **vt.** 1. to enroll in some branch of the armed forces 2. to win the support of; get the help or services of [to *enlist* men in a cause] 3. to get (another's help, support, etc.) —**vi.** 1. to join some branch of the armed forces 2. to join or support a cause or movement (with *in*) —**en·list·ee′ n.**

enlisted man any man in the armed forces who is not a commissioned officer or warrant officer

en·list·ment (-mənt) **n.** 1. an enlisting or being enlisted ☆2. the period for which one enlists

en·liv·en (in liv′n) **vt.** to make active, lively, interesting, or cheerful; liven up or brighten [*to enliven* a party by playing games] —**en·liv′en·er n.** —**en·liv′en·ment n.**

en masse (en mas′; *Fr.* än mäs′) [Fr., lit., in mass] in a group; as a whole; all together

en·mesh (en mesh′) **vt.** to catch in or as in the meshes of a net; entangle

en·mi·ty (en′mə tē) **n., pl. -ties** [< OFr. < L. *inimicus*, ENEMY] the bitter attitude or feelings of an enemy or mutual enemies; hostility

SYN.—enmity denotes a strong, fixed feeling of hatred, whether hidden or openly shown; **hostility** suggests open enmity shown in active opposition, attacks, etc.; **animosity** suggests bitterness of feeling, usually in personal relationships, that tends to break out in open hostility; **antagonism** stresses the opposition of persons, forces, etc. that compete or work against each other

en·no·ble (i nō′b'l) **vt. -bled, -bling** 1. to raise to the rank of nobleman 2. to give a noble quality to; dignify —**en·no′ble·ment n.** —**en·no′bler n.**

en·nui (än′wē; *Fr.* än nwē′) **n.** [Fr.: see ANNOY] a feeling of being very bored and tired of everything; boredom

e·nor·mi·ty (i nôr′mə tē) **n., pl. -ties** [< Fr. < L. < *enormis*, irregular, immense < *e-*, out + *norma*, rule: for IE. base see KNOW] 1. great wickedness [the *enormity* of a crime] 2. a very wicked crime 3. enormous size or extent: generally considered a loose usage

e·nor·mous (i nôr′məs) **adj.** [see prec.] 1. very large or very great; huge 2. [Archaic] very wicked; outrageous —**e·nor′mous·ly adv.** —**e·nor′mous·ness n.**

en route (än rōōt′, en) [Fr.] on or along the way

Ens. Ensign

En·sche·de (en′skhə dā′) city in E Netherlands, near the German border: pop. 136,000

en·sconce (in skäns′) **vt. -sconced′, -sconc′ing** [EN- + *sconce*, a small fort] 1. [Now Rare] to hide; conceal; shelter 2. to place or settle snugly [*to ensconce* oneself in an armchair]

en·sem·ble (än säm′b'l) **n.** [Fr. < OFr. < L. < *in-*, in + *simul*, at the same time] 1. all the parts considered as a whole; total effect 2. a whole costume, esp. of matching or complementary articles of dress 3. a company of actors, dancers, etc. 4. *Music a)* a small group of musicians performing together *b)* their instruments or voices *c)* the performance together of such a group, or of an orchestra, chorus, etc.

en·shrine (in shrin′) **vt. -shrined′, -shrin′ing** 1. to enclose in or as in a shrine 2. to hold as sacred; cherish [*enshrined* in memory] —**en·shrine′ment n.**

en·shroud (-shroud′) **vt.** to cover as if with a shroud; hide; veil; obscure [towers *enshrouded* in mist]

en·sign (en′sin; *also, and for 4 always*, -s'n) **n.** [< OFr. < L. < *insignia*: see INSIGNIA] 1. a badge, symbol, or token of office or authority 2. a flag or banner; specif., a national flag, as one displayed on a ship 3. *Brit. Army* formerly, a commissioned officer who served as standard-bearer ☆4. *U.S. Navy* a commissioned officer of the lowest rank, ranking below a lieutenant junior grade —**en′sign·ship′, en′sign·cy n.**

en·si·lage (en′s'l ij) **n.** [Fr.] 1. the preserving of green fodder by storage in a silo 2. green fodder so preserved; silage

en·sile (en sil′) **vt. -siled′, -sil′ing** [Fr. *ensiler*] to store (green fodder) in a silo

en·slave (in slāv′) **vt. -slaved′, -slav′ing** 1. to put into slavery; make a slave of 2. to keep complete control over; dominate; subjugate [she was *enslaved* by her work] —**en·slave′ment n.** —**en·slav′er n.**

en·snare (-sner′) **vt. -snared′, -snar′ing** to catch in or as in a snare; trap —**en·snare′ment n.**

en·snarl (-snärl′) **vt.** to draw into a snarl or tangle

SYN.—**enormous** implies a going far beyond what is normal in size, amount, or degree [an enormous room; enormous expenses]; **immense** implies size beyond the usual measurements but suggests that great size is normal for the thing described [redwoods are immense trees]; **huge** usually suggests a great mass or bulk [a huge building; huge profits]; **gigantic, colossal,** and **mammoth** originally implied a likeness to a giant, the Colossus of Rhodes, and an extinct elephant (the mammoth), and therefore these words emphasize the idea of great size, force, importance, etc., now often in an exaggerated way; **tremendous** literally suggests that which causes awe or amazement because of its great size

e·nough (i nuf′) *adj.* [OE. *genoh*] as much or as many as needed or wanted; sufficient [*enough* money to pay the bills] —*n.* the amount or number needed or wanted —*adv.* 1. as much or as often as necessary; sufficiently [the stew is not cooked *enough*] 2. fully; quite [oddly *enough*] 3. just adequately; tolerably; fairly [he played well *enough*]

e·now (i nou′) *adj., n., adv.* [Archaic] enough

en·plane (en plān′) *vi.* **-planed′, -plan′ing** to board an airplane

en·quire (in kwīr′) *vt., vi.* **-quired′, -quir′ing** *same as* INQUIRE —**en·quir′y** *n., pl.* **-quir′ies**

en·rage (in rāj′) *vt.* **-raged′, -rag′ing** to put into a rage; make very angry; infuriate —**en·rage′ment** *n.*

‡**en rap·port** (än rà pôr′) [Fr.] in harmony; in sympathy; in accord

en·rapt (in rapt′) *adj.* enraptured; rapt

en·rap·ture (-rap′char) *vt.* **-tured, -tur·ing** to fill with great pleasure or delight: also **en·rav′ish**

en·rich (in rich′) *vt.* to make rich or richer; specif., *a*) to give more wealth to *b*) to give greater value or effectiveness to [to *enrich* a curriculum] *c*) to decorate; adorn *d*) to fertilize (soil) *e*) to add vitamins, minerals, etc. to (bread, etc.) for more food value —**en·rich′ment** *n.*

en·roll, en·rol (in rōl′) *vt.* **-rolled′, -roll′ing** 1. to record in a list 2. to enlist 3. to accept as a member —*vi.* to enroll oneself or become enrolled; register; become a member —**en·roll′ee′** *n.* **en·roll·ment, en·rol·ment** (-mant) *n.* 1. an enrolling or being enrolled 2. a list of those enrolled 3. the number of those enrolled

en·sue (in sōō′, -syōō′) [< Fr. *ensuer* ... *insequi* < *in-*, in + *sequi*, to follow] 1. to come afterward; follow immediately [we met and a long friendship *ensued*] 2. to happen as a consequence; result [the damage that *ensued* from the flood] —see SYN. at FOLLOW

en·sure (in shoor′) *vt.* **-sured′, -sur′ing** [< Anglo-Fr. *enseurer:* see EN- & SURE] 1. to make sure; guarantee [measures to *ensure* accuracy] 2. to make safe; protect [safety devices to *ensure* workers against accidents]

-ent (ant, 'nt) [< OFr. *-ent*, L. *-ens* (gen. *-entis*), stem ending of certain present participles] 1. *a suffix meaning* that has, shows, or does [insistent] 2. *a suffix meaning* a person or thing that [superintendent, solvent]

en·tab·la·ture (en tab′lə char) *n.* [MFr. < It. *intavolatura* < *in-*, in + *tavola* < L. *tabula*, TABLE] *Archit.* 1. a horizontal structure supported by columns and composed of architrave, frieze, and cornice 2. any structure like this

CORNICE
FRIEZE
ARCHITRAVE
ENTABLATURE

en·tail (in tāl′) *vt.* [< ME. < *en-*, in + *taile*, an agreement < OFr. < *tail-lier*, to cut: see TAILOR] 1. *Law* to limit the inheritance of (real property) to a specific line or class of heirs 2. to have as a necessary part or result; involve; require [the plan *entails* work] —*n.* 1. an entailing or being entailed 2. an entailed inheritance 3. the order of descent for an entailed inheritance —**en·tail′ment** *n.*

en·ta·moe·ba (en′tə mē′ba) *n. same as* ENDAMOEBA

en·tan·gle (in taŋ′g'l) *vt.* **-gled, -gling** 1. to make tangled, or catch in a tangle; ensnare or ensnarl [the fishing lines became *entangled*] 2. to involve in difficulty [they *entangled* him in a bad business deal] 3. to confuse; perplex —**en·tan′-gle·ment** *n.*

en·tente (än tänt′) *n.* [Fr. < OFr. < *entendre*, to understand] 1. an understanding or agreement, as between nations 2. the nations, etc. having such an understanding

en·ter (en′tər) *vt.* [< OFr. *entrer* < L. *intrare* < *intra*, within < IE. base *en-*, in] 1. to come or go in or into 2. to force a way

fat, āpe, cär; ten, ēven; is, bīte; gō, hôrn, tōōl, look; oil, out; up, fur; get; joy; yet; chin; she; thin, then; zh, leisure; ŋ, ring; ə for *a* in *ago, e* in *agent, i* in *sanity, o* in *comply, u* in *focus;* ′ as in *able* (ā′b'l); Fr. bäl; ë, Fr. coeur; ö, Fr. feu; Fr. mon; ô, Fr. coq; ü, Fr. duc; r, Fr. cri; H, G. ich; kh, G. doch; ‡foreign; ☆ Americanism; < derived from. See inside front cover.

(For use with exercises on page 21.) **Please Turn Book Sideways**

Part 2 The Multiple Meanings of Words

Many of the words listed in the dictionary have more than one meaning. A good way to develop your vocabulary is to learn additional meanings for words that are already part of your vocabulary.

Of course, you know the word *front*. But you may not know that *Webster's New World Dictionary of the American Language* (Student's Edition) gives 15 noun definitions for *front*, 2 adjective definitions, 5 definitions as a transitive verb, and 2 definitions as an intransitive verb—24 definitions in all.

Dictionary Entry for *front*

front (frunt) **n.** [< OFr. < L. *frontis*, genitive of *frons*, forehead]
1. outward behavior or appearance, esp. when merely pretended [to put on·a bold *front*] **2.** the part of something that faces forward; most important side **3.** the first part; beginning [toward the *front* of the book] **4.** the place or position directly before a person or thing **5.** a forward or leading position or situation ☆**6.** the first available bellhop, as in a hotel **7.** the land bordering a lake, ocean, street, etc. **8.** the most forward area, where actual fighting is going on in a war **9.** a specified area of activity [the home *front*] **10.** a broad movement in which different groups are united in order to achieve certain political or social aims ☆**11.** a person who serves as a public representative of a business, group, etc., as because of his prestige ☆**12.** a person, group, etc. used to cover up some activity, esp. an illegal one [the barber shop was a *front* for the numbers racket] **13.** a stiff shirt bosom, worn with formal clothes **14.** a face of a building; esp., the face with the principal entrance **15.** *Meteorol.* the boundary between two masses of air that are different, as in density —**adj. 1.** at, to, in, on, or of the front **2.** *Phonet.* sounded toward the front of the mouth [*i* in *bid* and *e* in *met* are *front* vowels] —**vt. 1.** to face; be opposite to [our cottage *fronts* the ocean] **2.** to be before in place **3.** to meet; confront **4.** to defy; oppose **5.** to supply or be a front to [white stone *fronts* the building] —**vi. 1.** to face in a certain direction ☆**2.** to be a front (senses 11 & 12) (with *for*) — **in front of** before; ahead of

---

Exercises The Multiple Meanings of Words

A. Study the dictionary entry for *front,* shown on page 24. Write a sentence for each specific meaning of *front.*

B. Study the following dictionary entry for the word *cell.* Write a sentence illustrating each meaning of *cell.*

Dictionary Entry for *cell*

cell (sel) **n.** [< OFr. *celle* < L. *cella* < IE. base *kel-,* to conceal, from which also come HALL, HELL & HULL¹] **1.** a small room or cubicle, as in a convent or prison **2.** a very small hollow, cavity, or enclosed space, as in a honeycomb, or in a plant ovary **3.** any of the smallest organizational units of a group or movement, as of a Communist party **4.** *Biol.* a small unit of protoplasm, usually with a nucleus, cytoplasm, and an enclosing membrane: all plants and animals are made up of one or more cells **5.** *Elec.* a container holding electrodes and an electrolyte, used either for generating electricity by chemical reactions or for decomposing compounds by electrolysis —**celled adj.**

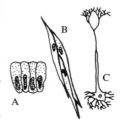

CELLS
(A, epithelial;
B, smooth muscle;
C, nerve)

C. The word *slip* is used in twelve different ways in the following sentences. Explain the meaning of the word as used in each sentence.

1. Ruth *slipped* softly from the room.
2. The ship *slipped* its moorings.
3. It must have *slipped* my mind.
4. We all wrote our names on a *slip* of paper.
5. Mother bought *slips* for the pillows in the guest room.

6. Ed *slipped* on a piece of ice yesterday.
7. The *Queen Elizabeth* occupies a special *slip* in the harbor.
8. She is a *slip* of a girl.
9. Marie asked for a *slip* of Aunt Susan's ivy.
10. Why don't you *slip* off your coat?
11. The hunter *slipped* his dog.
12. Bill made a bad *slip* while talking with the principal.

D. In the following sentences, the italicized word is used in a different sense from the usual one. Determine its meaning if you can. If not, consult a dictionary.

1. The men *scoured* the countryside for the lost boy.
2. An American *school* of painting began with Benjamin West.
3. I could not find the book I wanted in the *stacks*.
4. He converted his assets into *liquid* form.
5. Because of the dangerous *list*, the captain called all hands.

E. Each of the following words has several different meanings. Consult the dictionary entry for each word. Use each word in three sentences to illustrate three meanings.

1. rail   3. pledge   5. bark
2. tip   4. keep   6. square

Part 3   Refining Your Vocabulary

By now you should have some understanding of the importance of developing a large vocabulary. However, just knowing the meanings of a large number of words is not enough. You must use the words in your speaking and writing, and use them correctly. Developing your vocabulary also requires refining. As you add words to your vocabulary, you must constantly work to use the words correctly. You can help to refine or sharpen your vocabulary through the correct use of synonyms and antonyms.

Synonyms

Think for a moment of the color blue. What do you picture in your mind?

Now picture as many other shades of blue as you can.

Just as there are various shades of the color blue, there are various shades of meaning to the words we often call synonyms. Examine the synonymy given below for the word *quick*.

Dictionary Entry for *quick*

quick (kwik) **adj.** [OE. *cwicu*, living < IE. base *gwei-*, to live] **1.** [Archaic] living **2.** *a)* rapid in action; swift [a *quick* walk, a *quick* worker] *b)* prompt [a *quick* reply] **3.** lasting a short time [a *quick* look] **4.** able to understand or learn rapidly **5.** sensitive [a *quick* sense of smell] **6.** easily stirred; fiery [a *quick* temper] —**adv.** quickly; rapidly [come *quick*!] —**n. 1.** the living, esp. in **the quick and the dead 2.** the sensitive flesh under a fingernail or toenail **3.** the deepest feelings [cut to the *quick* by the insult] —**quick'ly adv. —quick'ness n.**
SYN.—**quick** implies a natural ability or tendency to respond rapidly in action, thought, or feeling [a *quick* mind]; **prompt** suggests a being willing or a being disciplined to respond immediately to a demand, request, etc. [*prompt* to obey; a *prompt* acceptance]; **ready** implies a being prepared, inclined, or willing to act at once in a specified way [her *ready* wit]—see also **SYN.** at AGILE and FAST[1]—**ANT. slow**

Note that this synonymy gives cross references to additional synonymies under the entries for *agile* and *fast*.

Dictionary Entry for *agile*

ag·ile (aj'l; *chiefly Brit.* -īl) **adj.** [Fr. < L. < *agere*, ACT] **1.** quick and easy of movement; nimble **2.** keen and lively [an *agile* wit] —**ag'ile·ly adv. —a·gil·i·ty** (ə jil'ə tē) **n.**
SYN.—**agile** and **nimble** both imply quickness and lightness of movement, but **agile** stresses general skill and ease in the use of the limbs, while **nimble** suggests quick sureness in carrying out a particular act [*nimble* fingers at the keyboard]; **quick** implies speed or promptness with no indication of the degree of skill; **spry** suggests nimbleness, esp. as displayed by a vigorous, elderly person; **sprightly** suggests liveliness, gaiety, etc.—**ANT. torpid, sluggish, lethargic**

Dictionary Entry for *fast*

fast (fast) *adj.* [OE. *fæst*] **1.** firm, fixed, or stuck [the car is *fast* in the mud] **2.** firmly fastened or shut [make the shutters *fast*] **3.** loyal; devoted [*fast* friends] **4.** that will not fade [*fast* colors] **5.** swift; quick; speedy **6.** permitting swift movement [a *fast* highway] **7.** lasting a short time [a *fast* lunch] **8.** showing a time that is ahead of the correct time [his watch is *fast*] **9.** *a)* reckless; wild [a *fast* crowd] *b)* sexually promiscuous ☆**10.** [Colloq.] glib and deceptive [a *fast* talker] **11.** [Slang] acting, gotten, done, etc. quickly and often dishonestly [out for a *fast* buck] **12.** *Photog.* adapted to very short exposure time [*fast* film] **13.** [Dial.] complete; sound [a *fast* sleep] — *adv.* **1.** firmly; fixedly **2.** thoroughly; soundly [*fast* àsleep] **3.** rapidly; swiftly **4.** ahead of time **5.** in a reckless, dissipated way; wildly **6.** [Obs.] close; near [*fast* by the river] —☆**a fast one** [Slang] a deceptive act [to pull *a fast one*] —**play fast and loose** to behave in a reckless and dishonest or insincere way
SYN.—fast and **rapid** are both used to express the idea of a relatively high rate of movement or action, but **fast** more often refers to the person or thing that moves or acts, and **rapid** to the action [a *fast* typist; *rapid* transcription]; **swift** implies great rapidity, but in addition often connotes smooth, easy movement; **fleet** suggests a nimbleness or lightness in that which moves swiftly; **quick** implies promptness of action, or occurrence in a brief space of time, rather than a high rate of speed [*quick* to take offense; a *quick* reply]; **speedy** intensifies the idea of quickness, but may also connote rapid motion [a *speedy* recovery; a *speedy* flight]; **hasty** suggests hurried action, and may connote carelessness, rashness, or impatience —**ANT.** **slow**

Exercises Using Synonymies

A. Use each word in the following three groups of synonyms in a sentence. Make sure that each sentence highlights the particular shade of meaning possessed by that word.

1. prompt   2. nimble   3. hasty
   quick   spry   fast
   ready   agile   swift

B. List at least four synonyms for each of the following words. Use each synonym in a sentence that illustrates the specific meaning implied.

1. error   2. crowd   3. pleasure

C. Each of the following groups of words may be considered synonyms. Consult the dictionary entries of synonymies for these words. Use each word in a sentence that illustrates the specific meaning of that word.

GROUP A	GROUP C
1. wind	1. secret
2. breeze	2. stealthy
3. gale	3. covert
4. blast	4. furtive
5. gust	5. clandestine
6. zephyr	6. surreptitious
	7. underhanded

GROUP B	GROUP D
1. rescue	1. go
2. deliver	2. depart
3. redeem	3. leave
4. ransom	4. withdraw
5. save	5. retire

Antonyms

Some words in English have exact opposites: day—night, short—long, hot—cold. Many other words do not have exact opposites, but they do have words whose meanings are different enough to be called antonyms. Antonyms are useful when you want to make a contrast in order to focus attention on a particular idea. Skillful use of antonyms will help you convey your meaning effectively and emphatically.

Exercises Using Antonyms

A. Following each of the three synonymies on pages 27 and 28, you will see an antonym or antonyms for the entry word. Use each of these antonyms in a sentence. If possible, use the contrasting entry word in the same sentence.

B. Give an antonym or antonyms for each of the following words.

1. careful
2. transitory
3. famous
4. humane
5. cheap

6. continue
7. cosmopolitan
8. prelude
9. combustible
10. despondent

c. Select five of the sets of antonyms you have given in Exercise B. Use each of these sets of antonyms in a sentence.

Part 4 Interesting Word Origins

Many English words have interesting origins. The word *senator* comes from the Latin word meaning "old." The Roman Senate was a council of elders.

A person who is fond of luxury, comfort, and costly pleasures may be called a *sybarite*. This word comes from Sybaris, an ancient Greek city in southern Italy famous for its luxury.

Exercises Interesting Word Origins

A. Each of the following words has an interesting history. Check the etymology of each word in a good dictionary. Write a brief description of the background of each word.

1. agriculture
2. belligerent
3. carnival
4. corduroy
5. curfew
6. czar
7. delta
8. intoxicate
9. landau
10. league

11. lieutenant
12. mob
13. nausea
14. ogle
15. emancipate
16. guerrilla
17. gymnasium
18. pedigree
19. sinecure
20. tenor (voice)

B. Look up the etymologies of these four words:

1. dexterous   3. gauche
2. adroit   4. sinister

Why do the first two words have favorable meanings, and the last two words uncomplimentary meanings?

Words Derived from People's Names

Many of the words we use are derived from the names of people or literary characters. The term *malapropism,* meaning "the act or habit of misusing words ridiculously," comes from Mrs. Malaprop, a character in Richard Brinsley Sheridan's eighteenth-century play *The Rivals.* Mrs. Malaprop was noted for her misuse of words. For example:

He is the very pineapple of politeness.

Exercise **Words Derived from People's Names**

Each of the following words is related to a person or a literary character. The etymology for each word in a good dictionary should tell you the person to whom the word is related. Check each word in a dictionary and write down the name of the person or character from whom it is derived. Then use each word in a sentence.

1. cereal	13. lynch
2. chauvinist	14. macadam
3. galvanize	15. martial
4. gerrymander	16. maudlin
5. guillotine	17. maverick
6. leotard	18. mercurial
7. mesmerize	19. sequoia
8. pantaloon	20. shrapnel
9. pasteurize	21. sideburns
10. quixotic	22. teddy bear
11. sandwich	23. vulcanize
12. saxophone	24. watt

Chapter 3

Combining Ideas in Sentences

Writing is a process of making choices. You must decide what ideas you want to express, which words are best to use, and how those words are to be arranged. Because writing occurs in sentences, the first step toward making yourself understood in writing is to write sentences that are clear and direct. The next step is to combine related ideas in your sentences.

A sentence is a group of words that expresses one main idea. Some main ideas, however, are made up of smaller ideas. If each smaller idea is expressed in a sentence of its own, the result is as choppy and monotonous as the following group of sentences.

> We were all hungry. It was after the game. We stopped at an all-night diner. We had hamburgers. We had clam chowder.

You can improve the choppy style by combining the ideas into one sentence.

> We were all hungry after the game, so we stopped at an all-night diner, where we had hamburgers and clam chowder.

The new sentence has only one main idea, but that main idea has several parts. The new sentence flows smoothly and shows how the ideas are related.

There are many ways to express any idea; one way may be more effective than another. Good writers choose the way that communicates an idea most clearly. This chapter will show you how to combine related ideas to create more effective sentences. It will also give you practice in making the choices a good writer must make.

Part 1 Joining Sentences

When two sentences express similar ideas that are of equal importance, they can usually be joined by a comma and the word *and*.

> Diane began work at noon. Sue joined her at one o'clock.
> Diane began work at noon, and Sue joined her at one o'clock.

When two sentences express contrasting ideas of equal importance, they can usually be joined by a comma and the word *but*.

> I went to bed early. I could not get to sleep.
> I went to bed early, but I could not get to sleep.

When two sentences express a choice between ideas of equal importance, they can usually be joined by a comma and the word *or*.

> Is Greg going to the game? Is he taking you to the movies?
> Is Greg going to the game, or is he taking you to the movies?

Exercises **Joining Sentences**

A. Join each pair of sentences by following the directions in parentheses.

1. Will Tom be able to rejoin the team? Will he have to sit out the whole season? (Join with **, or**.)

2. I remembered the eggs. I forgot the butter. (Join with **, but**.)

3. Jane sanded the tabletop. Phil assembled the base. (Join with **, and**.)

4. Would help arrive in time? Would we be stranded on the mountaintop all night? (Join with **, or**.)

5. Rain began to fall in torrents. The players sprinted for the shelter of the dugout. (Join with **, and**.)

6. Lucille is not as fast as Joan. She has more endurance. (Join with **, but**.)

7. Pine is much less expensive than oak. It is not as sturdy. (Join with **, but**.)

8. My parents are on a business trip. I'm staying with Jeff's family. (Join with **, and**.)

9. Shall I eat all this tomato soup? Would you like some? (Join with **, or**.)

10. The tax bill passed easily. The leash law was defeated by a wide margin. (Join with **, but**.)

B. Join each pair of sentences by using **, and** or **, or** or **, but**. Be prepared to explain your choices.

1. Jenny thought that she had finished the test. She had overlooked the last problem.

2. Chris ran after the bus. She was not able to catch it.

3. Add the cubed potatoes. Then simmer the soup for an hour.

4. You can walk from Knox Street to Third Avenue. You can take the crosstown bus.

5. Motorcycles are economical. A car offers better protection from the weather.

Part 2 Joining Sentence Parts

Sometimes the ideas expressed by two sentences are so closely related that some words are repeated in the two sentences. The repetition is unnecessary and awkward. The ideas would be much better expressed if they were joined in one sentence and the repeated words were eliminated. When the sentence parts express similar ideas of equal importance, they can usually be joined by *and*.

> Carl runs the hurdles. *He runs* the hundred-meter dash.
> Carl runs the hurdles *and* the hundred-meter dash.

When the sentence parts express contrasting ideas, they can usually be joined by *but*.

> We found the door. *We* could not open it.
> We found the door *but* could not open it.

When the sentence parts express a choice between ideas, they can usually be joined by *or*.

> Do you want enchiladas for dinner? *Do you want* spaghetti *for dinner?*
> Do you want enchiladas *or* spaghetti for dinner?

Exercises Joining Sentence Parts

A. Join the related parts in each pair of sentences by following the directions in parentheses. Eliminate the italicized words.

1. We will take the train to El Paso. *We will take* the bus *to El Paso*. (Join related parts with **or**.)

2. We led for most of the game. *We* lost in the final seconds. (Join related parts with **but**.)

3. Phil did not want to go at first. *Phil* changed his mind at the last minute. (Join related parts with **but**.)

4. Success may come overnight. *Success may come* after years of struggling. (Join related parts with **or**.)

5. I'd like to go to Denver. *I'd like to go to* San Francisco. (Join related parts with **and**.)

6. We have plenty of asparagus. *We have* no broccoli. (Join related parts with **but**.)

7. I stopped at Dan's house. *I* asked him to come to dinner. (Join related parts with **and**.)

8. Parker could inch his way along the narrow ledge. *Parker would have to* risk everything in a leap across the chasm. (Join related parts with **or**.)

9. The brown bear rolled over in the sun. *It* yawned. (Join related parts with **and**.)

10. Wash the cut with disinfectant to prevent infection. Bandage it carefully *to prevent infection*. (Join related parts with **and**.)

B. Join the related parts in each pair of sentences by using *and, but,* or *or*. Eliminate repeated words.

1. I want to become a biologist. I want to become a Grand National Stock Car driver.

2. I bought my mother some flowers. I took her out to dinner.

3. John was here this morning. John left before noon.

4. The shopping cart rolled down the hill. It rolled into the oncoming traffic.

5. I ran well at the start. I dropped out after the first hill.

Part 3 Adding Single Words

Sometimes only one word in the second sentence in a pair is really important to the meaning. All the other words in the sentence are unnecessarily repeated. The one important word can be added to the first sentence, resulting in one sentence that is a much tighter and more effective way of expressing the idea.

I like that puppy best. *It is* gray.
I like that gray puppy best.

Betty was able to fix our radiator. *It was* leaking.
Betty was able to fix our leaking radiator.

Chris stared at the fender. *It was* dented.
Chris stared at the dented fender.

Sometimes the form of the important word must be changed slightly before it is added to the other sentence.

Betty was able to fix our radiator. *It had a* leak.
Betty was able to fix our leaking radiator.

Chris stared at the fender. *It had a* dent.
Chris stared at the dented fender.

Exercises **Adding Single Words**

A. Combine each of these pairs of sentences by adding single words. Eliminate the italicized words. Follow any special directions.

1. Susan had a cold. *The cold was* severe.

2. John returned all the books. *They were* overdue.

3. Detective Bass studied the window. *The window was* broken.

4. A boy stood in the aisle. *He was* whimpering.

5. The reports are in that pile. *They are* complete. (End the important word with **-ed**.)

6. Ethel took the tea kettle from the stove. *The kettle was making a* whistle. (End the important word with **-ing**.)

7. The silence was shattered by a wolf. *It* howled. (End the important word with **-ing**.)

8. A buzzard glided toward the ground. *It made* circles. (End the important word with **-ing**.)

9. A dog had been following me to school every day for a week. *It had* spots. (End the important word with **-ed**.)

10. Mrs. Walker spoke of her childhood memories. *She* treasures *them*. (End the important word with **-ed**.)

B. Combine each of the following pairs of sentences by adding the important word from the second sentence. Decide on your own whether to change the form of the important word.

1. We had some of Jon's lasagna for dinner. It was delicious.

2. Officer Page caught the car at the light. It was speeding.

3. Jane walked along the street. The street was deserted.

4. This glass should be thrown out. It has a crack.

5. A cat was curled up in a spot of sun. It was asleep.

Part 4 Adding Several Single Words

You may be able to add several single words to a sentence. Adding several words will allow you to combine more than two sentences if one states the main idea and each of the others adds only one important detail to the main idea.

> Cathy told a story to a group of children. *The story was* thrilling. *It was an* adventure. *The children were* delighted.
> Cathy told a thrilling adventure story to a group of delighted children.

Sometimes you will have to use a comma when you add more than one word to a sentence.

> Jackson hit a home run into the upper deck at Yankee Stadium. *It was* long *and* towering.
> Jackson hit a long, towering home run into the upper deck at Yankee Stadium.

Sometimes you can join the words with *and.*

> My attention wandered during the second act. *The second act was* long. *It was also* tedious.
> My attention wandered during the long and tedious second act.

Remember that changes in the endings of the important words may be necessary.

> A building dominates the downtown area. *It is made of* glass. *It* glitters.
> A glittering glass building dominates the downtown area.

Exercises Adding Several Single Words

A. Combine each group of sentences on the next page by adding the important words. Eliminate the italicized words and follow any special directions given in parentheses.

1. At the end of the film, a snake crushed several buildings. *The snake was* huge. *The buildings were* tall.

2. Frank threw a pitch to Becky. *It was* low *and* outside. (Use a comma.)

3. Becky hit a line drive right at Jeff on third. *It* sizzled. (End the important word with **-ing**.)

4. The fox circled the chicken coop. *He was* crafty *and* old. (Do not use a comma.)

5. A slice of sun peeked over the horizon. *The slice was* thin. *The sun was* fiery *and* red. (Do not use a comma.)

6. In the light I could just make out a face *The light was* dim. *The face was* weathered.

7. We reached the summit after a climb. *The climb was* long. *It was also* exhausting. (Join the important words with **and**.)

8. Strips of orange peel add flavor to a stew. *The strips should be* thin. *The orange peel is* zesty. *The flavor is* unusual.

9. John gave a sigh of relief. *It was* long. *It was* low. *It was* heartfelt. (Use commas.)

10. The next meet will be held in Westlake's pool. *This is the next meet on the* schedule. *Westlake's pool has* heat. (End the important words with **-ed**.)

B. Combine each group of sentences by adding the important words from the second sentence to the first sentence. Remember that changes in the endings of the important words may be necessary.

1. Dan found a letter in a book on the shelf. The letter was crumpled. It was old. The book was dusty. The shelf was at the top.

2. The mysterious stranger stood alone in the night. It was still and damp.

3. The commuters enjoyed their ride on the cars. The ride was swift. It was also comfortable. The cars were new and lightweight.

4. The cry of the loon is unmistakable. It is a cry made of laughs and whoops.

5. I'll have eggs and tomato juice. Fry the eggs and chill the tomato juice.

Part 5   Adding Words with *-ly*

When you take a single important word from one sentence and insert it into another sentence, you may have to change the word so that it ends with *-ly*.

> My uncle visited us in Richmond. *It was a* brief *visit.*
> My uncle visited us briefly in Richmond.

Often, the word ending in *-ly* can be placed in any of several positions in the sentence.

> My uncle appeared with an armload of gifts. *His appearance was* unexpected.
> Unexpectedly, my uncle appeared with an armload of gifts.
> My uncle appeared unexpectedly with an armload of gifts.

Exercise Adding Words with *-ly*

Combine each pair of sentences by adding the important word, ending it with **-ly**. Eliminate the italicized words.

1. Kurt smiled at me. *His smile was* strange.

2. Jim dreamed of playing shortstop for the Yankees. *He kept this dream a* secret.

3. Detective Bass inspected the fingerprints. *It was a* close *inspection.*

4. Diana talked about her mountain-climbing adventures. *The talk was* endless.

5. Mr. Swanson had parked on the bridge. *Such parking is* illegal.

Part 6   Adding Groups of Words

You may find that one sentence contains an important group of words that can be added to another sentence. When the group of words gives more information about someone or something, it should be added near the words that name the person or thing.

The man had a suspicious look. *He was* beside my father.
The man beside my father had a suspicious look.

A box stood in the corner. *It was* filled with old clothes.
A box filled with old clothes stood in the corner.

I was startled by a shadowy figure. *It was* standing in the doorway.
I was startled by a shadowy figure standing in the doorway.

I was startled by a shadowy figure. *I was* standing in the doorway.
Standing in the doorway, I was startled by a shadowy figure.

In some cases you will have to separate the group of words from the rest of the sentence with a comma or a pair of commas.

My dream was to climb Everest. *Everest is* the world's highest peak.
My dream was to climb Everest, the world's highest peak.

My friend is a football fanatic. *My friend is* Al Peters.
My friend, Al Peters, is a football fanatic.

Alaska is twice the size of Texas. *Alaska is* our largest state.
Alaska, our largest state, is twice the size of Texas.

When the group of words describes an action, it should be added near the words that name the action.

Our cat was hiding. *She was* under the sofa.
Our cat was hiding under the sofa.

When the group of words adds more information to the entire main idea of the other sentence, it may be added at the beginning or at the end.

I drove to the abandoned factory. *I drove there* in the late afternoon.
In the late afternoon, I drove to the abandoned factory.
I drove to the abandoned factory in the late afternoon.

I decided to change my plans. *I did it* for Joan's sake.
For Joan's sake, I decided to change my plans.
I decided to change my plans, for Joan's sake.

Exercises **Adding Groups of Words**

A. Combine each group of sentences by adding a group of words or groups of words to one of them. Eliminate the italicized words.

1. Mr. Perkins was waiting. *He was* in the lobby.

2. A tall woman stood on the corner. *She was* carrying a briefcase.

3. *I was* opening the envelope. I found three pages. *They were* from my laboratory report.

4. We watched without moving. *We were* dazzled by the beauty of the falls.

5. A brilliant rainbow arched across the sky. *This happened* after the storm.

6. Katy spent every summer in the country. *She stayed there* with her grandmother.

7. John Layne praised the opposition. *This happened* after the game. *He is* our starting quarterback.

8. My first class each morning was biology. *Biology was* my favorite subject.

9. Diana was chosen for the all-star team. *She was* a short girl. *She was* playing in her first full season.

10. The downtown area was entirely reconstructed by 1884. *It had been* destroyed by fire in 1882.

B. Combine each group of sentences by adding a group of words or groups of words to one of them. Decide on your own what words should be eliminated.

1. Cliff had no idea that he was being watched. He was standing alone. He was beneath a streetlamp.

2. We had been reading *I Am Third*. *I Am Third* is the autobiography of Gale Sayers.

3. Archeologists flocked to the site of the ancient city. It had been discovered by Professor Greene and her students.

4. Dr. Watson settled back and began a story. The story was about one of Holmes's famous cases. This happened after dinner.

5. Rosa was concentrating fiercely. She was concentrating on her paper. Rosa did not hear the telephone. It was in the next room.

Part 7 Combining with *-ing*

Read the following pair of sentences.

> *She* jogged to school and back every day. *This* helped to increase her stamina.

Notice that the word *This* in the second sentence refers to the entire idea expressed by the first sentence. This pair of sentences, and others like it, can be combined in one smoothly flowing statement.

> Jogging to school and back every day helped to increase her stamina.

The word *jogged* was changed to *jogging,* and the italicized words were eliminated.

Here is another example of two sentences combined by using *-ing.*

> *He had* watched the sun rise over the ocean each morning. When he moved to Utah, Brad missed *that.*
>
> When he moved to Utah, Brad missed watching the sun rise over the ocean each morning.

Notice that the word *watched* was changed to *watching,* and that the italicized words were eliminated.

Exercises Combining with *-ing*

A. Combine each group of sentences by using **-ing**. Eliminate the italicized words.

1. *Renee* worked at an after-school job. *This* kept Renee from joining the track team.

2. *Phillip* refused to pay his debts. *That* led Phillip into serious trouble.

3. *Martha* visited the statewide science fair. *This* was the beginning of Martha's interest in science.

4. *Some people* get a good night's sleep before a test. *Others* cram until late at night. *The first* is a much better idea than *the second.*

5. *People* recycle paper. *This* saves forests, energy, and money.

6. *We* booed when the other team took the court. *That* was a mistake that we later regretted.

7. *Mrs. Benson* competed in the city marathon. *That* climaxed Mrs. Benson's fitness program.

8. *They* discussed politics and world affairs at dinner. They enjoyed *that*.

9. *We will* hold our meetings in the evening. We hope that *that* will increase attendance.

10. *People can* listen to a record. *People can* see a live performance. *The first* can never take the place of *the second*.

B. Combine each pair of sentences by using **-ing.** Decide on your own what words should be eliminated.

1. Maria missed the last bus home. That meant that she would be at least an hour late.

2. He climbed the Matterhorn at sixty years of age. That brought Mr. Daniels his greatest thrill.

3. People have to rest in bed after an illness. That can be depressing for an active person.

4. I discovered Parkinson's true identity. That enabled me to solve the mystery.

5. Cliff slipped as he rounded the final turn. That cost Cliff first place.

Review Exercises **Combining Ideas in Sentences**

A. Join each pair of sentences by using **, and** or **, or** or **, but**.

1. Would you like to borrow my pen? Do you prefer to use a pencil?

2. The birds haven't discovered the feeder. The squirrels have.

3. I made that feeder myself. Then I mounted it on a tall pole.

4. Would a taller pole discourage the squirrels? Will I just have to put up with them?

5. Time was running out. I still had three questions to answer.

B. Join the related parts in each pair of sentences by using **and, or,** or **but**. Eliminate the italicized words.

1. You might make the table with ash. *You might make the table with* birch.
2. They peered through the window. *They* couldn't see anyone inside.
3. Glen asked several questions. *Glen* still wasn't certain that he understood the problem.
4. We can meet today at noon. *We can meet* tomorrow at three.
5. I have relatives living in St. Louis. *I have relatives living in* Oakland.

C. Combine each of the following pairs of sentences by adding the important word. Eliminate the italicized words and follow any special directions in parentheses.

1. A wind blew from the mountains. *The wind was* frigid.
2. I had just begun my job. *It was my* first.
3. Detective Bass questioned the witness. *She was* nervous.
4. This project could not have been completed without the help of many people. *They were* tireless.
5. Sunlight glittered on the windowpanes. *They had* frost *on them.* (End the important word with **-ed.**)

D. Combine each group of sentences by adding the important words. Eliminate the italicized words and follow any special directions in parentheses.

1. Early that morning, a message arrived from the crew members. *The message was* mysterious. *The crew members were* missing.
2. Parker gave a speech. *It was* calm *and* thoughtful.
3. Could my voice be heard over the crowd? *My voice* trembled. *The crowd* screamed. (End the important words with **-ing.**)
4. I started the day with a plate of eggs. *They were* fluffy. *They were* scrambled. (Do not use a comma.)
5. A dog loped along beside me as I ran. *It was* large. *It was* shaggy. *It was* gray. (Use two commas.)

E. Combine each pair of sentences by using **-ly**. Eliminate the italicized words.

1. Ann stepped into the center of the mat. *She was* careful.

2. Carl visited the patients in the children's wing of the hospital. *His visits were* frequent.

3. Detective Bass questioned every suspect. *His questions were* extensive.

4. Marsha wandered through the park. *Her wandering was* aimless.

5. Mr. Johnson was attempting to get our attention. *His attempt was* frantic.

F. Combine each group of sentences by adding a group of words or groups of words to one of them. Eliminate the italicized words.

1. Mrs. Daniels was standing. *She was* at the side of the stage.

2. A trio of music students wandered through the park. *They were* playing violins.

3. *I was* turning the corner. I ran into two people. *They were* from my old neighborhood.

4. We sat motionless in our seats. *We were* stunned by the ending of the film.

5. Confetti littered Main Street. *This was* after the victory parade.

G. Combine each group of sentences by using **-ing**. Eliminate the italicized words.

1. *I* finished my history paper. *That* gave me a real sense of accomplishment.

2. *The Andersons* refinish old furniture. *That* has brought the Andersons a second income.

3. *Lucille* explained her position in a calm and logical way. *That* won Lucille the respect of everyone in the audience.

4. *Bill* brags. *That* has cost Bill many friends.

5. *People* plan ahead. *This* can prevent wasted time and effort.

Chapter 4

Improving Your Sentences

The problems of writing are largely problems with sentences. If you improve your sentences, you will almost automatically improve your paragraphs, reports, and letters.

One way to produce a good sentence is to do it on your very first try. However, not even the most talented professionals trust their first drafts. Even such highly acclaimed writers as Katherine Anne Porter and James Baldwin use their first drafts only as a point of departure. They *revise* until their sentences say exactly what they want them to say.

Revising is the surest way for you to improve your writing. As you reread your first drafts, you may find the following problems.

Some sentences lack ideas or do not give enough information.
Some sentences contain too many ideas and should be broken up.
Some sentences do not make sense.

This chapter deals with these sentence problems and shows you how to solve them.

The sentences you will be revising were written by young people like you. They did not have the opportunity to revise the sentences. You will be doing the revising for them.

You will be using a new method of writing improvement that has been tested with thousands of students. For many of them it has worked dramatically. This new method does not rely on the principles of grammar. Instead, it focuses on writing problems as problems of meaning and sense.

Part 1 Avoiding Empty Sentences

> The reason I like the Pittsburgh Steelers is that they are my favorite team.

Sentences that say too little are **empty sentences.** Grammatically they may be complete, yet they are lacking in ideas, in substance. One reason is that they may contain words or groups of words that repeat the idea contained earlier in the sentence. Here is an example of this kind of writing.

> The reason I like the Pittsburgh Steelers is that they are my favorite team.

This is writing in a circle. The idea of *liking* is repeated. The writer begins by saying that he *likes* the team. He ends with the same idea expressed in the word *favorite*. The sentence is empty because no reasons for liking the team are given. The writer could have said this:

> The Pittsburgh Steelers are my favorite team because they have a strong passing game, an aggressive defense, and a winning spirit. I particularly admire Terry Bradshaw's ability to pass the football.

Sentences are empty because the writer does not take the trouble ahead of time to think about what he or she wants to say. The reader then gets the impression that the writer is just trying to fill up space.

Exercises **Revising Empty Sentences**

A. Revise the following sentences.

Suggestions

1. Read each sentence. Ask yourself, "What idea is repeated?"
2. Supply the necessary facts or ideas.
3. Write more than one sentence if you need to.

1. I am interested in ceramics because it is an interesting hobby.

2. It is impossible to learn a new language so quickly because people are not able to do it.

3. I wanted to play on the team because I always wanted to be a basketball player.

4. During those few days I began to admire her qualities because her character was so fine.

5. Mike had three reasons for choosing the book he was reading, and his reasons were all good ones.

6. If you're just starting, the $75 Yamaha is a good guitar for a beginner.

7. The fight, of course, was silly, and we were both foolish for fighting.

8. The hero was the typical kind of man that you have seen many times in everyday life.

9. I liked the Robert Redford movie because it was an excellent movie.

10. My sister Fran is always joking, and she never does anything but joke around.

B. Revise these sentences.

1. I'd like to be a lifeguard because I'd love to do that and get paid for it, too.

2. I flunked the test because I didn't deserve to pass.

3. You should always put stereo speakers at least ten feet apart from each other because ten feet apart is the best distance for them to be.

4. Scott Joplin is popular because a lot of people like his songs.

5. More women are going into politics than ever before, and there should be more people like Ella Grasso and Jane Byrne running for office.

6. Inflation has become a huge problem, and everyone has to pay higher and higher prices for food, clothing, TV repairs, and other things, and these prices keep going up.

7. I think I should tell you everything in the story up to the ending, but I don't think I should tell you the ending.

8. I prefer to be with some people because they are my friends.

9. My freshman year was a good one because it was my first year.

10. I liked the waltzing bear best because it could dance.

Part 2 Avoiding Padded Sentences

> In my opinion, I think soccer is the best team sport ever invented.

Padded sentences are sentences that are stretched out with unnecessary words. Such sentences are ineffective and lacking in force.

Padding can result from the following:

repetition of the same word or idea
repetition of *that*
use of such fillers as

> *on account of the fact that . . .*   *what I believe is . . .*
> *the reason is that . . .*   *the thing . . .*

Repetition of the Same Word or Idea

PADDED: *In my opinion, I think* soccer is the best team sport ever invented.

(An opinion is a thought. Eliminate one or the other.)

BETTER: In my opinion, soccer is the best team sport ever invented.

BETTER: I think soccer is the best team sport ever invented.

PADDED: This book is a *biography of the life of* Jimmy Carter. (Since *biography* means *the life of,* one of these is unnecessary.)

BETTER: This book is a biography of Jimmy Carter.

BETTER: This book is about the life of Jimmy Carter.

Repetition of *That*

PADDED: It is obvious *that* since I like music so much *that* I should study it.

BETTER: It is obvious *that* since I like music so much, I should study it.

PADDED: The captain thought *that* if she turned south *that* she would run out of the storm.

BETTER: The captain thought *that* if she turned south, she would run out of the storm.

The Use of Fillers

PADDED: When the boys ran away, *the reason was that* they were frightened.

BETTER: The boys ran away because they were frightened.

PADDED: *On account of the fact that* we still depend on foreign oil, we may have more energy problems.

BETTER: Because we still depend on foreign oil, we may have more energy problems.

PADDED: *What I believe is* that love solves many problems.

BETTER: I believe that love solves many problems.

PADDED: *The thing* I am looking forward to being is a social worker.

BETTER: I am looking forward to being a social worker.

Long sentences can sometimes be simplified without losing any of their thought by reducing clauses to phrases or to appositives:

PADDED: We have a garage *that has an automatic door opener.* (adjective clause)

BETTER: We have a garage *with an automatic door opener.* (prepositional phrase)

PADDED: We attended the demonstration *that was given in the laboratory.* (adjective clause)

BETTER: We attended the demonstration *given in the laboratory.* (participial phrase)

BETTER: We attended the demonstration *in the laboratory.* (prepositional phrase)

PADDED: Jo Anne Smith, *who is our top-ranking student,* won a scholarship to Yale. (adjective clause)

BETTER: Jo Anne Smith, *our top-ranking student,* won a scholarship to Yale. (appositive)

Exercises Revising Padded Sentences

A. Revise the following sentences. Omit the padding.

1. The beginning of the unpleasantness started when Sue refused the invitation.

2. The reason why Agnes decided on a green dress was on account of the fact that she has red hair.

3. In his opinion, he thought I owed the teacher an apology.

4. The unbelievable number of accidents that are caused by sheer carelessness on our highways is staggering.

5. I did not like to retrace my footsteps back down the deserted street.

6. Jo thought that if she acted quickly that she could get the job.

7. Since I have finally reached the ripe old age of sixteen years of age, I hope to get a job this summer.

8. What the salesman wanted us to know was the fact that we did not have to pay the total cost in order to have the bicycle delivered.

9. The reason that Mike wanted to lose a few pounds was that his favorite slacks did not fit him.

10. The class prepared a program that was dedicated to Mozart, who was a great musician.

B. Revise these sentences.

1. The beginning of it all started with fighting in the streets.

2. During the Vietnam War there was a great change in people's attitudes at the time.

3. I believe it is time for a great leader to come along who will really lead our country, like Abraham Lincoln or Franklin D. Roosevelt.

4. Deaf people are usually safe drivers because they are aware of their handicap of not being able to hear.

5. On account of the fact that our house has been sold, we will be moving away soon.

6. The thing I am bothered about most is about my weight.

7. Dan did not have any gray paint to paint the steps with, so he used brown paint to paint the steps.

8. What I don't like about shirts is a shirt that has no pockets.

9. The reason that we were late was the fact that we missed the plane.

10. I saw a woman who was a suspicious-looking character slip into the telephone booth.

Part 3 Avoiding Overloaded Sentences

I want to be a doctor because I want to help people who suffer, but I will have to study many long years in medical school before I will be qualified as a doctor.

Overloaded sentences are sentences that say too much. They carry too many ideas. They mix up important ideas with unimportant ones, and the reader is unable to sort them out. In some cases, ideas are even repeated.

What can you do to avoid overloaded sentences?

1. First, decide on the main ideas.
2. Decide which ideas can be combined into one sentence.
3. Write the main ideas as one sentence, following the usual sentence pattern of subject—verb—object.
4. Write separate sentences for the other ideas.
5. Write simply and clearly.

The following sentence tried to say too much.

> I want to be a doctor because I want to help people who suffer, but I will have to study many long years in medical school before I will be qualified as a doctor.

Let's look at the steps necessary to revise that sentence. These are the main ideas.

> I want to be a doctor.
> I want to help people who suffer.
> I will have to study for many years to be qualified.

Two of these ideas can be combined smoothly into one sentence: the desire to be a doctor and the reason for the desire.

> I want to be a doctor because I want to help people who suffer.

The remaining ideas, which are also related, should be expressed in another sentence.

> To be qualified as a doctor, I will have to study for many years.

This is how the original overloaded sentence now reads.

> I want to be a doctor because I want to help people who suffer. To be qualified, I will have to study for many years.

The following are additional examples of overloaded sentences. In the revisions, unimportant words and ideas have been omitted. Study these sentences carefully. Think about how you can use the same revision techniques in your own writing.

OVERLOADED: I drove out of town on a dark, lonely road, and I happened to see a car pulled up at the side of the road, which made me feel sorry for the poor people standing beside it, and, like the Good Samaritan I am, I stopped to see if I could help.

REVISED: As I drove out of town on a dark, lonely road, I happened to see people standing near a car pulled up at the side of the road. Like a Good Samaritan, I stopped to see if I could help.

OVERLOADED: The Canadian government is still allowing hunters to kill baby seals, because the demand for their skins is so great, and when I watched that TV program and watched hunters shooting baby seals from a helicopter, I got sick to my stomach.

REVISED: The Canadian government is still allowing hunters to kill baby seals because of the great demand for their skins. When I watched a TV program in which hunters were shooting baby seals from a helicopter, I got sick to my stomach.

OVERLOADED: I like all kinds of books, and it makes no difference to me whether other people think a book I am reading is dull, as long as I like it.

REVISED: I like all kinds of books. It makes no difference to me whether other people think the book I am reading is dull, as long as I like it.

Exercises Revising Overloaded Sentences

A. Revise each of the following sentences.

Suggestions

1. Look for the main idea and concentrate on putting it into a sentence.
2. Leave out words or ideas that get in the way.
3. Write more than one sentence if necessary.

1. There was a science fair at the museum, and Jack Gorman's robot caused a great deal of excitement, and people came from miles around to watch him give a demonstration of it.

2. Scientists say that foods eaten as soon as possible after picking contain more vitamins and that prolonged cooking results in a lack of these very essential substances.

3. A teen age girl may be a little upset if she is not experienced in what to wear on a date, how to be attractive to the boy she is with, and what to talk about, and I don't mean about the boy she went out with the week before but a boy she has never gone out with.

4. Mathematics is a subject that trains your mind and helps you to solve problems, which helps in future life because so many people can't think straight or solve their problems.

5. He liked playing baseball and played it well, which is unusual because in 1900 there weren't many good players and baseball wasn't a popular game.

B. Revise these sentences.

1. The owners realize that we will annoy them for only three months, and when September comes again we will go back to school, and all the fun we had during our summer vacation will be only a pleasant dream.

2. I liked the movie more than the book because the movie made the characters seem more real, and they don't seem real in the book.

3. While I am covering various stories, I will be able to learn many new things and understand things I know even better and also help the paper's readers to be able to learn and understand different things that happen in the world.

4. No one even asked me to go home with her, but as I was walking home by myself thinking of my first unhappy day of school and of the dreary days ahead, a friendly voice called out behind me, "Hi! I'm Patsy Walker."

5. To me, sleeping is fascinating because I consider it as a time of dreams that can come in a very special place, or it may be any place I happen to be thinking of, or it may be a place that does not exist at all.

c. The following sentences contain the kinds of problems you have been working with. Revise the sentences. Some of them are empty, padded, *and* overloaded.

1. I want to be a deep-sea diver, and my reason for choosing this profession is that this is the thing that interests me most in life.

2. *All the President's Men* is a movie about Watergate, and Robert Redford and Dustin Hoffman are the leading characters, who take the parts of the two reporters who investigated the Watergate break-in and brought things into the open.

3. What I believe about criticism is that some kinds of criticism are good, but other kinds of criticism are harmful, and harmful criticism is criticism that tears a person down instead of helping him.

4. We have two English setters, Melissa and Storm, and English setters are such a rare breed that whenever we take them walking people stop and ask what kind of dogs they are.

5. Billy the Kid was America's best-known outlaw, and not many people know that he had a baby-faced look and did not look like a killer at all, and never used his real name, Henry McCarthy.

Part 4   Keeping to the Point

Omit details that interrupt the meaning of a sentence and have no connection with the main idea.

What's wrong with the following sentence?

The editor of the school paper, who has six Siamese cats, called a meeting of the staff and gave out the assignments for the final issue.

The editor's interest in cats has nothing to do with the staff meeting. The clause *who has six Siamese cats* is, therefore, a detail that interrupts the sentence and has no connection with the main idea. It should be omitted.

Do not allow irrelevant details to slip into your writing. Keep your ideas clear and to the point.

Exercises Keeping to the Point

A. Revise the following sentences. Omit details that do not belong.

1. Harold's older brother, who has three children, is completely different from Harold in appearance and interests.

2. The school band, which had brand new uniforms, was invited to play at a band competition in Washington, D.C.

3. Supersonic passenger planes, which make a terrible noise when they take off, have made it possible for people to travel around the world in a single day.

4. The all-girl rock group, in which there are several redheads, toured the state all summer.

5. The book I am reading, which has a blue cover and many illustrations, contains information about the most recent developments in the field of electronics.

6. Many of my friends, who are tall and very pretty, are fond of bowling.

7. Last Saturday I saw a basketball game, which I prefer to football, that went into double overtime.

8. At Grandmother's house, a table was prepared on which there was an abundance of bread, butter, cake (which my father is not allowed to eat because of his diet), colored eggs, ham, chicken, and other food.

9. The play was about two soldiers who became friends during World War II, which started for us when the Japanese attacked Pearl Harbor, and who were reunited years later.

10. I want to work in television or radio because the audience will be doubled in ten years, when I'll be ten years older and will have my own car, and more technicians will be in demand.

B. Revise these sentences. Each sentence may have more than one problem. Keep in mind that sentence problems can sometimes be solved in more than one way.

1. While I am on this earth, I want to do something that the people I leave behind me after I am gone will remember me for.

2. I used to live with my parents in Woodland Hills, which is a suburb of Los Angeles, but now I live with my mother in an apartment in the city, which is called "the city of angels" in spite of my presence.

3. It wasn't until last year, after Uncle Dan died in St. Francis Hospital, that I realized what a wonderful friend I had lost.

4. Since the Miami police had only one clue, which was a piece of cord from a Venetian blind, the police started their investigation by interviewing all cord wholesalers in Miami, which doesn't have a very high crime rate.

5. Chicago, which has been called "the city that works," was run by Richard J. Daley, who had been the mayor for twenty years and he died suddenly while in office in December, 1976.

Part 5 Keeping Related Sentence Parts Together

Do not separate sentence parts that belong together by inserting constructions that should be written elsewhere. Doing so causes your readers to lose the train of thought and makes it difficult for them to pick it up again. In addition, the sentences sound choppy.

AWKWARD: I *am*, as soon as I have saved enough money, *going to buy* a portable radio. (Parts of the verb phrase are separated.)

BETTER: As soon as I have saved enough money, I *am going to buy* a portable radio.

AWKWARD:	*Julie,* after falling from her bike, *assured* us she was not hurt. (Subject and verb are separated.)
BETTER:	After falling from her bike, *Julie assured* us she was not hurt.

AWKWARD:	I *found,* inside the envelope that Mother handed me, *an invitation* to a surprise birthday party. (Verb and object are separated.)
BETTER:	I *found an invitation* to a surprise party inside the envelope that Mother handed me.

Exercises Keeping Related Parts Together

A. Revise each of the following sentences. Bring the separated parts closer together.

Suggestions

1. Read each sentence to yourself. Read it in more than one way, moving the parts around. Listen to the sound and sense of the sentence as you say it with the parts in different places.
2. Revise the sentence to bring the separated parts closer.

1. The coach wouldn't, no matter how much we reasoned with him, put Jack back in the game.

2. The crippled plane, because the pilot wanted to use up most of the fuel before landing, circled the field for three hours.

3. We could have, if we had worked together, won the state championship last year.

4. I feel that I could, if I had an interest in chemistry, learn the subject more thoroughly.

5. College graduates receive, on account of their additional training and knowledge, higher salaries.

6. I, because I was in town, decided to buy my parents their Christmas presents.

7. Are there people on other planets who are discovering, by methods that we do not know, important facts about the earth?

8. My parents are, for the whole month of August, renting a bungalow at the shore.

9. I have, although my friends would not believe it, two medals for diving.

10. The gleeman, since there was neither television nor radio at the time, reported news of current happenings to the people.

B. Revise these sentences.

1. This 1924 airmail stamp is, I am told, worth $400.

2. There have been, throughout history, only seven basic jokes.

3. Wolves, in spite of what many think, never attack people.

4. The Hawaiian Islands were, in 1778, discovered by Captain James Cook.

5. The coach announced that she had resigned right after the game.

6. Most of Sam's snapshots had, until he got his new Leica, a washed-out look.

7. My bicycle and I are frankly no longer friends.

8. It had, even though it was a late-model car, a suspiciously low price.

9. Many offices have electric pencil sharpeners, keeping up with progress.

10. According to a psychologist, people are not very trustworthy who wear bow ties.

Part 6   Combining Ideas Effectively

Avoiding Overuse of *and*

Although *and* is a useful conjunction for joining ideas that have a relationship indicating *addition*, its overuse creates a decidedly uninteresting style. Careful writers avoid using *and*'s to join a string of ideas like the following:

I went to the library, and when I got there it was closed, and I was worried because I had to get a book for English, and I knew I would get into trouble if I didn't have it, and I read the sign and noticed that the hours were listed, and . . .

A reader quickly loses interest in a string of ideas like this. The writer's responsibility to a reader is to present ideas in a logical, coherent way. The secret of good writing is to take the time to *reread, revise,* and *rewrite.*

Using Compound Sentences Correctly

To the reader, the value of a compound sentence is that it joins related ideas.

Some people act before they think, and they live to regret it.

Sometimes a writer joins unrelated ideas because he or she does not take time to plan beforehand. Sometimes a writer leaves out an in-between thought through carelessness or haste. The reader is confused and has to stop and ask, "What is the connection between the first and the second idea?" There is no clear connection; the ideas are not related.

You can handle this problem by expressing the thought omitted. It may be necessary to write two sentences to do so.

CONFUSING: The time hand on the electric scoreboard stopped, and the visiting team won the game.

IMPROVED: The time hand on the electric scoreboard stopped. *As a result, extra seconds were allowed for play,* and the visiting team won the game.

CONFUSING: The rain came down in torrents, and the janitor's wife had to entertain the visitors alone.

IMPROVED: The rain came down in torrents. *Because the janitor was working late to take care of the flooded cellar,* his wife had to entertain the visitors alone.

Using Linking Words Correctly

Conjunctive adverbs and other linking words are also used to combine related ideas:

RESULT	ADDITION	
consequently	also	in fact
hence	besides	likewise
therefore	furthermore	moreover
thus	indeed	

EXCEPTION OR CONTRAST		ALTERNATIVE
however	still	at the same time
nevertheless	yet	on the other hand
nonetheless		otherwise

Notice the specific relationships made clear in these sentences.

Joe made the varsity; *consequently,* he will have to spend many hours in after-school practice. (result)

Studying languages disciplines your mind; *furthermore,* it makes communication with other nationalities possible. (addition)

The play had been widely promoted; *nevertheless,* the audience was small. (contrast)

It may snow tonight; *on the other hand,* there may be just a light frost. (alternative)

The choice of different connecting words can change the meaning of a sentence.

Auto racing is a dangerous sport; *nevertheless,* he wants to try it. (exception or contrast)

Auto racing is a dangerous sport; *therefore,* he decided not to try it. (result)

Exercises Combining Ideas Effectively

A. Revise the following sentences. Some of them contain too many *and*'s. Others are compound sentences joining unrelated ideas.

Suggestions:

1. Check the sentence for too many *and*'s.
2. Pick out the main ideas.
3. Combine related ideas.
4. Locate the compound sentences that join unrelated ideas.
5. Supply the details needed to make good sense.
6. Write more than one sentence if necessary.

1. The plane zoomed overhead, and it made a great deal of noise, and it was a 747 and was flying nonstop to California.

2. The game went into overtime, and the coach did not appear for his broadcast at the local studio.

3. I love to watch the snow start its long journey from the sky and fall to the ground, and the snowflakes lie there in all shapes, big ones, little ones, round ones, and people finally step on them or shovel them away.

4. He was watching a television play, and he decided it was the worst he had ever seen, and he was disappointed that this channel would offer such a program, and he turned it off.

5. The bugle corps lined up for the precision drill and maneuvers, and they carried the trophy home in triumph.

6. The train pulled out of the station, gradually picking up speed, and Jim went home disappointed.

7. The girl who had the leading role in the school play got the measles, and I hoped they would let me try out for the part, and they did, and I had only three days to rehearse.

8. The audience filed into their places for the first performance of the school show, and the total box-office receipts were very high.

9. I thought my mother and father didn't love me any more on account of my new baby sister, and my mother sensed my feelings, and she told me she loved all of us and not one more than the other.

10. The traffic was very light, and we all got bad sunburns at the beach.

B. In each of the following sentences, supply a linking word that makes clear the relationship between the parts. If an additional linking word can be used to indicate a different relationship, be prepared to explain what the relationship is.

1. He did not want to go; ⎯⎯⎯⎯⎯⎯, I insisted upon his making an appearance.

2. Perhaps it would take me years to learn the procedure; ⎯⎯⎯⎯⎯⎯, I might master it in six or seven months.

3. There is very little scenery in this play; ⎯⎯⎯⎯⎯⎯, you must use your imagination.

4. I'm not a poor driver; ⎯⎯⎯⎯⎯⎯, the traffic officer always stops me and threatens to give me a ticket.

5. Mr. Black acknowledged that it was Art's fault; ⎯⎯⎯⎯⎯⎯, he pointed out that Bob was responsible to a certain extent, too.

6. Amy felt like going to bed early; ⎯⎯⎯⎯⎯⎯, she had promised to write to Trisha that night.

7. Many of the girls I know ski very well; ⎯⎯⎯⎯⎯⎯, they are willing to take me along with them.

8. I have always wanted to be a teacher; ⎯⎯⎯⎯⎯⎯, I am interested in observing the methods used by my own teachers.

9. Farming had been a tradition in my family; ⎯⎯⎯⎯⎯⎯, my interest in it was not surprising.

10. He had eaten more than anyone else; ⎯⎯⎯⎯⎯⎯, he did it in half the time.

11. Everyone says that the show was the best we've ever had; ⎯⎯⎯⎯⎯⎯, we sold very few tickets.

12. You will have to sign the documents; ⎯⎯⎯⎯⎯⎯, you will have to be accompanied by your parents.

13. By reading a book you can find yourself floating down the Mississippi on a riverboat; ⎯⎯⎯⎯⎯⎯, you can experience the thrill of climbing the Swiss Alps.

14. You must follow the directions that came with the kit; ⎯⎯⎯⎯⎯⎯, you will not be able to assemble the model.

15. The cast of the annual school play was posted; ⎯⎯⎯⎯⎯⎯, Jane's name did not appear on the list.

Part 7 Subordinating Ideas Correctly

Another way to join ideas effectively is to use the complex sentence. The main idea is then expressed in the main clause and the less important idea in the subordinate clause.

SUBORDINATE IDEA   MAIN IDEA
After I had located the article, I read it rapidly.

It must be emphasized that only the writer of the sentence can determine whether ideas are of equal value or whether one is subordinate to the other. To one writer, the ideas in the following sentence may be equally important.

I located the article, and I read it rapidly.

(Turn to Section 1.7 in your Handbook for a list of subordinating conjunctions and the precise relationships they show between main and subordinate ideas.)

Problems in Joining Ideas

Two additional problems in joining ideas are *faulty coordination* and *faulty subordination.*

Faulty Coordination. Although it is true that the writer alone knows what the main idea in a sentence is, there are times when he or she may mistakenly coordinate two ideas that obviously are not of equal value and cannot be joined by *and.* The reader is uncomfortably aware that one idea is dependent upon the other in some way.

> FAULTY: The rainfall was not sufficient, and the roses drooped on their stems.

Here, logic determines that the roses drooped *because the rainfall was not sufficient.* Therefore, the sentence is an example of faulty coordination.

REVISED: *Because the rainfall was not sufficient,* the roses drooped on their stems.

FAULTY: The furniture was old and dilapidated, and my parents were not eager to entertain guests.

REVISED: *Because the furniture was old and dilapidated,* my parents were not eager to entertain guests.

Faulty coordination can be corrected by changing one of the clauses into a subordinate clause, a phrase, or an appositive.

FAULTY: Some students do not concentrate on their work, and they have difficulty in learning.

REVISED: Some students have difficulty in learning *because they do not concentrate on their work.* (subordinate clause)

FAULTY: She listened to John's excuse, and she broke out laughing.

REVISED: *After listening to John's excuse,* she broke out laughing. (phrase)

FAULTY: Joy won first prize in the state instrumental competition, and she is a soloist in our orchestra.

REVISED: *Joy, a soloist in our orchestra,* won first prize in the state instrumental competition. (appositive)

Faulty Subordination. Faulty subordination occurs when the writer states the main idea in the subordinate clause. The meaning thus becomes confused. This confusion may result from a sentence structure in which an idea that should precede another is placed after it.

FAULTY: Because the coat was too expensive for me, it was an imported cashmere.

REVISED: Because the coat was an imported cashmere, it was too expensive for me.

FAULTY: Everyone else was in swimming while Buzz and Joe tied all the clothes in knots.

REVISED: While everyone else was in swimming, Buzz and Joe tied all the clothes in knots.

Exercises Coordinating and Subordinating Ideas

A. Revise the sentences to correct mistakes in faulty coordination.

1. I listened to my father's advice, and I decided to take chemistry.

2. Edna Sloan won the cross-country race, and she is our best runner.

3. The pictures did not turn out well, and I had taken every precaution.

4. Mark Twain became a very popular writer, and he had great obstacles to overcome.

5. My older sister bought a new car, and it is a 1980 Pinto.

6. We won the league games for three successive years, and we have permanent possession of the trophy.

7. I had prepared my lesson thoroughly the night before, and I wasn't worried about the test.

8. Dolores has decided on her career, and it is marine biology.

9. All preparations had been carefully made, and the rocket exploded.

10. Bacteria have built up an immunity to certain antibiotics, and new drugs have to be produced.

11. Our school has many brilliant students, and we did not get a National Merit Scholarship.

12. Don was listening to his new stereo recordings, and he did not notice how late it was.

13. Fred kept looking and he still couldn't find the ball.

14. I sometimes think about death, and it is something that happens to everyone.

15. Mr. Novak told me to interview Miss Carnahan, and she is the personnel manager at the Sara Lee plant.

B. Revise the sentences to correct mistakes in faulty subordination.

1. Not being able to knit the sweater, she could not read the directions.

2. Joan is the top-ranking student in her class, although she is not going to college.

3. Yesterday I was walking down the street when I met a friend I hadn't seen in years.

4. Hurrying to help him, Ted saw his little brother in tears.

5. There was to be an important meeting of the student officers after school, although the president left at the regular time.

6. Wolves are rare because they are on the endangered species list.

7. I stepped off the plane at Kennedy Airport, when I noticed a crowd waiting behind the fence.

8. Dad was busy with his monthly report because he hardly heard a word I said.

9. Dashing out of the house, she grabbed a sandwich from the tray.

10. People who don't like this neighborhood really value privacy.

Part 8 Making Sentence Parts Parallel

The coordinating conjunction *and* joins sentence parts of equal value: noun and noun, verb and verb, phrase and phrase, clause and clause. The constructions are then **parallel.** If *and* is used to join constructions of different kinds, there is a **lack of parallelism.**

Study the following sentences and determine what constructions are joined by *and*. Note the revisions made to achieve parallelism.

FAULTY: Pat wanted a *view* of the West and *to ride* horseback. (noun and infinitive)

REVISED: Pat wanted *to see* the West and *to ride* horseback. (infinitive and infinitive)

FAULTY:	Everyone needs *sympathy* and *to be noticed*. (noun and infinitive)
REVISED:	Everyone needs *sympathy* and *attention*. (noun and noun)

FAULTY:	The principal asked us *to stand* and *that we remain silent for one minute*. (infinitive and clause)
REVISED:	The principal asked *that we stand* and *that we remain silent for one minute*. (clause and clause)

FAULTY:	She requested *help* with her exercise and *that I explain the procedure again*. (noun and clause)
REVISED:	She requested *help* with her exercise and another *explanation* of the procedure. (noun and noun)
REVISED:	She requested *that I help her with her exercise* and *that I explain the procedure again*. (clause and clause)

Lack of parallelism often occurs when the pronouns *which* and *who* are used in a sentence. Avoid using *and who* or *and which* unless there is a preceding *who* or *which* to balance it.

FAULTY:	This is a popular *book* and *which you can get in the school library*. (*and* joins a noun and a clause.)
REVISED:	This is a popular book, which you can get in the school library.
SIMPLER:	You can get this popular book in the school library.

FAULTY:	Ted is a brilliant *boy* and *who has a great future*.
REVISED:	Ted is a brilliant *boy*, and *he has a great future*.
REVISED:	Ted is a brilliant boy who has a great future.
SIMPLER:	Ted is a brilliant boy with a great future.

The fault can be corrected by making sure that the *and* joins two similar constructions. In the revision, *and* may be omitted altogether.

Exercises **Parallelism**

A. Revise these sentences to make the constructions parallel.

1. Dad visited his birthplace and where he grew up.

2. At last I came to a road I knew and which would take me home.

3. When you first meet him, you consider him to be a little odd and that he needs special medical attention.

4. We are going on a trip to Atlantic City and which is a popular resort.

5. In high school chemistry, you will learn about distilling water and to analyze compounds.

6. In this course you will learn accuracy and to work fast.

7. Everyone wants to avoid accidents and being sick.

8. Our neighbors are the Deckers and who won a trip to Mexico last month.

9. Jo had to choose between taking singing lessons and to learn ballet.

10. My brother wanted a trip around the world and to fly in a supersonic plane.

B. Revise these sentences.

1. She has many accomplishments: horseback riding, dancing, skin-diving, and a champion swimmer.

2. We decided to investigate further and that we might find clues in the locked room.

3. The coach was a man of experience and who never got impatient.

4. My brother has a job gassing up cars, picking up trash, and he runs errands.

5. The woman was old, sick, and had no teeth.

6. Gloria Steinem did not want a job taking dictation or be a filing clerk.

7. Following the trail is easier than to cut through the woods.

8. The salad dressing splattered on the table, on the rug, and got spots on Mr. Grimly's suit.

9. The typical American changes jobs seven times, and a change of career three times.

10. Laura is a good babysitter and reliable.

Review Exercises **Revising Sentences with Various Problems**

A. Revise the following sentences. They contain various problems you have dealt with in this chapter.

1. In my opinion, I think the leather jackets in the basement are better buys than the ones on the main floor.

2. Although we enjoyed the trip, the roads were terrible.

3. I like to watch professional tennis because it is an exciting sport to watch.

4. How to program a computer is something I haven't learned how to do yet.

5. I think that it was really fortunate that we had a spare tire.

6. The mayor personally cut the cake herself.

7. I'm afraid that I have to admit that I bungled the job.

8. Dad was in a state of shock because he was shocked by the size of the dinner check.

9. The last person on the show, who was a stand-up comedian, was a very funny fellow.

10. The electrician touched a live wire when she was electrocuted.

B. Revise these sentences:

1. Hank Aaron hit more home runs in his career than any other baseball player, and he hit 733 home runs.

2. I was startled by Selma's remark because I just sat there and said nothing.

3. Our trip to Disney World was, in spite of the long waits in line, fun for every member of the family.

4. When my brother Jack came home from college, he said his grades were so low he needed a snorkel, but I knew he was only joking because he always gets good grades.

5. My grandmother is a successful accountant, a professional clarinetist, and raises German shepherds.

6. Dad found two matching wedding bands in McDonald's driveway, so what he did was put a notice in the paper.

7. When I was only three years old, my family moved from Boston to Louisville, and we have lived in Louisville ever since.

8. The Queen of England can fix your car because she is a trained mechanic, and she learned how to fix cars during World War II.

9. Our fuel pump broke and our car had to be towed to the garage and so we missed the first act of the play.

10. Scientists have landed some equipment on Mars, including a seismometer, and they have studied the earthquakes that take place on Mars, but they call the earthquakes on Mars "Marsquakes."

Chapter 5

The Process of Writing

Learning to write is a continuing process. Once you have learned the basic elements of writing, you can begin to refine your writing. Writing as often as you can becomes increasingly important. You learn to use a more precise vocabulary. You learn to tighten your sentence structure. You begin to find your own "voice" in writing, which enables you to develop a style. You gain a sense of audience for the different kinds of writing you will be doing.

Whenever you write, however, there will always be something that remains the same: the process of writing. There are steps you can follow: pre-writing, writing a first draft, and rewriting, or revising. These steps are critical to the process of writing. They help you decide what to write about, how to organize what you write, and how to rewrite, or revise, what you have written.

Pre-Writing	

	1. *Possible Topics*
	  my first horseback ride
	  dentists' image
	  Starved Rock State Park
	
	2. *Selected Topic*
	  dentists' image

Writing the First Draft	
	need a change of image. *Dentists,* ~~have never been~~ ~~treated fairly. My father is a~~ ~~dentist.~~ *For years, they have* *been, the objects of scorn,* *(a source of fear,) and the targets* *of hundreds of jokes.*

Rewriting, or Revising	
	Dentists need a change of *image. For years, they have* *been a source of fear, the objects* *of scorn, and the targets of* *hundreds of jokes.*

Part 1 Pre-Writing

Sometimes you write in response to an assignment. Sometimes you write in order to communicate something important to you. Whatever you write, and whenever you write, you will find the beginning steps, called pre-writing, very important.

Before you write, you need to focus on your subject. Take your time at this point in the process of writing. Choose a subject that interests you. Use all of your senses to bring your subject clearly into focus. Make a list of possible topics. Select one topic and narrow it so that you can handle it in a given length.

Next, make a list of interesting details that you could use to develop your topic. List as many as you can think of. You can always eliminate those that do not work.

Finally, jot down any notes or ideas related to your topic. You do not have to use all of them. If you need to learn more about your topic, do that, too.

Here is an example of pre-writing notes.

1. Possible Topics
   Uncle John's Workshop
   Ann's new job
   storm at camp
   hot summer day
   the biology lab

2. Selected Topic
   hot summer day

3. Specific Details
   heavy, hot air of August
   afternoon sun
   animals in sprinkler
   no rain -- 19 days
   Ann and Mark arguing
   stillness of Lincoln Street
   no breeze, no energy
   burned lawn

4. Notes
   kind of paragraph - descriptive
   point of of view - third person
   develop with sensory details
   show mood

Part 2   Writing the First Draft

At this point in the process of writing, you are ready to write. Do not fuss with the writing. Do not worry about organizing ideas. Do not fret about spelling or punctuation. Do not get trapped by trying to make anything perfect at this stage. Let whatever happens, happen. Just write. This is only your first draft. You will rewrite, or revise, later.

Here is an example of a first draft of a paragraph.

FIRST DRAFT

It hadn't rained in nineteen days. The hot, thick air hung over the city like a blanket. A sprinkler sprayed the burned-out patch of lawn. The water had attracted sparrows and a large dog. Kathy Newman sat on the front steps, fanning herself with a newspaper. She barely had the energy to move her arm. Inside, her sister and brother, their tempers fueled by the heat, argued noisily. Kathy sighed and looked at the sky for the much-needed rain.

Part 3   Rewriting, or Revising

Now read what you have written. At this stage of the process you will need to work carefully and thoughtfully. You have to check what you have written.

Did you stick to your topic? Did you include everything you wanted to? Did you leave out unnecessary details? Do you like what you have written? Is it lively and interesting?

Read aloud what you have written. Often your ears will catch what your eyes do not. Listen to the rhythm of your writing. Do your ideas flow smoothly?

Concentrate on every word. Is your idea clearly expressed? Did you *show* your reader what you want to say? Is each word the right word?

Is your writing organized logically? Is there a beginning, a middle, and an end to the development of your idea? Take the time to read your writing and to think about it carefully.

Here is the rewritten, or revised, paragraph. Compare it with the first draft. Think about the changes that were made. Notice how the ideas are expressed in a different way.

REWRITTEN, OR REVISED, PARAGRAPH

There had been no rain for
^ ~~It hadn't rained in~~ nineteen days.
motionless, sweltering
The, ~~hot, thick~~ air hung over the
city like a blanket. *On Lincoln Street,* ~~A sprinkler~~
the Newman's sprinkler hissed as it
sprayed the, ~~burned-out~~ patch of
small, scorched *several*
lawn. The water had attracted, sparrows
, panting *Nearby,*
and a large, dog. Kathy Newman sat
slowly
on the front steps, fanning herself
the day's
with, a newspaper. ~~She barely had~~
~~the energy to move her arm.~~
the house
Inside, her sister and brother, their
tempers fueled by the heat, argued
searched
noisily. Kathy sighed and, ~~looked at~~
signs of
the sky for, the much-needed rain.

Proofreading

It is important to make your writing correct, as well as clear and lively. Check your spelling. Check capitalization and punctuation. Use whatever references you have available to check your work.

Finally, when you are satisfied that your writing is clear and correct, write it in its final form. Write carefully. Make your work as neat as possible. Be sure to follow the manuscript form that your teacher requires, including heading and margins.

When you have finished your final copy, proofread your work. Read your writing aloud, to yourself, one final time.

Here is the final copy of the paragraph. Compare it with the two preceding paragraphs.

FINAL COPY

There had been no rain for nineteen days. The motionless, sweltering air hung over the city like a blanket. On Lincoln Street, the Newman's sprinkler hissed as it sprayed the small, scorched patch of lawn. The water had attracted several sparrows and a large, panting dog. Nearby, Kathy Newman sat on the front steps, slowly fanning herself with the day's newspaper. Inside the house, her sister and brother argued noisily. Kathy sighed and searched the sky for signs of the much-needed rain.

Guidelines for the Process of Writing

Pre-Writing

1. Choose a subject that interests you.
2. Make a list of possible topics.
3. Select a topic and narrow it.
4. Make a list of interesting details that you could use to develop your topic.
5. Jot down any notes or ideas related to your topic.
6. Learn more about your topic if you need to.

Writing the First Draft

1. Begin to write.
2. Continue to write, without stopping to fuss over or correct anything at this stage. Let your thoughts flow freely.

Rewriting, or Revising

1. Read what you have written.
2. Did you stick to your topic?
3. Did you include everything you wanted to?
4. Did you leave out unnecessary details?
5. Do you like what you have written?
6. Is it interesting and lively?
7. Read aloud what you have written.
8. Do your ideas flow smoothly?
9. Are your ideas clearly expressed?
10. Is each word the right word?
11. Is your writing organized logically, with a beginning, a middle, and an end?
12. Rewrite, or revise, wherever necessary.

Proofreading

1. Read your rewritten, or revised, first draft.
2. Check for correct capitalization.
3. Check spelling. Use a dictionary, if necessary.
4. Check to see that all punctuation is correct.
5. Make a neat, final copy.
6. Follow required manuscript form.
7. Read your final copy aloud, to yourself.

Chapter 6

Writing Effective Paragraphs

Your goal as a writer is to communicate your ideas clearly to your readers. To accomplish this goal, you need to develop many skills. Among the most important is the ability to organize your ideas into paragraphs. In this chapter you will first examine the basics of paragraph construction. Then you will practice expressing your ideas in different kinds of paragraphs.

Part 1 What Is a Paragraph?

A paragraph is a group of sentences dealing with a single topic or idea. Usually, one sentence, called the topic sentence, states the main idea of the paragraph. All the other sentences are related to this topic sentence. They further explain or support the main idea.

Well written paragraphs are characterized by unity and coherence. Unity is the relationship of the sentences in a paragraph to the topic sentence. Coherence is the relationship of the sentences to each other.

Unity. When all of the sentences in a paragraph are related directly to the topic sentence, the paragraph has unity. Unity can be destroyed by the inclusion of one or two sentences that do not relate to the topic sentence. Sometimes the lack of unity is so pronounced that what you have is a series of disconnected sentences, not a paragraph.

Coherence. When the sentences in a paragraph are arranged in logical order, the paragraph has coherence. Logical orders vary, depending on the subject of the paragraph. The three most common orders are chronological, spatial, and order of importance. Each of these orders is discussed in detail in Chapter 7, Developing the Paragraph.

EXAMPLE 1

Study the following paragraph.

> After six weeks of feeding the lemon shark from the target, we gave him the big test. We put the target into the water at the appointed time but with no food on it. The shark rushed at the target with his mouth open, then swerved aside when he found no food. The second time, and for eight more times, he came in slowly, looking over the target without touching it. Finally, he nuzzled the empty target and set off the automatic bell. We quickly tossed out a reward piece of food wrapped in string that hit the water with a splash just to the left of the target. The shark quickly grabbed the food, cutting the string with his teeth. After that he repeatedly pushed the empty target and then took the food tossed to him, proving that he had associated pressing the target with getting food.—Dr. Eugenie Clark

This is a well written, well organized paragraph, one that exhibits the characteristics of unity and coherence. In the topic sentence, the writer states: "After six weeks of feeding the lemon shark from the target, we gave him the big test." She then describes what happened during the big test. Organizing her ideas in chronological order, she explains what happened first, what happened next, and so on. Every sentence in the paragraph relates back to the topic sentence.

EXAMPLE 2

Study the following example.

> Life at 1308 Carlisle Street was like a circus, with something always going on in at least three places at once. You never had time to think about yourself; you just tried to deal with each emergency as it same up—a fight between the twins, a bone stuck in little Randolph's throat, the baby crying—and go on to the next one. It was fun, like any circus, but going to the circus once a year was one thing, Louretta thought; living with it all the time was something else.—KRISTIN HUNTER

Example 2 is also characterized by unity and coherence. In the topic sentence, the writer describes life at 1308 Carlisle Street as a circus. In the rest of the paragraph she develops this comparison by noting similarities between her home and a circus and by pointing out an important difference. She organizes her ideas in order of importance, ending with the most important idea: Louretta's personal reaction to the circus-like atmosphere.

EXAMPLE 3

Now study this example.

> Preschool children are the single largest television audience in America, spending a greater number of total hours and a greater proportion of their waking day watching television than any other age group. According to a recent survey, children in the two-to-five age group spend an average of 30.4 hours each week watching television, while children in the six-to-eleven group spend 25.5 hours watching. The weekly average for adult viewers is 23.3 hours. Action for Children's Television is a parent-founded organization dedicated to improving the quality of programming for children. Watching television is essentially a passive experience for both children and adults. Another survey documented a weekly viewing time of 34.56 hours for preschool boys and 32.44 hours for preschool girls. Still other surveys suggest figures up to fifty-four hours a week for preschool viewers. Even the most conservative estimates indicate that preschool children in America are spending more than a third of their waking hours watching television.

Example 3 begins with a topic sentence that states the main idea of the paragraph: preschool children are the single largest television audience in America. The second and third sentences support this idea with several statistics. The fourth and fifth sentences, however, introduce ideas that are related to the general topic of television, but do not develop the specific idea of the paragraph. These sentences weaken the unity of the paragraph and should be removed, leaving a revised paragraph that reads as follows:

Preschool children are the single largest television audience in America, spending a greater number of total hours and a greater proportion of their waking day watching television than any other age group. According to a recent survey, children in the two-to-five age group spend an average of 30.4 hours each week watching television, while children in the six-to-eleven group spend 25.5 hours watching. The weekly average for adult viewers is 23.3 hours. Another survey documented a weekly viewing time of 34.56 hours for preschool boys and 32.44 hours for preschool girls. Still other surveys suggest figures up to fifty-four hours a week for preschool viewers. Even the most conservative estimates indicate that preschool children in America are spending more than a third of their waking hours watching television.

EXAMPLE 4

Read the following paragraph.

The problems of urban growth are painfully apparent. One of the worst is "urban sprawl." Many cities face tax starvation. Homes, schools, stores, factories, and highways spread across open land in an unplanned crazy-quilt pattern, smothering the countryside with confusion. They continue to depend on many of the services—hospital care, sewer lines, water supplies, and amusements—which are highly developed in the central cities. Another problem is the clash between the spreading city and the older political units—towns, villages, and counties—which lie in its path. Some authorities cite Los Angeles as a prime example of both problems and wryly call it "a hundred suburbs in search of a city."

After reading the topic sentence, you assume that all the ideas in the paragraph are going to relate to the problems of urban growth. All the ideas do, in fact, relate to these problems. However, the ideas are so disorganized that you probably had trouble understanding the relationship.

To begin an analysis of the paragraph, look at Sentence 1. It is a clear, well written statement of the main idea of the paragraph. Sentence 2 begins to explain the idea by identifying one of the problems of urban growth. Sentence 3, however, does not continue with the discussion of this problem. It introduces the new idea "tax starvation" without relating it to urban growth. This sentence should, therefore, be deleted.

Sentence 4 returns to the original idea of the paragraph. It defines "urban sprawl," the problem identified in Sentence 2. Sentences 2 and 4 can be combined to make a new sentence that reads, One of the worst is "urban sprawl," in which homes, schools, factories, and highways spread across open land in an unplanned crazy-quilt pattern, smothering the countryside with confusion.

Sentence 5 has a different kind of problem. It begins with the pronoun *they*, which refers to the homes, schools, stores, factories, and highways named in the previous sentence. The connection that the pronoun establishes between the two sentences is faulty. Homes, schools, stores, factories, and highways do *not* depend on hospital care, sewer lines, water supplies and amusements; people do. Sentence 5, therefore, should be removed.

Sentences 6 and 7 return once again to the original idea, the problems of urban growth. They should be retained because they explain the main idea of the paragraph.

After making the specified changes, the paragraph reads as follows:

> The problems of urban growth are painfully apparent. One of the worst is "urban sprawl," in which homes, schools, stores, factories, and highways spread across open land in an unplanned crazy-quilt pattern, smothering the countryside with confusion. Another problem is the clash between the spreading city and the older political units—towns, villages, and counties—which lie in

its path. Some authorities cite Los Angeles as a prime example of both problems and wryly call it "a hundred suburbs in search of a city."

The paragraph is now well written and well organized. All the ideas fit together to achieve a feeling of unity—a feeling that all the ideas stick to the point.

Exercise Identifying Well Written Paragraphs

Study the following groups of sentences. Identify those that are well organized paragraphs and those that are not. Revise the latter by rearranging sentences, by dropping sentences, by adding information, or by making other changes that transform the groups of sentences into unified paragraphs.

1   No one could escape from the city. The mainland was two miles away, across an expanse of wild water that no boat could survive. All four bridges were down. Men, women, and children crouched in their houses, staying close to the walls because that was the safest place if the roof came down. Houses were collapsing; people were dying. No one knew how many, no one knew when his or her turn would come. The wind blew on—and on—and on.

2   The opening shock of the orange chute jerked McIver straight up. He threw his head back to check the rigging. It was perfect. He pulled on the toggle held in his left hand, allowing a jet of air to escape from an opening in the back of the chute. This maneuver compensated for the strong wind, and he drifted steadily toward the landing site.

3   Native Americans have contributed a great deal to American farming methods. The white settlers in Colonial America might have starved if they had not copied Indian farming methods. Many places in the United States have names of Indian origin. Approximately half of the states have Indian names. At least one group, the Pima, had a well developed irrigation system.

4   As the first mist of morning rose over the hills, Vyry poked among the rubble and the warm ashes of her gutted home, trying to salvage any possible possession. At first, she was just another part of the gray mist that enfolded her, the gray shawl she was wearing, and the gray sky against whose grayness she was stooped alone in gray relief. Occasionally she found an iron pot or a fork and a spoon in the charred remains piled near the blackened chimney that had been the chimney of her kitchen. A little wind blew among the ashes, and sometimes the dust blew into her face. Then she would slowly straighten up and, carefully blinking her eyes, let the tears wash her eyes clean before bending down to continue her dismal search.

5   About five in the afternoon we submerged and set our course for the North Pole. The geographic North Pole does not coincide with the magnetic North Pole. All through the night, as we sped northward, the ice detector and television scanned the surface in vain for patches of thin ice. The nuclear submarines Nautilus and Skate reached the North Pole in 1958 and 1959, respectively. Our belief that we would find thin ice frequently enough to surface at will began to seem overly optimistic. Our plan to surface precisely at the North Pole began to look hopeless.

6   It was a warm, sunny day without a cloud in the sky. The day before had also been bright. I was standing by a weathered old tenement house. The paint had peeled from the walls; and what had been a front porch was now a mass of splintered, rotted wood. The house had once been the elegant home of a meat-packing tycoon. Servants had scrubbed the steps and polished the brass and answered the door in starched uniforms. Down the dirty street, I could see a little girl standing in the shadows. She held a doll with a broken head in her arms. She had long, blonde hair, and she was crying.

7   The road that passed the cabin lay like a thread dropped on a patchwork quilt. Stalk land, fallow fields, and brushland, all appeared to be sewn together by wide, fencerow stitches of trees. Their bare branches spread out to join together the separate patches of land. Weeds grew on either side of the road in summer, and a thin strip of green clung to life between the dusty tracks. In summer, a horse and wagon made almost no noise in the soft earth. In winter, when the ground was frozen, the rattle of wheels and each distinct hoofbeat puctuated the winter quiet. When the wind blew, little clouds of dust would rise in the road and follow the wind tracks across the fields.

8   I found a dead bat on the floor and sat down on the bench at the front of the store to examine it. It had a very unpleasant smell, but it was such an interesting creature that I ignored the odor. It had rather large, pointed ears and very sharp little claws. Its wings were webbed like the feet of ducks, with a thin membranelike tissue that was attached to the body, reaching from the front legs, or arms, to the back legs and attached to the sides. The body was small in comparison to the wide sweep of those curious wings. I stretched its wings out and they looked like the inside of an opened umbrella, and I couldn't help admiring them. I began to think of all the things I'd heard said about bats, "blind as a bat," and the word *batty* meaning crazy. I tried to figure out why *batty* means "crazy," and decided it's probably because a bat's behavior doesn't make sense to a human being. Its fast, erratic flight looks senseless.

9   Who are the Mexican people? That may be an impossible question to answer because we are so highly diverse and even unpredictable. We are peace-loving and friendly, yet we started the first bloody revolution in the twentieth century. We are vindictive and unforgiving, yet for three centuries we patiently worked on our own land as peons for those who had taken it from us in conquest. We are fiercely emotional and hot-blooded, yet in ancient times we were intellectual enough to chart the heavens with startling accuracy and build magnificent pyramids with geometrical precision. We are a cosmic people whose racial identity spanned an ocean and enshrined the best of two worlds.

10   As you move toward the baggage-claim area, you may see a family group which you can identify by the striking similarity in the way they walk. Walking away from the departure area, you see three travelers in telephone booths. Others on their way to the

baggage-claim counter who have been met by family or friends usually appear the happiest and walk with a great deal of enthusiasm. An airport is an excellent spot for viewing the entire human emotional spectrum. Those who are waiting to be met keep rising on their toes and looking around.

Part 2 The Topic Sentence and Its Function

In order to write a good paragraph, you must be able to write a good topic sentence. As defined earlier, a topic sentence states the main idea of a paragraph. The rest of the sentences must develop this single idea. The topic sentence, by containing the main idea, controls the content of the entire paragraph.

The topic sentence sometimes appears in the middle of a paragraph and sometimes at the end. Its usual position, though, is at the beginning of a paragraph. When the topic sentence is the opening statement, it establishes a type of contract between writer and reader. The writer is saying, in effect, "Look, I have an idea that I want to explain to you." The reader is responding, "All right, explain it to me." If the writer holds to the contract, the rest of the paragraph will explain the idea introduced in the topic sentence.

EXAMPLE 1

Here is an example of a topic sentence.

> Computers can make extremely fast calculations, millions of them a second, using facts stored in their electronic memories, yet these remarkable machines have a basic limitation.

In this sentence, the writer makes a contract in which she says, "I want to tell you about a limitation of computers." She then proceeds to fulfill her contract by explaining the limitation.

> *Computers can make extremely fast calculations, millions of them a second, using facts stored in their electronic memories,*

yet these remarkable machines have a basic limitation. They can only do what they are instructed, or "programmed," to do. They are no more skillful or accurate than the people who work on them, for if the programming is wrong, the answers will be wrong.

All the ideas in the paragraph are related to the topic sentence. This sentence controls the content of the entire paragraph.

EXAMPLE 2

Here is a second topic sentence.

> There was not much beauty here, only a gray, dirty, sad world we had lived in for nine months.

The contract implied by the writer of this sentence is, "I want to describe a gray, dirty, sad world." The writer, however, does not hold to this contract, as seen in the remainder of the paragraph.

> *There was not much beauty here, only a gray, dirty, sad world we had lived in for nine months.* In the alleys the snow packed down hard on the mounds of garbage and provided us with hills for sliding. It leveled the uneven sidewalks. It even painted the buildings and filled the holes in the streets and in yards, and laid lawns, for once, over all the neighborhood. It was clean. It was pure. It was good.

The topic sentence tells you that the paragraph will be about "a gray, dirty, sad world." Instead of developing this idea, however, the rest of the paragraph describes the beautiful transformation of the neighborhood caused by the clean, pure, good snow.

Key Words. In Example 2 the idea that controls the content of the paragraph is contained in the key phrase "gray, dirty, sad world." This is true of most topic sentences; the main idea is presented in one or several key words within the sentence. For example:

1. Pierrot was a gentle dog.
2. The calmness of the night was almost oppressive.
3. Breakfast on Saturday mornings was lazy and unhurried.

In topic sentence 1 the key word is *gentle;* in sentence 2 it is *calmness.* In sentence 3 the key phrase is *lazy and unhurried.* Each word or phrase sets the direction of the entire paragraph. Paragraph 1 will focus on Pierrot's gentleness. Paragraph 2 will give details that reinforce the idea of calmness. Paragraph 3 will explain what made the breakfasts so lazy and unhurried.

Paragraph Length

The length of a paragraph is also controlled by the topic sentence. A paragraph must be long enough to develop the single idea stated in that sentence. If the idea is simple and familiar, the paragraph will most likely be brief. If, however, you have chosen a complex idea or experience, the paragraph probably will be long and detailed.

A paragraph that is too short for its subject leaves the readers with a feeling of incompleteness. The following is an example of such a paragraph.

> Look at it this way, Mom and Dad. If I had my own car, you'd be free. Besides that, I could run a lot of errands for the family and be helpful.

This paragraph presents a brief and not very convincing argument. To be effective, it must be expanded.

> Look at it this way, Mom and Dad. If I had my own car, you'd be free. I could come and go as I had to, without bothering anybody or borrowing somebody else's car. The way it is now, if I use the family car, you're stuck until I get back; and if you use it when I need it, I'm stuck. That means I have to depend on my friends for rides and trust my life to whichever driver wants to take me along. You know that some of my friends drive dangerously, but I'm a careful driver. I'd always be home on time, too, because I'd be in charge of the car. Besides that, I could run a lot of errands for the family and be helpful.

The paragraph now communicates with far greater clarity and is, therefore, more satisfying to the reader.

Exercise **Analyzing Paragraphs**

Read the following paragraphs carefully. Identify those in which the writers have kept their contracts with their readers by developing the idea in the topic sentence and by giving enough information about it. Suggest possible revisions for those paragraphs in which the writers have not kept their contracts.

1   Kitty O'Neil has earned the title "fastest woman alive." She has driven superpowered vehicles on land and water. Handicapped children are her special interest. Herself deaf since infancy, she encourages deaf children to set high goals for success. Ms. O'Neil eats mostly spinach and other vegetables to keep in shape for her demanding job as a television and movie stuntwoman. She is the only woman member of Stunts Unlimited, a group of highly trained performers whose services are always in great demand.

2   There are laws of nature that I doubt we shall ever understand. Take such a simple matter as the twining of vines that climb by twisting their stems around a stronger support. They twist, with few exceptions, counterclockwise. Smoke rising from a chimney also twists counterclockwise. Hurricanes move in the same direction as they come whirling up the coast from the Caribbean. And water whirlpooling down the kitchen sink makes the same counterclockwise motion. Why is this so?

3   I always thought I'd like to sky dive. When I was little, I used to like to go swimming. Near the lake was a huge tree with a branch that reached out over the water. The other kids would climb up there—ten, maybe fifteen feet—hold their noses, and jump off; but I was always afraid of heights.

4   I knew with a terrifying certainty that I was no longer alone in the house. The hall clock chimed with comforting regularity. Rex yelped softly in his sleep. Outside a loose shutter banged familiarly against the shingles.

5   One day we heard Mrs. Cook's dog barking down beside the swamp at the base of the cornfield. We ran out to see what had

happened. When we got there, the dog was standing still, with his tail straight up in the air, barking hysterically. There, lying beside a log, was a big, old snake with fishy scales all over his body. Aldine, Junior, and I stood there in a trance looking at it, too scared to move. We had never seen one like this. It was so big it didn't even look like a snake. It looked big enough to swallow us whole. Finally the snake slowly made its way back into the swamp, leaving a trail of mashed-down grass behind it.

A moose was standing in the water among the lily pads on the far shore, his great antlered head and humped neck silhouetted clearly against the pale moon. He thrust his head again and again under the water, raising it high into the air after each immersion, and arching his neck. Two or three water hens swam out from the reeds, a little crested grebe popped up like a jack-in-the-box in the water beside them, and the spreading ripples of their wake caught the light of the moon. The moose squelched slowly out of the muddy water, shook himself, and turned, cantering up the bank out of sight.

Most diets are so weird that people don't follow them for long. There are some exceptions, of course. Dieters need to select foods from the four basic food groups.

Numerous reports of the yeti, or Abominable Snowman, have come from the Himalayas for some two hundred years. Villagers relate stories about it that date back many generations, and some claim to have recently seen the yeti. The first Westerner to have published an account of the yeti was B. H. Hodgson in 1832. Since then, more than forty Westerners have described sighting the yeti or its footprints.

Catching the Reader's Attention

The primary purpose of a topic sentence is to control the paragraph. The secondary purpose is to catch the reader's attention.

Look at the following topic sentences.

1. I am going to tell you about the excitement of grass skiing.
2. My trip to Lake Tahoe last summer was interesting.
3. Solar power is an important source of energy.

Each sentence could be developed into a paragraph, yet many readers might not be interested in reading the paragraph because of the dull opening sentence.

In contrast, the following sentences would most likely intrigue the reader enough to read beyond the opening sentence.

1. Simon was tough, intelligent, and determined to live.
2. Salt Lake City, Utah, has a law against carrying an unwrapped ukelele on the street.
3. Having an overly friendly dog cost me a job.

After reading each of these sentences, you probably found yourself asking questions such as these: What was wrong with Simon? Why was he so determined to live? How did such a silly law get passed? Does Salt Lake City have any other silly laws? What did the dog do? How could a dog's behavior cause a person to lose a job? Each sentence has caught your attention and has made you want to read further.

Part 3 Characteristics of the Topic Sentence

In Part 2, you learned that the topic sentence controls the entire paragraph; it controls both its content and its length. In order to function in this way, a topic sentence must have two basic characteristics.

1. It must be a general statement.
2. It must be a limited statement.

Although these two characteristics seem contradictory, they come together harmoniously in the good topic sentence.

A Topic Sentence Is a General Statement

A topic sentence must be broad enough so that it can be supported or explained by specific detail. It must be wider in scope, or more general, than the rest of the sentences in the paragraph.

Here are three good topic sentences that are general statements.

1. Anpao stopped and stared at the ground.
2. Los Angeles has a vaguely Mexican atmosphere, which cannot be captured in words or concepts.
3. The fall was a beautiful scarf of warm, hazy days that trailed leisurely over the Panhandle.

These sentences contain very little specific information. Each states what the paragraph is about. Each is general enough to be developed with specific details.

Let's see how the writers of the three topic sentences explained their general statements.

1   *Anpao stopped and stared at the ground.* On the trail lay the most beautiful objects he had ever seen. There was a war shirt, a shield, and a bow and arrows. Anpao had never seen such handsome weapons. He had never seen such a noble war shirt. His own clothes had become shabby from the long journey in the desert. His last pair of moccasins was torn, and his hair was knotted and filthy. He crouched so he could gaze at the beautiful things on the ground. It seemed as if someone had surely left them there so any passerby could take them. But Anpao would not touch them. He got up and walked carefully around the objects and continued on his way.—JAMAKE HIGHWATER

The writer first makes the general statement, "Anpao stopped and stared at the ground." Then he gives specific information about what Anpao sees on the ground; about what Anpao looks like, which affects his response to what is on the ground; and about Anpao's reaction to what he sees.

2   *Los Angeles has a vaguely Mexican atmosphere, which cannot be captured in words or concepts.* The Mexicanism—delight in

decorations, carelessness and pomp, negligence, passion and reserve—floats in the air. I say "floats" because it never mixes or unites with the other world, the North American world based on precision and efficiency. It floats, without offering any opposition; it hovers, blown here and there by the wind, sometimes breaking up like a cloud, sometimes standing erect like a rising skyrocket. It creeps, it wrinkles, it expands and contracts; it sleeps or dreams; it is ragged but beautiful. It floats, never quite existing, never quite vanishing.—Octavio Paz

Here again, the writer opens with a general statement, "Los Angeles has a vaguely Mexican atmosphere, which cannot be captured in words or concepts." Then he describes the way Mexicanism "floats" in the air of the city.

3   *The fall was a beautiful scarf of warm, lazy days that trailed leisurely over the Panhandle.* Along the Niobrara River, the silvery-gray strips of buffalo-berry bushes flaunted clumps of blood-red creeper. Back from the river, large, solitary cottonwoods rustled golden leaves in the light wind, and along the bluffs tall ash stood like slim, golden maidens against the darker brush.—Mari Sandoz

The writer makes a general statement about the fall, then follows with details about the trees and bushes that grew near the Niobrara River.

A Topic Sentence Is a Limited Statement

A topic sentence makes a general statement—a statement that is broader in scope than the rest of the paragraph. However, if a topic sentence is *too* general, the remainder of the paragraph will have to be either extremely long in order to explain the idea, or it will have to contain nothing but general statements. A topic sentence, therefore, must be a limited statement that presents an idea that can be developed completely in one paragraph.

Here are examples of topic sentences that are too broad.

1. He liked all kinds of fresh fruit.
2. I like comedies, especially film comedies.
3. Mathematics is useful in many areas of everyday life.

Each of these topic sentences would require several paragraphs for adequate development. If an attempt were made to develop any one of them in one paragraph, the paragraph would contain nothing but several broad generalizations, as in the following example.

> He liked all kinds of fresh fruit. He liked the way they felt in his hand, and he liked the way they smelled. Best of all, he liked the way they tasted.

To develop the idea in the topic sentence completely, the writer would have had to describe fruits such as apples, pears, peaches, plums, apricots, oranges, and grapes. She would have had to describe their feel, smell, and taste. As this was impossible within the confines of a single paragraph, she relied on generalizations that failed to explain why the person in the paragraph likes fresh fruit.

To communicate the basic idea of liking fruit more clearly, the topic sentence must be limited to a specific kind of fruit and to a specific situation, as in the following sentence.

> The cherry was a smooth, shiny marble in the child's possessing hand.

The idea in this sentence can be developed into a paragraph with the addition of specific details.

> The cherry was a smooth, shiny marble in the child's possessing hand. He stared at its roundness in fascination and thought he had never seen anything so beautifully red. It was flowers and summer days, and the brightest stones under the warmest streams. He held all these starry things burning together in his palm and smiled a secret smile that he felt to the tips of his toes. He pressed the fire-jewel, the robin feather, the drop of blood hard between thumb and finger and felt it squish into water. A warm, sweet smell rose up; and, with the tip of a small tongue, he licked the tart juice from his fingers. "The sun would taste like this if you could bite it," he sighed.

Exercises **Working with Topic Sentences**

A. From each pair of sentences, select the one that is more general.

1. a. First my alarm didn't go off, and I overslept.
   b. It had been a bad day.

2. a. Companionship is necessary for everyone.
   b. Infants who are alone for long periods of time fail to thrive.

3. a. Art and music are used in the treatment of disturbed children.
   b. Therapists study the drawings of children to identify emotional problems.

4. a. The air was warm for early June, and, as the hours passed, it lingered warm.
   b. It was a magnificent afternoon.

5. a. Fascinated, I watched the student rewire the lamp.
   b. Every movement was precise and purposeful.

6. a. I wish to hear the silence of the night.
   b. The silence of the night is positive.

7. a. Listening is an active, not a passive, endeavor.
   b. At least half of communicating is listening.

8. a. Highways block animal migration routes.
   b. Highways can destroy our precious wildlife.

9. a. Interviewers look for many qualities when they speak with a job applicant.
   b. The first thing an interviewer notices about a job applicant is his or her appearance.

10. a. The "happy talk" format of many news shows has come under severe criticism.
    b. Increasing pressure is being felt by television networks to revamp their news shows.

B. From each pair of sentences, select the one that is sufficiently limited to be developed in one paragraph.

1. a. According to the Surgeon General, smoking is hazardous to your health.
   b. Medical studies show that smoking is a leading cause of lung cancer.

2. a. An important requirement for scuba-diving is good breathing habits.
   b. Scuba-diving has many strenuous requirements.

3. a. Calf roping is a traditional rodeo competition.
   b. The Calgary Stampede, the oldest rodeo in Canada, has several main events.

4. a. San Francisco is a beautiful and interesting city.
   b. Fisherman's Wharf in San Francisco has many wonderful seafood restaurants.

5. a. Photography requires a sense of composition.
   b. Photography is an interesting and educational hobby.

6. a. A kid brother can be one of the world's worst nuisances.
   b. Last Sunday my brother Jason played a trick on me.

7. a. History has taught that cheating never pays.
   b. Joe was expelled from history class when he was caught cheating on a test.

8. a. To become a doctor, my friend, Ms. Williams, put in many long years of study and practice.
   b. A doctor can choose from many different specialties.

9. a. Chicago's Lakefront Festival is one of the city's most popular events.
   b. The most popular show at Chicago's Lakefront Festival was the comedy theatre.

10. a. Ray Harryhausen is one of the best known special effects experts in Hollywood.
    b. Special effects have been the main drawing force of several recent movies.

c. In the following paragraphs, the topic sentences have been removed, leaving only the supporting details. For each paragraph, write a topic sentence that is more general in scope than the details, but is limited enough to be adequately developed by the details.

1   In height, a bamboo plant can range anywhere from a dwarf twig, barely three inches tall, to a climber thrusting 200 feet skyward. In width, it can be a slender tendril of *sasa* one-tenth of an inch across or a hulking, seven-inch-wide pillar of *madake*.

2   The eyes, a camel's only truly beautiful feature, are double-lashed in a heavy fringe that screens out blowing sand. The ears and nostrils can be closed up tightly for the same purpose. The feet, disproportionately large at the bottom of skinny shins, are splayed and padded, the better to move over sand without sinking.

3   A calculator was propelled through a snowblower last winter; another was run over by a trailer truck. Both proved still usable after minor repairs. A calculator lost by a California survey crew on a 5000-foot mountain, where summer temperatures soar above 100 degrees and winter brings ten feet of snow, blinked instantly to life when found by a hunter a year and a half later.

4   The dunes were covered with mats of sand flowers, which are red and have tiny eyes that are sometimes pink and sometimes white. Yuccas grew tall among the rocks of the ravine. Their heads were clustered with curly globes no larger than pebbles and the color of the sun when it rises. Lupines grew where the springs ran. From the sunny cliffs, in crevices where no one would think anything could grow, sprang the little red and yellow fountains of the comul bush.—Scott O'Dell

5   Somehow I like, as often as possible, to touch nature, not something that is artificial or an imitation, but the real thing. When I can leave my office in time so that I can spend thirty or forty minutes in spading the ground, in planting seeds, in digging about the plants, I feel that I am coming into contact with something that is giving me strength for the many duties and hard places that await me out in the big world. I pity the man or woman who has never learned to enjoy nature and to get strength and inspiration out of it.—Booker T. Washington

D. Following is a list of subjects. Choose two and write topic sentences that could be developed into effective paragraphs. Then select two topic sentences from any of these sources: (1) the sentences you have written for this Exercise, (2) the general statements you identified in Exercise A, or (3) the limited sentences you chose for Exercise B. Write two paragraphs for the topic sentences you have chosen.

1. Frisbee throwing
2. First-aid
3. Nutrition
4. Careers
5. Advertising slogans
6. Television drama
7. Communities
8. Animal behavior
9. Nonverbal communication
10. A neighbor
11. Saving money
12. Comic books
13. After-school jobs
14. Saturday mornings
15. Study habits

Chapter 7

Developing the Paragraph

The preceding chapter examined the characteristics of the well written paragraph. Its primary emphasis was on the topic sentence and its controlling function within the paragraph. In this chapter, the emphasis shifts to the sentences that explain or support the idea presented in the topic sentence. The chapter takes a close look at four types of paragraphs—narrative, descriptive, explanatory, and persuasive—and explores the development of each into unified, coherent paragraphs.

Part 1   The Narrative Paragraph

The narrative paragraph is a natural form of writing that may be based on fact, on the imagination, or on a combination of both. Defined simply, a narrative paragraph is the telling of events. "Last night while I was watching a movie a strange thing happened," "Did you hear about Frank's accident at the football game," or "My sister did the nicest thing this morning" are examples of the kinds of sentences that begin narratives.

A narrative paragraph usually is developed in chronological order; that is, the events are related in the order in which they happened. Often a writer will open a narrative paragraph with a description of the first event rather than with a topic sentence. Although this is a common and acceptable practice, the examples in this chapter follow the established pattern of a general statement developed with specific details.

Some narrative paragraphs relate events that are part of longer pieces of writing. The following two examples illustrate this type of narrative:

1 Anpao and Grandmother Spider lived very happily in the tipi near the green gourd field. In the golden light of Anpao's great father, Grandmother Spider made bowls of clay and baked them in the sunshine until they dried. Then she baked them again in the embers of her cooking fire. She gathered the thorny leaves of the yucca and coiled them into baskets. Then Anpao and Grandmother Spider went out into the autumn days to collect dried plants and to bring them home, where they were stored for the winter in the new baskets. They hung the yellow gourds to dry and they smoked meat over the fire.—JAMAKE HIGHWATER

2 Jennie was not listening to these words. She had fallen into a trance-like meditation. Her lips twitched. She chewed her gums and rubbed her gnarled hands nervously. Suddenly she leaned forward, buried her face in the nervous hands, and burst into tears. She cried aloud in a dry, cracked voice that suggested the rattle of fodder on dead stalks. She cried aloud like a child, for she had never learned to suppress a genuine sob. Her slight old frame shook heavily and seemed hardly able to sustain such violent grief.—ARNA BONTEMPS

Other narrative paragraphs are complete within themselves. They resemble miniature short stories in that they build to a climax, often achieved in the final sentence. Following are three examples of such paragraphs:

1 As an attendance clerk in a junior high school for seven years, I was sure that every possible excuse for an absence had crossed my

desk. Thus I was delighted when, during a week of beautiful fall weather, a seventh-grader handed me this note from her mother: "Friday I took my family out into the glorious golden day. Dana, therefore, was absent from school, but not, I trust, absent from learning experiences. Such days have flooded the senses of poets and resulted in great contributions to literature."

2   It was George Crum, an American Indian, who chipped the first potato. In 1853 Crum was employed as a chef at a posh resort in Saratoga Springs, New York. One evening a particularly fussy guest kept returning his french fries because they were "too thick." Crum grabbed a potato, sliced it into paper-thin pieces, and plunged them into boiling fat. The resulting golden, curling chips were proclaimed delicious by the stubborn diner. They were known as Saratoga chips until the turn of the century. Thereafter, they were called potato chips.—BRUCE FELTON AND MARK FOWLER

3   My dad's a tinkerer with a creative bent, and he leaps at a chance to solve difficult problems. When a friend complained of being unable to rid his attic of a colony of squirrels, Dad immediately volunteered his services, suggesting the use of a flashing yellow light to scare them out. The two men installed it one Saturday afternoon and, after an hour, slowly opened the attic door. The light was working, but not in the way my father had expected. Around it, in a perfect semicircle, sat the squirrels, staring in fascination at the yellow light.—DAVID TOBIT

Exercises Developing Narrative Paragraphs

A. Following is a list of topic sentences written by professional writers. Read and think about the sentences one at a time. Then, for each, describe what might happen in the rest of the paragraph.

1. As one disreputable character to another, I frequently told Lacey Jordan that he was simply out of this world.

2. Miss Burton was always careful about giving money to street beggars.

3. At the cemetery it was a little group, not many of us, standing there in the autumn sunshine.

4. He was nothing but a wasted little piece of humanity, with the body of a half-grown boy and the eyes of a dreamer.

5. I almost ran over the snake before I could stop the tractor.

6. There was an eeriness about him as he moved through the night.

7. I was coming home from school when I passed Gavin's poolroom and saw the big guys hanging around.

8. Sam Wolinsky was seventeen, and a month had passed since he had begun to shave; now he was in love.

9. I guess being raised on a ranch, a fellow comes by his love of horses naturally.

10. Chuck squeezed into the grease pit under the race car and knocked the mud off the fitting.

11. Even in such obvious trouble, even with the police officer's grip still firm on his wrist, Johnnie Dakin's eyes had a flat, steady defiance in them.

12. With the closing of the door, Ellen left one of her lives behind and entered upon the other.

13. It was Paul's afternoon to appear before the Assistant Principal to account for his various misdemeanors.

14. I certainly made a fool of myself that time.

15. Nothing I did seemed to change Avey's indifference to me.

B. Following is a list of topics, each of which may be developed into a narrative paragraph. Choose two, or make up topics of your own. Then, drawing from your own experiences, the experiences of others, or your imagination, write two narrative paragraphs. Be sure to begin each paragraph with a topic sentence.

1. A Bad Day at School
2. The Day _____ Died
3. A Family Celebration
4. A Night To Remember
5. A New Kid Comes to School
6. It Pays To Be on Time

Part 2   The Descriptive Paragraph

A descriptive paragraph paints a word picture that appeals to the senses: sight, hearing, taste, touch, and smell. Some descriptive paragraphs appeal to one sense only. However, most appeal to a combination of the senses, as in the following example.

> The twilight was white, and it lasted for a long while. The sky became a curious blue-green that soon faded to white. The air was soft gray, and the arbor and trees were slowly darkening. It was the hour when sparrows gathered and whirled above the rooftops of the town, and when in the darkened elms along the street there was the August sound of the cicadas. Noises at twilight had a blurred sound, and they lingered—the slam of a screen door down the street, voices of children, the whir of a lawnmower from a yard somewhere.—CARSON McCULLERS

The writer of the paragraph creates an impression of twilight with carefully chosen words and precise details. She develops the paragraph by using phrases that appeal to the reader's sense of sight.

1. The twilight was white

2. The sky became a curious blue-green

3. The air was soft gray

4. the arbor and trees were slowly darkening

5. the darkened elms

She also uses phrases that appeal to the sense of hearing.

1. sound of the cicadas
2. Noises . . . had a blurred sound
3. the slam of a screen door
4. voices of children
5. the whir of a lawnmower

Each phrase contributes to the word picture that is evoked in the mind of the reader.

The writer of the next description appeals to all five senses.

> With the subtlest of incidents, he knew that this day was going to be different. It would be different also, because, as his father explained, driving Douglas and his ten-year-old brother Tom out of town toward the country, there are some days compounded completely of odor, nothing but the world blowing in one nostril and out of the other. And some days, he went on, were days of hearing every trump and trill of the universe. Some days were good for tasting and some for touching. And some days were good for all the senses at once. This day now, he nodded, smelled as if a great and nameless orchard had grown up overnight beyond the hill to fill the entire visible land with its warm freshness. The air felt like rain, but there were no clouds. Momentarily, a stranger might laugh off in the woods, but there was silence.—RAY BRADBURY

The writer first explains how his father classified days according to their sensory appeal. He then gives his father's description of one day that was "good for all the senses." He includes the following details.

1. smell/taste: as if a great and nameless orchard had grown up overnight to fill the entire visible land with its warm freshness
2. touch: The air felt like rain
3. sight: there were no clouds
4. hearing: a stranger might laugh . . . there was silence

Organizing Visual Details

Many descriptions of places and objects are primarily visual in appeal. These descriptions contain details that are organized in spatial order. Some spatial orders are direct and easy for the reader to follow. For example: from side to side, from top to bottom (or the reverse), or from near to far (or the reverse). These orders often are clarified through the use of words and phrases that indicate direction, such as *to the left, next to, above, at the top of, behind,* and *in front of.*

In more sophisticated writing, less structured patterns of spatial organization are common. In these paragraphs, direction words and phrases are essential, for without them a reader could not follow the descriptions.

The writers of the two sample paragraphs clearly indicate changes in direction with a variety of phrases.

1   Terminal Island pointed like a finger into the ocean outfalls of Long Beach. On the northeast half of the island, where the narrow channel was bridged into Long Beach proper, stood the vast complex of Long Beach Naval Station, home port to many of the ships destroyed at Pearl Harbor. At the island's lower end was the Federal immigration and customs facility and the low and fenced spread of Terminal Island Prison. The channel itself, between San Pedro, Fort MacArthur, and the Lomita oil fields, bristled with the slips and quays of busy and vital Los Angeles Harbor. Here stood shipyards, drydocks, and the oil storage tanks servicing the vast petroleum commerce out of one of the busiest harbors in the world.—PAUL BAILEY

2   I opened the gate and stepped into a beautiful garden. Huge poppies in vivid rows of orange and yellow nodded sleepily in the hot August sunlight. Back of these, tall spires of larkspur in a gamut of brilliant blues waved their lovely arms and trembled at each butterfly's shy kiss. The riotous marigold flaunted her golden gown against the lush cool green of an untrimmed privet hedge. In the center of a grassy circle, a flock of sparrows quarreled with two bluejays over the right to bathe in a white marble bird bath. But

in a nearby syringa bush, a cheery robin, oblivious to the confusion, sang lustily. Three weeping willow trees at the rear of the garden sheltered a rustic bench. In the midst of all this loveliness I sat and dreamed.—RAY BRADBURY

Describing a Person

Describing a person is different from, and in many ways more difficult than, describing a place or object. That is because the writer must try to capture intangible qualities such as personality and character. The skillful writer can do this by describing the person's external characteristics in such a way as to indicate inner realities, by describing the person's inner qualities directly, or by doing a little bit of both.

The writer of the following paragraph concentrates on observable qualities. He gives details about the fisherman's appearance, disposition, and approach to work.

> Jukichi Oyama, master fisherman, owner of the *Taihei-maru*, had a face like leather well tanned by sea winds. The grimy wrinkles on his hands were mixed indistinguishably with old fishing scars, all burned by the sun down into their deepest creases. He was a man who seldom laughed but was always in calm good spirits, and even the loud voice he used when giving commands on the boat was never raised in anger. While fishing, he seldom left his place on the sculling platform at the stern, only occasionally taking one hand off the oar to regulate the engine.—YUKIO MISHIMA

From the description of external characteristics, a reader can infer many things about the fisherman's inner qualities. For example:

1. He is a hard worker.
2. He respects those who work for him.
3. He is at peace with himself.
4. He is a disciplined person.
5. He is dedicated to his work.

The writer of the next paragraph takes an entirely different approach. He includes no details about physical appearance, but focuses directly on the character of his father.

> My father was a quiet, unpretentious man. He was naturally conservative and cautious, and generally displayed common sense in what he said and did. He never went to school; such education as he had was self-acquired. Later in life I appreciated the fact that his self-development was little less than remarkable. He had a knowledge of general affairs and was familiar with many of the chief events and characters in the history of the world. The quality in my father that impressed me the most was his high and rigid sense of honesty. I could not conceive of him as a party to any transaction that was questionable in the least. I think he got his greatest satisfaction in life out of the reputation he had built up as a man of integrity.—JAMES WELDON JOHNSON

Exercises Writing Descriptive Paragraphs

A. Following is a list of topics that may be developed into descriptive paragraphs. Choose one, or make up a topic of your own. Decide how you will organize the details within your paragraph. Then write a paragraph that appeals to at least two of the senses.

1. A summer morning
2. Riding a motorcycle
3. A drugstore
4. Eating an apple
5. Walking barefoot after a rainstorm
6. A school gymnasium during a basketball game
7. Bathing a dog
8. Sitting outside at night
9. A classroom during a test
10. A school dance

B. Following is a list of topics that may be developed into paragraphs describing people. Choose one, or make up a topic of your own. Then write a paragraph that reveals some of the inner qualities of the person.

1. A gymnast at an important meet
2. An instructor at a dog obedience school
3. A girl listening to her favorite record
4. A little boy trying to tie his shoes
5. A teen-age boy crying
6. An artist at work
7. A patient in the waiting room of a clinic
8. A roller skater
9. A favorite relative
10. A bus driver

Part 3 The Explanatory Paragraph

A friend wants to know how you like your new job. Mother wants to know why you are not wearing the new outfit she bought you last week. Your history teacher asks you to name the events leading to the Vietnam war. A stranger in your neighborhood wants to know the location of the nearest bus stop. In each of these situations, you are being asked to explain something.

An explanation can be written as a paragraph. This type of paragraph is called an *explanatory paragraph*. It can be developed in a variety of ways, depending on the purpose of the writer and on the subject of the paragraph.

Giving Instructions

The simplest form of the explanatory paragraph is the paragraph that gives instructions.

> The nearest hotel is the Sea View Inn on Second Avenue. To get there from here, go straight west on Fifth Street for three blocks. At that point, Fifth Street makes a northward curve down Brewery Hill and merges into Fourth Street. Go west on Fourth Street for nine more blocks. This will take you to Main Street. Cross Main Street and continue west for one more block. You will then be at Second Avenue and the front entrance of the Sea View.

In order for the reader to follow instructions easily, they must be as clear and precise as possible. They must also be well organized. Most explanatory paragraphs that give instructions are organized in chronological order, as in the following example.

> The forward roll will give you your first sensation of being upside down in tumbling. You have probably done this stunt many times, but let us analyze the correct movement. To get into the starting position, put your hands flat on the mat, shoulder width apart, your fingers pointing forward, knees between your arms. From here, push off with your feet and rock forward on your hands. Just as you feel yourself falling off balance, tuck your head down between your arms. Keep your chin on your chest and put the back of your head on the mat. Keep rolling, and as the weight comes off your hands and you roll onto your back, grasp your shins and pull yourself up onto your feet. That's all there is to the forward roll.—NEWTON C. LOKEN

The writer of the paragraph gives six steps for doing a forward roll.

1. Get into the starting position.
2. Push off with your feet and rock forward on your hands.
3. Tuck your head between your arms.
4. Keep your chin on your chest and put the back of your head on the mat.
5. Roll forward.
6. As the weight comes off your hands and you roll onto your back, grasp your shins and pull yourself up onto your feet.

The directions are given in the order in which the actions should be performed.

Exercise Developing an Explanatory Paragraph That Gives Instructions

Choose a physical activity that you do well. It can be an exercise such as sit-ups or deep-knee bends or a skilled activity such as pitching a baseball or doing a cartwheel. Write a paragraph that gives instructions for the activity.

Using Facts or Statistics

An explanatory paragraph can be developed by the use of statistics, as in the following example.

> The so-called typical American family—made up of a bread-winning father, a homemaking mother, and two dependent children—is no longer typical. According to recent government statistics, 7.3 percent of American households are made up of single parents with one or more children at home. Of the total number of households, 28 percent consists of both a father and a mother who are wage earners. A surprising 32.4 percent consists of married couples with no children or none living at home. In all, only 17 percent of American households fit the traditional pattern.

The writer begins with a general topic sentence. She then supports her main idea with four statistics. The first three statistics are organized from the least significant—the lowest percentage—to the most significant—the highest percentage. The final statistic strongly reinforces the idea in the topic sentence.

Following is an example of an explanatory paragraph developed with facts. In this paragraph also, the writer has organized her facts from the least important to the most important.

> London is the city of cities. It has been itself, for better or worse, for some two thousand years. It has spawned and abandoned the greatest empire known to history. It was the first great industrial capital, the first parliamentary capital, the arena of social and political experiments beyond number. Mozart wrote his first symphony in London, and Karl Marx began *Das Kapital* there. It is a city of innumerable spies, of novelists, auctioneers, surgeons, and rock stars.—JAN MORRIS

The writer gives historical facts about London that explain its long-time preeminence among cities. In her final sentence she focuses on the present, thus emphasizing that London remains the "city of cities."

By presenting facts and statistics from the least important to the most important, a writer can build to a climax, as in the first example, or emphasize a point, as in the second example.

Exercise Developing a Paragraph by Using Facts or Statistics

Following is a list of subjects, each one of which lends itself to paragraph development through the use of facts or statistics. Choose two of the subjects listed, or make up subjects of your own. Research your subjects. Then develop each into a paragraph in which the facts or statistics are organized from the least important to the most important.

1. Our vanishing wildlife
2. New American immigrants
3. The Olympic Games
4. The care and feeding of pets
5. Major highway accidents
6. Coal as a form of energy
7. Fish hatcheries
8. Minorities in the work force
9. New ways to predict the weather
10. Highway safety
11. Food additives
12. Spectator sports
13. Home computers
14. The recording business
15. Washington, D.C.

Using One or More Examples

Some explanatory paragraphs may be developed best through the use of examples, either one extended example or several brief ones. Following is a paragraph developed with one example.

Datsolalee, the greatest designer and weaver of baskets among the Washo people, created works of art that are treasured by collectors of American handicrafts. One of her most famous baskets, "Myriads of Stars Shine over the Graves of Our Ancestors," contains 56,590 single stitches, over thirty-six stitches to the inch. Requiring more than a year to create, its design reflects her view of tribal history and life.

The writer begins the paragraph with a general statement about the artist and her importance. She then describes one basket that is representative of the artist's finest work.

In the following paragraph the writer uses several specific examples to support the general idea in the topic sentence.

> In the untamed man's world that was the Old West, women went through unimaginable ordeals to stay alive, to reach their goals, to contribute in some way to the development of the frontier. Sarah Royce, traveling with a pitifully small and ill-equipped party, faced death from starvation in the desert before she reached California, there to bear a son who would become a prominent educator and philosopher. Bethenia Owens endured the dismay of other women and the derision of men to become a licensed, practicing physician. Clara Shortridge Foltz fought social pressure to study and practice law. Abigail Scott Duniway raised a family, supported an invalid husband, and was pelted with rotten eggs when she barnstormed for women's right to vote.

The writer begins with a general statement that concerns the ordeals endured by women in the Old West. He supports the statement with four examples of women who survived and achieved despite trials and hardships.

Exercise Developing a Paragraph by Using One or More Examples

Following is a list of subjects. Choose two that interest you, or make up subjects of your own. Write two topic sentences. Then develop each into a paragraph through the use of one or more examples.

1. The influence of "big money" on sports
2. Styles of sneezing
3. Television coverage of major events
4. Supermarkets: non-food items
5. Great cities
6. Noncompetitive sports
7. Challenging games

Using an Incident or an Anecdote

Developing a topic sentence through the use of an incident or anecdote can give a more personal or informal touch to an explanatory paragraph. In this type of writing, the topic sentence presents a general idea; the body of the paragraph illustrates the idea through an incident or anecdote taken from the writer's own experiences.

Sometimes the topic sentence is an aphorism, or a statement of a general truth, such as, "Kids say the darndest things," "Money is the root of all evil," or "A stitch in time saves nine." The rest of the paragraph then relates an incident that illustrates the truth.

Development by incident or anecdote is similar to development by one example. The difference is that the incident or anecdote is usually drawn from personal experience, while the example is generally more impersonal.

An explanatory paragraph developed by incident or anecdote is also similar to a narrative paragraph. The main difference is in purpose. In an explanatory paragraph, the events are used to support a general idea. In a narrative paragraph, the events are related for the purpose of telling a story.

The following is an example of an explanatory paragraph developed by using an incident.

> Adults often have vivid memories of childhood experiences that at the time seemed insignificant. I have never forgotten something that happened to me when delivering the laundry that my mother washed and ironed. We were in need of money, and Mother had hurried through this batch of laundry so that it could be delivered and we could be paid for the weekend. I took the bundle of clothes to a small apartment in a private house, entered, and called out.

No one answered. I called out again and again; then I went into the next room, part of which was cut off by a screen. I peeped around the screen and caught a glimpse of the young woman whose laundry I was delivering. She was sitting as quietly as a mouse, a book in her hands. I suspect she knew who was calling, and I can only guess that she did not answer because she did not have the money to pay. I could not bring myself to let her know that I knew she was there. I left the laundry and went home without the money. Mother did not scold me; somehow she managed that weekend.—Marian Anderson

The writer could have developed the topic sentence with several impersonal statements about childhood experiences that are long-remembered. Instead, she relates an incident that illustrates her point. The paragraph "comes alive" with the description of that one incident.

Exercises Developing a Paragraph by Using an Incident or an Anecdote

A. Here is a list of aphorisms, each one of which may be developed into a paragraph by using an incident or an anecdote. Choose one, or use another familiar saying. Then, drawing from your personal experiences, write a paragraph.

1. Rules are meant to be broken.
2. As the twig is bent, so the tree grows.
3. Beauty is in the eye of the beholder.
4. A picture is worth a thousand words.
5. A bird in the hand is worth two in the bush.
6. Good things come in small packages.
7. A penny saved is a penny earned.
8. Two heads are better than one.
9. Look before you leap.
10. People in glass houses shouldn't throw stones.

B. Here is a list of topic sentences. Choose one, or write a sentence of your own. Then develop it into a paragraph by relating an incident or anecdote drawn from your personal experiences.

1. Jealousy can destroy friendships.
2. Complaints sometimes result in actions.
3. Relatives can also be friends.
4. Some things you just have to learn for yourself.
5. Loneliness can be an excellent teacher.
6. My father/mother is an understanding person.
7. I met an important challenge—and won.
8. Learning to cook isn't as easy as it looks.
9. Daydreams can come true.
10. People can be unexpectedly generous.

Using Comparisons or Contrasts

In developing an explanatory paragraph by using comparisons or contrasts, you, the writer, must point out the similarities or the differences between two things. You may use facts, examples, or incidents. The important thing to remember is that, in using comparisons, you are showing how the facts, examples, or incidents are *alike*. In using contrasts, you are showing how the facts, examples, or incidents are *different*.

Using Comparisons. In the following paragraph, the writer compares, or points out, the similarities between two cities.

> Writing in the Boston *Globe* in 1970, Ian Menzies suggested that Boston and San Francisco are "the two most exciting cities in the nation." There are certainly strong similarities. Both have water on three sides, strikingly similar skylines, and almost equal land areas. Both have a similar mix of academe, of history, and of the arts. While one has a Puritan heritage, the other Spanish, both are dominated by an Irish-Italian political culture which is yielding its monopolistic control to emergent minority populations.

The writer introduces the idea of comparison in the second sentence. He then procedes to point out several similarities between Boston and San Francisco, similarities in physical, cultural, and political characteristics. By repeating the word *both*, he reinforces the idea of comparison throughout the paragraph.

Using Contrasts. In the following paragraph, the writer emphasizes differences.

> I could scarcely believe the man coming out of the house to be the same one who had so recently entered it. Surely, this alert young fellow with flushed, eager face and shining eyes had nothing in common with the pale, dejected-looking creature who a few minutes before had passed me. I had carefully observed him then and had noted the beaten, hopeless look in his eyes. How his shoulders had sagged, and his footsteps had lagged as though bound on a fruitless errand! Now his upright figure, with its squared shoulders, was vibrant with life. His lips were parted in a half smile; and as he passed me, he was humming a lilting tune.

The "before" and "after" description of the young man in this paragraph creates a sharp contrast. Something wonderful or exciting has happened to him, and the contrast points this up.

Exercises Studying and Writing Explanatory Paragraphs

A. Read the following list of subjects carefully. Decide whether the best method of development for each is comparison or contrast. Choose two of the subjects, or make up two of your own. Research the subjects if necessary. Then write a paragraph on each.

1. A city street before and after a rainstorm
2. Your town or city and one of equal size
3. Some aspect of modern medicine and medicine 100 years ago
4. A vacation at a mountain lake and a vacation at a beach
5. Last year's basketball team and this year's team
6. A van and a pick-up truck
7. A football uniform and a hockey uniform
8. Your education and that of your grandparents
9. A television program and a live play staged in a theater
10. An alligator and a crocodile
11. Your eating habits and those of a friend
12. The individual styles of two singers

B. In a newspaper or magazine, find a good example of an explanatory paragraph. Read it to the class. Identify the method used to develop the paragraph. Explain why you think it is a good paragraph.

Part 4   The Persuasive Paragraph

A persuasive paragraph is a kind of explanatory paragraph, set apart from other kinds by its purpose and by the nature of its topic sentence.

The purpose of a persuasive paragraph is to convince readers to accept the rationality of an opinion or to adopt the opinion as their own. The choice of subject matter is limited to ideas about which there are at least two more or less reasonable ways of thinking.

The topic sentence of a persuasive paragraph states the writer's way of thinking about a subject. It establishes the writer's point of view, which is justified by the supporting statements in the rest of the paragraph.

Giving Opinions and Reasons

Persuasive paragraphs are of two basic types. In the first, the element of persuasion is weak. The purpose of the paragraph is to convince readers to accept the rationality of an opinion. To accomplish this goal, the writer states an opinion in the topic sentence, then follows with reasons to support that opinion. The opinion might be signaled by phrases such as *I think, I like,* or *I believe.* However, it is more likely that the opinion in the topic sentence will be presented without such clues, as in the following example.

> I was born in the wrong century. The signs of my out-of-placeness are everywhere. My shelves are filled with Victorian novels. I don't have a food processor. I eat fatback. I spank my children. I think everyone should take Latin. I believe in duty, work, fidelity, and suffering. I think too much fun is not a good thing.—Suzanne Britt Jordan

The writer opens with an opinion: "I was born in the wrong century." She supports the opinion with facts and with further supporting opinions. She uses these facts.

1. My shelves are filled with Victorian novels.
2. I don't have a food processor.
3. I eat fatback.
4. I spank my children.

She uses these further supporting opinions:

1. I think everyone should take Latin.
2. I believe in duty, work, fidelity, and suffering.
3. I think too much fun is not a good thing.

Notice that these supporting opinions contain the signal phrases *I think* and *I believe*.

In all, the writer presents seven reasons to convince readers that she was born in the wrong century.

Because an opinion is by nature neither right nor wrong, a paragraph that includes opinions is open to challenge. For example, a friend of the writer who believes that she was born in the wrong century might counter her opinion with one of his own, such as, "You are a twentieth-century woman." He might then give several reasons to support his opinion.

Stating Propositions and Supporting Arguments

In the second type of persuasive paragraph, the element of persuasion is much stronger. Its purpose is to convert the readers to the opinion held by the writer.

The topic sentence in this type of paragraph is a definite proposition of belief. It is a clear statement of a conclusion that the writer has reached and that the writer wishes the readers to reach by way of the arguments presented in the paragraph. At first reading, a proposition of belief might appear to be a statement of fact. Closer analysis, however, will reveal that it deals with a question or problem that is open to debate.

The following are three examples of propositions of belief.

1. The passion of Americans is not politics, baseball, or money, but education.

2. Our football team is the best in the state.

3. The threat of famine facing the United States is even greater and more imminent than that descending upon the hungry nations.

Every persuasive paragraph contains two parts: a *what* and a *why*. The proposition of belief stated in the topic sentence is the *what*. The arguments given to support the what are the *why*.

> All of us must be conscientious about brushing our teeth regularly after eating. Food residue clings to the surfaces of the teeth and, if not removed by thorough brushing, will form acids. These acids destroy the tooth enamel, and then decay sets in. Bad breath is one result. More seriously, teeth may be lost, abscesses may form, and infection may spread to other parts of the body. The ultimate result will be lengthy, perhaps painful, and certainly expensive trips to the dentist.

The *what* in this paragraph is "All of us must be conscientious about brushing our teeth regularly after eating." This is followed by several *why's*; acids will form; decay sets in; bad breath is one result; teeth may be lost; abscesses may form; infection may spread; a trip to the dentist may be the ultimate result. The writer has supported the *what*—his proposition—with specific facts.

When you wish to write a strong persuasive paragraph, keep these three things in mind.

1. To present an effective argument for one side of a question, you must be familiar with the other side as well. You must study and understand the arguments that support the opposite point of view.

2. Your audience consists of readers whose beliefs about the question at hand are different from yours. You are not writing for readers who already think the way you do. Therefore, your arguments must be as convincing as possible.

3. Your supporting arguments can take the form of facts, statistics, examples, anecdotes, comparisons, or contrasts. In other words, you have available all the methods you used for developing other kinds of explanatory paragraphs.

Exercises **Writing Persuasive Paragraphs**

A. Following is a list of topic sentences that may be developed into persuasive paragraphs. Study the list carefully; then choose one topic and write a paragraph. You may, if you wish, choose an opposite point of view from that stated in the topic sentence.

1. Teenagers are safer drivers than adults.
2. English should be a required subject every year in high school.
3. All grades should be abolished.
4. A dog is a more satisfactory pet than a cat.
5. Small high schools are better than large ones.
6. Anti-intellectualism is a danger to America.
7. We need an honor system for taking exams.
8. We need a serious tax reform.
9. Americans are free people.
10. Progress has meant the progress of technology, not of people.
11. It is the role of the writer to criticize society.
12. Reading poetry is a worthwhile pastime.
13. People must establish roots in their communities.
14. Life is everlasting change.
15. Americans are not geared to the past but to the future.

B. Following is a list of subjects. Choose one, and write an opinion or proposition of belief about some aspect of the subject. Then develop your idea into a persuasive paragraph.

1. The American teenager
2. The extended family
3. Compulsory education
4. The quality most necessary in a friend
5. Keeping well informed
6. Living in harmony with nature
7. The most valuable of the five senses
8. The challenges of the future
9. Materialism
10. Television comedy
11. Remaining frontiers

Checklist for Writing Paragraphs

This Checklist will help to remind you of the qualities necessary for good paragraphs. However, your writing procedure should also follow the steps in Guidelines for the Process of Writing on page 83.

1. Is the paragraph a group of sentences dealing with only one main idea?

2. Does the paragraph have a topic sentence that states the main idea?

3. Does the topic sentence make a general statement about what is to follow?

4. Does the topic sentence control and limit the ideas that are discussed in the rest of the paragraph?

5. Does the paragraph have unity? Does each sentence relate to the main idea?

6. Is the paragraph long enough to explain the idea clearly?

7. If it is a narrative paragraph, are the events developed in chronological order?

8. If it is a descriptive paragraph of a place or an object, does it use sensory details? Are details organized in a spatial order?

9. If it is a descriptive paragraph of a person, does it try to capture the essence of the person? Does it appeal to the senses?

10. If it is an explanatory paragraph that gives instructions, are the instructions clear and precise? Are they organized in chronological order?

11. If it is an explanatory paragraph that uses facts or statistics, are they organized from the least important to the most important?

12. If it is an explanatory paragraph that uses examples, does it have one well developed example or several brief but pertinent examples?

13. If it is an explanatory paragraph that uses an incident or anecdote, is it drawn from first-hand experience?

14. If it is an explanatory paragraph that uses comparisons or contrasts, do the comparisons involve similarities? Do the contrasts involve differences?

15. If it is a persuasive paragraph, does it present convincing reasons or arguments?

Chapter 8

Writing a Composition or a Report

By now you are familiar with the main types of paragraphs and the various ways they may be organized. A paragraph, however, rarely stands alone. It is usually a unit within a longer composition. Sometimes a composition is called a "report." In this chapter you will study the development of the longer composition or report from idea to finished product.

Part 1   What Is a Composition?

At the beginning of Chapter 6, the paragraph was defined as follows:

> A paragraph is a group of sentences dealing with a single topic or idea. Usually, one sentence, called the topic sentence, states the main idea of the paragraph. All the other sentences are related to this topic sentence. They further explain or support the main idea.

The definition of the composition is only slightly different:

A composition is a group of paragraphs dealing with a single topic or idea. Usually, one paragraph, called the introductory paragraph, states the main idea of the composition. All the other paragraphs are related to the introductory paragraph. They further explain or support the main idea.

The following examples illustrate the similarities between the organization of the paragraph and the organization of the composition.

A PARAGRAPH

The destruction caused by the tidal wave was total. On the beach where the village had stood not a house remained, no wreckage of wood or fallen stone wall, no little street or shops, no docks, not a single boat. The beach was as clean of houses as if no human beings had ever lived there. All that had been was now no more. —PEARL S. BUCK

A COMPOSITION

THE BIG WAVE

The purple rim of the ocean seemed to lift and rise against the clouds. A silver-green band of bright sky appeared like a low dawn above the sea. The castle bell began to toll a warning, deep and pleading. Would the people hear it in the roaring wind? Their houses had no windows toward the sea. Did they know what was about to happen?

Under the deep waters of the ocean, miles down under the cold, the earth had yielded at last to the fire. It groaned and split open and the cold water fell into the middle of the boiling rocks. Steam burst out and lifted the ocean high into the sky in a big wave. It rushed toward the shore, green and solid, frothing into white at its edges. It rose, higher and higher, lifting hands and claws.

The wave came nearer and nearer, filling the air with its roar and shout. It rushed over the flat, still waters of the ocean. It reached the village and covered it fathoms deep in swirling water, green laced with fierce white foam. The wave ran up the mountainside, until the knoll where the castle stood was an island. All who were still climbing the path were swept away—black, tossing scraps in the wicked waters.

Then with a great sucking sigh, the wave swept back again, ebbing into the ocean, dragging everything with it, trees and stones and houses. It swept back over the village and returned slowly again to the ocean, subsiding, sinking into a great stillness.

Upon the beach where the village had stood not a house remained, no wreckage of wood or fallen stone wall, no little street of shops, no docks, not a single boat. The beach was as clean of houses as if no human beings had ever lived there. All that had been was now no more.—PEARL S. BUCK

The paragraph deals with a single idea—the destruction caused by a tidal wave. The topic sentence states this idea. The other sentences support the main idea by describing the destruction.

The composition also deals with a single idea. However, the idea is broader than that of the paragraph. Rather than focus on one aspect of the tidal wave, such as its causes or results, the composition describes the entire process of destruction. The introductory paragraph implies that something dangerous is about to happen. The rest of the paragraphs further explain this idea by giving details about what does happen.

Notice that the composition has five paragraphs. Although compositions vary in length, those selected as examples for this chapter are all made up of five paragraphs.

Part 2 Deciding on a Subject

"What shall I write about?" is the first question you will probably ask when faced with writing a composition. Before answering, you need to think about the things that interest you. They most likely will include not only familiar things, but also things that you would like to learn more about. Only by taking time to choose a subject that interests you will you be able to write a composition that creates interest on the part of your readers. This is the first step in the Process of Writing.

In general, subjects fall into two categories: (1) those that relate to the personal experiences of the writer, and (2) those that require knowledge from sources other than the writer's own experience.

Subjects That Relate to Personal Experience

You are an individual. You are unique. There is no other person in the world just like you. No one looks the same; no one acts the same; no one thinks the same. No one else has lived a life exactly like yours. Your experiences, your thoughts, your feelings provide an almost endless source of subjects for interesting compositions.

The writer of the following composition drew from his own uniqueness, from his own experiences, to explain what "growing up" meant to him.

UNDERSTANDING OF A SORT

On a hill I stood and whispered to the far sea. I was ten, not really much younger than I am now, though almost a decade separates that little boy I was from the bigger boy I am. Understanding of a sort has come between us—or perhaps it is a loss of understanding.

The sea was bluer then, I think. Ten years ago the little boy thought that seas are blue because the water is blue—all the way to the bottom. Now the bigger boy knows that seas are blue because they reflect the sky, and the bigger boy wishes that the little boy had never found out.

The tide is coming in. Tides, the bigger boy has been told, come in because of the magnetism of the moon. The little boy thought the tide comes in because on the shore a good water mother calls it to her arms. Lying on the hill, the little boy used to wait and try to hear her call, but she always called so softly that he never could hear her. If ever he had heard her, he planned to run down the hill to the beach and hunt until he found her in one of the coves. She would have room in her arms, he was sure, for him as well as for the sea.

When the little boy, ten years ago, stood on the hill and

watched the sea, he stood in another land, apart from the country of drab people and dingy towns. They did not exist for him. But the years have brought a growing in the towns and people about him. The vines of reality climbed over him and after a while he became part of them. Now they are forever with him.

The bigger boy I am cries again to be the little boy I was; but the voice comes back to me as a hollow echo, thwarted by the wall of understanding that the years have built between us. But there— the water mother is calling in the sea. I think I almost hear her.

Exercise Listing Possible Subjects

Study the following suggestions for composition topics. On a sheet of paper, list those that interest you. Then think about your own experiences. Add at least ten topics to your list. *Keep your list for future reference.*

1. My Fondest Dream
2. My Family at the Dinner Table
3. My Own Pet Prejudice
4. Thoughts on Growing Up
5. Souvenirs I Have Collected
6. My Kid Sister/Brother
7. The Day I Learned Fear
8. I Like the Quiet Times
9. Things I Can Do Without
10. My Nicest Compliment—I Think
11. The Worst Party I Ever Attended
12. He/She Is My Best Friend
13. My Dog Taught Me a Lesson
14. A Perfect Day
15. A Kind Gesture
16. I Went Out for the Team and Lost/Won
17. My Imagination
18. My First Date Was Almost My Last
19. My Biggest Mistake
20. A Person I Learned To Like/Dislike

Subjects Outside the Writer's Experience

Although some of your compositions will recall personal experiences, most will be based on information acquired from outside sources. This is the kind of composition that lends itself to a report. One possible source of information is people who have had unique experiences or who are authorities in a certain area. The most familiar and accessible source, however, is published material in magazines, nonfiction books, newspapers, pamphlets, and reference works.

In looking for possible subjects, you will want to consult the sources available to you. Friends, relatives, neighbors, or other people in your community might be able to suggest subjects. School and public libraries have hundreds of books on a great variety of subjects. Your textbooks often mention people, places, and events that are potential subjects.

When thinking about possible subjects, keep in mind that you will have to spend some time learning about a subject. Therefore, it is important that the subject you choose interests you.

In the following example, the author has chosen a subject outside his own personal experience and has become familiar enough with it to write with authority.

SUMO TOURNAMENTS

A special type of Japanese wrestling is called *sumo*. Sumo is probably Japan's oldest sport. It began hundreds of years ago as a part of a Shinto religious ceremony. Some Shinto shrines had special buildings built for sumo matches, held to honor the gods. In the year 858, it is said, the two sons of the emperor wrestled to see who would succeed to the throne.

Today sumo is so popular that tournaments are held every year in the large cities. Thousands go to the huge stadiums to watch the matches. Others view them on television. The sumo wrestlers are tall and heavy, sometimes weighing 300 pounds. Each wrestler wears only a ring about his waist and a loincloth. The place where they perform is a circle that measures fifteen feet across.

Before the wrestlers begin a match they throw salt into the ring to drive away the evil spirits. Then they step out and practice balancing exercises. After this more salt is thrown, and there are more exercises. Finally they are ready, and the referee flips his fan.

The wrestlers charge at each other. Each tries to lift or push the other out of the ring. If any part of the wrestler's body except his feet touch the ground, or if one wrestler steps out of the ring, the match is over. The whole contest takes no longer than about one minute.

There are usually about fifteen matches in one afternoon. The tournament continues for several days until all the wrestlers have been in the ring. The winner is called a grand champion. No one in Japan is more admired than a Sumo Grand Champion.—LEE W. FARNSWORTH

Exercises Choosing a Subject

A. Study the following examples of subjects for compositions. Then make a list of ten subjects of your own. If any of the subjects given here interest you, add them to your list. *Keep your list for future reference.*

1. Sky Diving
2. Women in the Work Force
3. The Chicanos in America
4. Disco Dancing
5. Bird Migration
6. The Japanese Game of Go
7. Photography
8. America's Relationship with Great Britain
9. Soccer
10. Endangered Species
11. Superstitions
12. The History of Advertising
13. Synthetic Fuels
14. Is Our Weather Changing?
15. The Modern Olympic Games
16. School Athletics

B. You now have two lists of subjects—one listing subjects that relate to personal experience, the other listing subjects that require knowledge gained from outside sources. Study the two lists. Then choose the one subject that interests you most.

Part 3   Narrowing the Subject

In writing a paragraph, you must choose an idea that can be treated adequately and satisfactorily within the limits of the paragraph. The same holds true in writing the composition. You must choose a subject that is narrow enough to be developed completely in a few paragraphs.

Some subjects are too broad for treatment in a composition, such as "The History of Music in America." That subject could fill an entire book. Even when narrowed to "Music in Twentieth-Century America," the subject is still too broad for a five-paragraph composition. The subject "The History of Music in America," however, does contain many narrow, more specific topics, such as these:

> Who Really Wrote "Yankee Doodle"?
> Francis Scott Key and "The Star-Spangled Banner"
> W. C. Handy: The Father of Jazz
> Scott Joplin and Ragtime
> Louis Armstrong: Jazz Musician
> Marian Anderson: The Singer, the Person
> Bessie Smith Sings the Blues
> Elvis Presley and the Rise of "Rock"
> Sarah Caldwell and the Opera Company of Boston

Each of these specific topics is appropriate for a short composition or report.

Another example of a subject that is too broad for a composition is "The Contributions of Japanese-Americans to American Society." Again, the subject contains numerous specific topics, such as these:

Daniel K. Inouye: Soldier and Statesman
Seiji Ozawa: A New Breed of Symphony Conductor
Dr. S. I. Hayakawa: World Authority in Semantics
Minoru Yamasaki: Distinguished American Architect
Dr. Hideyo Noguchi: World-Famous Bacteriologist

The Narrowing Process

Subjects taken from personal experience often do not have to be narrowed. That is because, when selecting this type of subject, you usually have one specific experience in mind. On the other hand, subjects that require research most likely need to be narrowed at some point. Narrowing such subjects is a two-step process. The first step is preliminary research. This involves spending some time in the school library, in the public library, or with some authority for the purpose of locating books on your general subject.

Exploring Library Sources. In the library, begin with the card catalog. When you come across a book you think you might use, write the name of the book, the author's name, the call number, and the place where you found the book on a 3x5 card. Number each card in the upper right-hand corner.

One writer decided to write a composition on American music. She found a book listed in the card catalog whose title sounded interesting. She wrote the following information on a 3x5 card.

Call Number — 780 / EL78n ①

Title — *The National Music of America and Its Sources*

Author — Louis C. Elson

Place — School Library

The second step in the narrowing process is checking the Table of Contents in several books on your subject. From the many specific topics listed, choose the one that is the most interesting to you. If necessary, narrow the topic further, either by studying any subheads contained in the Table of Contents or by skimming the chapter.

The writer of the composition on American music had listed several books, among them *A Short History of Music in America*. She checked the Table of Contents for this book and found the following general headings.

Each of these subjects was too broad for her composition. She found, however, that the Table of Contents was broken down into narrower topics. She reread the Table of Contents, and under "The Second Decade and World War I" she discovered the following:

From the three specific topics suggested by this part of the Table of Contents, the writer chose the following:

The Origins of Jazz

Exercise Narrowing Your Subject

In your last assignment you decided on a subject for your composition. If you chose a subject to develop through research, narrow it by using the two-step process described in this lesson. If you chose a subject that relates to your personal experience, make sure that it is narrow enough for a short composition. If you find that it is too broad, think of several specific topics within your subject, and choose one for your composition.

Part 4 Deciding on the Audience and the Purpose

Before you begin to write a composition, you must decide for whom you are writing and your purpose for writing.

1. **Know your audience.** It is important, first of all, to know the age group for whom you are writing. The reason for this is simple. If you are writing for young children or if you are writing for adults, the words you choose, the amount of information you include, and the explanations you give will be quite different than if you were writing for your classmates.

Besides the age of your audience, you should know whether you are writing for readers with some knowledge of the subject or for readers who are unfamiliar with it. This, too, will influence the amount and difficulty of information you will select and present.

To clarify this point, read the following two paragraphs, both written on the same subject for two entirely different audiences.

MOHENJO DARO, AN ANCIENT CITY IN INDIA

From what was found in Mohenjo Daro, we know much about the people who lived there. The citizens of this city knew how to make bricks. With the bricks they built houses for themselves. They planned their cities and kept them clean by laying drainpipes to carry away dirty water. They built huge public baths, and broad streets for chariots and carts. They made fine pots of clay and weapons of copper and bronze. They decorated their pottery with figures of animals and gods. They made beautiful necklaces of beads and ornaments of gold and ivory. They knew how to write, although we do not yet know how to read what they wrote.
—Sheila Dhar

MOHENJO DARO, AN ANCIENT CITY IN INDIA

The most striking of the few large buildings in Mohenjo Daro was the great bath. This was an oblong pool thirty-nine by twenty feet in area and eight feet deep, constructed of beautiful watertight brickwork. The pool was surrounded by a covered walkway onto which opened a number of small rooms. Like the "tank" of a Hindu temple, the bath probably had a religious purpose, and the rooms may have been the homes of priests. The special attention paid by the people to cleanliness indicates that, like the later Hindus, they had a strong belief in the purificatory effects of water.—A. L. Basham

The first paragraph is written for young readers; the second for older, more knowledgeable readers. The writers chose their words and details for their specific audiences.

2. **Know your purpose for writing.** Before writing, you must decide whether you wish to tell your readers a story, to describe something for them, or to explain something to them. You must also decide on the *tone* and *mood* for your composition. Do you want it to be humorous? sad? serious? Do you want your readers to laugh? to cry? to be moved by the beauty or ugliness of the scene you are describing? to think seriously about the idea you are presenting?

Once these decisions are made, you are ready to begin gathering information for your composition.

Deciding on the Audience and the Purpose

A. Decide on the audience for your composition.

B. Decide on the purpose for writing your composition.

Part 5　Planning the Composition

Planning is a necessary part of writing a composition. The planning process involves four separate, equally important steps.

1. Gathering information
2. Grouping ideas
3. Making a working outline
4. Organizing the Composition

By following these steps, you can be confident that your composition not only says something, but also says it in such a way that your readers can easily understand your ideas. Planning your composition is an important part of the pre-writing process.

Gathering Information

Writing a successful composition depends to a great degree on how much you know about your subject. This principle holds true for both types of compositions—those based on personal experience and those based on learned information.

If you are going to write about a personal experience, you are already familiar with your subject. You have all the information you need, stored in your memory. To retrieve this information, you must first spend some time thinking about your subject. You can then write the ideas you want to include in your composition on 3x5 cards, using one card for each idea.

If, however, you are going to write about a subject outside your own experience, you must gather information through research. You need to collect as much information as possible so that you know more about the subject than your readers.

Throughout this discussion you are directed to take notes on 3x5 cards. This is a good method because it allows you to group and regroup your ideas easily.

Finding and Recording Information

Begin your search for information with the cards that you prepared for Part 3. Use the call numbers on the cards to locate the books on the library shelves. Read the appropriate sections of each book and jot down pertinent information on 3x5 cards, using one card for each idea.

Next, check reference books, such as encyclopedias, biographical dictionaries, and yearbooks for information. For each reference that you use, record the title and, if applicable, the volume number of the book, the title and page numbers of the entry, and the place where you found it. Number each of your source cards.

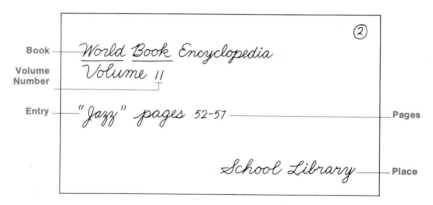

Write the information that you learn from reference books on 3x5 cards, putting one idea and the page where you found it on each card. Number each note card with the corresponding number on your source card. In this way, you can recheck your ideas quickly if you need to.

For some subjects, magazines are good sources of information. To locate magazine articles, start with the *Readers' Guide to Periodical Literature.* When you find a title that sounds interesting, record the title, author, and pages of the article and the name, date, and volume number of the magazine. Also include the place where you found it.

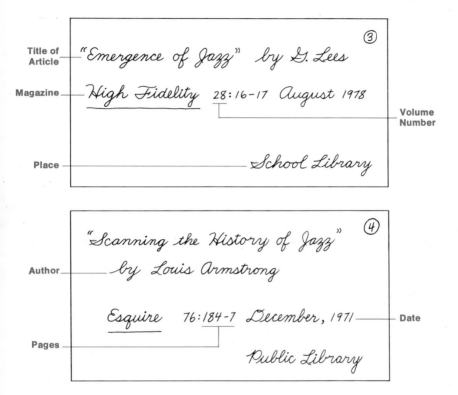

As you read each magazine article, write your ideas on separate cards. Number the cards to correspond with the number on your source card.

As part of your preliminary research, you might have talked with an expert on your subject. Now is the time to return to that expert. The information that you gather from this source should also be recorded on 3x5 cards. Include the name of the expert and the date of the interview.

The writer who chose the subject "The Origins of Jazz" for her composition researched her topic in several sources and recorded dozens of ideas on 3x5 cards. Four of her cards are shown here.

Each Sunday, slaves in ② Congo Square, New Orleans, danced, clapped and beat drums.
page 54

Rag or Ragtime: ② Syncopated rhythm
page 55

slave spirituals: ③ one source of "the blues"
page 16

New Orleans: ③ Congo Square celebrations called "bamboulas"
page 17

Exercise Writing Down Ideas

Collect the information you need for your composition—from your memory, from printed materials, or from experts. Record your ideas on 3x5 cards.

Grouping Ideas

Whether you are writing a composition based on personal experience or one based on learned information, your next step in planning is to organize your ideas in relation to each other; that is, to group similar ideas together.

The writer of the composition "The Origins of Jazz" learned that jazz developed from three basic roots: the beat, the brass bands, and the blues. She made three general headings.

    I. The beat
   II. The brass bands
  III. The blues

Next she sorted her 3x5 cards into three piles according to where each idea fit into her overall three-part scheme. She reread each group of cards, then listed specific ideas under each general heading.

I. The beat
   clapping and dancing
   Congo Square
   drums played by slaves

II. The brass bands
   Ragtime
   military bands
   French quadrilles
   syncopation

III. The blues
   spirituals
   work songs
   plantation cries
   field "hollers"

Exercises Grouping Your Ideas

A. Following is a list of ideas. Decide which two should be general headings. Then list the remaining ideas under the appropriate headings.

1. provide adequate street lighting
2. pedestrians often cause their own injuries
3. they cross streets diagonally
4. they cross streets in the middle of the block
5. they walk with their backs to traffic on the highway
6. pedestrian lives can be saved
7. they step into traffic from parked cars
8. provide traffic lights for pedestrians
9. they step from behind parked cars
10. give traffic tickets to pedestrians
11. they cross against lights
12. they don't watch for traffic

B. From the following list of ideas, choose the three general headings. Then group the remaining ideas under those headings.

1. service to society
2. description of career
3. specific attitudes
4. income
5. qualifications needed
6. personal satisfaction
7. physical and personal qualities
8. rewards of this career
9. opportunities
10. kinds of work involved
11. education and other training
12. places where such work is done

C. Organize the ideas you have gathered for your composition by grouping specific, related ideas under three headings.

Making a Working Outline

Making a **working outline** is the next step in planning your composition. Because you now have all your ideas in related groups, this step is not difficult. It involves deleting those ideas that are of little importance and reorganizing the remaining ideas into a logical order. A logical order is an order that is easy for your readers to follow. Unfortunately, there is no simple, one-two-three order for a composition. Each composition presents an organizational problem of its own.

Organizing Ideas in Chronological Order. The simplest and most natural order is *chronological*; that is, placing the ideas in order of time—first things first.

    I. The beat
       A. Drums played by slaves
       B. Clapping and dancing

II. The brass bands
   A. Military bands
   B. French quadrilles
   C. Ragtime
III. The blues
   A. Work songs
   B. Plantation cries
   C. Field "hollers"
   D. Spirituals

Notice that the writer dropped "Congo Square" and "syncopation." These are less important ideas that will be mentioned in the discussion of other ideas.

Organizing Ideas in Order of Importance. Ideas can also be organized in *order of importance;* that is, from the least important to the most important.

THE DEAD WATERFOWL

  I. The threats
    A. Loss of wildlife
    B. Loss of water supplies
 II. The causes
    A. Accidental seepage of industrial waste
    B. Accidental collisions of oil tankers
    C. Deliberate piping of industrial wastes directly into water
    D. Deliberate flushing of tankers' oil compartments on the high seas
III. The remedies
    A. Informal individual and collective action
    B. Formal national and international legislation

In this example, the writer is concerned about the death of wildlife and the loss of water supplies. The most important ideas that she will present are the remedies for these losses. These ideas come at the end of the outline.

Exercises Making Outlines

A. Following are three lists of ideas. Rearrange each of the lists into an outline, using the order that seems best for the subject.

1. MARKET GARDENING
    selling the products
    selecting seed
    planting
    preparing the soil
    deciding what to plant
    gathering the products
    cultivating
    preparing the products for market

2. TENNIS: A GOOD GAME FOR STUDENTS
    increase in mental alertness
    relaxation from study
    joy of competition
    health
    pleasure
    interaction with others
    improvement in circulatory system

3. AUTOMOBILES SHOULD BE BANNED FROM CITIES
    Public transportation is more efficient than the automobile.
    The automobile is the major source of air pollution.
    Accidents involving pedestrians and automobiles are common.
    Automobiles contribute to noise pollution.
    Dependence on automobiles hurts everyone.
    Automobiles are inefficient for moving large numbers of people.
    New freeways remove more land from residential, business, and recreational use.
    Money spent on new roads and road repairs could be put to better use elsewhere.
    The automobile is a nuisance and a health hazard.
    Many automobiles carry only one driver.

B. Organize your list of ideas for your own composition into a working outline containing three major headings.

Organizing the Composition

Earlier, a composition was defined as follows:

> A composition is a group of paragraphs dealing with a single topic or idea. Usually, one paragraph, called the introductory paragraph, states the main idea of the composition. All the other paragraphs are related to this introductory paragraph. They further explain or support the main idea.

To this definition, you now can add this:

> A good composition always contains a *beginning*, a *middle*, and an *end*.

When you made your working outline, you completed the organization of the middle, or body, of your composition. To make a final outline, you need to add the beginning, or introductory paragraph, and the end, or conclusion. Your finished outline will follow this pattern:

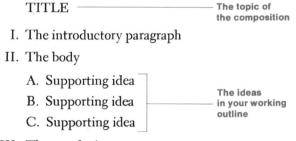

TITLE ———————————— The topic of
                                    the composition

   I. The introductory paragraph

  II. The body

     A. Supporting idea
     B. Supporting idea   —— The ideas in your working outline
     C. Supporting idea

  III. The conclusion

When writing your composition, your outline will work as a guide to help keep your ideas moving in a logical direction.

Exercise Making a Final Outline

Make the final outline for your composition, using your working outline to complete section II.

Part 6 Writing the Composition

A major part of your work is now finished. Your topic has been selected, your audience and your purpose have been decided, and your ideas have been organized into a logical pattern. You are now ready to begin writing the first draft of your composition, the second step in the Process of Writing.

The Introductory Paragraph

The introductory paragraph of a composition serves two important functions and must, therefore, be written with great care. First, a good introductory paragraph catches the reader's attention. Second, it gives the reader an indication of what the composition is about.

Catching the Reader's Attention. A good writer avoids dull and uninteresting opening statements, such as these:

1. In this paper, I am going to tell you about the origins of jazz.
2. Hang-gliding is an exciting sport.
3. There are three important reasons why automobiles should be banned from our cities.

There is nothing in these sentences to make the reader want to read further. How lacking in interest they are compared with the following:

1   The roots of American jazz were planted long before this century was born. These roots were the beat, the music of the brass bands, and the blues—three roots which eventually joined together to form the most American of music—Jazz!

2   "What am I doing here?" A surge of panic raced through my body as I felt the wind begin to tug at the contraption strapped to my arms. "I could break a leg, an arm. I could be killed!" At that moment, the full pressure of the wind caught at the hang-glider's sail, and I was lifted upward, upward, held aloft only by the rising currents of air.

3   The automobile has got to go! We have reached a point in the history of our cities where we can no longer allow this primitive mode of transportation to eat up our land, pollute our atmosphere, and press our citizens into financial ruin.

In these introductory paragraphs, not only have the writers given an indication of what their compositions will be about, but they have done so in a way that catches their readers' attention.

Types of Introductory Paragraphs.   There are many types of introductory paragraphs. Each embodies a different approach to the material that will be presented in the composition. When choosing the approach that will be the most effective, the writer must consider both the subject and the purpose of the composition.

Four types of introductory paragraphs are illustrated by the following examples.

1. THE PARAGRAPH THAT MAKES A DIRECT APPEAL

If you like riddles, try this one: What do teeth fillings, engagement rings, eyeglasses, and toasters have in common with gasoline, fiber-glass curtains, synthetic fertilizers, and the catalytic converters in most 1976 automobiles? Answer: All of these products rely on one of earth's most expensive and least publicized metals— platinum.—RONALD SCHILLER

In this type of introductory paragraph, the writer gets directly to the point, leaving no doubt about the subject of the composition. This approach is particularly effective for compositions that give many facts about their subjects.

2. THE PARAGRAPH THAT USES A PERSONAL APPROACH

Halloweens I have always considered wilder and richer and more important than even Christmas morn. The dark and lovely memories leap back at me as I see once again my ghostly relatives, and the lurks and things that creaked stairs or sang softly in the hinges when you opened a door.—RAY BRADBURY

In this type of introductory paragraph, the attitude of the writer toward the subject is immediately apparent. A composition that begins with this approach will probably go on to describe a personal experience and the writer's feelings about the experience.

3. THE PARAGRAPH THAT DESCRIBES AN OVERALL EFFECT

November chills. Raw rain flays the sullen fields and black roofs. Sunlight touches the earth, but shyly. Most mornings are dusted with frost. Storm sashes rattle in the wind. Snow flurries swirl from a lonely sky and whip the flinty earth. It is the time for man-made warmth.—HERB DANIELS

This type of paragraph is effective in "setting the scene" for a composition. It often is used as the opener for a description or for a narrative based on an experience of the writer or on an imaginary experience. A writer who uses this approach must be careful to evoke a mood that will be consistent with the content of the composition.

4. THE PARAGRAPH THAT AROUSES CURIOSITY

Suppose there were no critics to tell us how to react to a picture, a play, or a new composition of music. Suppose we wandered innocent as the dawn into an art exhibition of unsigned paintings. By what standards, by what values would we decide whether they were good or bad, talented or untalented, successes or failures?
—MARYA MANNES

This type of paragraph invites the reader to find the answer to a question by reading the rest of the composition. It is especially effective for compositions whose purpose is to explain an idea.

Exercises Writing Introductions

A. Read the following opening statements and decide which ones have definite reader appeal. Rewrite those that are lacking in appeal. You may use more than one sentence in your revision if you wish.

1. Habits are first cobwebs, then cables.
2. This composition is about learning to ski.
3. My kid sister is a difficult person to live with.

4. Nobody goes to the hardware store for a loaf of bread.

5. I would like to tell you about an interesting trip I took to Chicago.

6. Today we need all the help we can get in sifting food facts from food fads.

7. Say "New Orleans" to somebody who has been there, and you get a most predictable response: "Ah, the food."

8. Jerusalem is as important as it is unique.

9. Our camping trip turned out to be an exciting experience.

10. My teacher has asked me to write a paper about censorship.

11. The first time I met Joe Benton, I thought he was a great guy; now I think he's crazy.

12. My father works in a local filling station.

13. My friend Andrea is very intelligent.

14. Accidental swallowing of tabs and rings from soft-drink cans can be a serious problem.

15. It is a picture that has haunted me for months.

B. Write the introductory paragraph for your own composition. Revise it until you are satisfied that it will catch your readers' attention and that it states accurately the subject of the composition.

The Body

The major part of a composition is the body. It is in these paragraphs that the ideas indicated in the introductory paragraph are developed or explained. As an example, let's look once again at the composition on "The Origins of Jazz."

The introductory paragraph of that composition is this:

> The roots of American Jazz were planted long before this century was born. These roots were the beat, the music of the brass bands, and the blues—three roots which eventually joined together to form that most American of music—Jazz!

The paragraph indicates that the writer will discuss the beat, the music of the brass bands, and the blues. The outline for the composition also indicated that the body paragraphs will be concerned with these three ideas. The writer consulted her notes and, following her outline, wrote these paragraphs:

> The beat, the first root of jazz began with the varied rhythms of African slaves in New Orleans. Each Sunday these slaves would gather on Congo Square for a celebration, a *bamboula*. There they recalled the rhythms of their homeland, rhythms passed down from parent to child. As some of the musicians beat their intricate rhythms on drums of many sizes, others would dance and clap. Thus, the beat was born.
>
> The second root of jazz was also planted in New Orleans. Through its years as a French colony, the people who lived in this city on the Delta had heard the strident music of the military brass band, and had danced to the rhythms of French quadrilles played by some of these same bands. These sounds and rhythms they combined with the beat of the Congo drums into a music of their own, a syncopated form of melody which became known as "rag" or "Ragtime." This music was also played by small brass bands made up of the descendants of those earlier slaves who had established the "beat"in Congo Square.
>
> No one knows who first made up the blues. It is fairly certain, however, that its roots were firmly planted in the work songs, the plantation cries, the field "hollers," and the spirituals heard and sung by the early slaves as they gave vent to their loneliness, frustration, and sorrow.

This example illustrates two more important points about the composition.

1. **The composition is always divided into paragraphs.** The division of a composition into paragraphs has a psychological effect upon the reader. Often, if a reader sees a page covered with writing, with no blank space to relieve the monotony, he or she may not even attempt to read that page.

Also, paragraph indentations signal the reader that a new idea is about to be introduced. The reader then knows that he or she is moving to the next point of development, or the next point of information in the composition.

2. **Each paragraph of the composition usually begins with a topic sentence.** As you know from your previous study, the topic sentence of a paragraph gives an indication as to what the paragraph will be about. That is true not only when the paragraph stands alone, but also when it is part of a composition.

To clarify these ideas, let's analyze the following folktale.

MESSAGE IN THE SKY

When the earth was young, the beasts roamed the world. One was a snake of many colors. The snake was a sight to behold, for the Creator had endowed him with beauty. The other creatures admired him. Never had they seen so many colors on any one animal.

The snake's beauty brought him fame in the animal kingdom. With fame came the friendship of all the animals. The animals complimented him until, one day, he thought more highly of himself than all others. He became boastful, claiming to be the King of Beauty.

The animals were tolerant, but not the Creator. Upon hearing the boasts, the Creator sent a warning message to the snake to cease his boasting, but the snake would not listen, and kept on boasting. The Creator was angered and was determined to put an end to the silly snake's boasts. He sent a great white eagle to seize the snake and fly with him into the sky, then lower him to earth.

Once more safe on the earth, the snake discovered he no longer was beautiful. So angered was he that he developed the venom of hate. The defiant snake lifted his head to curse the Creator, only to see his coat of many colors in a bow across the sky. Now the beauty of the colors was to be enjoyed by everyone and not just one.

Thus, after every rainfall the rainbow comes out to remind the snake of his fall to earth, leaving behind him his coat of many colors.—GLENDA CELESTINE

From a psychological point of view, the composition appeals to the eye. It is broken up into short paragraphs with enough blank space to assure the readers that they are not going to lose themselves in long, involved ideas.

The introductory paragraph indicates that the composition is going to be about a beautiful snake of many colors. The body paragraphs develop this main idea.

Each paragraph in the body begins with a topic sentence that states what the paragraph is about.

1. The snake's beauty brought him fame in the animal kingdom.
2. The animals were tolerant, but not the Creator.
3. Once more safe on the earth, the snake discovered he no longer was beautiful.

The supporting details in each paragraph are directly related to the topic sentence, and each paragraph is directly related to the introductory paragraph. Thus, the composition is well written and well organized. Also, it has *unity*; everything is tied together and is not merely a series of isolated ideas.

Transitional Devices

The good writer makes use of **transitional devices** to give a composition a feeling of unity. These devices tie the ideas of the composition together by referring either to the idea that precedes, or to the idea that follows, or to both.

There are six basic transitional devices.

1. **Using a Word That Indicates Time.** Such words include the following:

first	before	meanwhile	until
next	after	in the meantime	finally
then	afterwards	eventually	today

The chief servant clapped his hands and a door opened through which there came servants, all with wings on their backs, bearing golden trays laden with meat, fish, pomegranates, and persimmons, pineapples, and peaches. A tall servant with a long white beard carried a golden goblet full of wine. Atzel was so starved that he ate ravenously. The angels hovered around him, filling his plate and goblet even before he had time to ask for more.

When he had finished eating, Atzel declared he wanted to rest. Two angels undressed and bathed him. Then they brought him a nightdress of fine embroidered linen, placed a nightcap with a tassel on his head, and carried him to a bed with silken sheets and a purple velvet canopy. Atzel immediately fell into a deep and happy sleep.—Isaac Bashevis Singer

2. **Using a Word That Shows the Relationship Between ideas.** Such words include the following:

also	because	therefore	moreover
too	and	besides	similarly

In the dining room, my father still sat on the floor. His shoulders sagged and he looked up at me with dull, unseeing eyes. Within a single morning, on a perfect June day, my young father had become an old man. Looking down at my father, I deliberately ignored the soldiers and their authority to tell me what I might and might not do—and asked for my father's permission to go to my mother. He nodded and patted my hand.

My mother too had changed. Usually she was composed and fastidiously groomed, but now her face was flushed and her beautiful crown of braids was tumbling down. . . .—Esther Hautzig

3. **Using a Word That Shows an Opposite Point of View.** Such words include the following:

but	while	on the other hand	nevertheless
however	although	in contrast	yet

I ordered stock and played records on request, emptied ashtrays and dusted the windows' cardboard displays. Louise and her partner, David Rosenbaum, showed their pleasure by giving me a raise; and although I was grateful to them, I could exhibit my feelings only by being punctual in coming to the shop and being efficient at work and coolly, grayly respectful.

At home, however, life shimmered with beautiful colors. I picked up my son from the baby-sitter's every evening. He was five years old and so beautiful his smile could break the back of a brute.—Maya Angelou

4. Using a Word That Repeats a Word Used Earlier.

Barclay's attitude to the railroad was about the same as toward the modern world in general. He had entered light-heartedly into the whirl and crash and crush, the grand babel of building, the suction and spouting, groaning and whining and breaking of steel —all the riotous, contagious movement around him.

He had entered into the rough camaraderie of the railroad with all the hot energy of youth. It was a rugged, new experience that kindled his vagabonding mind and body. There was rude poetry in the roar and rush and rattle of trains, the sharp whistle of engines and racing landscapes, the charm of a desolate mining town and glimpses of faces lost as soon as seen. He had even tried to capture some of those fleeting, piled-up images in writing.—CLAUDE MCKAY

5. Using a Synonym for a Word Used Earlier.

Standing in front of the lioness, he shouted something unintelligible in a raucous voice. The fur all over her body seemed to stand up, and she backed away from him apprehensively. Then he began talking to her in a soft, cooing voice. She relaxed at once and came closer to him. As he backed away from her she followed him. Then he barked a command in a sharp voice and although he continued to back away, Mumma stood still, watching him.

Without taking his eyes off the animal, he said to me, "The most important part of controlling an animal is the tone of your voice. Once you can get an animal to react to your tone, you can control it completely.—DAMOO DHOTRE

6. Using a Pronoun That Refers to a Word Used Earlier.

Dame Agatha Christie died recently in her eighty-sixth year. Next to the Bible and the plays of Shakespeare, her writings have reached a wider audience than those of any author who ever lived. She has been called "one of the most imaginative and fertile plot creators of all time," a "champion deceiver," and "the mistress of mystery."

Except for her unparalleled success, her life contained little out of the ordinary. She grew up in the solid, upper-middle-class English countryside that figures so prominently in her books.

Giving Credit

One important note of caution to keep in mind when writing the body of your composition is this: Never take credit for someone else's work. If you use information from another source, you must not copy the material word for word and claim it as your own. You can, however, quote the exact words or use the ideas of another person, as long as you give credit to that person.

Exercises Studying and Writing Body Paragraphs

A. Study the following pairs of paragraphs carefully. Identify the transitional device, or devices, that each writer has used to tie the paragraphs together.

1   After I had returned from India, I entered into a correspondence with Ved, whose letters were surprisingly mature for a boy in his teens. They were clearly the work of a resourceful mind. What impressed me particularly was his supple use of the English language.

     I met Ved for the first time in the spring of 1952. He came to our home with his father, then in the United States as a visiting Fulbright professor. There was nothing about Ved that suggested a handicapped person. He used no cane. He had no Seeing Eye dog. He didn't wait for people to lead him from one place to another. Not once did his father take him by the hand. Yet he moved about easily.—NORMAN COUSINS

2   Pavlov discovered he couldn't make dogs salivate on signal until he put them into artificial, controlled environments. By controlling space, sound, temperature, and food, he made them respond to his slightest signal.

     Disney made the same discovery. *Control* was his favorite word. He controlled every stage in the production and marketing of his films. He developed the "wrap-around screen," which was an effort at total environment. His studio was a controlled environment and served as the prototype for Disneyland.—EDMUND CARPENTER

3　For seven years there had been too little rain. The prairies were dust. Day after day, summer after summer, the scorching winds blew the dust, and the sun was brassy in a yellow sky. Crop after crop failed. Again and again the barren land must be mortgaged, for taxes and food and next year's seed. The agony of hope ended when there was no harvest and no more credit, no money to pay interest and taxes. The banker took the land. Then the bank failed.

In the seventh year a mysterious catastrophe was worldwide. All banks failed. From coast to coast the factories shut down, and business ceased. This was a Panic.—LAURA INGALLS WILDER

4　Marget was my first love. I met her when she joined our sixth-grade class.

She stood before the class, her blue, frightened eyes sweeping back and forth across the room until they came to rest on my face. From that very first day we became friends—Marget, just fresh from Sweden, and I, a sixth-generation American.—CARRIE A. YOUNG

5　The heat pressed down on me, as if suddenly in league with gravity. My pack sagged. And then all at once, a thread of clear water was sparkling on bare rock. I walked up beside it with light and springing step. The thread broadened. Half a mile, and I camped in the shade of some green creekside bushes. Soon I was stretched out cool and naked on my sleeping bag.

The little creek, still less than a foot wide, bubbled and babbled past so close that I could reach out whenever I wanted to and scoop up a cupful of cool drinking water. All I could see was green foliage and a hint of glaring rock beyond. That, and the sparkling creek and the oddly humped, blue-gray rock over which it flowed. —COLIN FLETCHER

6　I was about ten feet in front of Kitty as we got near the corner. The thing about Kitty is that you have to beat her to the corners if you're going to win a bicycle race that she's in. She always slowed down more than most people when she got to the corners, but she made up for it when she got on the straight runs. The only people on the block that she couldn't beat were Kwami and me, but she was getting pretty close to me, too. Anyway, I was just about ten feet in front of her when we hit the corner. I reached down and switched into fifth gear and leaned into that corner perfectly and was just about ready to straighten out and really do it to the finish line when I saw this lady named Drusilla.

Well, I saw her and then again I didn't see her. That is, I didn't see her in time. All of a sudden she popped up from between two parked cars, and I jerked my handlebars so I wouldn't hit her. I think I shouted "Watch out!" or something like that, too. When I jerked the handlebars, the bike started skidding and went right at her. I went over the handlebars and smack into the middle of the street. I hit so hard I thought I was going to pass out. I actually bounced!—WALTER DEAN MYERS

7   Ollie spent the early afternoon sitting on the rail in front of The Chicken Shack Restaurant, watching the cooks sling the wire baskets of chicken in and out of the frying fat. They were too sweaty and tired to tell her to move from in front. "Ruining the business," the owner used to fuss.

Later she stood between the laundry and shoe store, watching some men pitch pennies against the building. She waited for a while, squeezing a rubber ball in her hand. If I can just get the wall for a minute, she thought, maybe somebody'll come along and we'll have us a good game of handball. But the men went right on pitching while other ones were waiting their turn. They'd be there for hours, so Ollie left.—TONI CADE BAMBARA

B. Complete the body of your own composition. Make certain that you have used appropriate transitional devices to tie your ideas together into a unified, smoothly flowing composition. Make sure also that each paragraph is directly related to your introductory paragraph.

The Conclusion

After you have finished writing the body of your composition, your final step is to write the conclusion. The concluding paragraph ties all the ideas together and indicates to the reader that the composition is finished.

The writer of the composition "The Origins of Jazz" wrote this concluding paragraph:

> Eventually, interest in the blues grew until it joined with the beat and the music of the brass bands. From this union, a new and completely American form of music was born—Jazz!

You will notice that the conclusion *repeats* some of the ideas from the introductory paragraph.

In "Message in the Sky," you may recall, the writer ended her composition in this manner:

> Thus, after every rainfall the rainbow comes out to remind the snake of his fall to earth, leaving behind him his coat of many colors.

In this short, concluding statement, the writer has effectively *summarized* her story.

The following is another effective ending:

> What of the heroic horseman who aroused the Minutemen on that April night? Henry Wadsworth Longfellow lifted him from a footnote of history to a place in American poetic literature with a ballad that includes these words:
>
> So through the night rode Paul Revere;
> A cry of defiance and not of fear,
> A voice in the darkness, a knock at the door,
> And a word that shall echo forevermore!

This writer ended with an appropriate stanza of poetry that indicates "finish" to the reader.

Exercise Completing Your Composition

Write the concluding paragraph of your own composition. Make sure that it ties in well with the rest of the paragraphs. Then title your composition. You can take the title from your outline or write an original new one.

Rewriting, or Revising

With the completion of your first draft, you are ready to rewrite, or revise your composition, the third step in the Process of Writing. Review the third step of the Guidelines on page 83. You may also wish to review the Checklist for Writing Paragraphs on page 129 and the Checklist for Writing Compositions or Reports.

Proofreading

Follow the steps for Proofreading on pages 82 and 83. Use the Handbook section at the back of this book.

Checklist for Writing Compositions or Reports

As you write a composition or report, follow the steps in Guidelines for the Process of Writing on page 83. Use this Checklist after you have written your first draft.

1. Has the subject been narrowed to a topic that can be covered in a few paragraphs?
2. Does the composition or report deal with a single topic or idea?
3. Does it have an introduction, a body, and a conclusion?
4. Does the introduction present the main idea? Does it catch the reader's interest?
5. Does the body explain or support the main idea?
6. Does the conclusion restate the main idea, summarize the information, or comment upon it?
7. Do the paragraphs work together to develop a single topic or idea that is the subject of the composition or report?
8. Is the composition or report appropriate for the audience for which it is intended? Is the purpose clear?
9. Are the ideas presented in a clear, logical order?
10. Does the composition or report have unity? Are the supporting ideas in each paragraph related to the topic sentence? Is each paragraph directly related to the main idea in the introductory paragraph?
11. Are there transitional devices that tie the paragraphs together?
12. Is the title meaningful and interesting?

Chapter 9

Types of Compositions

Just as there are several types of paragraphs, there are also several types of compositions. In Chapter 7, you became familiar with narrative, descriptive, explanatory, and persuasive paragraphs. In this chapter, you will apply your knowledge of these paragraphs to the same four types of compositions. You will also gain further practice in applying the principles of composition development, which were presented in the preceding chapter.

Part 1 The Narrative Composition

The narrative paragraph relates something that happened; in other words, it tells a story. The narrative composition does the same thing. There are two main types of narrative compositions: the simple narrative and the complex narrative. As its name implies, the complex narrative is longer and more complicated than the simple narrative. Both, however, contain the same basic elements of character, setting, and conflict.

The **characters** are the people in the story. Those who are active in the narrative, and upon whose action the story depends, are the *major characters*. Those whose actions are less significant are the *minor characters*. Because of its short length and simple structure, a simple narrative will often have only one character. A complex narrative, on the other hand, will often have several characters, both major and minor.

The **setting** is the place where the events in a narrative happen. Setting includes the time frame of the story and the conditions under which the events occur. In some narratives, the setting is a key element, having an impact on both the characters and the events. In other narratives, the setting plays a minor role.

The **conflict** is the struggle or problem that is central to the narrative. Conflict usually is brought about because of something the character, or characters, want. There are four basic types of conflict.

THE INDIVIDUAL AGAINST A SUPERNATURAL FORCE: the struggle against God or the gods (as in the ancient myths and legends) or against the devil.

THE INDIVIDUAL AGAINST NATURE: the struggle to survive natural catastrophes, such as floods, earthquakes, and hurricanes that might destroy human life. This would also include the struggle against any members of the animal or plant world.

THE INDIVIDUAL AGAINST SOCIETY: the struggle against social forces, such as injustice, prejudice, and loss of individual freedom. It also includes the struggle of one individual against another.

THE INDIVIDUAL AGAINST HIMSELF: the struggle within the mind or conscience of an individual as he or she attempts to make a personal decision.

The conflict—the cause of it and the resolution of it—forms the framework of the narrative. In the simple narrative, the conflict is presented and resolved in just a few paragraphs. In the complex narrative, the framework, or plot, is more highly developed. Often the writer will attempt to arouse feelings of curiosity, uncertainty, and suspense in the mind of the reader.

To summarize, the three basic elements of the narrative composition are these:

CHARACTERS: major and minor

SETTING: the place, time, and conditions in which the action occurs

CONFLICT: the struggle that forms the framework of the narrative

Unity, Coherence, and Emphasis

The well written narrative composition exhibits the characteristics of unity, coherence, and emphasis.

Unity in the narrative means sticking to the story. Each event in some way contributes to the unfolding of the plot.

Unity is enhanced by transitional devices that tie together the paragraphs and the ideas within the paragraphs. In the simple narrative, unity is also enhanced by structure. The main idea is given in the introductory paragraph and each paragraph that follows explains or supports that idea.

Coherence in the narrative is the relation of one event to another and the order in which these events are described. In most narrative compositions, events are related in chronological order.

Emphasis is a matter of proportion and position relative to the central idea of the composition. Events that are important to the central idea are treated in greater detail than those that are less important. Each detail in the composition in some way relates to the central idea.

The Simple Narrative

In the simple narrative, the writer makes no attempt to lead up to a climax, merely to a conclusion. Following is an example of such a narrative.

A MESSAGE

I went out of doors and looked around. The air was pure. A cliff on the edge of the airport stood in profile against the sky as if it were daylight. Over the desert reigned a vast silence as of a house in order. Here, though, were a green butterfly and two dragonflies knocking against my lamp. A dull ache that might as easily have been joy as fear came up from the depths of me, so vague that it could scarcely be said to be there. Something was calling to me from a great distance. Was it instinct?

Later, I went out once again. The wind had died down completely. The air was still cool, but I had received a warning. I guessed, I believed I could guess, what I was expecting. Was I right? Neither the sky nor the sand had made the least sign to me, but two dragonflies and a moth had spoken.

I climbed a dune and sat down, face to the east. If I was right, the thing would not be long coming. What were they after here, those dragonflies, hundreds of miles from their oases inland? Wreckage thrown up on the beach bears witness to a storm at sea. Even so did these insects declare to me that a sandstorm was on the way, a storm out of the east that had blown them out of their oases.

Solemnly, for it was filled with danger, the east wind rose. Its flame wrapped me round once, only once, in a caress that seemed dead. I knew, in the seconds that followed, that the Sahara was catching its breath and would send forth a second sigh; that before three minutes had passed the air-sock of our hangar would be whipped into action; and that before ten minutes had gone by, the sand would fill the air. We should shortly be taking off in this. conflagration, in this return of the flames from the desert.

That was not what excited me. What filled me with a barbaric joy was that I had understood a murmured monosyllable of this secret language, had sniffed the air and known what was coming, like one of those primitive men to whom the future is revealed in such faint rustlings. It was that I had been able to read the anger of the desert in the beating wings of a dragonfly.—ANTOINE DE SAINT EXUPERY

In this composition, the writer describes one person's intimation of an impending sandstorm. That person is the only character. His experience takes place at night, at an airport in the Sahara desert. This is the setting of the narrative. Central to the narrative is the conflict of the individual against nature. Specifically, it is the struggle of the character to "tune in" to the secret language of nature.

The writer achieves unity by describing only the events that relate to the main idea of the composition. He does not stray from the main idea by describing the airport, his experiences as a pilot, or previous sandstorms.

The writer achieves coherence by organizing the narrative in chronological order. He describes what happened in the order that it happened.

The writer achieves emphasis by the skillful selection and arrangement of details. The emphasis throughout is on the writer's thoughts and feelings about the coming sandstorm. All the other details are included because they have some direct or indirect relationship to these thoughts and feelings.

The writer has grouped all the details around the central idea of the composition. In the first paragraph, he describes a vague and as yet unnamed feeling. In the second paragraph, he gives further details about the source and meaning of that feeling. In the third paragraph, he relates the feeling to the sandstorm. This is the central idea of the composition. It is identified in the third paragraph, or center, of the five-paragraph composition. In the final two paragraphs, the writer gives details about the sandstorm and summarizes the main idea of the composition.

Point of View

Every narrative composition, whether it is a simple narrative or a complex narrative, has a narrator through whose eyes the story is told. The writer of the composition can choose to have the narrator relate events either in the first person (as in the simple narrative used as an example) or in the third person.

First-Person Narration. In this type of narration the narrator can be either an observer of the action or a participant in it. In either case, the description of events is limited to what the narrator can know and see at any one time. The description of thoughts and feelings is limited to those of the narrator only. He or she does not have access to, and therefore cannot relate, the thoughts and feelings of the other characters.

Following are two sentences written in the first person. In the first, the narrator is an observer of the action. In the second, she is a participant.

1. Looking through the bars of the fire escape, I saw a German Shepherd pawing through the garbage piled next to the building.

2. With great effort, I summoned the last of my depleted strength and jumped the final hurdle.

Third-Person Narration. In this type of narration, the narrator functions in one of three ways. He or she may "see" and describe all the externally observable events, even those that take place at the same time. The narrator may not, however, describe what is going on in the minds of the characters.

A second kind of third-person narrator relates events through the eyes of one character. He or she has access only to the thoughts and feelings of that character and to the events observed by the character.

A third kind of narrator is omniscient. He or she knows everything, including what goes on in the minds of all the characters.

Following are three sentences written in the third person. In the first, the narrator describes external events only. In the second, the narrator describes the thoughts of one character. In the third, the narrator reveals the thoughts of two characters.

1. Raul pushed aside the heavy blue drape and entered the dimly lit room.

2. Henry hesitated for a moment, reluctant to commit himself to such drastic action.

3. Robin and Eric examined the arrowhead carefully, each anticipating the fine addition it would make to his collection.

Exercise Writing a Simple Narrative

Consider possible subjects for a narrative composition. They can be based on events in which you participated, on events that were observed by you, or on events that were described for you by someone else. Select one subject. Think about the characters, setting, and conflict involved in the events. Choose an appropriate point of view.

After you have thought about your subject, develop a composition following the steps presented in Chapter 8. When revising your composition, make sure that it is characterized by unity, coherence, and emphasis.

Follow the Guidelines for the Process of Writing on page 83 and the Checklist for Writing Compositions or Reports on page 165.

The Complex Narrative or Short Story

The complex narrative, or short story, contains the same basic elements of character, setting, and conflict as the simple narrative. In the complex narrative, however, these elements are developed with much greater detail.

A more significant difference between the simple and the complex narrative lies in their structures. In the simple narrative, the writer describes events that lead to a conclusion, achieved in the final paragraph. In the complex narrative, the writer builds to a climax, the turning point or high point of the story. Usually, the climax takes place close to the end of the story. The events that follow the climax resolve the conflict with which the characters have struggled throughout the narrative.

In addition to a unique structure, most short stories have the following five identifiable characteristics.

1. Dialogue, or conversation, that gives a feeling of naturalness, or believability, to a story and that brings the characters to life.
2. An immediate introduction of the reader to the setting of the story, followed by an introduction to the major characters and the beginnings of the conflict.

3. A tight structure in which every detail is significant.
4. A structure in which the end is enfolded in the beginning. What happens at the end of the story is a direct result of what was set up at the beginning.
5. A title whose meaning does not become clear until the end of the story.

Story 1

Here is an example of a short story. Read it first for pleasure. Then reread it and try to identify its main elements, the techniques used by the writer to achieve unity, coherence, and emphasis, and the characteristics of the short story that it illustrates.

TEST

Robert Proctor was a good driver for so young a man. The turnpike curved gently ahead of him, lightly traveled on this cool morning in May. He felt relaxed and alert. Two hours of driving had not yet produced the twinges of fatigue that appeared first in the muscles in the base of the neck. The sun was bright, but not glaring, and the air smelled fresh and clean. He breathed it deeply, and blew it out noisily. It was a good day for driving.

He glanced quickly at the slim, gray-haired woman sitting in the front seat with him. Her mouth was curved in a quiet smile. She watched the trees and the fields slip by on her side of the pike. Robert Proctor immediately looked back at the road. He said, "Enjoying it, Mom?"

"Yes, Robert." Her voice was as cool as the morning. "It is very pleasant to sit here. I was thinking of the driving I did for you when you were little. I wonder if you enjoyed it as much as I enjoy this."

He smiled, embarrassed. "Sure I did."

She reached over and patted him gently on the arm, and then turned back to the scenery.

He listened to the smooth purr of the engine. Up ahead he saw a great truck, spouting a geyser of smoke as it sped along the turnpike. Behind it, not passing it, was a long, blue convertible, content to drive in the wake of the truck. Robert Proctor noted the arrangement and filed it in the back of his mind. He was slowly overtaking them, but he would not reach them for another minute or two.

He listened to the purr of the engine, and he was pleased with the sound. He had tuned that engine himself over the objections of the mechanic. The engine idled roughly now, but it ran smoothly at high speed. You needed a special feel to do good work on engines, and Robert Proctor knew he had it. No one in the world had a feel like his for the tune of an engine.

It was a good morning for driving, and his mind was filled with good thoughts. He pulled nearly abreast of the blue convertible and began to pass it. His speed was a few miles per hour above the turnpike limit, but his car was under perfect control. The blue convertible suddenly swung out from behind the truck. It swung out without warning and struck his car near the right front fender, knocking his car to the shoulder on the left side of the turnpike lane.

Robert Proctor was a good driver, too wise to slam on the brakes. He fought the steering wheel to hold the car on a straight path. The left wheels sank into the soft left shoulder, and the car tugged to pull to the left and cross the island and enter the lanes carrying the cars heading in the opposite direction. He held it, then the wheel struck a rock buried in the soft dirt, and the left front tire blew out. The car slued, and it was then that his mother began to scream.

The car turned sideways and skidded part of the way out into the other lanes. Robert Proctor fought against the steering wheel to straighten the car, but the drag of the blown tire was too much. The scream rang steadily in his ears, and even as he strained at the wheel one part of his mind wondered coolly how a scream could so long be sustained without a breath. An oncoming car struck his radiator from the side and spun him viciously, full into the left-hand lanes.

He was flung into his mother's lap, and she was thrown against the right door. It held. With his left hand he reached for the steering wheel and pulled himself erect against the force of the spin. He turned the wheel to the left, and tried to stop the spin and careen out of the lanes of oncoming traffic. His mother was unable to right herself; she lay against the door, her cry rising and falling with the eccentric spin of the car.

The car lost some of its momentum. During one of the spins he twisted the wheel straight, and the car wobblingly stopped spinning and headed down the lane. Before Robert Proctor could turn it off the pike to safety a car loomed ahead of him, bearing down on him. There was a man at the wheel of that other car, sitting rigid, unable to move, eyes wide and staring and filled with fright. Alongside the man was a girl, her head against the back of the seat, soft curls framing a lovely face, her eyes closed in easy sleep. It was not the fear in the man that reached into Robert Proctor; it was the trusting helplessness in the face of the sleeping girl. The two cars sped closer to each other, and Robert Proctor could not change the direction of his car. The driver of the other car remained frozen at the wheel. At the last moment Robert Proctor sat motionless, staring into the face of the onrushing, sleeping girl, his mother's cry still sounding in his ears. He heard no crash when the two cars collided head-on at a high rate of speed. He felt something push into his stomach, and the world began to go grey. Just before he lost consciousness he heard the scream stop, and he knew then that he had been hearing a single, short-lived scream that had only seemed to drag on and on. There came a painless wrench, and then darkness.

Robert Proctor seemed to be at the bottom of a deep black well. There was a spot of faint light in the far distance, and he could hear the rumble of a distant voice. He tried to pull himself toward the light and the sound, but the effort was too great. He lay still and gathered himself and tried again. The light grew brighter and the voice louder. He tried harder, again, and he drew closer. Then he opened his eyes full and looked at the man sitting in front of him.

"You all right, Son?" asked the man. He wore a blue uniform, and his round, beefy face was familiar.

Robert Proctor tentatively moved his head, and discovered he was seated in a reclining chair, unharmed, and able to move his arms and legs with no trouble. He looked around the room, and he remembered.

The man in the uniform saw the growing intelligence in his eyes and he said, "No harm done, Son. You just took the last part of your driver's test."

Robert Proctor focused his eyes on the man. Though he saw the man clearly, he seemed to see the faint face of the sleeping girl in front of him.

The uniformed man continued to speak. "We put you through an accident under hypnosis—do it to everybody these days before they can get their drivers' licenses. Makes better drivers of them, more careful drivers the rest of their lives. Remember it now? Coming in here and all?"

Robert Proctor nodded, thinking of the sleeping girl. She never would have awakened; she would have passed right from a sweet, temporary sleep into the dark heavy sleep of death, nothing in between. His mother would have been bad enough; after all, she was pretty old. The sleeping girl was downright waste.

The uniformed man was still speaking. "So you're all set now. You pay me the ten dollar fee, and sign this application, and we'll have your license in the mail in a day or two." He did not look up.

Robert Proctor placed a ten dollar bill on the table in front of him, glanced over the application and signed it. He looked up to find two white-uniformed men, standing one on each side of him, and he frowned in annoyance. He started to speak, but the uniformed man spoke first. "Sorry, Son. You failed. You're sick; you need treatment."

The two men lifted Robert Proctor to his feet, and he said, "Take your hands off me. What is this?"

The uniformed man said, "Nobody should want to drive a car after going through what you just went through. It should take months before you can even think of driving again, but you're ready right now. Killing people doesn't bother you. We don't let your kind run around loose in society any more. But don't you worry now, Son. They'll take good care of you, and they'll fix you up." He nodded to the two men, and they began to march Robert Proctor out.

At the door he spoke, and his voice was so urgent the two men paused. Robert Proctor said, "You can't really mean this. I'm still dreaming, aren't I? This is still part of the test, isn't it?"

The uniformed man said, *"How do any of us know?"* And they dragged Robert Proctor out the door, knees stiff, feet dragging, his rubber heels sliding along the two grooves worn into the floor.
—Theodore L. Thomas

Analysis

Basic Elements. The following outline shows the basic narrative elements as they appear in this short story.

    I. CHARACTERS
        A. Major: Robert Proctor
        B. Minor
            1. Proctor's mother
            2. Driver of the oncoming car
            3. Passenger in the oncoming car
            4. Blue-uniformed man
            5. Two white-uniformed men
    II. SETTING
        A. Time
            1. Morning
            2. May
        B. Place
            1. Inside a car on a turnpike
            2. Place where driving tests are given
    III. CONFLICT: Robert Proctor's struggle against loss of control

Point of View. The story is told in the third person through the eyes of one character, Robert Proctor.

Unity, Coherence, and Emphasis. Unity is achieved by the writer's relating only the events surrounding the driving test.

Coherence is achieved by telling the story in chronological order.

Emphasis is achieved by treating the central idea, the last terrifying moments of the accident, in great detail. This, in fact, is the climax of the story, the point at which Proctor surrenders the last remnants of control. The events that come before the climax lead up to it. The events that come after lead away from the climax to the resolution of the conflict.

Notable Characteristics. The writer uses dialogue at the beginning and at the end of the story. He gets immediately into the story by introducing the main character and by describing the setting in the first paragraph. In the next several paragraphs, he builds up the feeling that the main character is in complete control of the situation. When the loss of control occurs, it is as much a jolt to the reader as to the character. By the end of the story, the loss of control is complete, and the main character is divested of even his own personal freedom. In the final paragraphs, the meaning of the title "Test" becomes clear.

Story 2

Here is another short story. Read it first for pleasure. Then reread it and try to analyze the elements of the story. To what extent does the story achieve what you have learned thus far about a well constructed complex narrative?

THE PASSING

Ever since Mama married Miguel we had lived in the country. He had built a tall, single-walled, two-room house on the land of his family above the big bend of Fish Creek, and it stood there, lean and unpainted among the trees back from the road. Even after Mama and I came to live there it remained unpainted. It was built of unfinished sawmill planks and had two stovepipe chimneys sticking through its green roof. Right across the road was the Indian church.

The house stood above a steep, boulder-littered and heavily wooded slope and the creek that ran below. I had developed a swimming hole there, and across the creek on the wooded slopes I played at hunting. It had been almost two years since we had settled there, and I had already explored the surrounding countryside for miles in winter and summer so that I now usually stayed close to the house. Summer had grown old, and I was becoming restless.

One evening as I played cars with pieces of wood in the dust beside the house, Mama saw the boy coming along the road. She stopped gathering the clothes from the line and took the clothespins from her mouth. I looked after her gaze and beyond. Through the shadows and trees I saw how the road curved and disappeared quickly into the dusk and woods. I looked back to her when she spoke.

"Sonny, there goes Joe Willow," she said. Then she paused and put the shirt she was holding into the basket at her feet. "He sure does work hard. I hope old Jimmy Bear and Fannie appreciate it, those two."

She shook her head and began to gather the rest of the clothes. I sat back on my heels and wondered at the tone of her voice. I had never really noticed Joe Willow before, but I knew the rest of the family from church meetings. And once I had seen where they lived.

It was about a mile beyond the curve, far back from the road and reached by a rutted drive that skirted the Indian graveyard. I knew the graveyard because near it were some pecan trees from which I gathered the nuts each fall. Their house was very old and unpainted. It sat low and gray under a group of large blackjack oaks and within a grassless yard that was pressed closely by the thick, surrounding woods.

Joe Willow's mother, Fannie, was a short, round woman with mottled brown skin and a high, shiny forehead that wrinkled when she laughed. Jimmy Bear was her second husband, and they used to pass our house often on their way to town. They had once driven an old Dodge, but it no longer ran, and it now sat lopsided and windowless among the weeds beside their lane. Jimmy Bear was a skinny man, but he had a round, protruding belly and wore his belt under it so that it looked as if he carried a basketball inside. He had gaps in his teeth and a rough, guttural laugh and walked with a shuffle. Mama told me that Fannie had once had money, but that they had long since used it up.

The next evening when Joe Willow passed the gate I got up and ran to hang on it as I watched him pass on up the road. The sun, being low and to his back, sent a long finger of shadow ahead of him. I could hear the crunch and whisper of his footsteps between the squeaks of the bucket he carried until they began to fade with the coming of the breeze through the tall grass alongside the road. The bucket creaked faintly and the breeze dropped for a moment.

I called to him.

"Hello, Joe Willow," I said.

In the stillness my voice carried, and he turned, his shadow pointing into the woods, and lifted his hand. He squinted into the sun and smiled. I waved, and he turned back up the road and soon faded against the shadow and trees.

I sat on the gate for a while until a deeper darkness crept from the woods and began to fuse with the trees. I heard the trees begin to sigh and settle down for the night, the lonely cooing of a dove, and from somewhere across the creek the hoot of an owl. Then I hurried back to the house in the new coolness and stood near my mom for a while as she moved about the warm iron cookstove preparing supper.

Almost every evening of August that summer the young Indian passed along the road in front of our gate. I saw him several times a week as he came up from the bridge, always carrying a small, empty lard bucket whose handle squeaked faintly as he passed by and out of sight. He walked like someone who is used to walking, slowly, without spirit, but with the strength seen in a young workhorse.

Many evenings I swung back and forth on the gate and waited for him to come by. I had no brothers or sisters as yet, but Mama was expecting Miguel's first child before spring. Miguel was my stepfather, and since he said very little to me and because I couldn't be around Mama all the time, I waited for Joe Willow to pass by, although I seldom spoke except to reply to his greetings. Often I didn't even show myself at all and only sat among the grapevines next to the gate until the darkness sent me home.

I remember one of the last times I saw him. It was early in September, and I was sitting on the gate watching the sun caught on the treetops, noticing how the leaves looked like embers across its face as it settled into them, when Joe Willow appeared like a moving post upon the road. I had just gotten down from the gate and sat on the large rock that propped up our mailbox when Miguel called for me to eat supper. Instead, I began to sift sand into little conical piles as I waited. I looked down the road past the young worker to where the sun had fallen behind the trees. It looked trapped. The wind was very soft and smelled of smoke and dust. A few birds chuckled above me in the trees, and the insects of the evening buzzed in the weeds below.

Miguel called again and I looked up.

"Howdy, Joe Willow," I said. "You coming home from work?"

He stopped and grinned.

"That's right," he said. He leaned on the mailbox, and we said nothing for a few moments until he spoke again. "You're Miguel's boy, aren't you?"

"Huh-uh. I belong to Rosa."

"Oh." He squatted down. "You know what? I'm the same way. Everybody calls me Jimmy Bear's boy, but I'm not. He's not my daddy."

We both shifted around and watched where the sun had gone down.

"You see what happens when the sun goes down?" He pointed to the evening star and motioned toward the other stars that had appeared in the east. "When the daddy goes to bed, all the little children come out." His teeth gleamed in the gathering darkness, and I smiled, too.

We had watched the stars for only a moment when Miguel called again.

"You better get on home," Joe Willow said. "That's your daddy calling you."

"I'm Rosa's boy," I said.

"I know," he said, "but you better get on back." He looked up again at the deepening sky and laughed softly. "I'll see you some other time—'Rosa's boy.'"

After September came, I started school and no longer saw Joe Willow pass our gate. One day I asked Mama about him, and she said that he had gone to the free Indian boarding school in the northern part of the state, just south of the Kansas line. It was when winter was just melting into spring, a few weeks after

Mama had returned from the hospital with my baby brother, that I remembered him again.

Just before supper Miguel came into the kitchen, stamping the bits of dirty snow from his overshoes.

"Jimmy Bear's boy's been killed by the Santa Fe train at Chillocco," he said. "But they say they ain't sure how it happened." He warmed his hands over the stove and sat down.

I looked at Mama. She said nothing and rocked the baby. On the stove the beans bubbled softly, and their smell filled the room. I watched the lid on the pot jiggle as the steam escaped and I heard the wind rattle gently at the window. Miguel struggled with his overshoes and continued:

"Fannie tol' me a railroad man was down the first thing and said they was willin' to pay." He grunted and shoved the overshoes near the stove. "The funeral's Tuesday," he said.

Mama nodded and handed me the baby and got up to put the food on the table. She touched my head, and we sat down to supper.

At the funeral Joe Willow's family cried, and old Fannie even fainted at the grave site when they started to cover him. Jimmy Bear had to struggle to keep her from falling. The dirt sounded on the wooden vault, and the little houses over the older graves looked gray and damp with the people standing among them. I went over to the pecan trees and kicked among the damp mulch looking for good nuts, but I couldn't find any.

That evening after supper I stepped out onto the back stoop, and the yellow lamplight behind me threw my shadow onto the patches of snow and earth, enclosing it in the rectangle that the doorway formed. I looked up. The spotty clouds looked like bits of melting snow pressed into the darkness, and the stars were out, sprinkled into the stillness beyond. The black trees swayed, and the cold wind was familiar.

Behind me Mama moved around the kitchen, and I heard the chink and gentle clatter of the plates and pans as she put those things away. I shivered. And I knew that soon, as it did every spring, the clouds would come and it would begin to rain, a cold, heavy drizzle, and the land would turn to mud.—DURANGO MENDOZA

183

Analysis

Characters. The major character is an unnamed young boy. The minor characters are Rosa, the boy's mother; Miguel, his step-father; and Joe Willow.

Setting. The setting is a small, run-down house in a rural area. The time is the present, from August to the following spring.

Conflict. The conflict is the young boy's struggle against loneliness.

Point of View. The story is told in the first person, through the eyes of the young boy.

Unity, Coherence, and Emphasis. Unity is achieved by the writer's relating only those events concerning the young boy's relationship with his mother, his step-father, and Joe Willow.

Coherence is achieved by telling the story in chronological order.

Emphasis is achieved by treating the central idea, the boy's loneliness, in great detail. The climax of the story is the death of Joe Willow. The events before the climax lead up to it. The events after the climax resolve the conflict.

Notable Characteristics. The setting is an integral part of the story because it parallels the lonely, bleak, spiritless existence of the boy. The constant, detailed descriptions of the landscape help you understand the young boy's dreary, gray, empty life. He finds some release from his loneliness in brief talks with Joe Willow. He identifies with Joe. Both of them are "mother's" boys; both have step-fathers who are strangers to them. The writer uses dialogue to reveal the characters to you. He shows through their actions what kinds of people they are.

After Joe Willow's death, the climax, the story ends quickly, and the title achieves deeper meaning. At one level, "The Passing" refers to Joe Willow, who passes the house and helps to relieve the boy's loneliness. At another level, the title refers to Joe's death, his passing away. At a third level, it takes on added meaning for the resolution of the conflict. It refers to the rite of passage, the movement from youth to maturity. After Joe Willow's death, the young boy realizes that he is trapped in his environment, that the coming spring will not be a renewal of life, but rather, a sky of relentless rain and a land turned to mud.

Exercises Writing a Complex Narrative or Short Story

A. Choose another short story that interests you and analyze it in the same way as above, referring to the previous outline and the procedures for writing the complex narrative.

B. From personal experience or from imagination (or a combination of the two), create an outline for a complex narrative, using the same outline form used in the analysis.

After you have created your outline, write a complex narrative. Working in groups of three or four students, discuss any possible changes and revise where necessary.

In discussing your narrative, and considering ways of improving it, use the following questions.

1. Have I kept to my story?
2. Have I aroused and kept the reader's interest?
3. Are my characters real people?
4. Does my dialogue sound like actual conversation?
5. Is my conflict believable?
6. Have I given emphasis to the events of greatest importance?
7. Should I shorten any incidents for the sake of proportion?
8. Does my narrative move forward rapidly?
9. Is the resolution of my conflict meaningful in terms of my story?
10. Is my title interesting?
11. Have I correctly paragraphed my story?

Part 2   The Descriptive Composition

Description is usually used in conjunction with other types of writing. There are instances, though, when writers communicate their ideas and feelings in the form of descriptive compositions.

As is the narrative composition, the descriptive composition is written from a definite point of view. It also exhibits the same characteristics of unity, coherence, and emphasis. The way that these four characteristics are present in descriptive writing, however, is slightly different from the way they are present in the narrative.

Point of View

In the narrative composition, point of view refers to the way that the narrator tells the story. In the descriptive composition, point of view refers to the physical place from which the writer views the object of description. It can also refer to the writer's mental attitude toward the subject.

Physical Point of View. The details in a descriptive composition, as in a descriptive paragraph, must be arranged in some logical order. These orders include from left to right (or the reverse), from bottom to top (or the reverse), from near to far (or the reverse). They also include chronological order and any number of original orders conceived and carried out by the writer.

No matter what organizational pattern you follow, you must choose a position from which to view the object or scene that is the subject of your composition. This position is your physical point of view.

By selecting a specific point of view, you narrow your subsequent choice of details to those that can be sensed from that given point. For example, if you decide to describe a traffic jam from the top of a tall building, you will include those things that can be heard, seen, touched, tasted, and smelled from that vantage point. If you decide to place yourself in the midst of the traffic jam, your choice of details will be entirely different.

Mental Point of View. Mental point of view can vary according to the mood of the writer. Suppose you are looking down at a city street. The sky is dark. Heavy, black clouds are moving in from the west. The wind is blustery, and thunder rumbles in the distance. You may feel depressed, melancholy. This is the mental point of view that will be reflected in your description of the scene.

On the other hand, suppose that the morning sun is shining down on the rain-washed street. The sky is a cloudless blue, and the air is invigorating. In the distance you hear someone singing. You may feel happy, carefree. This is the mental point of view that will be evident in your writing.

Unity, Coherence, and Emphasis

Unity. The purpose of the descriptive composition is to create a single, unified impression in the mind of the reader. You achieve this by maintaining a definite point of view. You include only those details that contribute to the desired impression. You make sure that each sentence relates to the topic sentence of the paragraph and that each paragraph relates to the introductory paragraph. You use transitional devices to tie the ideas together.

Because it strengthens the impression in the mind of the reader, precise language reinforces the unity of a descriptive composition. The writer creates precise language in three main ways.

1. By using strong verbs; for example, *grabbed* instead of *took* and *marched* instead of *walked*.

2. By using specific nouns; for example, *collie* instead of *dog* and *daisy* instead of *flower*.

3. By using adjectives and adverbs and prepositional phrases as adjectives and adverbs; for example, *the sprightly old woman* instead of *the woman*, tumbled *head-over-heels* instead of *tumbled*, and *slept quietly under the cherry tree* instead of *slept*.

Coherence. Coherence, or clarity, in description is achieved through the logical arrangement of ideas. The logical orders specific to description were discussed previously in the section on point of view.

Emphasis. Emphasis in description is achieved by choosing a center of interest or dominant image or idea. It may be a mountain, a unique architectural detail, or an interesting play of light or color. All the details are presented in relation to it. Those details that relate directly are emphasized. Those that relate indirectly are de-emphasized.

The Practical Description

There are two types of descriptive compositions: practical and artistic. The practical description appeals to the intellect. It is an objective description that holds strictly to external details and facts, as in the following example.

SRI LANKA

Between the parallels of 5°55′ and 9°51′N and 79°43′ and 81°53′ E is the island of Sri Lanka. It is 270 miles long and 140 wide and has a total area of 25,332 square miles. Within this small island is a variety of landscapes that few larger countries could equal, and each scenic region has a characteristic climate.

Around the palm-fringed coast and up the wide plains of the South and West, the climate is warm and often wet. In the jungle plains of the Southeast and North-Center, the unique Tank Country, it is hot and generally dry. At the island's center, which climbs to a peak of 8,298 feet, the climate varies from cool to cold, from wet to dry, and from grassy downland to luxuriantly wooded mountains down which waterfalls tumble.

The Northern Peninsula is distinct and different from all the South. For the most part it is hot and dry, yet its terrain ranges from sandy desert to verdure unsurpassed in better watered regions. The Peninsula is ringed by islands as romantic and tenuous on the horizon as any South Sea atoll.

Sri Lanka encompasses wide variations in rainfall, elevation, and temperature. Precipitation measures anywhere from 25 to 250 inches annually. Elevations go from sea level to above 7,000 feet.

Occasionally temperatures drop below freezing, but generally they hover near the nineties.

This is no ordinary island in the sun. In a brief journey—you can make no single trip in this microscopic paradise more than 350 miles long—you can put yourself in the environment of your choice.—SRI LANKA TOURIST BOARD

In this composition the writer has used a moving point of view. That is, he does not describe the island from a fixed position. Because this is a practical description, the writer's mental point of view, beyond his appreciation for the variety offered by the island, is not easily perceived. However, if you take a close look at the composition, you will note a few emotionally laden words such as *luxuriantly*, *romantic*, and *paradise*. These words indicate a favorable attitude toward the subject. Overall, though, the description is highly objective and factual.

In the introductory paragraph, the writer states: "Within this small island is a variety of landscapes few larger countries could equal, and each scenic region has a characteristic climate." He goes on to give many details about the landscapes and climates found on the island. By holding to this subject, the writer achieves unity.

He achieves coherence by organizing the details in logical order. He focuses first on the landscapes and climates found in the main part of the island, moves to the unique Northern Peninsula, then discusses the characteristics of the entire island.

The writer achieves emphasis by selecting the variety of the island as his central idea, then giving details that bring out that variety.

Exercise Writing a Practical Description

Choose a subject suitable for development into a practical descriptive composition. Then, drawing from fact, from imagination, or from both, write a five-paragraph composition. Be sure to follow the steps for writing a composition that were presented in Chapter 8. Also keep in mind a specific physical point of view and the techniques for achieving unity, coherence, and emphasis in the descriptive composition. Follow the Guidelines for the Process of Writing on page 83 and the Checklist for Writing Compositions or Reports on page 165.

The Artistic Description, or Personal Essay

The artistic description appeals to the emotions and to the imagination. It includes details that cause the reader to feel much as the writer felt about the object or scene being described. In contrast to the practical description, the artistic description is primarily subjective. Therefore, the mental point of view of the writer is very important in this type of composition.

The following is an example of an artistic description.

WINTER HAPPENING

Once in the year there comes *the snow*. There are all manners of snow, both cruel and kind, but there is one snow that people think of as *the snow*. It actually comes very seldom but is the symbol of all snows, the childhood miracle that remains forever an image larger than all the bitter snows that come before and after.

The snow falls slowly in soft clusters like fairy snowballs. The clusters are so slow, so far apart that children can stand and catch them on their tongues. The snow clings where it falls, pure as wool blankets. The thistles become flowers. The wild carrot blooms again. Everything is unbelievably still.

The snow falls to the proper depth, to the exact moment when all ugliness is covered, to the weight that the twig and branch can bear without breaking. It knows precisely when to stop. All night *the snow* remains motionless unless a twig is shaken by an owl or a weasel. It hardens a little with a light crust, to bear the weight of the wild things walking in the night, and to preserve itself for the daylight.

The morning comes slowly and begins with a gray whiteness. The ground is stitched with tiny tracks that end suddenly in round, damp holes, or vanish where a small thing flew upward. Rabbit tracks wander along the raspberry thickets, and the sycamore balls have little caps of fur. It is best in this white grayness before the sun has come through the ascending clouds. The brooding, silent, closed-in world of *snow* and whiteness, motionless except for the birds, a timeless moment like an enormous pearl, a moment of stillness before the sun, and the thousand-diamond glitter and the rainbowed sound of light.

Even children, whose first thought is to tramp it and scrape it into balls, stand for a moment in awe. They drink in the miracle that is to become forever *snow* for the rest of their lives, *the snow* that is almost too beautiful to be borne.—JOSEPHINE W. JOHNSON

The writer's physical point of view is in the midst of the snow. Her mental point of view is one of serenity, of peace.

The single, unified impression communicated to the reader is one of serenity. The writer creates this impression by maintaining a consistent point of view—both physical and mental—and by carefully choosing details that elicit feelings of serenity in the reader. These details include phrases such as "soft clusters," "unbelievably still," "the snow remains motionless," "The brooding, silent, closed-in world," "motionless except for the birds," "a timeless moment like an enormous pearl," "a moment of stillness," and "the thousand-diamond glitter and the rainbowed sound of light."

The writer also achieves unity by repeating the phrase "the snow" and by constructing the composition so that each paragraph develops the main idea presented in the introductory paragraph.

The writer achieves coherence through the logical arrangement of ideas into chronological order. She describes the snow falling at night, then its appearance in the morning.

The writer achieves emphasis by including numerous details in the body paragraphs to describe "the snow," the central idea of the composition. The falling of the snow and its appearance in the morning are the two most important ideas in relation to the central idea. The writer, therefore, gives these two ideas the largest amount of space.

Exercise Writing an Artistic Description

In the previous exercise, you wrote a practical description. Now write a second description, or personal essay, on the same subject, this time making it an artistic description. Follow the steps that you followed in writing the practical description. This time, however, keep in mind a mental point of view as well as a physical one.

Follow the Guidelines for the Process of Writing on page 83 and the Checklist for Writing Compositions or Reports on page 165.

Part 3 The Explanatory Composition

The explanatory composition, like the explanatory paragraph, can give instructions. It can also explain an idea by using facts or statistics, one or more examples, an incident or an anecdote, or comparisons or contrasts.

The explanatory composition must also have unity, coherence, and emphasis. These three characteristics are achieved in much the same way as in narrative and descriptive compositions. Unity is created by maintaining a consistent attitude toward the subject matter; by a tight structure in which each paragraph and sentence is related either directly or indirectly to the main idea of the composition; by details that reinforce the main idea; and by transitional devices that tie ideas together.

Coherence is created by arranging ideas in logical order. In the explanatory composition, logical order means the order that best fits the particular content of the composition, whether that order is chronological, spatial, order of importance, or order of familiarity.

Emphasis is achieved by selecting one central idea to which all the other ideas are related and by devoting the most space to the most important supporting ideas.

As with the descriptive composition, there are two types of explanatory compositions: practical and artistic.

The Practical Explanatory Composition

In Part 2 you learned that the practical description appeals to the intellect. It is an objective description that holds strictly to external details and facts. The same definition can be applied to the practical explanatory composition. This type of composition is written when clarity and conciseness are important and when emotional involvement would stand in the way of communication. It would be written, for example, to give instructions or to explain a problem.

Here is an example of a practical explanation.

ICEBERGS ON THE MOVE

As the population of the world increases and the standard of living rises, the need for water—for homes and cities, industry and agriculture—grows steadily too. Even though water covers three-quarters of the earth's surface, about ninety-seven percent is salt water, which is of little use to human development on land. Most of the remaining three percent is frozen as glaciers, "rivers of ice" that creep down cold mountain valleys and drain off the frigid land in broad ice sheets. Many glaciers melt while still on land, but some reach the coast, where large pieces break off from the glacial sheet and fall into the ocean to form icebergs. For more than a century, both dreamers and realists have thought about towing icebergs thousands of miles to the coasts of warm, dry areas where they would provide water for thousands, perhaps millions, of people. So far the obstacles to such an undertaking have proven to be nearly overwhelming.

The most obvious obstacle is that icebergs are extremely dangerous to approach. If you look at an ice cube floating in a glass of water, you will see that most of the cube is beneath the surface. As it melts, it changes shape, and its center of gravity shifts. An iceberg does much the same thing. As its weight and shape change, it may roll over suddenly, churning the water violently and bringing large, submerged parts into the air—endangering any vessel nearby.

Even if an iceberg could be approached and prepared for transportation, several obstacles still remain. One problem is the melting that occurs when an iceberg reaches warm water. Only if it could be steered directly to a desired location, with no loss of time, might it still be large enough to yield a substantial volume of water. Glacier ice is colder than regular ice, so it melts more slowly. However, only a very large iceberg could be worth transporting, and that would cost an enormous amount of money. Then, even if this iceberg could be brought to its destination, it could not be towed in close to shore. Because eighty-five to ninety percent of an iceberg is underwater, it would be grounded on the ocean floor far from land. Even from this distant position, an iceberg would probably change the environment somewhat. It might create cool breezes or fog and lower the air and water temperature. The decrease in water temperature, along with the changes in the salt content of the water, could affect the marine plants and animals in the area.

Recently the National Science Foundation developed an elaborate plan for towing icebergs from Antarctica to Los Angeles. The plan seems to surmount many of the major obstacles, particularly those involved in moving the icebergs and in getting water from iceberg to shore. Satellites, photographing earth from space, would be used to spot icebergs of the desired size and shape for towing. Several large, solid, flat, streamlined bergs would be linked together with cables, like a string of barges. They would be insulated with quilted plastic sheeting to slow melting, so that in the year-long trip to Los Angeles, less than one-tenth of the ice would melt. Power would be drawn from escort ships. Tugs, helicopters, and a crew would travel with the iceberg train. At Los Angeles the train would serve as a long breakwater or be taken apart. Meltwater would be collecting in floating dams, or pieces of quarried ice could be brought inland, perhaps on a convey or belt. Water might also be channeled into hollows or collection points on the berg.

Despite great physical and financial risks, iceberg importing, once a fantastic dream, may become a reality. Someday, glistening white icebergs may float in warm harbors through the world.
—Gwen Schultz

Exercises Studying and Writing a Practical Explanation

A. Answer the following questions about the composition "Icebergs on the Move."

1. What is the purpose of the composition?

2. What technique does the writer use to develop the composition?

3. What is the central, or main, idea of the composition?

4. Does the writer take an objective or a subjective approach to the topic?

5. How does the writer achieve unity of structure?

6. Does she use transitional devices? If so, what are they?

7. In what order does the writer present her ideas?

8. How does the writer achieve emphasis?

B. Choose a subject suitable for development into a practical explanatory composition. Then, following the steps for writing a composition, develop your subject into a five-paragraph explanation that exhibits the characteristics of unity, coherence, and emphasis.

Follow the Guidelines for the Process of Writing on page 83 and the Checklist for Writing Compositions or Reports on page 165.

The Artistic Explanatory Composition, or Essay

There may be times when you wish to involve your reader emotionally as well as intellectually in your explanatory writing. You will then write an artistic explanatory composition. As with the artistic description, the artistic explanation is primarily subjective. Therefore, your attitude toward the subject, or mental point of view, is important, as in the following example.

THE GREAT DEEPS

There is a night world that few human beings have entered and from whose greatest depths none have returned alive—the abyssal depths of the sea. Darwin's associates dreamed of its hovering and intangible shapes as possibly those of the lost Paleozoic world. The great naturalist himself pleaded with outbound voyagers: "Urge the use of the dredge in the tropics; how little we know of the limit of life downward in the hot seas."

Anything that has been supposedly dead for a hundred million years is monstrous when you find it alive and pulsing in your hand.

This was the experience of Sir Charles Thomson, one of the few explorers of the North Atlantic sea bed. Few people in the years since have laid hands or eyes upon living denizens of the fossil kingdom, and this was an adventure no one could forget. The discovery influenced directly the formation of the world's largest oceanographic expedition and made Sir Charles its leader. Speaking of his find, long afterwards, he said: "It was like a little round red cake. And like a little round red cake, it began to pant there in my hand. Curious undulations were passing through it, and I had to summon up all my resolution before handling the weird little monster."

Now to the ordinary person, that little round red cake would have been a sea urchin, and whether it panted would have meant nothing at all except that it was alive. Nevertheless, the ordinary person would have been wrong. The fact *was* monstrous and the little red sea urchin more startling still. Even the "panting" had significance. No living sea urchin had ever been observed in such a performance. The known forms are all too rigid. The undulations of this little beast were a sure sign of its relationship to a more leathery and flexible ancestral group.

As a living fossil, it had been dredged out of the North Atlantic sea bed almost a solid mile below the surface. A mile today is not a great depth compared with the six-mile depression of the Tuscarora Deep, but in the sixties of the last century—Sir Charles Thomson's time—it was below the level at which life was generally supposed to exist. Anything below three hundred fathoms was Azoic, lifeless—so wrote Edward Forbes, the first great oceanographer of the eighteen forties. Like many pioneers he was destined to be proved wrong, yet looking back, it is possible to sympathize. The cold, the dark, the pressure of those unknown depths was frightening to contemplate. The human mind shied subconsciously away from the notion that living beings had groped their way down into the primeval slime of the sea floor. It was the world of the abyss, supposedly as lifeless as the earth's first midnight.

Today we know that the abyss is haunted. Through it drift luminous jack-o'-lantern faces with wolf-trap mouths and meager bodies, as though a head floating in that enormous darkness were more important than a body, which could almost be dispensed with in the lean economy of the night. It is a world of delicately groping, yard-long antennae, or of great staring eyes that can pick up remote pinpoints of light and follow them through the restless luminescence of a firefly darkness. To Sir Charles Thompson, however, the abyss was more than haunted. It was the world of the past.—Loren Eiseley

The writer of this composition carefully chose words and ideas that convey to the reader his feeling for the great mysteries in the depths of the ocean.

Exercises Studying and Writing an Artistic Explanation

A. Explain in a few sentences how the writer of the sample artistic explanation achieved unity, coherence, and emphasis. Then cite at least five examples of phrases that have emotional appeal.

B. Choose a subject suitable for development into an artistic explanatory composition, or essay. As you follow the steps for planning and writing a composition, keep in mind your mental point of view and the techniques for achieving unity, coherence, and emphasis in the explanatory composition.

Follow the Guidelines of the Process of Writing on page 83 and the Checklist for Writing Compositions or Reports on page 165.

Part 4 The Persuasive Composition

The persuasive composition is closely related to the explanatory composition in that it seeks to explain an idea through the use of facts or statistics, one or more examples, an incident or an anecdote, or comparisons or contrasts. The difference between the two types of compositions lies in their aims. The explanatory composition explains something with no desire, necessarily, to persuade the reader to the writer's way of thinking. In the persuasive composition, however, the whole purpose is to persuade the readers to believe or act as the writer does.

In Chapter 7, the following sentences were used to describe the persuasive paragraph.

The choice of subject matter is limited to ideas about which there are at least two more or less reasonable ways of thinking.

The topic sentence of a persuasive paragraph states the writer's way of thinking about a subject. It establishes the writer's point of view, which is justified by the supporting statements in the rest of the paragraph.

Chapter 7 also included these points to keep in mind when writing a persuasive paragraph.

To present an effective argument for one side of a question, you must be familiar with the other side as well. You must study and understand the arguments that support the opposite point of view.

Your audience consists of readers whose beliefs about the question at hand are different from yours. You are not writing for readers who already think the way you do.

The same four ideas are also true for the persuasive composition. Because the persuasive composition is written for readers whose beliefs are different from yours, this type of writing is both constructive and destructive.

1. It is constructive because it involves the presentation of reasons that compel the reader not only to acknowledge your view as valid, but also to accept it as his or her own.

2. It is destructive because it involves an awareness of the doubts and objections in the mind of the reader and efforts to satisfy and answer those doubts and objections.

An outline, or "brief," for a persuasive composition appears on the next page.

PROPOSITION OF BELIEF: The jury system should be abolished.

    I. It makes just verdicts hard to secure.
        A. Juries are often uninformed.
        B. Juries are often prejudiced.
            1. Many are influenced by church or society affiliations.
            2. Many are prejudiced against large business corporations.
    II. The trial of all cases by judges would be better.
        A. Judges are experienced in working with complicated legal cases.
        B. Most judges are aware of their prejudices and try to rise above them.
        C. Judges are less likely to be moved by the eloquent arguments of lawyers.
        D. Judges are not easily deceived by witnesses.
    III. The substitution of judges for juries would not be a dangerous innovation.
        A. Appellate and Supreme Courts function without juries.
        B. Many lawyers have long favored the substitution.

As with the persuasive paragraph, the writer begins with a proposition of belief. She clearly states the conclusion that she has reached and that she wishes the reader to reach. She then gives three reasons, or arguments, to support her proposition.

    I. It makes just verdicts hard to secure.
    II. The trial of all cases by judges would be better.
    III. The substitution of judges for juries would not be a dangerous innovation.

In anticipation of the arguments that the opponents of this proposition might raise, the writer has listed, under the main headings, supporting statements that are constructive to her own arguments and destructive to those of her opponents.

In the following example of a persuasive composition, the writer presents a proposition of belief in the first paragraph: that young people can take action to protect the environment. Then, in each succeeding paragraph, he deals with a specific kind of action.

BE AN ECOLOGIST

Most people agree that pollution is a continuing threat to the land, air, and water on this planet. Many people, though, especially young people, are not aware of what they can do as individuals to protect the environment. Here, then, are three suggestions for immediate action.

One easy way to decrease the amount of refuse that litters highways, streets, and beaches and that ends up piled high in unsightly garbage dumps is to avoid buying disposable products. These products are designed to be thrown away after one use, even though many could be reused. They include "no-deposit, no return" soft drink bottles, plastic tableware, pop-top aluminum cans, and paper towels, napkins, plates, and cups. Disposables are almost always more expensive, either in actual cost or in cost-per-use, than reusable items. Therefore, by switching to reusable products, you will help the environment and save money.

You can help to preserve the air that you breathe by avoiding products in aerosol cans. Aerosols release fluorocarbons into the air. These fluorocarbons attack the layer of ozone that protects the earth from the harmful rays of the sun. Aerosol cans add to the bulk of your garbage because they cannot be reused as spray bottles can, and they are potentially explosive. Aerosol sprays can be dangerous to the eyes and to the respiratory system. Also, aerosol products are almost always more expensive than the same products in nonaerosol form.

A third way to protect the environment is to use only those detergents that are labeled "biodegradable." This means that they do not contain phosphates or other pollutants that poison the earth's water supply permanently.

Our planet needs everyone's help to survive. It needs the help of scientists and industrialists, engineers and government officials. It needs your help, too. Your wise choice of products can contribute to the continued existence of the earth as you know it.

The writer has created unity in this composition by keeping to one basic belief: that there are things young people can do to protect the environment. He presents only those ideas that support this belief.

The writer has achieved coherence by arranging the three main supporting ideas from the least familiar to the most familiar.

He has achieved emphasis by treating the two suggestions that young people will most likely follow—avoid buying disposables and avoid buying aerosols—in greater detail than the third suggestion.

Exercise Writing a Persuasive Composition

Think of several subjects that are currently being discussed in your school or community. Choose one about which you have a strong and well founded opinion and write a proposition of belief. Then, following the process explained in Chapter 7, write a five-paragraph persuasive composition. After you have completed a rough draft, check to make sure that your composition is characterized by unity, coherence, and emphasis.

Follow the Guidelines for the Process of Writing on page 83 and the Checklist for Writing Compositions on page 165.

Chapter 10

Letters, Applications, and Résumés

Before this time, most major decisions were probably made for you. You are now adopting a more adult life-style and find that you are faced with a number of choices for your future. Would you like to work at a resort or national park next summer? Are you wondering which college or trade school to attend after high school? Perhaps a summer in a foreign country is in the back of your mind. How would you go about investigating any of the many opportunities and courses open to you?

There is only one way to receive specific, accurate information, and that is to deal directly with the source. The one efficient way to accomplish this purpose is to write a business letter. You will receive the information you have requested, have it available to study and compare time and again, and establish a contact for any additional facts you need.

Schools and colleges have specific offices for requests from future students. Employment agencies and corporations will inform you as to the availability of jobs—permanent, part-time or temporary. Travel agencies are loaded with information they are eager to mail. Park and resort areas hire seasonal help yearly and they are waiting for requests from potential employees.

In this chapter you will learn how to write business letters: what to write, where to write, and what to do with the replies you receive.

Part 1   The Forms of Letters

Just as the business letter has a specific purpose, it also has a specific form. This form is as important as the layout of a baseball diamond. You would not switch first base with the pitcher's mound, or move the catcher in front of the batter. If you did, the game would be confusing to the regular fan. The same kinds of rules apply to a business letter. The reader is accustomed to looking at a certain part of the page for specific information. If you change the form, you will confuse the reader.

While there are different business letter forms, the information is always in the same order and consists of six parts. Compare the examples that follow, noting the parts and their names.

Choose the form that appeals to you and master it. You will be using it frequently in the years ahead.

The **heading** of the letter consists of your address and the date. You always use three lines. The first line contains your street address. The second line is the city, state, and ZIP code. Note that there is always a comma between the city and the state, but none between the state and zip code. The third line is the date the letter is written. If you live in a small town that has no street addresses for mailing purposes, or if your mail is delivered to a post office box, you would use a slightly different heading, as shown in the examples on the next page.

P.O. Box 169   Edmore
Rochester, New York 14617   North Dakota 58330
July 16, 1981   July 16, 1981

Block Form   (used only when the letter is typewritten)

1563 New Salem Drive
St. Louis, Missouri 63141   Heading
July 14, 1981

Manager
Specific Personnel Agency, Inc.   Inside Address
620 Broadway
New York, New York 10006

Dear Sir or Madam: Salutation

                                        Body

....
....
....

....
....

Yours truly,   Closing

John H. Levine   Signature

John H. Levine

1563 New Salem Drive
Heading   St. Louis, Missouri 63141
July 14, 1981

Office of Admissions
University of Hawaii
2444 Dole Street   **Inside Address**
Honolulu, Hawaii 96822

Dear Sir or Madam: **Salutation**

                                     Body

....
....
....

....
....

       Closing   Sincerely,

       Signature   *John H. Levine*

                   John H. Levine

The **inside address** includes the department or person to whom you're writing on the first line; the name of the company on the second line; the street address or post office box number on the third line; and the city, state, and ZIP code on the fourth line. If you are not writing to a specific person or department, you would have a three-line address and simply eliminate the first line.

One space is left blank between the inside address and the next part, the **salutation.** This can be one of many, depending upon the inside address.

FOR A DEPARTMENT OR A COMPANY

```
Gentlemen:
Ladies and Gentlemen:
Dear Sir or Madam:
```

FOR A SPECIFIC PERSON, NAME UNKNOWN

```
Dear Sir:
Dear Madam:
Dear Sir or Madam:
```

FOR A SPECIFIC PERSON, NAME KNOWN

```
Dear Mr. Jones:
Dear Mrs. Sorenson:
Dear Miss Sorenson:
Dear Ms. Sorenson:
```

A blank space is left between the salutation and the **body** of the letter, which is the most important part of your letter. You should state your purpose clearly, briefly, and politely. It is always helpful to make a rough draft of this portion of the letter to be certain you have given the necessary information and no more, and that you have no errors in punctuation, spelling, or grammar. This is the only impression the receiver will have of you; make it a good one.

A blank space is left between the body of the letter and the **closing.** This is kept as simple as possible, with only the first word capitalized.

```
Sincerely,     Yours truly,   Respectfully yours,
Truly yours,  Cordially,     Very truly yours,
```

Type or print your name four spaces below the closing, and write your **signature** in the space between.

Whenever you write a business letter, you should have a copy for yourself. This does not mean you write the letter twice, only that you use a piece of carbon paper to make a carbon copy. Carbon paper is readily available and easy to use, particularly if you type. If you are writing your letter in longhand, you must buy carbon paper made for this purpose.

Typists may sometimes find that their letters do not look as attractive as they should because the letters are short. In this case, double-space the entire letter, leaving extra spaces between the six parts.

Exercises The Forms of Letters

A. Put the following addresses in proper inside-address form, punctuating and capitalizing correctly. Below each address use the correct salutation for the particular address.

1. western airlines vacation department p o box 92931 world way postal center los angeles california 90009

2. personnel manager general telephone co of florida 610 morgan street tampa florida 33602

3. quantas 360 post street san francisco california 94108

4. employment office yellowstone company yellowstone park wyoming 82190

5. admissions office colorado women's college montview boulevard and quebec denver colorado 80220

B. Using one of the letter forms shown, write a letter on a plain piece of paper to one of the addresses in Exercise A. Label all six parts of the letter in the right margin.

Part 2   The Envelopes

A standard 9½″ x 4″ envelope is preferred for a business letter. This size allows sufficient room for the receiver's address and your return address. Also, the insertion of the letter is much easier than with a smaller envelope. You need to learn only one form.

In the upper left-hand corner, write your name on the first line; the street address or post office box on the second line; and city, state, and ZIP code on the third line. Then, in a position in the middle of the envelope, copy the inside address from your letter, line for line. Write from the middle of the envelope to the right, so the address actually ends up in the bottom corner of the envelope. Be sure to check the back of the envelope before addressing to make certain it is right side up.

```
Ms. Jane Tyler
1462 Downington Avenue
Salt Lake City UT 84105


                    Office of Admissions
                    University of Hawaii
                    2444 Dole Street
                    Honolulu HI 96822
```

In order to ensure that your letter reaches the correct party, check the address, street and ZIP code. The ZIP code is of primary importance today, as it enables the postal department to sort your letter for delivery as rapidly as possible. If you do not know the ZIP code, call your local post office. Someone will be happy to give you the correct ZIP code for any address in the United States and the territories.

You will notice in the second example that the state has been abbreviated. The United States Postal Service has published a list of approved abbreviations for states, which may be used on the envelopes. If you use these abbreviations, you *must* use the ZIP code with them. When using these abbreviations, it is not necessary to separate the city and state in the address with a comma; if you do not use the abbreviations, you must use the comma. The list of approved abbreviations is shown on the next page.

Abbreviations of State Names

Alabama	AL	Montana	MT
Alaska	AK	Nebraska	NE
Arizona	AZ	Nevada	NV
Arkansas	AR	New Hampshire	NH
American Samoa	AS	New Jersey	NJ
California	CA	New Mexico	NM
Canal Zone	CZ	New York	NY
Colorado	CO	North Carolina	NC
Connecticut	CT	North Dakota	ND
Delaware	DE	Ohio	OH
District of Columbia	DC	Oklahoma	OK
Florida	FL	Oregon	OR
Georgia	GA	Pennsylvania	PA
Guam	GU	Puerto Rico	PR
Hawaii	HI	Rhode Island	RI
Idaho	ID	South Carolina	SC
Illinois	IL	South Dakota	SD
Indiana	IN	Tennessee	TN
Iowa	IA	Trust Territories	TT
Kansas	KS	Texas	TX
Kentucky	KY	Utah	UT
Louisiana	LA	Vermont	VT
Maine	ME	Virginia	VA
Maryland	MD	Virgin Islands	VI
Massachusetts	MA	Washington	WA
Michigan	MI	West Virginia	WV
Minnesota	MN	Wisconsin	WI
Mississippi	MS	Wyoming	WY
Missouri	MO		

After the letter has been written and the envelope addressed, you must fold the letter to fit the envelope. This can be accomplished by folding the letter into thirds so that you will have only two creases in the paper. Start at the bottom of the letter and fold up. When folded, your letter should fit easily into the envelope.

Exercises **Addressing Envelopes**

A. Using a plain sheet of paper, turn it sideways and draw two 9½″ x 4″ envelopes on each side, a total of four envelopes. On one side, choose two of the first five items in the exercise and address the envelopes correctly, using your return address. On the other side of the paper choose two of the numbers 6 thru 10 and address these envelopes. Use your telephone directory, magazines, or your local library to locate correct addresses.

1. Advertising Department, Revlon, Inc., 767 5th Avenue, New York, New York 10022
2. Reservations, Aladdin Hotel of Las Vegas, 3667 Las Vegas Boulevard South, Las Vegas, Nevada 89109
3. *Mad* Magazine, E. C. Publications, Inc., 485 Madison Avenue, New York, New York 10022
4. Public Relations Department, Ford Motor Company, The American Road, Dearborn, Michigan 48121
5. Subscription Department, Field & Stream, 75 Huntington Avenue, Marion, Ohio 43302
6. A trade or business school
7. The personnel office of a national company
8. A travel agency
9. The personnel office of a local company
10. A college in which you are interested

B. Using the letter form you've chosen, write a letter to an imaginary person at an imaginary company. Use the correct form, including salutation and closing. On the back of the paper draw an envelope and address it. You may choose one of the suggestions below or use your imagination.

1. The manager of a book store
2. The proprietor of a summer resort
3. The owner of an obedience school for dogs
4. The manager of a recycling plant
5. The manager of a radio station

Part 3   Kinds of Business Letters

Business letters are written to achieve a wide variety of purposes. There are letters requesting information, letters inquiring about employment, letters to colleges and other schools, and many more. They all require that you remember the following guidelines.

1. Use plain white 8½″ x 11″ paper. Pastels and decorated stationeries are not appropriate.
2. Use a standard form.
3. Keep a carbon copy for your reference.
4. Use a standard envelope. A letter folded nine times to fit a small envelope looks messy.
5. Check the address and include the ZIP code.
6. Keep the body of the letter brief and specific.
7. Stay within your vocabulary range. Do not use technical terms if you are not certain of their correct usage.
8. Make a rough draft of your letter and check carefully for errors before writing the final copy.
9. Make your handwriting as legible as possible.
10. Approach letters with a positive attitude.

Letters Requesting Information

The one type of business letter you will use more than any other is the request for information. It is used to inquire about employment, college requirements, vacation ideas, or anything else in which you have an interest.

The body of the letter should be brief, with the main emphasis on what information you need and why you need it. If you are writing regarding employment or college, the dates you plan to work or attend are necessary. The order of these three W's— What, Why, and When—will change, but it is much easier on the reader if you write what you want first. The Why should be as concise as possible. A detailed explanation is not only unnecessary, but unwanted. Remember, you are asking for information; make it easy for the reader to reply to your letter. Being polite, of course, is a necessity.

General Requests for Information

There are times when you will need more information for a major assignment than is available in the school library. Perhaps you are curious about some particular place, person, or hobby. If you take the time to write a letter requesting this particular information and find an address where it is available, you will undoubtedly receive a reply.

---

413 Acacia Avenue
Palo Alto, California 94306
August 2, 1981

Energy Research and Development Administration
U.S. Government
20 Massachusetts Avenue, N.W.
Washington, D.C. 20019

Dear Sir or Madam:

At the present time I am preparing a research paper on energy alternatives for my high school science class. Could you please supply me with some current information regarding the development of solar energy or any other substitutes for current energy sources?

Also, if you have any publications available on this matter, I would appreciate being informed of their titles and cost.

Yours truly,

Rosa M. Ortega

Rosa M. Ortega

Exercise Requesting Information

Choose one of the subjects below and write a rough draft of a letter requesting information. Include all six parts of the letter in your rough draft. Then find two additional addresses to which you could mail the same letter and write them on the other side of the paper.

1. Child Abuse	6. TV Violence
2. Population Control	7. Drug Abuse
3. The Women's Movement	8. Earthquakes
4. Environment Conservation	9. Pollution
5. Alcoholism	10. Civil Rights

Letters About Employment

Letters regarding employment must include specific facts, such as the kind of job in which you are interested and any previous experience you have had. State clearly whether you are looking for full-time, part-time, or temporary employment. **Full-time employment** is forty hours per week, fifty-two weeks per year (excluding holidays and vacation). **Temporary employment** is forty hours per week also, but only for a specific period during the year, such as summer or Christmas vacation. **Part-time employment** is less than forty hours per week, but you would be expected to work the entire year. For most students, only part-time or temporary employment is practical.

State your age or grade in school and the date you will be available to work. If you have any particular reason for looking for a job with a certain company, include that in your letter. A furniture store might be more interested in hiring you if they know you plan to major in interior design; an interest in hotel management could help if you are contacting a large hotel chain. Remember that there are more teenagers looking for jobs than there are jobs available. Give yourself every opportunity to appear valuable to a potential employer. That means writing a letter that will give a good impression.

If you are writing to a small company and you know the name of the owner or manager, address the letter directly to him or her. If you are writing to a large concern, the Personnel Department handles all the hiring, regardless of the department. If the company is in your area, you might request an interview.

                                    1496 Oakridge Road
                                    Fort Worth, Texas 76135
                                    March 22, 1981

Personnel Department
Neiman-Marcus Company
Main and Ervary
Dallas, Texas 75201

Dear Sir or Madam:

   I am interested in temporary employment as a sales clerk for Neiman-Marcus Company. I am sixteen years old and have taken courses in retailing and sales procedure at Bradley High School. I am interested in retail sales as a profession.

   I will be available June 4, 1981, and could work until the resumption of school on September 7, 1981. If a position is not available for temporary work, do you have any openings presently for part-time sales personnel? I would appreciate an appointment for an interview at your convenience.

                              Sincerely,

                              Susan Houston

                              Susan Houston

```
          1496 Oakridge Road
          Fort Worth, Texas 76135
          March 23, 1981

          Personnel Manager
          The Yellowstone Company
          Yellowstone Park, Wyoming 82190

          Dear Sir or Madam:

          I am interested in working at Old Faithful Lodge
          this summer. Could you please advise me as to
          jobs available?

          I will be available from May 30 through
          September 7. I am seventeen years old and at
          present am attending high school. I have had some
          experience as a waiter and busboy, and have taken
          courses in accounting and office machines.

          Any information you could provide would be
          appreciated.

          Yours truly,

          Douglas Jackson
          Douglas Jackson
```

Exercise Letters About Employment

Choose one of the items below. Write a letter expressing interest in employment. Make a carbon copy of the letter and address an envelope.

1. A part-time job with a large corporation in your area
2. A summer job with a local department store
3. A summer job with a local summer recreation program
4. A part-time job in a local hotel or restaurant
5. A summer job at a vacation resort

Letters to Colleges and Other Schools

Letters to schools follow the same basic pattern, whether they are addressed to colleges, universities, or vocational schools.

936 Queen Avenue
Yakima, Washington 98902
March 22, 1981

Northwest Technical School
418 King Street
Yakima, Washington 98906

Dear Sir or Madam:

I am interested in enrolling in Northwest Technical School after my graduation from North High School this June.

Could you please tell me what courses you have in photography, particularly commercial photography? I would also like to know the total costs for this course of study.

Sincerely,

Louise Sanders

Louise Sanders

1421 Kenneth St.
Shreveport, Louisiana 71103
February 21, 1981

Admissions Office
University of Oklahoma
660 Parrington Oval
Norman, Oklahoma 73069

Dear Sir or Madam:

Would you please send me information about the
entrance requirements for the University of
Oklahoma. I will be graduating from high school in
the spring of 1983, and plan to enter the
university the following fall.

I am interested primarily in your tuition, board
and room, and any other major expenses involved
in obtaining a degree in Pharmacology.

I would appreciate a copy of your catalog.

Respectfully,

Anthony Lebeaux

Anthony Lebeaux

Be specific about the information you would like. If you are
interested in costs, ask about them. If you are "shopping around"
and comparing a number of schools, request a catalog. There
might be a charge for the catalog, but they will inform you. If you
have already decided on a specific major field, state what it is.

218

There may be different requirements for that field, such as specific preparation, a longer course, more expenses. Direct your letter to the Admissions Office. *Barron's Profiles of American Colleges* or a similar reference book in your local library will supply you with the required information for the address.

```
1420 Inca Lane
St. Paul, Minnesota 55112
April 14, 1981

Scholarships Office
St. John's University
Collegeville, Minnesota 56321

Dear Sir or Madam:

I have applied for admission to St. John's
University in the fall of 1983. Would you tell me
what types of scholarships are available? I intend
to major in Secondary Education.

I am presently attending Northwest High School in
St. Paul, and will be graduating on June 6,
1983.

Yours truly,

Russell Christianson

Russell Christianson
```

With the costs of higher education rising, you may be looking into scholarship possibilities. Write directly to the Scholarships Office at the school, asking for information on available scholarships for the year you plan to enter. It is not necessary to go into detail regarding your finances, GPA, or any test scores. The school will send you forms to fill out on which these will be included.

Exercise **Letters to Colleges and Other Schools**

Choose a college, university or vocation school in the United States. Write a letter requesting enrollment information. Make a carbon copy, address the envelope, and mail the letter. If each student writes to a different school, your class should have a helpful up-to-date library of information to compare.

Part 4 Application Forms

Once you have written and mailed your letter, you may think you are finished. However, the one reason to write a request for information is to elicit a reply. Then you face the next step of what to do with the reply. If you were writing to a particular company about a job and they have no openings, you have to write another letter to a different company. If you are fortunate, you will receive a reply on one very important form, an **application form.** Whether it is an application form for a job or for admission to a school, it requires attention, time, and a degree of skill to answer all the questions. You will receive only one copy, so you cannot make errors.

First, get a good pen and practice printing, or be prepared to type. Read the instructions carefully, particularly those in fine print. A prospective employer learns a great deal about you by your ability to follow directions, and to follow them neatly. Think before you write, but if you do make an error, erase carefully. Do not cross out a mistake.

All application forms have a number of questions in common. The sooner you are prepared for these, the easier it will be for you to fill in all the application forms necessary to survive in this paperwork world. Your name is one of the first items. Read carefully. Some forms ask for the first name first, and some for last name first.

Your address, date of birth, sex, height, weight, color of hair and color of eyes are normal application entries. Do not make the common mistake of putting the current year for the date-of-birth entry. You will find that there is never enough space for the information requested. When you can, abbreviate. This means that you would put 10–31–64 rather than October 31, 1964.

There may be questions on the application form that you cannot answer. These may be "Military Service," "Number in Family" etc. There is one standard guideline for filling out applications —answer everything! An empty line looks as if you forgot to answer, did not know the answer, or did not want to answer. If the information does not apply to you, insert the initials N.A. This means "not applicable"; it does not apply to you.

Application forms consistently ask for references. They sometimes specify personal references; at other times they ask for the names of former employers. A personal reference does not mean your best friend. An employer would like the name of a responsible adult who has known you for a long period of time, who has some idea of your capabilities, and whether or not you are honest and trustworthy. Family physicians, former employers, teachers, and family friends are ideal. Contact them first and ask if you may use them as references. Have their full names and home addresses ready for the application form.

Fill in every item as accurately and completely as possible. Do not underestimate yourself. Do not exaggerate. Be honest.

Exercise Application Forms

On pages 222 and 223 are examples of different application forms that you may encounter. Number a sheet of paper to correspond with the questions on these applications. Fill in the answers as completely and neatly as possible.

Undergraduate Application For Admission

University of Utah   **Salt Lake City, Utah 8411⁁**

Date _____

Personal Data

1. Social Security No. _____

2. Legal name ☐ Mr. ☐ Miss ☐ Mrs. _____
   Last Name   **First**   **Middle**
   Names different from above, such as maiden name, that appear on your academic records. _____

3. Applying for 19 ____ (Check one) Beginning: Summer Quarter ☐ Autumn Quarter ☐ Winter Quarter ☐ Spring Quarter ☐
   yr.

4. Check appropriate status: ☐ Freshman ☐ Undergraduate transfer.

5. Birth date: _____   6. Birthplace (City and State): _____

7. Home address:

   _____
   Number and Street   **City**   **State**   **Zip**   **Telephone (In case of emergency)**

8. If you live in Utah, how long have you continually resided in this state? _____

9. Please check all boxes that apply: ☐ Male ☐ Married ☐ Veteran ☐ Immigrant
   ☐ Female ☐ Unmarried ☐ U.S. Citizen ☐ Student Visa (A special application is required)

10. Applicant's parents: (List names even if deceased)

Father's Name	Mother's Name
Number and Street Address	Number and Street Address
City State Zip	City State Zip
Number of years resident of state above: _____	Number of years resident of state above: _____
Occupation _____	Occupation _____

11. Has either parent ever attended the University of Utah? ☐ Yes ☐ No

12. If both parents are deceased, who is guardian or nearest relative?

   _____
   Name   **Number and Street Address**   **City**   **State**   **Zip**

Education

13. Is above person your legal guardian? ☐ Yes ☐ No   Applicant's relationship to above: _____

14. Have you ever attended the University of Utah? ☐ Yes ☐ No. If yes, when? _____ as   Quarter   Year   (Check one) Day ☐ Evening ☐   Special Student ☐

15. List in chronological order the last high school and all colleges you have attended, regardless of length of attendance and even if no work was completed:

Name of Institution	Location	Date Entered Mo.	Yr.	Date Left or Will Leave Mo.	Yr.	Degree Earned or Expected	Yr. Degree Earned or Expected

Major Field of Study

16. Please select a major of interest to you by checking one of the areas listed below. This is for the purpose of assigning you a faculty advis⁁ only. After you arrive at the University, you may change your major at any time. If you have not chosen a major or have no preference, the⁁ check the last item on the list: ''No Preference.''

____Accounting (Pre)
____Anthropology
____Architecture (Pre)
____Art (Pre)
____Biology
____Business (Pre)
____Chemical Engineering
____Chemistry
____Child Development and
____Family Relations
____Civil Engineering
____Clothing and Textiles
____Computer Science

____Economics (Pre)
____Education, Elementary
____certification (Pre)
____Education, Secondary
____certification (Pre)
____Electrical Engineering
____Engineering
____English
____Finance (Pre)
____French
____Geology
____Geography
____German

____Greek
____Health Sciences
____History
____Home Economics
____Industrial Engineering
____Journalism and
____Mass Communications
____Latin
____Management (Pre)
____Marketing (Pre)
____Mathematics
____Mechanical
____Engineering

____Medical Technology (Pre)
____Metallurgical
____Engineering
____Meteorology
____Mining Engineering
____Music
____Nursing (Pre)
____Nutrition Science
____Pharmacy
____Philosophy
____Physical Education
____Physical Therapy (Pre)
____Physics

____Political Science
____Pre-Dentistry
____Pre-Law
____Pre-Medicine
____Psychology
____Russian
____Sociology
____Spanish
____Special Education (Pre)
____Speech
____Communication
____Theatre
____No Preference

17. If you have any physical impairment or handicap, please check here and list nature of handicap. ☐ _____
   You will be sent information concerning available resources and services.

18. Additional comments which you consider pertinent to your application to the University of Utah: _____
   _____
   _____

Signature

19. All the answers I have given in this application are complete and accurate to the best of my knowledge. If admitted, I agree to observe th⁁ rules and regulations of the University of Utah and to pay all fees and charges assessed thereunder.

   _____

   Signature of Applicant

   Freshman Applicant: Please give this application for admission, the applicatio⁁ for financial aids (if desired) and the $15 application fee to your high school office⁁

Application for Employment
STATE NATIONAL BANK

Date _____

Name _____ 3. Soc. Sec. No. _____
      Last   First   Middle or Maiden

Present Address _____ 5. Tel. No. _____

How Long Have You Lived at Above Address? _____

Previous Address _____ 8. How Long Did You Live There? _____

Do You Rent ☐   Own Your Home ☐   Live with Parents ☐   Or Room ☐

Date of Birth _____ 11. Are You a Citizen? _____

Marital Status   Single ☐   Married ☐   Widowed ☐   Divorced ☐

Number of Dependents _____   No. of Children _____   Ages _____

Person To Be Notified in Case of Accident or Emergency _____

Name _____   Address _____   Phone _____

How Much Time Have You Lost from Work or School Because of Illness? _____

Position Applied for _____ 17. Are There Any Experiences, Skills, or

Qualifications Which You Feel Would Specially Fit You To Work with the Company? _____

On What Date Will You Be Available for Work? _____

RECORD OF EDUCATION

School	Name and Address of School	Years Attended To From	Check Last Yr. Completed	Grade Average or Class Rank
Elementary			5 6 7 8	
High			1 2 3 4	
College			1 2 3 4	

Current Military Classification _____ 23. If Previously in Service,

Indicate Branch _____ Rank _____ 24. Date of Discharge _____

Check the Following Office Operations with Which You Have Had Experience:

☐ Adding Machine   ☐ Dictaphone   ☐ Addressograph
☐ Proof Machine (IBM)   ☐ Shorthand   ☐ Bookkeeping Machine
☐ Switchboard   ☐ Typewriter   ☐ Other

PERSONAL REFERENCES (Not Former Employers or Relatives)

Name and Occupation	Address	Phone No.

I hereby affirm that my answers to the foregoing questions are true and correct and that I have not knowingly withheld any information which would, if disclosed, be considered sufficient cause for dismissal.

In the event of my employment, I promise to faithfully comply with all the rules and regulations presently in effect, or which may hereafter become effective, relating to the conduct and performance of the employees of the State National Bank.

Applicant's Signature _____

Part 5 Résumés

Many employers and graduate schools request résumés instead of, or in addition to, applications. A **résumé** is a personal inventory of your life as it applies to a career. An employer accomplishes a great deal by asking you for one. First, he finds out if you are sufficiently educated to know what a résumé is. Second, he can determine how well you are able to compile factual information. Third, he can rapidly see your experience, education, and special skills and interests. You may be required to submit a résumé before you will be given an interview. This is one way an employer can narrow the field of applicants to a select few.

Once you have written one résumé, it is easy to add to it as your education and experience progress.

Résumé

NAME   **Street Address**
                                                  City, State and ZIP
                                                  Telephone number

Objective

Experience

Education

Personal

References

Once again, you are going to have to present material in a certain form. However, before you are ready to write your final copy, you must go through a process of inventorying. The instructions that follow will give you practice in making a rough draft, or worksheet. You will later revise your rough draft into the final copy to be sent to a prospective employer.

Start by writing your **name, address** and **telephone number,** including the area code.

James A. Bennett

1433 Blaine Avenue
Salt Lake City, Utah 84105
Telephone: 801-485-5826

The next step is to determine what your **objective** is. This can be narrowed down to a specific job, or stated broadly to apply to a general field.

OBJECTIVE: Position as a sales trainee in a retail organization that gives opportunities for advancement to a position in management.

OBJECTIVE: Salesman in Sporting Goods Department of Johnson Brothers Company

Now answer the following questions regarding **experience.** Always list your most recent job first, and work back to your first job. Do not be concerned if your experience seems a little sparse right now; you will be surprised how quickly it will increase in the next few years.

1. Period employed

   Name and address of firm

   Position held

   Duties

2. Period employed

   Name and address of firm

   Position held

   Duties

If you have had no job experience, your next entry is your **education.** This is also listed from the most recent to the earliest. However, most employers are not interested in anything before high school.

School attended

Place

Special Subjects

The next general category is **personal.** These are the items you should list:

Place and date of birth

Marital status

Health

Professional memberships

Community groups

Other curricular or extra-curricular activities
(academic, athletic, student government, etc.)

Hobbies or special interests

Special skills

The last category is your **references.** You should give the names and addresses of three people who will give you a good reference. It is helpful if one is a previous employer, one a former teacher or school administrator, and one a family friend.

1. Name
   Address

2. Name
   Address

3. Name
   Address

Your worksheet, in rough form, is now complete and will probably look something like this:

James A. Bennett

1433 Blaine Avenue
Salt Lake City, Utah 84105
Telephone: 801-485-5826

Objective: Salesman in the Sporting Goods Department of Johnson Brothers Company.

Experience:
1. period employed June to September 1980
2. name and address Parker's Tackle Shop, 726 South Main Street, Salt Lake City, Utah 84101
3. position held salesperson
4. duties sold fishing supplies - delivered purchases - stocked shelves

1. period employed November, 1979 to May, 1980
2. name and address Ferguson's Grocery, Bingham, Utah 84006
3. position held stock clerk
4. duties stocked the shelves - bagged groceries

Education:
school attended East High School
place Salt Lake City, Utah
special subjects took a lot of courses in business

Personal:
place and date of birth Bingham, Utah, May 4, 1964
health great
community groups Eagle Scout - work as a volunteer at the YMCA - 10th grade president -

hobbies or special interests ham radio operator - like to ski
special skills speak French

References:
Joseph Parker
Parker's Tackle Shop
726 Main Street
Salt Lake City, Utah 84101

Dr. James Evans
431 Laird Avenue
Salt Lake City, Utah 84115

James A. Foster
East High School
840 13th East
Salt Lake City, Utah 84102

Now that your rough worksheet is complete, you are ready to revise it into a final copy. The wording in a résumé is quite different from the kind of writing you are used to in school. For one thing, you do not use personal pronouns. The reader knows you are referring to yourself.

RIGHT: Born in Bingham Canyon, Utah,
September 4, 1964

WRONG: I was born in Bingham Canyon, Utah,
September 4, 1964

Another difference is that you do not use complete sentences. This is a compilation of facts, not a paragraph assignment. If the name of a school or employer is all that is necessary, that is all you write.

RIGHT: East High School
Salt Lake City, Utah
Special courses in retailing, accounting,
business machines

WRONG: I attended East High School in Salt Lake
City, Utah, where I took many special courses.
Some of those of particular interest were
retailing, accounting, and business machines.

Before you write the final copy, here are some important guidelines:

1. Use 8½″ x 11″ white paper.
2. Type your résumé or have it typed.
3. Proofread carefully for misspelled words.
4. Do not write too much. A résumé should be no more than two pages in length.

Exercise Preparing a Résumé

Take the worksheet you have just completed for your own résumé. Revise it into final form. Either type or write out your final copy. The following résumé is the corrected final copy of the sample worksheet on page 227. Use this final copy as a guide.

Résumé

JAMES A. BENNETT   1433 Blaine Avenue
                          Salt Lake City, Utah 84105
                          Telephone: 801–485–5826

Objective   Salesperson in Sporting Goods
                 Department of Johnson Brothers Company

Experience   Parker's Tackle Shop, 726 South Main
                 Street, Salt Lake City, Utah 84101
  June 1980   Salesperson
     to   Sold fishing supplies,
  Sept. 1980   delivered purchases, stocked shelves

  Nov. 1979   Ferguson's Grocery, Bingham, Utah 84006
     to   Stock Clerk
  May 1980   Stocked shelves, bagged groceries

Education   East High School
                 Salt Lake City, Utah
                 Special courses in retailing

Personal   Born in Bingham, Utah, May 4, 1964
                 Excellent Health
                 Eagle Scout, Volunteer at YMCA,
                 10th Grade Class President,
                 Hold FCC Radio Operator's License

References   Mr. Joseph Parker,
                 Parker's Tackle Shop, 726 Main Street,
                 Salt Lake City, Utah 84101

                 Mr. James A. Foster,
                 East High School, 840 13th East,
                 Salt Lake City, Utah 84102

                 Dr. James Evans,
                 431 Laird Avenue,
                 Salt Lake City, Utah 84115

Chapter 11

Using the Library and Reference Works

Knowing how to use library resources will save you time and energy in completing assignments that require outside information, either for English or for other studies.

Understanding how books are classified, how they are arranged on the shelves, and how to use the card catalog to find them are the first steps in using library resources efficiently.

Reference works are another important source of information. These are usually kept in a separate section of the library. Reference works are often the quickest way to obtain information.

This chapter will give you the basic information you need to make efficient and intelligent use of the library.

Part 1 How Books Are Classified and Arranged

It is important for you to understand the classification and arrangement of books in a library. Knowing how and where books are placed will enable you to find any book you need.

The Classification of Books

Fiction. Novels and short-story collections are usually arranged in alphabetical order by author. For example, if you wanted to read the novel *A Separate Peace,* by John Knowles, you would first look for the section in the library marked FICTION. Then you would look for books that have authors whose last names begin with *K* and find the book in its alphabetical position. If the book is not there, someone else has borrowed it, or a browser has carelessly returned it to the wrong position. You would be wise to check part of the shelf to see if the book has been returned out of alphabetical order.

Nonfiction. Most libraries classify nonfiction books according to the Dewey Decimal System. This system, which is named for its originator, the American librarian Melvil Dewey, classifies all books by number in ten major categories.

000–099 **General Works** (encyclopedias, handbooks, almanacs, etc.)

100–199 **Philosophy** (includes psychology, ethics, etc.)

200–299 **Religion** (the Bible, theology, mythology)

300–399 **Social Science** (sociology, economics, government, education, law, folklore)

400–499 **Language** (languages, grammars, dictionaries)

500–599 **Science** (mathematics, chemistry, physics, biology, etc.)

600–699 **Useful Arts** (farming, cooking, sewing, nursing, engineering, radio, television, gardening, industries, inventions)

700–799	**Fine Arts** (music, painting, drawing, acting, photography, games, sports, amusements)
800–899	**Literature** (poetry, plays, essays)
900–999	**History** (biography, travel, geography)

As you can see from the major categories of the Dewey Decimal System, each discipline has a classification number. For example, all science books have a number between 500 and 599, and all history books have a number between 900 and 999. The system becomes more detailed as each of these major groups is subdivided. The table below shows how the subdividing works in the literature category (800–899).

800–899 **Literature**	810–819 **Literature Subdivided**
810 American literature	810 American literature
820 English literature	811 Poetry
830 German literature	812 Drama
840 French literature	813 Fiction
850 Italian literature	814 Essays
860 Spanish literature	815 Speeches
870 Latin literature (classic)	816 Letters
880 Greek literature (classic)	817 Satire and Humor
890 Other literatures	818 Miscellany
	819 Canadian-English literature

Arrangement of Books on the Shelves

You will see at a glance that books are arranged on the shelves numerically in order of classification. Most libraries prominently mark their shelves with the numbers indicating the books to be found in each particular section. Within each classification, books are arranged alphabetically by authors' last names. An exception is individual biographies and autobiographies. These books are arranged alphabetically by the last name of the *person written about.*

Biography. The Dewey Decimal System division for Biography is 920. However, large libraries will often place biographies in a separate section because of the large number of these books. In this case they will have a "B" on the spine of the book and on the catalog card. If you are looking for a particular biography and are unable to locate the 920 division, ask the librarian for assistance.

Reference Books. Reference books of particular types or specific subjects are also shelved together, often with the letter *R* above the classification number.

Exercises How Books Are Classified and Arranged

A. In which category would the following information be found?

1. Flying saucers
2. Cost of a college education
3. Rules for soccer
4. History of Buddhism
5. Plays with two characters
6. Tasaday Indians
7. Recipes for pizza
8. Picture of a medieval castle
9. African art
10. Population explosion

B. Using the Dewey Decimal system listed on pages 232 and 233, assign the correct general classification number to each of these books.

1. *Words from the Myths,* by Isaac Asimov.
2. *How Does a Poem Mean?* by John Ciardi.
3. *Your Legal Rights As a Minor,* by Robert H. Loeb, Jr.
4. *The Aztec Indians of Mexico,* by Sonia Bleeker.
5. *Developing Your Personality,* by Martin Panzor.
6. *I Like Jazz,* by Donald Myrus.
7. *Modern English and Its Heritage,* by Margaret Bryant.
8. *Everyday Life in Classical Athens,* by T. B. Webster.
9. *Math Menagerie,* by Robert Kadesch.
10. *Modern Sociology,* by Marvin Koller.

Part 2 Using the Card Catalog

To determine whether the library has a book you want and where to find it, use the **card catalog.** The card catalog is a cabinet of small drawers or file trays containing alphabetically arranged cards. Each card bears the title of a book that the library has on its shelves. The card also carries the classification number, or as librarians say, **call number** in the upper left-hand corner. (See the illustration on the next page.)

To find your book, write down the call number on a slip of paper. If it is a literature book—for example, *The Red Pony* by John Steinbeck—the call number will be in the 800 range. (Specifically, American fiction will be found in 813.)

Go to the section of shelves marked 813, and you will find your book alphabetically placed among those authors' last names that begin with S. The same call number you found on the catalog card will be imprinted on the spine of the book near the bottom.

There are usually three cards for the same book in the card catalog: the *author card,* the *title card,* and the *subject card.*

The Author Card. Perhaps you are researching a topic concerning space vehicles. It is the topic of one such book by Robert M. Powers. You will find the author card in the card catalog, and it will look like this:

Y629.45   **Powers, Robert M.**

       Shuttle: the world's first spaceship/by
       Robert M. Powers. Stackpole. c 1979
       255 p., ill.

                     ◯

Author cards for all books by an author will be filed together alphabetically according to title. Notice also that books *about* the author are filed *behind* his author cards.

The Title Card. Suppose you do not know the author's name, but do know the title of the book about a space vehicle. Look in the card catalog for a card bearing the title at the top as follows:

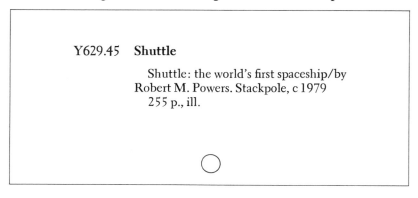

Y629.45   **Shuttle**

        Shuttle: the world's first spaceship/by
        Robert M. Powers. Stackpole, c 1979
        255 p., ill.

The place of the title card in the catalog is determined by the first letter of the first word in the title. (*A, An,* and *The* do not count as first words.)

The Subject Card. You may not know whether a book has been written about space vehicles. However, because it is of current interest you suspect that there may be a book about them. If you look through the cards cataloged under the subject space vehicles, you will find the following:

Y629.45   **SPACE VEHICLES**

        Shuttle: the world's first spaceship/by
        Robert M. Powers. Stackpole, c 1979
        255 p., ill.

Subject cards are most useful when you want information on a specific topic from a variety of sources. Cards for all books on a particular subject are cataloged together. The subject card may also indicate whether a book has chapters on a single aspect of the topic you are interested in. The publication date on the card will help you find the most-up-to-date book on your subject.

Card Information

Notice that all three types of catalog cards (author, title, subject) give the same information.

1. The call number
2. The title, author, publisher, and date of publication
3. The number of pages, and a notation on whether the book has illustrations, maps, tables, or other features

The catalog card will often provide additional information.

4. A brief description of the nature and scope of the book (This will help you decide whether the book will be useful to you.)
5. A listing of other catalog cards for the book

Cross Reference Cards

Occasionally, in looking up a subject, you will find a card that reads *See* or *See also*. The "See" card refers you to another subject heading in the catalog that will give you the information you want. Let's say you want a book on movies, and you find this card.

```
Movies

        see

Moving pictures
```

It means that the library catalogs all books on movies under the heading of moving pictures.

The "See also" card refers you to other subjects closely related to the one you are interested in. A "See also" card looks like this:

```
Moving pictures

    see also

Comedy films
Experimental films
Horror films
Indians in motion pictures
Social problems in motion pictures
War films
Women in moving pictures
```

Guide Cards

Besides the catalog cards, you will find guide cards in the cabinet trays. These are blank except for the guide word (general subject heading) on a tab that projects above the other cards. Guide cards aid you in finding other catalog cards quickly. For example, if you want books on the metric system, you will find them easily by means of alphabetically arranged guide cards such as the following:

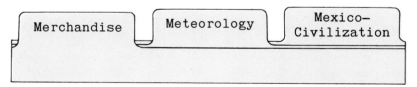

Exercises Using the Card Catalog

A. The figure on the next page represents six trays of a card catalog. The items at the right name authors, titles, and subjects that would be filed in these trays. Copy the list at the right on a separate sheet of paper and write the numbers in the blanks to show in which trays you would find the items listed.

1—	**A—Be**	_____ *Don Quixote*
2—	**Bi—Ca**	_____ Badminton
3—	**Ce—Cr**	_____ *A Bell for Adano*
4—	**Cu—Do**	_____ City Planning
5—	**Du—Er**	_____ *An American Dilemma*
6—	**Es—Fu**	_____ Charlotte Bronte
		_____ *The Environmental Handbook*
		_____ Acting
		_____ Charles Beard
		_____ *A Friend of Caesar*

B. Use the card catalog to find the title, author, call number, and publication date of the following books. Number your paper from 1 to 10 and write the answers.

1. A book of haiku poetry
2. A book by Willa Cather
3. A book on fighting gear in World War I
4. A book on Neanderthal man
5. A book by Jesse Stuart
6. A book about women's rights
7. A book on consumer credit
8. A book on Catherine the Great
9. A book on knighthood and chivalry
10. A book with mathematical puzzles

C. What subject cards would give you information about the following topics? Discuss your answers in class.

1. Bali dances
2. The powers of the president
3. Jewelry designs
4. Automobile insurance
5. Writing a research paper
6. Dieting
7. Salem witchcraft trials
8. Ballads of the Civil War
9. Life on Mars
10. Atomic submarines

D. Using the card catalog, list the author, title, call number, and publication date of all books about two of the following people:

1. Abigail Adams	6. Richard Wright
2. Duke Ellington	7. Joan of Arc
3. Golda Meir	8. George Gershwin
4. Adlai Stevenson	9. Queen Elizabeth II
5. Rachel Carson	10. Clarence Darrow

Part 3 Using Reference Works

One of the best ways to get information is to consult a reference work. Suppose your teacher were to ask you to write a brief biographical sketch of the American writer Carl Sandburg. One good source would be *Twentieth Century Authors*, by Kunitz and Haycraft. It may be found in the reference room of most libraries. Knowing the various types of reference works and where they are kept in your school and public library can save you valuable time.

Reference works are tools, and like tools, should be used in definite ways. Most reference works have prefaces that describe how information is arranged, show sample entries, and explain the symbols and abbreviations used in the book. Before using any reference work for the first time, you would be wise to skim the preface.

Nine basic types of reference works are described in this part.

1. Dictionaries. The most widely used reference books in the library are the general dictionaries. They may be classified in three major types. The first is the unabridged (complete) dictionary containing more than 500,000 words. Second, there are abridged (shorter) editions, commonly called "desk" or "collegiate" dictionaries. The third group are pocket-sized; they are convenient for checking the spelling of ordinary words, but too limited for high school and college use.

Here is a list of reliable dictionaries for your use.

The American Heritage Dictionary of the English Language
The Macmillan Dictionary
The Random House Dictionary of the English Language
Thorndike-Barnhart Dictionary
Webster's New World Dictionary of the American Language
Webster's Third New International Dictionary of the English Language

Another group of dictionaries are those dealing with certain aspects of the English language: synonyms and antonyms, rhymes, slang, Americanisms, etymology, and so forth. Finally, there are special-purpose dictionaries that deal exclusively with music, medicine, biography, and many other subjects. The list below is by no means complete, but it provides good source material for you. You may check your school and community library as to the availability of specific-subject dictionaries.

DICTIONARIES ON SPECIFIC SUBJECTS

Abbreviations Dictionary (Abbreviations, Acronyms, Contractions, Signs, and Symbols Defined)
Acronyms, Initialisms, and Abbreviations Dictionary
Brewer's Dictionary of Phrase and Fable
Comprehensive Dictionary of Psychological and Psychoanalytical Terms: A Guide to Usage
Compton's Illustrated Science Dictionary
Dictionary of Biology
Dictionary of Economics
Dictionary of Literary Terms
Dictionary of Science and Technology
A Dictionary of Slang and Unconventional English
A Dictionary of Word and Phrase Origins (3 volumes)
Gregg Shorthand Dictionary
Grove's Dictionary of Music and Musicians (10 volumes)
Harper's Dictionary of Contemporary Usage
Harvard Dictionary of Music
Mathews' Dictionary of Americanisms

The New Roget's Thesaurus in Dictionary Form
The Oxford Dictionary of English Etymology
Roget's International Thesaurus
Webster's Biographical Dictionary
Wood's Unabridged Rhyming Dictionary

2. Encyclopedias. These are collections of articles, alphabetically arranged on nearly every subject known to man. Guide letters on the spine of each volume and guide words at the top of the pages aid you in finding information. It is best, however, to first check the general index when looking for information. It may list several relevant articles. For up-to-date information on a topic, check the yearbook that many encyclopedias issue. (A word of caution: When you write essays and reports, you must enclose all material taken verbatim from encyclopedias and all other sources in quotation marks.) The following are some of the most reliable encyclopedias:

GENERAL ENCYCLOPEDIAS

Collier's Encyclopedia (24 volumes)
Compton's Encyclopedia (26 volumes)
Encyclopaedia Britannica (30 volumes)
Encyclopedia Americana (30 volumes)
World Book Encyclopedia (22 volumes)

The library has many special-purpose encyclopedias dealing with a wide variety of subjects. These encyclopedias are located in the library reference room or area.

ENCYCLOPEDIAS ON SPECIFIC SUBJECTS

The Baseball Encyclopedia
The Concise Encyclopedia of Archeology
The Concise Encyclopedia of English and American Poets and Poetry
The Concise Encyclopedia of Modern Drama
Encyclopaedia of Occultism
Encyclopaedia of Religion
The Encyclopedia of American Facts and Dates
Encyclopedia of Animal Care

Encyclopedia of Auto Racing Greats
Encyclopedia of Careers and Vocational Guidance
The Encyclopedia of Chemistry
Encyclopedia of Gardening
Encyclopedia of World Art (15 volumes)
Grzimek's Animal Life Encyclopedia (13 volumes)
The Illustrated Encyclopedia of Aviation and Space
The Illustrated Encyclopedia of World Coins
The International Encyclopedia of Cooking
International Encyclopedia of Social Sciences (17 volumes)
LaRousse Encyclopedia of Mythology
McGraw-Hill Encyclopedia of World Biography (12 volumes)
McGraw-Hill Encyclopedia of World Drama (4 volumes)
The Mammals of America
The New Columbia Encyclopedia
The Pictorial Encyclopedia of Birds
Universal Encyclopedia of Mathematics

3. Almanacs and Yearbooks. Published annually, almanacs and yearbooks are useful sources of facts and statistics on current events, as well as matters of historical record in government, economics, population, sports, and other fields.

Guinness Book of World Records
Information Please Almanac, Atlas and Yearbook
Statesman's Yearbook
Statistical Abstract of the United States
Women's Rights Almanac
World Alamanac and Book of Facts

4. Biographical References. There are brief biographical notations in dictionaries and longer biographical articles in encyclopedias. Often, however, a better source is one of these specialized works.

American Men and Women of Science
The Book of Presidents
Current Biography
Dictionary of American Biography
Dictionary of National Biography

The International Who's Who
Twentieth Century Authors
Who's Who
Who's Who in America
Who's Who in the East (and Eastern Canada)
Who's Who in the Midwest
Who's Who in the South and Southwest
Who's Who in the West
Who's Who in American Women

5. Books About Authors. Some excellent reference books are the following:

American Authors: 1600–1900
British Authors Before 1800
British Authors of the Nineteenth Century
Contemporary Authors
Twentieth Century Authors
Twentieth Century Authors: First Supplement
European Authors: 1000–1900
World Authors 1950–1970

6. Literary Reference Books. The following are valuable reference books on the history of literature, on quotations and proverbs, for locating poems and stories, and for finding information about writers.

Bartlett's Familiar Quotations
Cyclopedia of Literary Characters
A Dictionary of Literature in the English Language
Encyclopedia of World Drama
Granger's Index to Poetry
A Literary History of England
A Literary History of the United States
Mencken's *A New Dictionary of Quotations*
The Oxford Companion to American Literature
The Oxford Companion to English Literature
The Oxford Companion to the Theatre
Poetry Handbook

7. Pamphlets, Handbooks, and Catalogs. Many libraries have pamphlets, handbooks, booklets, and clippings on a variety of subjects including vocations, travel, census data, and program schedules. They also have a collection of college catalogs. All of these are kept in a set of file cabinets called the **vertical file.** This file can be an invaluable source to you when writing a report or looking for information on careers.

8. Atlases. We usually think of an atlas mainly as a book of maps, but it contains interesting data on a number of subjects. The excellent *National Geographic Atlas of the World,* for example, lists some of the following topics in its table of contents: "Great Moments in Geography," "Global Statistics," and sections on population, temperatures, oceans, and place names. Below is a list of other widely used atlases.

> *Atlas of World History*
> *Atlas of World Wildlife*
> *The Britannica Atlas*
> *Collier's World Atlas and Gazetteer*
> *Goode's World Atlas*
> *Grosset World Atlas*
> *Hammond's New World Atlas*
> *The International Atlas from Rand McNally*
> *The National Geographic Atlas of the World*
> *Rand McNally Commercial Atlas and Marketing Guide*
> *The Times Atlas of the World*
> *Webster's Atlas with Zip Code Directory*

9. Magazines. The *Readers' Guide to Periodical Literature* lists the titles of articles, stories, and poems published during the preceding month in more than 100 leading magazines. It is issued twice a month from September through June and once a month in July and August. An entire year's issues are bound in one hardcover volume at the end of the year. Articles are listed alphabetically under *subject* and *author* (and *titles* when necessary). You will find the *Readers' Guide* invaluable when looking for articles on a subject for a composition.

The following excerpt from the *Readers' Guide* illustrates how articles are listed:

Excerpt from the *Readers' Guide*

ARMSTRONG, Dave
Falling in love with four-wheel drive. J. A. La-   title of article
tham. il pors Esquire 91:23-30 Je 5 '79 *
ARMSTRONG, Joe
Between the lines. pors N Y 12:5 My 14 '79
ARMSTRONG, Louis
Louis Armstrong: release of Giants of jazz al-
bum. J. Vance. por Stereo R 42:142-3 My '79 *   name of magazine
ARMSTRONG, Neil A.
Footprints of Apollo II. E. Keerdoja. il pors
Newsweek 94:14+ Jl 2 '79 *
volume number
ARMSTRONG, Sonia
Between two worlds. N. M. Nichols. Seventeen
38:140-1 My '79 *   page reference
ARNESON, Howard D.
(ed) Economic diary (cont) Bus W p 18+ Mr
19: 16+ Je 4 '79   date of magazine
ARNETT Cobb Quartet. See Jazz groups
ARNIE'S (restaurant) See Chicago—Hotels, res-
taurants, etc.
ARNOLD, Walter   author entry
Trade winds (cont) Sat R 6:58 F 17; 50 Ap 14;
48 My 12; 47 Jl 7 '79
ARNOLD Bernhard & Company. See Bern-
hard, Arnold & Company
ARNOLDO Mondadori Editore. See Publishers
and publishing—Italy
ARNSON, Cynthia
Charge up Capitol Hill. Nation 228:755-6 Je 23 '79
ARON, Raymond
Democracy, yes. por Time 114:41 Jl 9 '79 *
ARONS, Stephen
Book burning in the heartland. il Sat R 6:24-6+   illustrated article
Jl 21 '79
ARREST   subject entry
Bum rap for former mental patients: study by
Henry Steadman. L. Asher. Psychol Today
12:102+ Ap '79
See also
Bail   "see also" cross reference
ARRHYTHMIA. See Heart beat   "see" cross reference

Exercises Using Reference Works

A. Find information on one of the following subjects by using the general index of three different encyclopedias available in your school or public libraries. Write a brief report on the topic. At the end of your report tell which encyclopedia was most useful and why.

The Kabuki Theater in Japan
Jet Propulsion
Television Advertising
Tools of the Stone Age
American Sculpture
Extrasensory Perception (ESP)
Sickle Cell Anemia
Space Travel
Urban Renewal
The Human Circulatory System
Water Pollution
Bioengineering

B. Using the dictionaries available in your library, write answers to the following questions. Write the title of the dictionary used after each answer. Use as many different dictionaries as possible.

1. What is the origin of the word *Motown?*
2. Give two definitions of the word *masthead.*
3. List three antonyms for the word *flimsy.*
4. Where was the word *juba* first used?
5. What is meant by the expression "French leave"?
6. Give three synonyms for the word *patience* and use each one in a sentence.
7. What is an ombudsman?
8. Define the word *allegory* and give an example.
9. What type of instrument is a dulcimer, and how is it played?
10. The word *radar* is an acronym. From what other words was it formed?

C. Use the current issue of *World Almanac* to answer the following questions:

1. How can you apply for a patent?

2. What is the address of the National Foundation of the March of Dimes?

3. When should the U.S. flag be displayed?

4. How many Americans have been awarded the Nobel Prize for Literature?

5. What does the 26th amendment to the Constitution provide for?

6. What historic event took place on January 25, 1915?

7. Who was the first woman in space?

8. When will Halley's comet next be visible from the earth?

9. What is the standard time in Tokyo when it is noon in New York City?

10. In which state could you visit North Cascades National Park?

D. Use the *Readers' Guide* to answer the following:

1. Turn to the "Key to Abbreviations" and write the meaning of the following symbols used in *Readers' Guide*:

Ap	Ja
il	supp
+	tr
por	Jl
S	abr
Ag	jt auth

2. Using the list of "Abbreviations of Periodicals Indexed," give the complete titles of the following magazines:

Motor T	Sci Am
Eng J	Sr Schol
Sports Illus	Phys Today
Good H	US News
Sat R	Bus W

3. Find three articles on any subject that interests you, giving the title of the article, the author (if given), the name of the magazine, volume number, date, and pages.

E. Using the special-purpose dictionaries, encyclopedias and biographical and literary reference works noted in this chapter, find answers to the following questions. Write the name of the reference work you used after each answer.

1. Define and give examples of a limerick.

2. What was Thomas Jefferson's role in the American Revolution?

3. What is the title of the poem that begins—"Some say the world will end in fire"? Who wrote the poem?

4. Find a picture of Queen Elizabeth II of England.

5. How did Sir Isaac Newton discover the law of gravitation?

6. How did the expression "the real McCoy" originate?

7. Where are the nuclear power reactors located in the United States?

8. What is the "Theater of the Absurd"?

9. What literary reference work includes a discussion of *The Bridge of San Luis Rey*?

10. Who wrote *Leaves of Grass*? Where and when was this writer born?

Chapter 12

Group Discussion

The most common method of exchanging information and ideas is through *informal discussion*. By this method you can exchange information about books, TV programs, sports, science, religion, or any other topic.

Informal discussion is also the method most commonly used for solving personal and group problems.

This chapter will show you how to participate effectively in group discussion. It will also show you that your own contribution can make or break an entire discussion. Your understanding of how groups function can help you—and your group—to reach decisions efficiently and fairly.

Your Duties as Chairperson

The degree to which you succeed as chairperson of a group discussion depends upon your familiarity with the subject under discussion and the way you carry out your duties as a leader.

1. **Prepare for the discussion.** Do some preliminary reading and thinking about the subject, and take notes on important points that should be considered.

2. **Introduce the topic or problem, and state the aim of the discussion.** You may also mention important points you think the group will want to consider.

3. **Allow time for (1) the introduction, (2) the discussion, and (3) a short summary of the conclusions reached.**

4. **Keep the discussion orderly.** Allow only one person to speak at a time. Ask members of the group to raise their hands if they wish to speak.

5. **Give everyone a chance to contribute.** If two or more persons wish to speak, call on the person who has so far had only a small share in the discussion.

6. **Keep the group's interest at a high pitch.** Ask stimulating questions from time to time—especially if the discussion begins to lag.

7. **Keep the discussion moving forward.** If its purpose is to reach a conclusion or consensus on a topic, keep this fact constantly in mind. If its purpose is to adopt a plan of action, guide the discussion toward that end.

8. **Take notes on key points made during the discussion.** These will come in handy when you make your summary.

9. **At the end of the discussion, summarize it briefly.** State any conclusions or plans of action that have been agreed on.

Your Duties as a Participant

The value of any discussion in which you take part will depend in great measure on how well you, as a participant, know your duties and carry them out. If you follow the guides given below, you will not only contribute to the success of the discussion but you will also gain the respect of your fellow participants.

1. **Take part in the discussion.** The purpose of discussion is to bring out different points of view. Even though you may not be as forceful a speaker as someone else, speak up anyway. Your ideas may be just as good as another person's.

2. **Speak only when the chairperson recognizes you.** In a very large group, you can get the chairperson's attention by standing. In a small group, you can simply raise your hand.

3. **Speak correctly and distinctly.** Be sure to use acceptable grammar and usage. If you do, your listeners can concentrate on *what you are saying;* if you do not, they will be unduly distracted by *how you are saying it.* Be sure also that you enunciate clearly and that you speak with enough volume so that everyone can hear you.

4. **Support your statements with facts, examples, or opinions of experts.** If you introduce facts or statistics, be sure they are accurate. If you cite examples, be sure they are relevant to the situation in all respects. If you give the opinions of experts, be sure that these opinions were intended to apply to the topic under discussion.

5. **Keep a sense of direction as the discussion advances.** You will help everyone present if you accompany your suggestion or comment with a reference to what has immediately preceded it and perhaps an indication of what is to follow.

6. **Listen thoughtfully.** Listen carefully to what is being said rather than trying to think how to refute it.

7. **Be courteous and tactful.** If you disagree with someone, do not confront him with a flat contradiction. Instead, ask questions: "Paul, don't you think that . . . ?" "Mary, is it possible that . . . ?"

8. **Try to understand the other person's point of view.** Reason along with him and try to see things as he sees them. Consider everyone present as your equal and accept even the least appealing remarks as worthy of your complete attention. Ask an occasional question that will draw out the wisdom hidden in some passing remark. Finally, be ready to recognize and accept an opinion or a solution that is better than one that you yourself may have proposed.

A Group Discussion for Analysis

The following is part of a class discussion. Read it and be prepared to answer the questions that follow it.

Should Every High School Graduate Go to College?

CHAIRWOMAN: We hear a great deal today about the importance of going to college. But is a college education really essential for success in life today? Many of our fathers didn't go to college, yet we would agree that they have made a success of their lives. The question, then, is: should we all aim at getting a college education?

JEFF: Madame Chairwoman.

CHAIRWOMAN: Jeff.

JEFF: It seems to me that things being what they are today, each of us—

TOM: (interrupting) You mean that everyone in our class should decide to go to college? Don't be silly.

JEFF: No, not necessarily. I mean that if we think we are college material, we should do everything in our power to assure ourselves of getting a college education. My reason for thinking so is that competition is much keener today, and the person who has a college education stands a much better chance of meeting that competition.

KATHY: Madame Chairwoman.

CHAIRWOMAN: Kathy.

(As the discussion continues, the chairwoman recognizes each speaker in turn and by so doing gives him or her the right to speak.)

KATHY: While Jeff has raised a good point, I believe there may be other points that we should discuss in regard to this matter of a college education. May we hear from those who have other arguments, either pro or con?

ANNE: Well, why don't you give your own point of view on this question, instead of holding out to get the opinions of others? Don't you *have* a point of view? Well, I have. I know plenty of people who have made a lot of money in business or in industry, and they never had a college education. So I think Jeff is all wrong.

NED: It's my opinion that Jeff has a very good argument, and I'd like to enlarge upon it. Educators and others who know about these things are constantly telling us that the college graduate gets the preference today in all fields leading to executive or administrative positions. Furthermore, we know that it is impossible to get into the professions today if we don't have a college background.

JOAN: I think Ned has backed up Jeff's statement very well, and I would like to add one more point. I read that there are more than four million students in our colleges today. With so many students graduating from college each year, does anyone think that an executive in business or industry would offer a job to a person without a college education when there are so many college graduates to choose from?

LEO: I agree with what has been said about the increasing value of a college education in this competitive world of ours. However, I want to say a word for the student who has ability and is enterprising but is not prepared to spend the time or the money it takes to get a college education. I don't think this student should feel discouraged about his future. He can go to a vocational school that will prepare him for some trade or service job. Later, he can take courses in evening schools that will help him to advance. Eventually he may have his own shop or become a small businessman. To some people, this kind of career is most satisfying.

KATHY: So far in this discussion we have talked about a college education only as an advantage in getting a good job that could increase one's earning power. I think there are other values to be considered. What about the social and cultural advantages of a college education?

ANNE: Kathy has a good point there. To me, the social and cultural values of a college education are just as important as the economic values. The social activities of campus life provide many opportunities for a girl or a boy to acquire poise, pleasing manners, and other personal characteristics that lead to social success.

NED: Kathy mentioned the cultural advantages. Let's not forget them. The culture one acquires through a college education can make one a well rounded person—one who has many interests and can converse on many different subjects— all of which contribute to social as well as economic success.

JEFF: To go back to the economic values again, I'd like to make another point. A business executive is often influenced by the fact that a candidate for a position in his or her firm has graduated from the same college. Many executives tend to favor their own alumni, and that is only natural.

CHAIRWOMAN: It seems to me that we have thrashed out this question pretty well. Before we try to come to a conclusion, however, do you think we should invite some experienced adults—business or professional people—to give us the benefit of their thinking on this question?

Exercises Holding Discussions

A. Answer the following questions about the discussion, "Should Every High School Graduate Go to College?"

1. How well did the chairwoman introduce the subject?
2. How would you rate each student's contribution? Give specific reasons for your answer.

B. Divide the class into three or four groups. Let each group elect a chairperson and discuss one of the following questions. Before you begin your discussion, review your duties as a participant, on pages 252 and 253. See how well you can put into practice what you have learned.

1. Should every high school graduate go to college?
2. Should capital punishment be restored as a deterrent to crime?
3. Does violence on TV affect people's lives?
4. What type of television programs are most rewarding?
5. Should private citizens be allowed to own handguns?
6. Should the United States feed the world?

Handbook

A detailed Table of Contents appears in the front of this book.

How To Use the Handbook

This Handbook is your reference book. In it the concepts of grammar and usage are organized so that you can study them efficiently and refer to them quickly.

To use the Handbook well, you should first leaf through it to become familiar with its organization and contents. Note especially the following:

Organization of the Handbook

Grammar (Sections 1–4)   Sections 1–4 provide a comprehensive treatment of English grammar. They give the rules and explanations for grammatical questions you want answered.

Usage (Sections 5–9)   Sections 5–9 are a guide to English usage. When you are puzzled about which form of a word to use in your writing, turn to the appropriate part of these sections.

Forms and constructions marked STANDARD are accepted as standard usage—the kind of usage that is appropriate at all times and in all places. Forms and constructions marked NONSTANDARD are not accepted everywhere. They may go unnoticed in the locker room, but in many other situations, they mark the user as careless or untrained in the English language.

Capitalization (Section 10)

Punctuation (Sections 11–14)

Spelling (Sections 15–16)

Good Manuscript Form (Section 17)

Outlining (Section 18)

Throughout the Handbook are many exercises that test your understanding of the concepts explained. These exercises are the first steps in putting what you learn here to practical use. The next steps are in your own writing and speaking.

1.0 The Classification of Words

In our language words are classified into eight large groups according to the jobs they perform in a sentence. These eight groups are called the eight **parts of speech.**

nouns	adjectives	conjunctions
pronouns	adverbs	interjections
verbs	prepositions	

In addition to the parts of speech, there are three kinds of words, formed from verbs, that do many different jobs. These words are called **verbals.** Verbals are all formed from verbs and have several of the characteristics of verbs. They are unlike verbs, however, in that no verbal can stand by itself as a complete verb. The verbals are the *infinitive*, the *participle*, and the *gerund*.

This section provides a comprehensive treatment of the parts of speech and the verbals. Understanding how words are classified will give you a deeper understanding of how our language works.

1.1 The Noun

Certain words in the language are used as labels. We use them to identify people and things.

A noun is the name of a person, place, or thing.

Things named by nouns may be visible, such as *clothes, trees,* and *chairs*. Things may be items that we perceive with our other senses: *smells, sounds, tastes*. Other things are abstract and not observed through the five senses: *beliefs, ideas, wishes,* and so on.

PERSONS	PLACES	THINGS
Benjamin Franklin	Boston	baseball
lawyer	cellar	charity
priest	country	Buddhism

A **common noun** is the name of a whole group of persons, places, or things. It is a name that is common to the whole group: *animal, dish, apple, tent*.

A **proper noun** is the name of an individual person, place, or thing.

A proper noun always begins with a capital letter.

COMMON NOUNS	PROPER NOUNS
dancer	Maria Tallchief
bridge	Golden Gate Bridge
country	Africa
business	Jordan Marsh Company
language	Spanish

As the above list shows, a noun may consist of more than one word. Each word in a proper noun is capitalized.

Any word that can be immediately preceded by *the* is a noun: *the* bridge, *the* dog, *the* language. Most proper nouns, but not all of them, can also be preceded by *the*: *the* Astrodome, *the* Buick, but not *the* O. J. Simpson or *the* Detroit.

Exercise A: Find all the nouns in the following sentences.

1. The announcer said that the plane for Minneapolis would leave in thirty minutes.
2. Dr. Cooper was in college with my mother.
3. John wanted to change the ribbon on his typewriter, but the ribbon would not cooperate.
4. There was a scream of skidding tires and then a metallic thud, followed by the sound of splintered glass.
5. Carl and his brother crossed the continent in their old car.
6. The boys drove through the desert at night.
7. Helen is president of the class, and her brother is secretary.
8. Al wrote a paper about Babe Didrikson and her life in sports.
9. Half of the people in the world can neither read nor write.
10. Georgia O'Keeffe is well known for her paintings of the desert.

Exercise B: Decide which are common nouns and which are proper nouns. Write the proper nouns, beginning each with a capital letter.

1. german, science, language, english
2. lake, lake erie, mountain, mount everest
3. park, joshua national monument, gulf, cape cod
4. village, fairfield township, country, saint paul
5. labor, labor day, good friday, birthday
6. senator nancy kassebaum, mayor tom bradley
7. judge, justice thurgood marshall, judge shirley m. hufstedler
8. uncle harry, bridge, rittenhouse square, boston common
9. cathedral, rabbi, saint patrick's cathedral, church
10. college, dartmouth college, university, jefferson high school

1.2 The Pronoun

It would be awkward and cumbersome to repeat the name of a person or thing every time we wish to refer to it. Instead, we sometimes use other words in place of names. These words are pronouns. They may be used in a sentence in any way that a noun is used.

A pronoun is a word used in place of a noun.

The noun for which the pronoun stands and to which it refers is its **antecedent.**

Sue had changed *her* dress. (*Sue* is the antecedent of *her.*)

The *boys* changed *their* jerseys. (*boys* is the antecedent of *their.*)

Sometimes the antecedent of a pronoun appears in a preceding sentence.

The fishermen cheered as *they* entered the harbor. *They* had not seen *it* for a month, and *they* longed for home. (*They* in each sentence refers to the antecedent *fishermen; it* refers to *harbor.*)

Indefinite pronouns do not often refer to any specific noun. The indefinite pronoun itself may be the antecedent of a personal pronoun.

The *students* were overjoyed. *Some* lifted the coach on their shoulders. (The antecedent of the indefinite pronoun *Some* is *students.*)

Has *anyone* lost *his* hat? (The antecedent of *his* is the indefinite pronoun *anyone.*)

There are six kinds of pronouns:

personal pronouns	demonstrative pronouns
compound personal pronouns	interrogative pronouns
indefinite pronouns	relative pronouns

Personal Pronouns

Pronouns used in place of persons' names are called **personal pronouns.** They permit us to identify the person speaking, the person spoken to, and the person spoken about. Personal pronouns are also used to refer to things.

First Person (the person speaking)
I, me, my, mine, we, us, our, ours

Second Person (the person spoken to)
you, your, yours

Third Person (the person or thing spoken about)
he, she, it, they
his, hers, its, their, theirs
him, her, them

Personal pronouns change their form, or spelling, for different uses in sentences. This change of form is called the **case** of pronouns. There are three cases: *nominative, possessive,* and *objective.* Personal pronouns also change their form to show the difference between singular (one) and plural (more than one). This change of form is called the **number** of pronouns.

The following table shows the forms of the three *persons,* for the three *cases,* and for the *number* of all of the personal pronouns.

Personal Pronouns			
Singular			
	NOMINATIVE	POSSESSIVE	OBJECTIVE
FIRST PERSON:	I	my, mine	me
SECOND PERSON:	you	your, yours	you
THIRD PERSON:	he, she, it	his, her, hers, its	him, her, it
Plural			
	NOMINATIVE	POSSESSIVE	OBJECTIVE
FIRST PERSON:	we	our, ours	us
SECOND PERSON:	you	your, yours	you
THIRD PERSON:	they	their, theirs	them

Third person pronouns that refer to male persons are in the **masculine gender.** Those that refer to female persons are in the **feminine gender.** Pronouns that refer to things are in the **neuter gender.**

Here are some important things to remember about pronouns:

The pronoun *it* is called a personal pronoun even though it refers to things more often than to persons.

Countries, ships, and airplanes are sometimes referred to by the feminine pronouns, *she, her, hers*. Animals may be referred to by *it* and *its* or by *he, his, him, she, her, hers*, depending on the sex of the animal.

The words *mine, yours, hers, ours,* and *theirs* are always used as pronouns. The words *my, your, its, our,* and *their* are always used as modifiers before nouns. They are **possessive pronouns.** *His* may be used either as a pronoun or as a modifier.

This hat is *mine*. (pronoun)
There is *my* record. (modifier)
The victory is *theirs*. (pronoun)
It was a gift from my mother to *his*. (pronoun)
We listened to *her* story. (modifier)

Exercise: In the following sentences find the personal pronouns. Find the antecedent of each pronoun.

1. The doctor told the boys that they could use his boat.
2. Bob, your father wants you to call for him.
3. Helen and Karen finished the test first. They found it easy.
4. The long run brought the crowd to its feet.
5. Ali has her own ideas, but the family does not agree with them.
6. The *Viking 2* spacecraft made its way to the northern hemisphere of Mars.
7. The boys cooked their meals in the open and made their beds of pine boughs.
8. When Jim's power mower broke, the neighbors let him use theirs.
9. Betty has a driver's permit, but she doesn't have it with her.
10. The police found the car, but they couldn't move it.

Compound Personal Pronouns

A **compound personal pronoun** is formed by adding *-self* or *-selves* to certain of the personal pronouns, as follows:

FIRST PERSON: myself, ourselves
SECOND PERSON: yourself, yourselves
THIRD PERSON: himself, herself, itself, oneself, themselves

There are no other acceptable compound personal pronouns. Never say *hisself* or *theirselves*.

Compound personal pronouns are used *intensively* for emphasis or *reflexively* to refer to a preceding noun or pronoun.

The President *himself* welcomed the ambassador. (intensive)

Dawn treated *herself* to a soda. (reflexive)

Exercise: Supply an acceptable compound personal pronoun in each of these sentences. Find the antecedent for each compound personal pronoun.

1. The doctor (_____) helped Ms. Brown into the car.
2. The students have no one but (_____) to blame for the failure of the fund raiser.
3. Eve talked (_____) into asking for a raise.
4. Harry (_____) answered the telephone.
5. You girls can see the results for (_____).
6. Jack blames (_____) for the accident.
7. Jane, you will have to solve this problem (_____).
8. The boys cleaned up the kitchen by (_____).
9. Before renting the mopeds, we tested them (_____).
10. The company president (_____) replied to our criticism.

Indefinite Pronouns

Some pronouns, such as *anyone* and *anything,* do not refer to a definite person or thing. They are called **indefinite pronouns.** Normally, indefinite pronouns do not have antecedents.

SINGULAR INDEFINITE PRONOUNS

another	anything	either	everything	no one
anybody	one	everyone	neither	someone
anyone	each	everybody	nobody	somebody

PLURAL INDEFINITE PRONOUNS

both   many   few   several

The pronouns *all, some, none, most* and *any* may be singular or plural, depending upon their meaning in the sentence.

All of the candy *has* been sold. (singular)
All of the skiers *have* returned. (plural)
Some of the money *is* counterfeit. (singular)
Some of the voters *were* angry. (plural)
None of the cider *is* sour. (singular)
None of the doors *were* locked. (plural)

Demonstrative Pronouns

The words *this, that, these,* and *those* are used to point out which one or which ones are meant. Since they point to, or demonstrate, what is meant, they are called **demonstrative pronouns.** They always refer to a definite person or thing. The words they refer to may come later in the sentence, or in another sentence altogether.

This is the *camera* I won. (*camera* is the word referred to.)

On his wall were several Picasso *prints. These* had been given to him by his uncle. (*prints* is the word referred to by *These.*)

Note: The demonstrative pronouns *this, that, these,* and *those* may also be used as adjectives: *this hat, those curtains.*

Interrogative Pronouns

The pronouns *who, whose, whom, which,* and *what* can be used to ask questions. When used in this way, they are **interrogative pronouns.**

Who took the pretzels?   *What* is the time?

Whom did you want?   *Which* do you like?

The shoes aren't mine. *Whose* are they?

Relative Pronouns

The words *who, whose, whom, which,* and *that* are sometimes used to introduce an adjective clause. They relate the clause to some other word in the sentence. When used in this way, they are called **relative pronouns.**

A relative pronoun is used to introduce a relative clause. It also has a use within the relative clause. See Section 3.6.

Exercise A: List the pronouns in these sentences. Tell what kind each pronoun is.

1. Nobody knew the answer to the question.
2. The teacher could not find her pen.
3. Some of the neighbors formed a car pool.
4. All of the clowns carried water pistols.
5. Who took the twins to their lessons?
6. Someone had dropped her purse into the pool.
7. What have you done to make Mike so upset?
8. This is a baffling problem.
9. Is this the watch you lost?
10. Have you had anything to eat?

Exercise B: Follow the same directions as for Exercise A.

1. Which of these coats is yours?
2. Whom did Dad call?
3. Many heard the story, but few believed it.
4. This is a job for someone with patience.
5. Anyone may join the camera club.
6. This is the recycling center.
7. Everything I learned was useful.
8. Neither of the girls could find anything to say.
9. That is the best course for anyone to follow.
10. Several of our students have won valuable prizes.

1.3 The Verb

Every sentence must contain a word that tells what is happening. This word is the verb.

A verb is a word that tells of an action or state of being.

Grammatically, the verb is the most important word in the sentence. If you can find the verb and manage it properly, many of your grammar and usage problems will be solved.

Most verbs change their form (their sound or spelling) to show past time or present time. They are the only words to do so. This fact can help you decide which word in a sentence is the verb.

The trains *were* on time. (past)
The trains *are* on time. (present)

The Smiths *loved* Arizona. (past)
The Smiths *love* Arizona. (present)

Most verbs also change their form to show the difference between singular and plural in the third person.

Joe *likes* country music. (third person singular)
Sue and Marcella *like* woodworking class. (third person plural)

Action Verbs

An action verb may tell of an action that can be seen.

> Loretta *knocked* on the door.
> The car *skidded*.
> Tony *rocked* the boat.

An action verb may also tell of an action that cannot be seen.

> Jane *wanted* a new cat.
> The ambassador *hoped* for success.
> Rita *liked* the movie.

Linking Verbs

A few verbs, such as *be*, link the subject to a noun, to a pronoun, or to an adjective. Hence they are called **linking verbs.**

> Aretha *is* co-captain.   Sherman *seems* unhappy.

The most common linking verb is *be*. It has the forms *be, am, are, is, was, were, been, being.*
Other linking verbs are *appear, become, seem, look, sound, grow, feel, smell, taste, remain,* and *stay.*

> The children *appeared* sleepy.   The radio *sounds* awful.
> The sky *became* threatening.   The crowd *grew* restless.
> Sheila *seemed* annoyed.   The mayor *feels* confident.
> The prospects *look* good.   The forest *smelled* dank.
> The victory *tasted* sweet to the new coach.
> The weather *remained* unchanged for two months.
> The flagpole *stayed* upright throughout the storm.

Some linking verbs may also be used as action verbs.

> We *looked* into the cage.   Paul *sounded* the gong.
> Linda *tasted* the waffles.   The cat *smelled* the lobster.
> We *grew* all our own vegetables last year.
> Tammy *felt* the bump on Anne's head.

Main Verbs and Auxiliaries

Many verbs consist of more than one word. They consist of a **main verb** and one or more helping verbs or **auxiliaries.** The last word in the phrase is the main verb.

There are three verbs that can be used either as main verbs or as auxiliaries. Here are their forms:

DO	HAVE	BE		
do	has	is	was	be
does	have	am	were	been
did	had	are		being

AS MAIN VERB	AS AUXILIARY
Lisa will *do* the work.	We *do* enjoy school shows.
Have you the strength?	They *have* lost it.
The marks *were* good.	The fans *were* watching.

The auxiliaries used most often are the forms of *be* and *have.* Other common auxiliaries are the following:

must	may	shall	could	would
might	can	will	should	

AUXILIARY	MAIN VERB	VERB
has	had	has had
had	been	had been
was	doing	was doing
had	done	had done
could have	gone	could have gone
might have been	seen	might have been seen
is being	improved	is being improved

Often the parts of a verb are separated by a modifier or modifiers that are not part of the verb.

We *had* certainly *known* it.   It *had* just *stopped* snowing.

Exercise A: Find the verb in each of these sentences. Include all the words that make up the verb. Do not include any word that separates an auxiliary from a main verb.

1. The lighthouse keeper had never seen such a storm.
2. When will the next pollutant be banned?
3. The truck driver was completely blinded by the flash.
4. Our people have always had enough to eat.
5. The new school will almost surely be ready by fall.
6. The new law has been poorly enforced.
7. Do you and your brother have enough blankets?
8. The freighter had apparently run aground in the fog.
9. The park benches had been freshly painted.
10. The swimmers were obviously nearing exhaustion.
11. The fog was now rapidly lifting from the field.
12. No one has ever returned from that desert.
13. The flaws can easily be seen under a magnifying glass.
14. Have you really been trying your hardest?
15. The oxygen supply in the submarine was slowly being exhausted.

Exercise B: Find each verb. Tell whether it is an action verb or a linking verb.

1. Everyone sat quietly during the speech.
2. Alice smelled smoke in the cellar.
3. The study hall remained quiet for the rest of the hour.
4. The proposal for a student discount sounded good.
5. Suddenly, the twelve o'clock whistle sounded.
6. For two hours we lay under the boat.
7. Nancy felt her way down the dark steps.
8. The coach seemed uneasy about something.
9. After the conference we all felt better.
10. The boys left the building immediately after school.
11. We looked everywhere for the keys.
12. The tornado appeared without warning.
13. Stan looks unhappy.
14. The house appears empty.
15. On the way to Boston, the team seemed unusually quiet.

The Principal Parts

The principal parts of a verb are those from which all forms of the verb are made. They are (1) the *present infinitive* (usually called simply the *present*); (2) the *past*; and (3) the *past participle*.

A **regular verb** is one that forms its past and past participle by adding *-ed* or *-d* to the present.

PRESENT	PAST	PAST PARTICIPLE
talk	talk*ed*	talk*ed*
dazzle	dazzle*d*	dazzle*d*
arrive	arrive*d*	arrive*d*

An **irregular verb** is one that does not form its past and past participle by adding *-ed* or *-d* to the present. See Section 8.1 for usage of irregular verbs.

PRESENT	PAST	PAST PARTICIPLE
burst	burst	burst
sing	sang	sung
freeze	froze	frozen

The **present participle** of a verb is formed by adding *-ing* to the present form: *see—seeing; play—playing; leave—leaving.*

The Progressive Forms

To show ongoing action, you use the **progressive forms** of the verb. They are formed by using the forms of *be* with the present participle.

She *is running.*
We *are going.*
The cars *were stalling.*
Someone *will be arriving.*

Rob *has been sleeping.*
The water *had been running.*
We *must be going.*
They *might have been shouting.*

The Emphatic Forms

You can give special emphasis to a statement by using *do*, *does*, or *did* with the present form of the verb. These are examples of **emphatic forms.**

> I *did enjoy* your speech.
> We *do like* the new cottage.
> Jo Ellen *does seem* pleased.

Transitive and Intransitive Verbs

A **transitive verb** carries the action from the subject to the object of the verb. An **intransitive verb** expresses an action that is complete in itself; it does not carry action to an object.

TRANSITIVE	INTRANSITIVE
Cara *completed* the **application.**	Mr. Jones *died.*
My neighbor *raises* **avocados.**	The motor *sputtered.*
José *entered* the **subway.**	Bret *sang* well.
Maria *bought* the **scarf.**	We *gazed* at the exhibit.

Many verbs may be transitive in one sentence and intransitive in another.

INTRANSITIVE	TRANSITIVE
Everyone *applauded.*	Everyone *applauded* **John Denver.**
Are you *selling?*	*Are* you *selling* your **home?**
Mr. Berra *called.*	Mr. Berra *called* the **lawyer.**

The Active and Passive Voice

When the subject performs the action expressed in the verb, the verb is in the **active voice.** When the subject receives the action of the verb, the verb is in the **passive voice.** The passive voice is formed by using some form of *be* with the past participle of the verb.

ACTIVE	Jeanne *threw* the *ball* out-of-bounds.
PASSIVE	The ball *was thrown* out-of-bounds.

ACTIVE	Fritz *is carving* the *turkey*.
PASSIVE	The turkey *is being carved* by Fritz.

A transitive verb can be put into the passive voice because it has an object. The object in the active form becomes the subject in the passive form.

An intransitive verb cannot be put into the passive voice because it has no object. There is no word to become the subject.

Gertrude Stein *wrote* the introduction. (active)
The introduction *was written* by Gertrude Stein. (passive)
Jim Childs *read* the minutes. (active)
The minutes *were read* by Jim Childs. (passive)

Exercise A: Find each verb. Decide whether it is a progressive or emphatic form.

1. What has Karen been doing this summer?
2. The punishment does seem a bit severe.
3. We are now exploring new energy sources.
4. We have been hoping for a new school for years.
5. Artificial respiration does save lives.
6. The lawyer will be filing her brief in court.
7. Geologists do not know the exact age of Earth.
8. Many scientists have been working on cures for cancer.
9. Has anyone been doing anything about decorations for the party?
10. The principal did approve the student council's plan.

Exercise B: Find each verb. Tell whether it is transitive or intransitive.

1. The band uniforms finally arrived just before Christmas.
2. The trainer stepped into the wounded leopard's cage.

3. The sophomore class has a good attendance record.
4. Greg walked unsteadily to the front of the stage.
5. The author tells a story of her childhood in Wyoming.
6. Our team played over its head in the first half.
7. Once a circus horse literally stuck his right hind foot into his mouth.
8. Helen enjoys responsibility.
9. The murderer does not appear in this act.
10. All cars have safety belts as standard equipment.

Exercise C: Find each verb. Tell whether it is active or passive.

1. The lights had been turned down.
2. We have been invited to the symphony concert.
3. My sister has already picked a career.
4. The next batter was hit by a pitched ball.
5. Many New York school children do not understand English.
6. Several of the games were played at night.
7. A new school will be constructed here.
8. The speaker told of her adventures in Africa.
9. More than 100 elements have been discovered.
10. Cynthia has bought a new book about sports cars.

Exercise D: Change the active verbs to passive. Change the passive verbs to active.

1. The speaker will be introduced by the class president.
2. Only Woodbridge has equaled our record.
3. Our class decorated the gym.
4. The influenza shots were given by the school doctor.
5. The game was ruined by the rain.
6. The team bus was delayed by a flat tire.
7. The citrus fruit was destroyed by frost.
8. The new bridge will be dedicated by the mayor.
9. A flaming explosion interrupted the rock concert.
10. My sister's class elected her president.

Tense

Tense means "time." Most verbs change their forms to show present, past, and future time. Each verb has three simple tenses and three perfect tenses. They are formed as follows:

1. **Present tense.** The present tense is formed from the present or simple form of the verb.

A verb in the present tense usually tells of something that exists at the present moment.

> The mail carrier *is* at the door. (right now)
> The jacket *feels* too tight. (at this moment)

The present tense of a verb is not always used to tell of actions that are going on at the moment, however. We do not usually say, "I read." We are more likely to use the **progressive form** "I am reading" or the **emphatic form** "I do read." An exception is the use of the present to describe ongoing sports events:

> Madlock *slides* and Bench *tags* him out.

The present tense is used to tell of repeated or regular and habitual action.

> We *go* to band practice on Thursday evenings.
> The factory *closes* at five o'clock.

The present tense is also used to tell of something that is generally true at all times.

> All politicians *need* a base of power.
> The sun *rises* in the east.
> Dr. Joyce Brothers *writes* about human behavior.

The **historical present tense** is used to tell of some action or condition in the past as though it were occurring in the present:

> The captain *orders*, "Abandon ship!" as the great vessel *lists*
> dangerously to starboard, its decks ablaze.

2. **Past tense.** Past time is usually told by the past tense, which is the second principal part of the verb: *We left, they cheered, nobody asked.* Continuing past action is shown by the **past progressive:** We *were having* a good time.

3. **Future tense.** Future time is shown by using *shall* or *will* with the present form of the verb: *We shall arrive, you will notice, I will listen.*

Future time may be shown by the present tense together with an adverb or phrase that tells time. Future time may also be shown by the use of a form of *be* with *going to.*

> We *get* the grades *tomorrow.* (*tomorrow* is an adverb telling time.)
> I *am going to* resign in January.
> The planes *are grounded until further notice.* (*until further notice* is an adverb phrase telling time.)

4. **Present perfect tense.** The present perfect tense is formed by using *has* or *have* with the past participle (third principal part) of the verb. This tense is used to refer to some indefinite time in the past.

> The mayor *has promised* his support.
> I *have* often *written* letters to the editor.

The present perfect is also used to show action that began in the past and continues into the present.

> We *have worked* here for ten years. (We still work here.)
> We *have been debating* long enough. (present perfect progressive)

5. **Past perfect tense.** The past perfect tense is formed by using *had* with the past participle (third principal part) of the verb. The past perfect tense tells of an action completed in the past before some other action.

EARLIER	LATER
We *had finished* the harvesting	before the storm *broke.*
Brenda *had been* pessimistic	until the acceptance notice *came.*
We *had been waiting* an hour	before the President *arrived.*

6. **Future perfect tense.** The future perfect tense is formed by using *will have* or *shall have* with the past participle of the verb (third principal part). This tense is used to tell of one action completed in the future *before* some other action in the future.

Before the season *ends,* the Mets *will have won* eighty games.
When the campaign *is* over, he *will have made* 150 speeches.

Note: The first verb, in the present tense, indicates far future action. The second verb, in the future perfect tense, indicates future action *before* the action of the first verb.

Conjugation of *Save*

Conjugation is a list of the forms of a verb. Usually, verbs are conjugated in the order shown here:

Principal Parts: save, saved, saved   **Present Participle:** saving
Present Infinitive: to save   **Perfect Infinitive:** to have saved

Present Tense

FIRST PERSON:	I save	we save
SECOND PERSON:	you save	you save
THIRD PERSON:	he, she, it saves	they save

PRESENT PROGRESSIVE: I am saving, you are saving, etc.
PRESENT EMPHATIC: I do save, you do save, he does save, etc.

Past Tense

FIRST PERSON: I saved   we saved
SECOND PERSON: you saved   you saved
THIRD PERSON: he, she, it saved   they saved

PAST PROGRESSIVE: I was saving, you were saving, etc.
PAST EMPHATIC: I did save, you did save, etc.

Future Tense

FIRST PERSON: I shall (will) save   we shall (will) save
SECOND PERSON: you will save   you will save
THIRD PERSON: he, she, it will save   they will save

FUTURE PROGRESSIVE: I shall be saving, you will be saving, etc.

Present Perfect Tense

FIRST PERSON: I have saved   we have saved
SECOND PERSON: you have saved   you have saved
THIRD PERSON: he, she, it has saved   they have saved

PRESENT PERFECT PROGRESSIVE: I have been saving, you have been saving, he has been saving, etc.

Past Perfect Tense

FIRST PERSON: I had saved   we had saved
SECOND PERSON: you had saved   you had saved
THIRD PERSON: he, she, it had saved   they had saved

PAST PERFECT PROGRESSIVE: I had been saving, you had been saving, he had been saving, etc.

Future Perfect Tense

FIRST PERSON: I shall have saved   we shall have saved
SECOND PERSON: you will have saved   you will have saved
THIRD PERSON: he, she, it will have saved   they will have saved

FUTURE PERFECT PROGRESSIVE: I shall have been saving, etc.

Exercise A: Find each verb and tell its tense.

1. We do not know the answer.
2. The workers handled the explosives carefully.
3. Mary always seems restless.
4. At the side of the road stood two state police cars.
5. The crew of the *Mary Jane* had vanished.
6. Will the new offices have air-conditioning?
7. Amateur rock-collectors are finding many valuable gems.
8. By 1980 the world population will have grown to nearly four billion.
9. The car had been behaving oddly on hills.
10. There have been lighthouses on our coasts since 1716.

Exercise B: Follow the same directions as for Exercise A.

1. Sue had lived in Duluth as a child.
2. The President now serves only two terms.
3. A new roller rink will open in September.
4. The girls' basketball team has won the state title.
5. Curt makes pizza with pepperoni and olives.
6. Martina Navratilova won the Wimbledon tennis tournament.
7. Ralph Nader has been organizing a consumer group for sports fans.
8. By eight o'clock tomorrow morning, the rocket will have passed the moon.
9. The band was playing the grand finale.
10. The Chicago Symphony returned yesterday from Europe, where it had played to enthusiastic audiences.

Mood

The mood of a verb shows the writer's attitude about the actuality of a happening. The **indicative mood,** which we use most of the time, shows that we are talking or writing about a fact. That is, we are speaking of something that has happened, is happening, or definitely will happen.

The **subjunctive mood** is used only to express wishes, commands, and conditions that are doubtful or contrary to fact. The forms of the subjunctive mood are like those of the present tense of the indicative mood, except in the third person where the *s* ending is omitted.

> INDICATIVE: He *uses* safety belts—even for short drives.
> SUBJUNCTIVE: We asked that he *use* safety belts—even for short drives.
> SUBJUNCTIVE: He asked that we *use* safety belts—even for short drives.

The subjunctive form of the verb *be* is a special case. With this verb, the form in the present tense for all persons and numbers is *be*.

> Mary asked that the order *be* cancelled.
> Phil moved that the amendment *be* accepted.

The past subjunctive form of the verb *to be* is *were*.

> If she *were* President, she would limit spending.
> I wish I *were* going to Europe this summer.
> If I *were* you, I would study harder.

The **imperative mood** is used to express a command or a request. The imperative mood has only one tense—the present—and only one person—the second.

> *Take* your books with you.   Please *call* me.
> *Find* all your errors.   *Be* quick.

1.4 The Adjective

We do not rely on nouns and verbs alone to express our point of view fully or to make our meaning clear and definite. We use other kinds of words to describe or limit the meaning. We call these words *modifiers*.

An adjective is a word that modifies a noun or pronoun.

Adjectives are used to tell *which one, what kind, how many,* or *how much* about nouns and pronouns.

WHICH ONE: this, that, these, those
WHAT KIND: tiny, old, yellow, shy
HOW MANY: few, three, both, twenty, most
HOW MUCH: more, less, enough, abundant

The Articles

The word *the* is called a **definite article** because it usually refers to a definite or specific thing or person.

The words *a* and *an* are called **indefinite articles** because they refer to no particular thing or person. A is used before words beginning with consonant sounds. An is used before words beginning with vowel sounds. The sound, not the spelling, makes the difference.

They went to *an* auction every Saturday.
I found *a* history book.
The bus was *an* hour late.
It was *a* heated argument.

Proper Adjectives

A word formed from a proper noun is a **proper adjective.** A proper adjective is always capitalized.

NOUN	ADJECTIVE	NOUN	ADJECTIVE
Ireland	Irish	East	Eastern
France	French	Shakespeare	Shakespearean
Canada	Canadian	Bible	Biblical
Australia	Australian	President	Presidential

Predicate Adjectives

An adjective is frequently separated from the noun or pronoun it modifies by a linking verb.

Karen seems *sleepy*. (separated)

We were *exhausted*. (separated)

An adjective in the predicate that modifies the subject is a predicate adjective.

Exercise A: Find each adjective and tell which word it modifies. Ignore the articles.

1. The old house had been empty for several years.
2. The second team played during the last quarter.
3. The new teacher was patient and helpful.
4. The poor elephant was suffering from a bad toothache.
5. The enormous jet cannot land at a small airport.
6. A magnetic field surrounds the entire earth.
7. The new atomic submarines are spacious and comfortable.
8. The water in this lake tastes salty.
9. Many young Americans are making scientific discoveries.
10. The two people in the other car seemed angry.

Exercise B: Follow the same directions as for Exercise A.

1. This little book contains some big ideas.
2. A cold wind drove the deep snow into huge drifts.
3. Steve Cauthen is the young jockey who has won many races.
4. Yesterday Carlita collected sixteen different coins.
5. This new tent easily sleeps several people.
6. Most European students can speak the English language.
7. The library charges fines for overdue books.
8. The hamburger tasted dry and gritty.
9. Some small economy cars are neither small nor economical.
10. Janet Guthrie became famous as the first woman racer in the Indianapolis 500.

Adjectives in Comparisons

We often compare the various qualities of persons and things. The comparison is made by use of two different forms of adjectives.

The **comparative** form of the adjective is formed in two ways:

1. All adjectives of one syllable and a few adjectives with two syllables add *-er*.

   warm—warmer   loose—looser   funny—funnier

2. Most adjectives with two syllables and all adjectives with more than two syllables use *more* to form the comparative.

   careful—more careful   optimistic—more optimistic

The **superlative** form of the adjective is formed by adding *-est* or by using *most*. Adjectives that form the comparative with *-er* form the superlative with *-est*. Those that form the comparative with *more* form the superlative with *most*.

COMPARATIVE	SUPERLATIVE
funnier	funniest
more mature	most mature

Irregular Comparisons

We form the comparative and superlative of some adjectives by changing the words themselves.

	COMPARATIVE	SUPERLATIVE
good	better	best
well	better	best
bad	worse	worst
little	less *or* lesser	least
much	more	most
many	more	most
far	farther *or* further	farthest *or* furthest

Exercise A: Find each adjective. Tell whether it is in comparative form or superlative form. Ignore the articles.

1. We gave the best performance on Friday.
2. Tokyo is now bigger than New York.
3. The pen is mightier than the sword.
4. The world's fastest bird is appropriately called the swift.
5. Jack was the most unhappy boy on the team.
6. Fruit is more plentiful than ever before.
7. Which is harder, calculus or algebra?
8. Where can I find a larger dictionary?
9. That was the worst mistake I ever made.
10. The largest crowds in history witnessed the World Series.

Exercise B: Follow the same directions as for Exercise A.

1. Sweden is larger in area than Norway.
2. Slowly the condition of the patient became worse.
3. Is Mt. Everest or Mt. McKinley higher?
4. The movie was funnier than I had expected.
5. The haircut I had today was the fastest on record.
6. During the last few weeks Kelly's grades improved.
7. Agatha Christie's most intriguing novel may be *Curtain*.
8. Chairs that recline are the most comfortable ones.
9. Does lemonade or cocoa sound more appealing?
10. Who says "Laverne and Shirley" is the most hilarious show on television?

1.5   The Adverb

Nouns and pronouns are modified by adjectives. Other parts of speech are modified by adverbs.

An adverb modifies a verb, an adjective, or another adverb.

MODIFYING A VERB: Barnes answered *angrily*.

MODIFYING AN ADJECTIVE: It was a *most* enjoyable trip.

287

MODIFYING AN ADVERB: They moved *rather* cautiously.

Adverbs tell *where, when, how,* or *to what extent:*

WHERE:	The family is *inside.*
WHEN:	I'll bring you the present *soon.*
HOW:	The storm struck *swiftly.*
TO WHAT EXTENT:	We did not *fully* understand the question.

Many adverbs are formed by adding *-ly* to an adjective: *perfect—perfectly, quiet—quietly, happy—happily.* However, not all modifiers ending in *-ly* are adverbs. The following, for example, are adjectives: *friendly, lively, lonely, ugly.*

Some words may be either adjectives or adverbs.

ADJECTIVE	ADVERB
a *fast* game	Run *fast.*
an *early* lunch	We left *early.*
a *high* building	The bird flew *high.*

Many adverbs do not end in *-ly.* The negatives *no, not,* and *never* are almost always adverbs. Many time-words, such as *later, often, always, soon,* are always adverbs.

Directive Adverbs

Adverbs that tell *where* (place or direction) about the verb are called **directive adverbs.** They normally follow the verb they modify.

We searched *near* and *far.*	The sign had fallen *down.*
They are waiting *outside.*	The conductor walked *in.*

Many of these directive adverbs are combined with verbs to make idioms: *put off, put through, put up.* An idiom is a group of words with a meaning different from the literal meanings of the words taken individually.

Position of Adverbs

A directive adverb normally follows the verb it modifies. An adverb modifying an adjective or another adverb usually comes immediately before the word it modifies. Other adverbs may be shifted from one place in the sentence to another.

DIRECTIVE: The elevator had gone *up.*

ADVERB MODIFYING MODIFIER: It was a *very* common name.

OTHER ADVERBS: *Suddenly,* he turned and ran.

He *suddenly* turned and ran.

Adverbs in Comparisons

Like adjectives, adverbs are used in comparisons. The comparative and the superlative are formed as follows:

1. Adverbs of one syllable add *-er.*

The wind blew *harder* yesterday.
The assignment took *longer* than usual.

2. Most adverbs ending in *-ly* form the comparative with *more.*

The second round of talks ended *more fruitfully.*
I walked into the baby's room *more quietly.*

3. The superlative form of the adverb is formed with *-est* or *most.* Adverbs that form the comparative with *-er* form the superlative with *-est.* Those that use *more* for the comparative use *most* for the superlative.

COMPARATIVE	SUPERLATIVE
harder	hardest
longer	longest
more fruitfully	most fruitfully
more quietly	most quietly

Note: See Section 1.4 for irregular comparisons of adjectives. Some of the words listed there as adjectives may also be used as adverbs and are compared in the same way.

Exercise A: Find each adverb and tell which word or words it modifies.

1. The bus almost always arrives late.
2. The entire class worked hard and successfully on the project.
3. Does your car usually start easily on cold mornings?
4. The streets have become rather crowded recently.
5. The auditorium was soon completely filled.
6. The heart of nearly every large city is deteriorating.
7. The doctor gave orders quietly and confidently.
8. Polio is sometimes rather difficult to diagnose.
9. Lately, the summers have been extremely hot.
10. There goes Dr. Harrison now.

Exercise B: Follow the same directions as for Exercise A.

1. The doctor approached the sick tiger carefully.
2. Did Carlotta send for the tickets yesterday?
3. Soon the class had finished the signs.
4. The plane's fuel supply was now nearly exhausted.
5. David raised his hand eagerly.
6. We had often explored the cave before.
7. Geologists have recently discovered oil below the Sahara.
8. The football field flooded almost completely.
9. On Sunday Helen's condition suddenly became worse.
10. Come in quietly and leave your boots outside.

1.6   The Preposition

The words in an English sentence are arranged in precise patterns. The words that go together are joined or linked in a variety of ways. One means of linking words is the **preposition.**

There are seventeen one-syllable prepositions in English.* They are used to show the following relationships.

LOCATION: at, by, in, on, near
DIRECTION: to, from, down, off, through, out, past, up
ASSOCIATION: or, for, with, like

Here are some two-syllable prepositions.

about	against	before	beside	except
above	along	behind	between	inside
across	among	below	beyond	outside
after	around	beneath	during	over
				under

A number of prepositions have been formed by combining some of the one-syllable prepositions.

into   upon   without   onto   within   throughout

Compound prepositions have been formed by combining a modifier with a preposition or by grouping prepositions.

according to	out of	on account of	aside from
prior to	owing to	instead of	by means of
in front of	subsequent to	because of	as to

Objects of Prepositions. A preposition never appears alone. It is always used with a word or group of words that is called its **object.**

A preposition relates its object to some other word in the sentence.

The object of a preposition usually follows the preposition. The only exception occurs in a sentence or clause introduced by an interrogative pronoun or a relative pronoun.

The President walked briskly *into* the *hall.*
The President walked briskly *from* the *hall.*

* The word *but* may be used as a preposition with the meaning of *except.*

W*hom* did you write the letter *to?*
The girls did not know *whom* the note was meant *for.*
Whose *party* did you go *to?*

The object of a preposition may be a single word or a group of words.

WORD: The box fell behind the *refrigerator.*
WORD: In *writing,* clarity is prized.

WORD GROUP: Before *signing the contract,* read it carefully.
WORD GROUP: Give the package to *whoever answers the door.*

Exercise A: Find each preposition and its object.

1. The truck was stopped at the border and searched for arms.
2. During the centuries, the continents have been drifting apart.
3. Booth jumped to the stage and screamed at the audience.
4. To whom is the announcement addressed?
5. After the game, the crowd rushed for the exits.
6. According to the paper, there will be no school on Friday.
7. The people of Quebec speak French instead of English.
8. Beyond the city limits there is no rule against fireworks.
9. At half time a band marched onto the field.
10. For many years, the old courthouse had been left in disrepair.

Exercise B: Follow the same directions as for Exercise A.

1. On the weekends Don babysits for his neighbors.
2. The pandas at Washington Zoo have been put on diets.
3. The dog sniffed around the kitchen for its dinner.
4. Raccoons scurried over immense piles of garbage.
5. Everyone but Marietta had seen the car approaching.
6. California's redwoods tower above the other trees.
7. Karen felt better after her talk with the coach.
8. All but one of the trees died during the winter.
9. Instead of the bus, Amy rode her bike to school.
10. Aside from the cost, there is no objection to the proposal.

1.7 The Conjunction

Another kind of word used to tie the parts of a sentence together is a conjunction.

A conjunction is a word that connects words, phrases, or clauses.

There are three kinds of conjunctions: coordinating conjunctions, correlative conjunctions, and subordinating conjunctions.

Coordinating Conjunctions

There are three conjunctions used only to connect similar sentence parts. They are called **coordinating conjunctions** because they tie together things of the same kind or order. These coordinating conjunctions are *and, but,* and *or.*

> Snow *and* sleet covered the roads. (connects nouns)
> The train was fast *and* comfortable. (connects adjectives)
> The traffic moved slowly *but* steadily. (connects adverbs)
> The rocket shot off the pad *and* into the air.
>   (connects prepositional phrases)
> We could take a walk *or* go for a swim. (connects predicates)
> The weather report said "rain," *but* the sun is shining brightly.
>   (connects clauses)

For is used as a coordinating conjunction only between clauses. *Nor* is used as a coordinating conjunction only when it is preceded by another negative word.

> The Senator ended her speech, *for* it was clear the
>   bill would pass.
> The workers had *no* organization, nor did they
>   have leaders.
> Betty did *not* have her skis, *nor* did she have her skates.

Correlative Conjunctions

A few conjunctions are used in pairs: *not only . . . but (also); either . . . or; neither . . . nor; both . . . and; whether . . . or.* Such conjunctions are called **correlative conjunctions.**

> Some cats are *not only* independent *but also* aloof.
> *Both* Laurel *and* her brother made the team.
> *Neither* the mayor *nor* his aide would comment on the report.
> We must decide *whether* to stand firm *or* to compromise.

Subordinating Conjunctions

Words used to introduce adverb clauses are called **subordinating conjunctions.** These words not only introduce the subordinate clause but link it to the main clause. They make the relation between the two clauses clear. Subordinating conjunctions show relationships of *time, place, cause, result, exception, condition,* and *alternative.* The most common subordinating conjunctions are these:

after	as though	provided	till	whenever
although	because	since	unless	where
as	before	so that	until	wherever
as if	if	than	whatever	while
as long as	in order that	though	when	

Conjunctive Adverbs

Certain adverbs are used to join main clauses. When so used, they are called **conjunctive adverbs.** A conjunctive adverb is preceded by a semicolon and followed by a comma. The most common conjunctive adverbs are these:

accordingly	hence	nevertheless	therefore
consequently	however	otherwise	yet
furthermore	moreover	also	

Exercise A: Find each conjunction and conjunctive adverb. Tell what kind each joining word is.

1. Neither the speeches nor the music was very exciting.
2. Both the Japanese and the Italian delegates opposed the investigation.
3. The search party worked quickly and carefully.
4. We must either sell more subscriptions or give up the paper.
5. The police officer beckoned us forward, but we could not move.
6. Although the odds were against him, Washington drove forward.
7. We were not at home when the package arrived.
8. The evidence sounded convincing; nonetheless, we believed Northrop innocent.
9. The dictionary is a valuable tool; however, not all dictionaries agree.
10. When the planes flew over, the sub was lying silently 300 feet down.
11. Think of us whenever you play the record.
12. We must leave at once; otherwise, we will be late.
13. You may have the car, provided you pay for the gas.
14. The outfielders wear glasses so that the sun won't blind them.
15. Wave after wave engulfed the tower, but the light still shone.

Exercise B: Find the conjunctions in the following sentences. Tell what kind of words or word groups they join.

1. The test was difficult but fair.
2. Neither Jenny nor Jean jogs alone.
3. We wanted to watch the game, but our television set was broken.
4. John Adams and Thomas Jefferson died on the same day in 1825.
5. Germanium is a rare but useful metal.
6. The burglars went down the alley, into the basement, and up the stairs.
7. Small children and injured persons were the first into the lifeboats.

8. We may take either biology or general science.
9. These school sweaters are not only warm but also attractive.
10. You will enjoy both *Old Yeller* and *The Home Place* by Gipson.

1.8 The Interjection

An interjection is a word or group of words interjected, or thrown, into the sentence. It is usually followed by an exclamation point.

An interjection is a word or word group used to express surprise or other emotion. It has no grammatical relation to other words in the sentence.

Help!   Oh!   Terrific!   Hold it!   Yeah!   Oops!

1.9 Words Used as Different Parts of Speech

Some words, such as *have, is, do,* are always verbs. The personal pronouns *I, me,* etc., are always pronouns. Many words, however, may be used in sentences in different ways.

The *fire* destroyed sixty acres of trees. (noun)
Among the chief duties of a ranger is *fire* patrol. (adjective)
The manager will *fire* that clerk. (verb)

Verb or Noun?

Some words may be used either as verbs or as nouns. Study these examples.

Where can we *store* the boxes? (verb)
The *store* closes early today. (noun)
Dip the meat in the sauce. (verb)
Let's take a *dip* in the pool. (noun)

Noun or Adjective?

A word used to name a person, place or thing is a noun. The same word may be used before another noun to tell "what kind." When so used, it is an adjective.

> *Jazz* has come of age in America's concert halls. (noun)
> Would you call Billie Holiday a *jazz* singer? (adjective)
> *Plastic* is now used in making most toys. (noun)
> They bought their child a *plastic* swimming pool. (adjective)

Adjective or Pronoun?

A demonstrative pronoun—*this, that, these,* and *those*—may also be used as an adjective. If the word is used alone in place of a noun, it is a pronoun. If used before a noun to tell "which one," it is an adjective.

> *This* is my Aunt Margaret. (pronoun)
> *These* are Ted's gloves. (pronoun)
> *That* composition is excellent. (adjective modifying *composition*)
> *Those* hamburgers are really good. (adjective modifying *hamburgers*)

In a similar way the words *what, which,* and *whose* may be used alone as pronouns or before nouns as adjectives.

> *What* should I say? (pronoun)
> *What* street is this? (adjective modifying *street*)
> *Which* is your painting? (pronoun)
> *Which* train do I take? (adjective modifying *train*)
> *Whose* can it be? (pronoun)
> *Whose* plan was accepted? (adjective modifying *plan*)

The words *your, my, our, his, her, their* are forms of the personal pronouns used to show possession. Used in this way, they perform the job of adjectives. The words *mine, yours, hers, ours,* and *theirs* are always pronouns. The word *his* may be used either as a pronoun or an adjective. See Section 1.2.

> The yellow Honda is *hers.* (pronoun)
> The new Volkswagen is *his.* (pronoun)
> That is *his* Uncle Charlie. (adjective use)

Adjective or Adverb?

Several words have the same form whether used as adjectives or adverbs. To tell whether a word is used as an adjective or as an adverb, decide what other words in the sentence it goes with, or modifies. This is a matter of sense, which you can get from reading the sentence. If the word modifies a verb, it is used as an adverb. If it modifies a noun or pronoun, it is used as an adjective. If it tells *where, when, how,* or *to what extent,* it is an adverb. If it tells *what kind,* it is an adjective.

> The plane flew *low.* (adverb telling *where* about *flew*)
> The song ended on a *low* note. (adjective telling *what kind*
>   about *note*)

Adverb or Preposition?

A number of words may be used either as prepositions or as adverbs. If the word is followed by a noun or pronoun, it is probably a preposition. The noun or pronoun is its object. If the word in question is not followed by a noun or pronoun, it is probably an adverb. If the word can be moved to another position, it is an adverb.

> Sue threw *out* her old bathing suit.
> Sue threw her old bathing suit *out.*
>   (In both sentences *out* is an adverb. It can be moved
>   without changing the meaning.)

The parakeet flew *out* the window.
  (*out* cannot be moved; it is a preposition.)
The sundial had been knocked *down*. (adverb)
Will you all please stand *up?* (adverb)
The cart rolled *down* the hill. (preposition)
The mountaineers struggled *up* Pike's Peak. (preposition)

Exercise A: Determine how the italicized words are used in these sentences.

1. A special plane stood waiting *for* the President.
2. It was a hard decision, *for* there were too few facts.
3. We started out with our packs full of food, cooking utensils, clothes, chocolate bars—everything *but* soap.
4. We telephoned on Saturday morning, *but* the office was closed.
5. *After* the accident Carmen drove with great caution.
6. *After* the doors had been closed, the judge rose to speak.
7. Are *these* your books?
8. *These* lucky discoveries have greatly benefited mankind.
9. *What* college does your sister attend?
10. *What* are you going to read for your report?
11. The clock is *slow*; it always runs *slow*.
12. *Outside* the window stood a tall, eerie figure.
13. Please take the dog *outside*.
14. *Inside* the house everything was in disorder.
15. We stood on the balcony watching the sun go *down*.

Exercise B: Follow the same directions as for Exercise A.

1. The *pull* of sun and moon on the earth creates tides.
2. *Which* is the problem that bothered you?
3. The wind blew *hard* all night long.
4. At the North Pole, the sea is very *deep*.
5. The scientists are boring *deep* into the earth's crust.
6. There will be no *afternoon* games next year.
7. The sun came out late in the *afternoon*.

8. My grandparents have a very *fast* boat.

9. Unfortunately, they cannot run the boat *fast* on the narrow river.

10. *This* paper is easy to read; *that* is not.

11. The fireplace was made of *brick*.

12. The *brick* wall was crumbling.

13. The builder tore into the windows and *bricked* up the opening.

14. The opossum was hanging head down from a lower *branch*.

15. Many American companies *branch* out into other parts of the world.

1.10 Verbals

There are a number of highly useful words in English that are difficult to classify. These are **infinitives, ·participles,** and **gerunds.** They are called verbals because they are formed from verbs. Like verbs, they may be completed by objects or predicate words. Like verbs, they may be modified by adverbs.

1.11 The Infinitive

Usually, but not always, the infinitive is preceded by *to*, which is called the "sign of the infinitive." The kinds of infinitives are as follows:

> ACTIVE PRESENT: to honor
> PASSIVE PRESENT: to be honored
> ACTIVE PERFECT: to have honored
> PASSIVE PERFECT: to have been honored

The infinitive may appear without the word *to:*

> No one saw Marguerite *leave*.
> She did not dare *call* her dentist.

The infinitive may be used as a noun. It may be subject or object of the verb, a predicate noun, or an appositive.

> *To win* was not our only goal. (subject of *was*)
> My little brother always wants *to argue*. (object of *wants*)
> Sherry's ambition is *to act*. (predicate noun)
> The mayor's last proposal, *to cut* the budget, was
>   rejected. (appositive)

The infinitive may also be used as a modifier. Used as an adjective, it may modify nouns and pronouns.

> Cape Cod is the place *to see*.

> The Dodgers are the team *to beat*.

As an adverb, the infinitive may modify adverbs, adjectives, or verbs.

> The suit was easy *to clean*. (modifying the adjective *easy*)

> Bob arrived too late *to help*. (modifying the adverb *late*)

> They started *to laugh*. (modifying the verb *started*)

The Infinitive Phrase. An infinitive itself may have modifiers. It may also have a subject, an object, or a predicate word. An **infinitive phrase** consists of the infinitive, its modifiers, and its subject, object, or predicate word.

The infinitive may be modified by adverbs, phrases, or clauses. These modifiers are part of the infinitive phrase.

> *To speak* confidently requires poise.
>   (The adverb *confidently* modifies *To speak*.)

> *To survive* in the nuclear age, we must disarm.
>   (The phrase *in the nuclear age* modifies *To survive*.)

> The teacher said *to study carefully* if we wanted passing grades.
>   (The clause *if we wanted passing grades* modifies *to study*.)

The infinitive may have a direct object, an indirect object, or a predicate word. These words, completing the meaning of the infinitive, are part of the infinitive phrase.

> *To start* the *motor,* first turn on the ignition.
> (*motor* is the direct object of *To start.*)
> We voted *to offer him* the *nomination.*
> (*him* is the indirect object and *nomination* is the direct object of *to offer.*)
> Connie asked *to be team manager.*
> (*team manager* is a predicate noun after *to be.*)
> The solution to the problem ought *to be easy.*
> (*easy* is a predicate adjective after *to be.*)

The infinitive may have a subject. The subject always follows the main verb and comes directly before the infinitive. Since it follows the main verb and is in the objective case, it is sometimes mistaken for an object of the main verb. The subject of the infinitive is part of the infinitive phrase. In the following examples, the entire phrase is the direct object of the verb.

> The commander ordered *them to charge.*
> The editor urged *her readers to vote.*
> Sylvia asked *Marilyn to drive.*

Note: If the main verb is a linking verb (a form of *be, appear, seem,* etc.), the noun following it is a predicate noun. If a predicate noun is followed by an infinitive, the infinitive modifies the noun.

> Sarah is the person to *ask.*   These are the sentences *to study.*

Exercise A: Find the complete infinitive phrase in each sentence.

1. The children are really trying to help.
2. The plan is to survey the bottom of the oceans.
3. Althea decided to accept the challenge.
4. I want to work on the problem slowly and carefully.

5. The giant radio antenna is designed to pick up sounds far out in space.

6. It was an honor to be invited to the dinner.

7. Everyone thinks he or she wants to be told the truth.

8. The last question was supposed to have had two parts.

9. We were glad to have been invited.

10. The lock appears to have been broken.

11. To gain admission to the Air Force Academy, one must be recommended.

12. The tourists asked to be given fuller directions.

13. The class voted to end the party at midnight.

14. We stayed up late to hear the election returns.

15. It takes patience, practice, and stamina to be a writer.

Exercise B: Find the complete infinitive phrase in each sentence.

1. We ought to leave now.

2. It would be a good idea to telephone home.

3. Your parents should be told that you are going to be late.

4. Did the propeller seem to be broken?

5. The cables appear to have been cut deliberately.

6. A raccoon always tries to wash its food.

7. Before we take any action, we want to be sure of the facts.

8. The person to help you with your tennis is Mr. Davis.

9. To get a better view, Lucy stretched on her tiptoes.

10. Ask your friend to come to our house for supper.

1.12 The Gerund

The gerund is a verbal noun that always ends in -ing. It is used in the sentence as a noun and in almost every way that a noun can be used.

Debating is Fred's favorite school activity. (subject of the verb)
Tanya likes *skating* and *skiing*. (object of the verb)
Before *writing*, be sure of your facts. (object of the preposition)

The Gerund Phrase. A gerund may be modified by adjectives or adverbs. It may be completed by objects or predicate words. A **gerund phrase** consists of the gerund together with its modifiers, objects, or predicate words.

The gerund may be modified by single adjectives and adverbs, by phrases, and by clauses.

> *Proper lighting* is necessary for studying.
> (*Proper* is an adjective modifying *lighting*.)
> Geraldine likes *walking briskly*.
> (*briskly* is an adverb modifying *walking*.)
> *Playing without adequate practice* demoralizes a team.
> (*without adequate practice* is a phrase modifying *Playing*.)
> *Swimming after eating a meal* is dangerous.
> (*after eating a meal* is a phrase modifying *Swimming*.)

Gerunds may be completed by objects or predicate words. These words are part of the gerund phrase.

> *Being president* of the group is an honor.
> (*president* is a predicate noun completing *Being*.)
> *Giving Phil those books* changed his whole life.
> (*Phil* is the indirect object and *books* is the direct object of *Giving*.)

Exercise A: Find the gerunds or the complete gerund phrases in the following sentences.

1. Walking is considered good exercise by some.
2. Making a speech was torture for Thomas Jefferson.
3. Some people enjoy standing in line.
4. Quick thinking saved the ship from disaster.
5. Ms. Rossetti saved money by painting the house herself.
6. Before raking leaves, decide what you will do with them.
7. Making new friends is something you can learn.
8. Spending more than you earn is an easy way to anxiety.
9. Horseback riding is Lisa's favorite sport.
10. Mike enjoys cooking Chinese food in a wok.
11. Many teen-agers earn money by mowing lawns.

12. Craig saved time by studying on the bus.
13. By backing down the hill, Sue finally started the car.
14. After winning her race, Elyse felt elated.
15. Before leaving the city, we took one more subway ride.

Exercise B: Follow the same directions as for Exercise A.

1. Cissy's biggest talent is managing money.
2. Studying is a lot like boxing; you have to be on your toes.
3. Disco dancing has become a fad.
4. We cannot avoid making decisions.
5. Pleasing the crowds is the performer's aim.
6. Some people invite trouble by talking too loud.
7. After waiting patiently for an hour, Malcolm left the office.
8. Our dog starts barking at 5:30 A.M.
9. The constant dripping of water will erode the hardest of stones.
10. Jacques Cousteau invented the aqualung, a device used in skin diving.

1.13   The Participle

There are several forms of the participle, all widely used.

PRESENT PARTICIPLE:	following
PAST PARTICIPLE:	followed
PERFECT PARTICIPLE:	having followed
PASSIVE PERFECT PARTICIPLE:	having been followed

The present participle always ends in *-ing*. The past participle is the third principal part of the verb, and its endings are various. (See Section 1.3.)

The participle is always used as an adjective to modify a noun or a pronoun. In the following examples, the arrow indicates the word modified by the participle.

Smiling, Laura accepted the award.

Elated, the class arrived in Washington.

Having been hired, Lana looked forward to her new job.

The *exhausted* players headed for the locker room.

The Participial Phrase. A participle may be modified by single adverbs or by phrases and clauses. The participle may also be completed by objects or predicate words. A **participial phrase** consists of the participle together with its modifiers, objects, or predicate words.

When a participle is modified by an adverb, a phrase, or a clause, these modifiers are part of the participial phrase.

Moving closer, we could see the tiger's teeth.
(*closer* is an adverb modifying *Moving*.)

Walking in pairs, the elephants lumbered into the ring.
(*in pairs* is a phrase modifying *Walking*.)

When a participle is completed by objects or predicate words, these words are part of the participial phrase. In the examples below, the arrow indicates the word modified by the participial phrase.

Having passed the test, Darla heaved a sigh of relief.
(*test* is the direct object of *Having passed*.)

Chet bent over his physics book, *looking perplexed.*
(*perplexed* is a predicate adjective completing *looking*.)

Giving the first mate the charts, the ship captain scanned the radar.
(*first mate* is the indirect object and *charts* is the direct object of *Giving*.)

Exercise A: Find each complete participial phrase and show which word it modifies.

1. Running at great speed, Pat broke the school's one-mile record.
2. The cyclist, straining every muscle, reached the crest of the hill.

3. The runner, trying for a double, was out at second base.

4. Working fast, Julia remodeled the room in a few weeks.

5. Smelling smoke, Coretta called the fire department.

6. Surrounded by enemy ships, Drake decided to attack.

7. The crowd, pleased with Grasso's victory, listened to the speech.

8. Early the next morning, the prospectors arrived in San Francisco, loaded with gold nuggets.

9. The defendant, waiting for a verdict, gazed at the judge.

10. Having been defeated twice, Purdue could not win the championship.

11. Calvin ordered a hot fudge sundae topped with marshmallows.

12. Walking carefully on the rocks, the hikers crossed the stream.

13. The toddler raced down the aisle, knocking over a stack of cans.

14. Beth found the terrier ripping up her math homework.

15. Trained for emergencies, the paramedics rushed into action.

Exercise B: Follow the same directions as for Exercise A.

1. Concentrating on his form, Roger did a perfect back dive.

2. Many people object to the violence shown on television.

3. Outdistancing her guard, Jane raced down the court, scoring easily.

4. With somber faces, the miners arrived at the surface, carrying their injured friend.

5. The little boat, careening wildly, crashed right into the dock.

6. The old cobbler, stricken with grief, remained in his shop for days.

7. Struck by a sudden idea, Sally turned back to her locker.

8. Having twice won the prize, Hal gained permanent possession.

9. The team ran out onto the field, determined to win.

10. The old sign, worn and battered by wind and rain, was almost illegible.

Exercise C: Find the verbals in these sentences. Label them as infinitives, gerunds, or participles.

1. Taking care of an aquarium is not an easy task.

2. I have learned to take notes in class.
3. Long-distance running makes many people feel healthy.
4. That free ice cream cone was an unexpected treat.
5. Denise likes to dance on roller skates.
6. There are courses to improve memory.
7. Playing fairly demands self-discipline.
8. Disappointed by their loss, the team left the field silently.
9. Having friends is important to most teen-agers.
10. Having passed the time trials, I could sign up for the race.
11. Charlie Chaplin made clowning an art.
12. Coreen wants to study auto mechanics.
13. Ignoring the traffic, the child darted across the street.
14. Most people want to succeed the easy way.
15. I spotted Brian turning somersaults down the hall.

REVIEW: THE CLASSIFICATION OF WORDS This exercise is a review of Section 1. Determine how the italicized words are used in each sentence. Tell whether each is a noun, pronoun, verb, adjective, adverb, preposition, conjunction, interjection, gerund, participle, or infinitive.

1. *Several* of the people *on* the beach played volleyball.
2. Cal *soon* learned that the *plant* with *three* leaves was poison ivy.
3. *Although* she *seemed* calm, Char was *nervous* about the play.
4. *Wow! That* really sailed out of the stadium!
5. The lighthouse *keeper sounded* the foghorn.
6. Scientists *are finding* many *uses* for the *laser* beam.
7. Belinda *guided* the chestnut-brown horse *along* a wooded trail.
8. Carlos celebrated *his* birthday by *going* to the carnival.
9. For supper we *ate some* of the vegetables that grew in our garden.
10. *Who* discovered *Antarctica?*
11. *Ashley* used both *palms* and ferns in her terrarium.
12. The cafeteria serves hamburgers *or* hot dogs *nearly* every day.
13. *Frequently,* Lisa *uses* a jump rope *to exercise.*
14. The game stopped *while* Derek hunted *for* his contact lens.
15. *Aha!* You're the *one* responsible!

2.0   The Parts of a Sentence

In English, single words are used widely to convey meaning. The words *stop, danger, poison,* for example, express full meaning to the reader. In general, however, meaning is expressed in English by groups of words acting together: *in the morning, playing tight end, Laura laughed.*

These groups of words are neither spoken nor written in haphazard order. The English sentence has fixed patterns into which words are placed to express meaning. These patterns are learned in childhood. They are learned because they are the chief means by which the child can express his or her feelings.

A knowledge of what these sentence patterns are and of how they work is essential for effective use of language in adult life.

2.1   The Sentence

Sentences are used to make statements and to ask questions. To be understood, they must express a complete thought, a complete idea, or a complete question.

A group of words must express a complete thought or it is not a sentence. We begin the study of the sentence with a partial definition:

A sentence is a group of words that expresses a complete thought.

INCOMPLETE: The man in the white suit (What about him?)
COMPLETE: The man in the white suit sells ice cream.
INCOMPLETE: Joe Garagiola, the sports announcer (Does what?)
COMPLETE: Joe Garagiola, the sports announcer, tells colorful baseball stories.
INCOMPLETE: Crossing the road (Who did what?)
COMPLETE: Crossing the road, we noticed some glass on the pavement.

Exercise A: Which of the following groups of words are sentences?

1. Immediately recognizing the danger
2. Nobody panicked
3. Like most small children on a roller coaster
4. Waited for the rain to stop
5. Libby answering our call
6. Quito, Ecuador, practically on the equator
7. This is an entirely new approach
8. Some highlights of his career
9. Her remarks influenced the campaign
10. An ice-skating rink in the park
11. The easiest way out
12. Quadraphonic sound at home in your living room
13. There is ample evidence to prove the statement
14. Will changes have to be made
15. Over the bridge to the main highway

Exercise B: Which of the following groups of words are sentences?

1. Actually, we were not at all surprised
2. No clear-cut plan or ready-made formula
3. Never spoke to us or even noticed us
4. They scraped and painted the walls
5. Disappearing in the fog
6. Always asking questions
7. Still trying to discourage the plan
8. Was too much emphasis placed on the commercial
9. The change in population throughout the country

10. Coming to a sudden stop in the middle of the intersection
11. The traffic officer waved furiously
12. Coming into the brightly lighted entrance hall
13. Renowned for its excellent service and cuisine
14. There at the pier was a glamorous cruise ship
15. Instead, he dictated a sharp reprimand

2.2 Kinds of Sentences

Sentences may be classified according to structure* or according to the purpose of the speaker or writer. There are four principal purposes served by sentences, as described below.

1. The **declarative sentence** is used to make a statement. The statement may be one of fact, wish, intent, or feeling.

> Naomi Jones sailed solo around the world in 1978.
> I would like to be a nuclear physicist.

2. The **imperative sentence** is used to state a command, request, or direction. The subject is always *You*. When the subject is not expressed, as is usually the case, *you* is "understood" to be the subject.

> (You) Please turn off the light.
> (You) Speak to the landlord tomorrow.
> (You) Take your first right at the traffic light.

3. The **interrogative sentence** is used to ask a question. It is always followed by a question mark.

> How much does it cost?
> Who wrote *To Kill a Mockingbird?*
> What does *ecumenical* mean?

4. An **exclamatory sentence** is used to express strong feeling. It is always followed by an exclamation point.

> What a surprise that was!   How lucky we were!

---

* For classification of sentences by form or structure, see Section 3.0.

Exercise A: What kind of sentence is each of the following?

1. Can anyone explain this problem?
2. Brasilia is the capital of Brazil.
3. Throw away those dirty old sneakers.
4. Where does the Queen of England live?
5. Please step aside and let the passengers off.
6. What a weird riddle that was!
7. What TV program shall I tune in?
8. Her remark was quite uncalled for.
9. Raisins are made by drying grapes.
10. What a day it was for a hike!

Exercise B: Follow the same directions as for Exercise A.

1. When is the next solar eclipse?
2. Keep your seatbelt fastened.
3. Airport controllers must be alert.
4. How crazy this plan seems!
5. Which states have ratified the Equal Rights Amendment?
6. I am taking a vacation from alarm clocks.
7. Oh, look at that magnificent rainbow.
8. Don't expect to learn a foreign language overnight.
9. For many years, Silas lived at the edge of town.
10. Turn left at the next corner.

2.3 Subject and Predicate

There are two parts in every complete sentence. . (1) The **subject** is the person, thing, or idea about which something is said. (2) The **predicate** is the idea expressed about the subject.

Every sentence contains a subject and a predicate.
The subject of the sentence is the person or thing about which something is said.

The predicate tells something or asks something about the subject of the sentence.

The word *predicate* means "to proclaim, declare, preach, or affirm." The predicate of a sentence, therefore, "proclaims, declares, preaches, or affirms" something about the subject.

We may say that a sentence is a group of words that tells something (*predicate*) about a person or thing (*subject*). Our definition of a sentence may now be expanded:

A sentence is a group of words expressing a complete thought by means of a subject and a predicate.

SUBJECT	PREDICATE
Dogs	bark.
The dogs in the street	bark at passing fire engines.
Light	shines.
The light at Kennedy's grave	shines as a beacon of courage.

2.4 The Simple Predicate

In every predicate, however long, the most important word—the key word—is the **verb.*** In fact, the verb is the key word in the entire sentence. Sentences may be constructed without nouns, pronouns, or other parts of speech; but without a verb there can be no sentence.

The simple predicate of the sentence is the verb.

The verb may be a phrase consisting of more than one word: *had seen, should have seen, was singing, had been singing.* The words making up the verb may be interrupted by a modifier. Such a modifier is not part of the verb.

were soon *found*   *had* just *left*
was never *finished*   *had* almost *toppled*

---

* The **complete predicate** consists of the verb, its modifiers, and complements. The **complete subject** consists of the simple subject and its modifiers.

The simple predicate, which we shall hereafter call the *verb,* may be compound. The word *compound* means "having more than one part of the same kind." The parts of a compound verb are joined by a conjunction (*and, or, neither-nor,* etc.).

> She **sang** well *and* **danced** beautifully.
> The motor **sputtered, coughed,** *and* **stopped.**
> You **can** *either* **go** *or* **stay.**

2.5 The Simple Subject

Every verb has a subject. It is the word or words that answer *who?* or *what?* before the verb.

> Holly called yesterday.   One of the ships sank.
> *Verb:* called   *Verb:* sank
> *Who called?:* Holly   *What sank?:* One
> *Subject:* Holly   *Subject:* One

The **simple subject** is the subject of the verb.

The subject of the verb may be compound. The parts of a compound subject are normally joined by a conjunction.

> The **brain** *and* **spinal cord** are parts of the central nervous system.
> A **quartet** by Haydn *and* a **quintet** by Mozart were played at the concert.
> *Either* **Sadowsky** *or* **Fisher** will start at quarterback.

Exercise A: Find the verb and its subject.

1. Robert Frost won the Pulitzer Prize.
2. Once again, the Yankees have won the World Series.
3. Streams and rivers flowed gently down to the sea.
4. The rocket orbits at an altitude of one thousand miles and circles the earth once every two hours.
5. Carly Simon and James Taylor are recording an album together.
6. The birch trees swayed and danced in the breeze.

7. Imported silks and domestic cottons are displayed at Kessler's.
8. The old dog rose slowly, stretched, and then shook himself.
9. All the club members helped with the decorations.
10. Oranges, grapes, and boxes of candy filled the basket.

Exercise B: Find the verb and its subject.

1. Soup, fruit, and whole-wheat bread make a nutritious lunch.
2. Tracy's most cherished possessions are her Beatles and Rolling Stones albums.
3. Many high schools have recently organized coed sports programs.
4. Are Natalia Makarova and Cynthia Gregory famous ballerinas?
5. Neither she nor her friend had come to our party.
6. At the noise, the pigeons took off and flew into the trees.
7. He changed his seat twice, fidgeted, and then left the hall.
8. The chill and the dampness of the old abandoned house depressed us.
9. Either the soprano or the alto will sing a solo.
10. Unjust punishment and excessive flogging had turned the officers and crew against Captain Bligh.

2.6 Subjects in Unusual Positions

In most sentences the subject appears before the verb. This subject-verb order is the normal pattern of English sentences. In many sentences, however, this order is reversed.

Questions. In most questions the subject appears between the words making up the verb phrase.

VERB	SUBJECT	VERB
Did	you	ask?
Have	you	eaten?
Can	you	go?
Could	you	have gone?

In most questions beginning with the interrogative words *where, when, why, how, how much,* the subject falls between the parts of the verb. In questions beginning with *who* or *what,* the verb may follow the subject in normal order:

> Who shouted?   What fell?

Sentences Beginning with *There* and *Here*. Many sentences begin with *There* or *Here* immediately followed by some form of *be: There is, There was, There will be, Here is, Here were,* and so on. Often, *Here* and *There* are introductory words used to get the sentence started. They are never the subject of the verb. In this kind of sentence, the subject follows the verb.

> Here is a new idea. (*idea* is the subject.)
> There were eight puppies in the litter. (*puppies* is the subject.)
> There will be a rehearsal on Saturday. (*rehearsal* is the subject.)

Note: Not all sentences beginning with *Here* and *There* follow the above pattern: *Here we can plant a garden. Here she comes. There he is.* In these sentences, *Here* and *There* are adverbs modifying the verb.

Sentences in Inverted Order. For emphasis or for variety of style, the subject is sometimes placed after the verb.

> Standing next to Barbara Jordan was her *secretary*.
> On the top of the mountain was a lookout *post*.
> Onto the runway roared the sleek *jet*.

Finding the Subject of the Verb. To find the subject of the verb in any sentence, find the verb first. Then ask *who?* or *what?* before it. If the sentence is not in normal word order, change it to normal order, and the subject will become clear.

> INVERTED: From the cellar came a low whine.
> NORMAL: A low whine came from the cellar.

Exercise A: Find the verb and its subject.

1. From the top balcony came many "bravos."
2. How much money did you lose?
3. Could you have seen the show from the back row?
4. Here are the missing keys.
5. Over the treetops rose the full moon.
6. Along the hedge crept the cat.
7. There was not a house in sight.
8. Should I have telephoned so early?
9. There might have been a serious accident.
10. Through the tall grasses leaped the kangaroo.

Exercise B: Find the verb and its subject.

1. Out of the night came the hoot of an owl.
2. There on the wet grass lay my lost scarf.
3. At the end of the parade came the sanitation trucks.
4. Did you ever see such a huge crowd?
5. Have you never heard the cry of the loon?
6. Out of the fog came the warning sound of the bell buoy.
7. Where else can you enjoy such beautiful scenery?
8. There will be a fire drill tomorrow.
9. For every participant there was a prize.
10. When will your sister hear about her bar examination?

2.7 The Direct Object

In many sentences the action verb carries action from the subject to some other word. It serves to tie these words together. The word to which the action is carried from the subject is the **direct object.**

Sometimes the direct object tells what receives the action of the verb. Sometimes it tells the result of the action.

RECEIVER OF ACTION: Sondra baited the *hook*. (baited what?)

RESULT OF ACTION: Sondra caught a *fish*. (caught what?)
RECEIVER OF ACTION: The lawyer took the *case*. (took what?)
RESULT OF ACTION: The lawyer won the *case*. (won what?)

The direct object is a word or group of words to which the verb carries the action from the subject.

The direct object may be a word, a phrase, or a clause.

SUBJECT	VERB		DIRECT OBJECT
Mary Ellen	changed	the	*tire.*
I	would like	your	*advice.*
The band	formed	a	*circle.*

Action verbs that carry the action from subject to object are called **transitive verbs.** Action verbs that are not followed by direct objects are called **intransitive.** Some verbs may be transitive in one sentence and intransitive in another.

The fans *were cheering* Chris Evert Lloyd. (transitive)
The fans *were cheering*. (intransitive)

In some so-called action verbs, the action is not visible. However, the verb does carry the thought from subject to object, tying them together.

Beth *has* high ideals. (has what?)
George *understands* Italian. (understands what?)
Adam *wants* a snowmobile. (wants what?)

The direct object may be compound.

I lost my *hat* and *coat*. (lost what?)
They wanted *to swim* and *to play* golf. (wanted what?)

A word that completes the meaning of the verb is called a **complement.** The direct object is one kind of complement.

Direct Object or Adverb? To find the direct object, ask *what?* after the verb. A direct object tells *what* after the verb. An adverb following an action verb tells *where, when, how,* or *to what extent* about the verb.

The dog follows the *mail carrier*. (what—direct object)
The dog is *outside*. (where—adverb)
The guests arrived *late*. (when—adverb)

2.8 The Indirect Object

The indirect object of the verb tells *to or for whom*, or *to or for what*, something is done.

We gave *Karen* the award. (*to* Karen)
Joe made his *brother* a sandwich. (*for* his brother)

A verb has an indirect object only if it also has a direct object.

SUBJECT	VERB		INDIRECT OBJECT		DIRECT OBJECT
Ms. Preston	showed		*us*	the	map.
Art	offered	the	*guests*	some	coffee.
I	sent		*Angela*	a	card.

The indirect object may be compound: I asked *Bert* and *Amy* the question.

The words *to* and *for* are never placed before the indirect object. When followed by a noun or pronoun, *to* and *for* are prepositions. The noun or pronoun following the preposition is the object of the preposition.

Alec gave *Lisa* a sweater. (*Lisa* is the indirect object.)
Alec gave a sweater to *Lisa*. (*Lisa* is the object of the
    preposition.)
My grandmother made *me* a pie. (*me* is the indirect object.)
My grandmother made a pie for *me*. (*me* is the object of the
    preposition.)

Exercise A: Find both the direct and indirect objects.

1. Jack sent Doreen a card from Hawaii.
2. The principal gave the student council her advice.
3. Dad wrote the mayor a letter of apology.
4. The committee offered Ward the job.
5. The contract guarantees you a month of vacation.
6. Phoebe told the teacher her excuse.
7. A passing motorist offered the boys a lift.
8. David passed Suzanne his eraser.
9. An usher handed me a program.
10. The forlorn Santa offered Sonia his job.

Exercise B: Follow the same directions as for Exercise A.

1. A sudden downpour brought Texas flash floods.
2. The police officer issued my sister a speeding ticket.
3. At graduation the superintendent awarded five students scholarships.
4. The economist sent Congress her recommendations.
5. The guide showed the visitors several of Mary Cassatt's paintings.
6. Danny sends you his best wishes.
7. Navy planes brought the party badly needed supplies.
8. The speaker showed us some slides of New Zealand.
9. The President awarded the ship a unit citation.
10. The explorers bid the islanders a happy farewell.

2.9   Predicate Words

The linking verb links its subject to a word in the predicate. The word in the predicate, so linked, is called a **predicate word.** The subject may be linked to a **predicate noun,** a **predicate pronoun,** or a **predicate adjective.**

My favorite holiday is *Christmas.* (predicate noun)

The motor scooter is *hers.* (predicate pronoun)

The quarterback felt *confident.* (predicate adjective)

A word that completes the meaning of a verb is called a **complement.** Predicate words complete the meaning of linking verbs. Since they refer to the subject, they are called **subject complements.**

Diagraming. The simple sentence with an action verb is diagramed as follows:

We sang.   We sang songs.

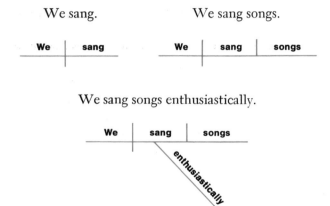

We sang songs enthusiastically.

Note: The single-word modifier goes on a slant line below the word it modifies.

The simple sentence with a linking verb is diagramed as follows:

George seems well.   Mary is president.

Note: The line following the linking verb slants toward the subject.

The action verb with an indirect object is diagramed as follows:

My aunt sent me a sweater.

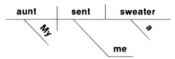

Exercise A: Find the predicate words.

1. This may be our last chance.
2. The new high school looks very modern.
3. Ann seems quite happy at college.
4. The stadium was nearly full of spectators.
5. Harry will probably be our next class president.
6. This is an unusual opportunity.
7. The demolished car was a depressing sight.
8. Billie's plans for the party sound exciting.
9. The captain of the ship is an old friend of ours.
10. Juanita is clearly the best player on the team.

Exercise B: Make five columns. Head them *Subject, Verb, Direct Object, Indirect Object,* and *Predicate Word.* Place those parts of the following sentences in the proper columns.

1. The commander gave the troops a stern warning.
2. We now have a permanent settlement at the South Pole.
3. After the concert, Jane Oliver gave us her autograph.
4. At the icy turn, four cars piled up in a single crash.
5. Has Jim read the directions carefully?
6. The new jets are sensitive to weather conditions.
7. Ghost towns appear throughout the mining country.
8. In 1907 two men rowed a boat across the Atlantic.
9. In the first airplane race, one plane was chased by an eagle.
10. Dr. Johnson wrote an excuse for Bob.
11. The rebels appear confident of success.
12. The shop has made us a new table.
13. In the last quarter, Deerfield scored two touchdowns.

14. New sources of energy will greatly change our lives in the next twenty years.

15. The leaders of the expedition were scientists from England.

2.10 Compound Parts of Sentences

Subjects, verbs, objects, predicate words, and predicates may all be compound. That is, they may consist of more than one part *of the same kind*. The parts are joined by a conjunction.

COMPOUND SUBJECT:	*Time* and *Stereo Review* are Jerry's favorite magazines.
COMPOUND VERB:	The plane *climbed* and *dived*.
COMPOUND DIRECT OBJECT:	We want *air* and *sunlight*.
COMPOUND INDIRECT OBJECT:	Pam gave *Joe* and *Felicia* the directions.
COMPOUND OBJECT OF PREPOSITION:	We drove steadily through the heavy *rain* and *sleet*.
COMPOUND PREDICATE WORD:	We felt *warm* and *cozy*.
COMPOUND PREDICATE:	The police *halted the bus* and *questioned all of the riders*.

Diagraming. Compound sentence parts are diagramed as follows:

Al and Sue *(compound subject)* sat and listened *(compound verb)*.

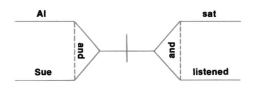

The teacher gave Louis and Josie (*compound indirect object*) the books and records (*compound direct object*).

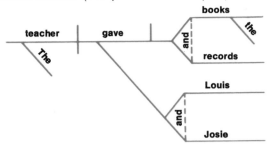

The speeches of the governor and the mayor (*compound object of the preposition*) were brief but informative (*compound predicate adjective*).

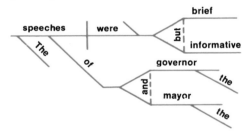

The critics praised the acting but disliked the play (*compound predicate*).

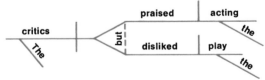

Exercise: Make five columns. Head them *Subject, Verb, Direct Object, Predicate Word, and Predicate*. Find the compound parts of the following sentences, and write these parts in the proper columns.

1. Robin washed and waxed the new Toyota.
2. The plane struck the runway and bounced high in the air.

3. Judy sounds tired and unhappy.

4. Bernstein led the orchestra and also played the piano.

5. You will need your school record and letters of recommendation.

6. The uniforms were bright and colorful.

7. The airplane patrols and ground search parties sought the missing elephant for three weeks.

8. The three longest rivers are the Nile, the Amazon, and the Mississippi.

9. The passengers and the crew were bickering with each other.

10. The fisherman baited his hook and tossed out his line.

11. Above the clouds, the sky was a brilliant blue and gold.

12. Fame and fortune are perishable.

13. The police arrived and looked around.

14. We want loyalty, sympathy, and patience from friends.

15. Tugs, fireboats, and ocean liners welcomed the gallant little ship.

2.11 The Phrase

A phrase is a group of words without a subject and a verb, used as one part of speech.

A phrase is used as one part of speech. A **verb phrase** is two or more words used as a verb: *would be, could have been.* A **noun phrase** is two or more words used as a noun: *Pan American Highway, Jane Addams High School.*

2.12 The Prepositional Phrase

The prepositional phrase consists of the preposition, its object, and modifiers of the object.

Behind the ramshackle red barn was an old workhorse.
The children ran *through the whirling lawn sprinkler.*

The object of a preposition is always a noun, a pronoun, or a group of words used as a noun.

> Esther went *to* the opera. (*opera* is the object of *to*.)
>
> The dog went everywhere *with* him. (*him* is the object of *with*.)
>
> *After* calling the Coast Guard, we resumed the search. (*calling the Coast Guard* is a gerund phrase used as a noun. It is the object of *After*.)
>
> Give the letter *to* whoever answers the door. (*whoever answers the door* is a noun clause, the object of *to*.)

The prepositional phrase is a modifier. It is used either as an adjective or as an adverb. A prepositional phrase that modifies a noun or pronoun is an **adjective phrase.** That is, it is a phrase used as an adjective.

> Kirstin is the student *with the most potential*. (*with the most potential* modifies the noun *student*.)
>
> The energy *of an atom* is tremendous. (*of an atom* modifies *energy*.)
>
> The treaty *between the two nations* was signed in Geneva. (*between the two nations* modifies *treaty*.)

An adjective phrase always comes immediately after the noun or pronoun it modifies.

A prepositional phrase that modifies a verb, an adjective, or an adverb is an **adverb phrase.** That is, it is a phrase used as an adverb to tell *where, when, how* or *to what extent* about the word it modifies.

> Megan put the stereo speakers *on the bookcase*. (*on the bookcase* tells *where* about the verb *put*.)

The movie was successful *beyond all expectations.* (*beyond all expectations* tells *to what extent* about the adjective *successful.*)

The hunters rose early *in the morning.* (*in the morning* tells *when* about the adverb *early.*)

When two or more prepositional phrases follow each other, they may modify the same word, or one phrase may modify the object in the preceding phrase.

They arrived *at the airport on time.* (Both phrases modify *arrived; at the airport* tells *where* and *on time* tells *when* about the verb.)

Cape Horn is *at the southernmost tip* of South America. (*at the southernmost tip* modifies *is; of South America* modifies *tip.* It tells *which* tip.)

Diagraming. Prepositional phrases are diagramed as follows:

Eric painted a portrait *of the President.* (adjective phrase)

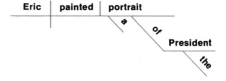

The guests left early *in the morning.* (adverb phrase)

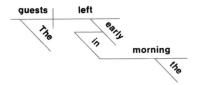

The key was stuck *in the door.* (adverb phrase)

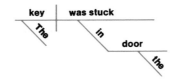

The novel *about life on Mars* has disappeared. (adjective phrases)

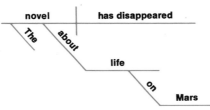

Exercise A: Write each prepositional phrase and the word or words it modifies.

1. In the late afternoon we had our first customer.
2. There was a spontaneous burst of applause.
3. John had once been lost on the Yukon River for three days.
4. The jewels had been hidden in a box of rubbish.
5. Can you work at the museum after school?
6. The sudden illness of the leading lady forced a change in our plans.
7. For twenty years the man in the iron mask captured everyone's imagination.
8. Before a holiday, a feeling of excitement pervades the school.
9. A cloud of smoke appeared on the horizon.
10. For two hours Dale clung to the rock with her fingertips.

Exercise B: Write each prepositional phrase and the word or words it modifies.

1. Early in the morning we arrived at the lake.
2. There was a strange cry in the middle of the night.

3. The radio towers were visible for a distance of ten miles.

4. Below the North Pole, the sea has a depth of nearly three miles.

5. At the South Pole there is a solid mass of ice.

6. During the storm the waves hurled heavy rocks onto the shore.

7. Jessie went cycling with her mother in the afternoon.

8. A crowd of angry people gathered outside the store.

9. Before the railroads, settlers traveled along the rivers.

10. For years the Pennsylvania Canal towed its boats over the mountains.

2.13   The Infinitive Phrase*

Usually the **infinitive phrase** begins with *to*. The phrase consists of *to*, the infinitive, its complements, and its modifiers. If the infinitive has a subject, that is also part of the phrase.

> I tried *to write better.* (The infinitive phrase is the object of the verb *tried.*)

> Jane was careful *to check her answers twice.* (The infinitive phrase modifies the adjective *careful.*)

> We plan *to play softball on Sunday afternoon.* (The infinitive phrase is the object of the verb *plan.*)

Diagraming. The infinitive phrase is diagramed as follows:

We want to have a beach party soon.

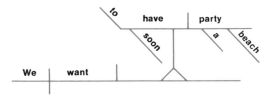

* See also Section 1.11.

To get a summer job was not easy.

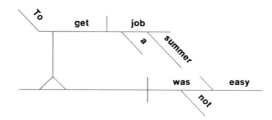

Exercise A: Find the infinitive phrases in the sentences below.

1. As soon as she arrived, Deena made plans to leave town.
2. Unfortunately, Don is sure to win this election.
3. Marla decided to read *Sounder* for her report.
4. Congresspersons like to get letters from the voters.
5. Are you planning to get a job next summer?
6. The Todds are trying to rent their house for the summer.
7. Three people volunteered to paint the fence.
8. Ms. Moss expects her students to be hard working.
9. People crowded the stadiums to watch Babe Ruth.
10. To pay his debts, Thomas Jefferson had to sell his library.

Exercise B: Follow the same directions as for Exercise A.

1. Emily's ambition is to write for a newspaper.
2. To study for the test, Molly outlined the chapters.
3. The candidate promised to halt inflation.
4. Record crowds went to see the King Tut exhibit.
5. To open the garage door, you push this button.
6. John Adams was the first President to live in the White House.
7. To keep plants healthy, fertilize them monthly.
8. *Jaws II* was meant to be more frightening than *Jaws*.
9. To clean the attic would take hours.
10. The performer asked the audience to sing along.

2.14 The Participial Phrase*

The **participial phrase** usually begins with the participle. The phrase consists of the participle, its modifiers, and its complements. The modifiers and complements may themselves be phrases and clauses.

We stood in line for three hours, *hoping to get tickets*.
(The participial phrase modifies the pronoun *we*. The infinitive phrase *to get tickets* is the object of the participle *hoping*.)

Angered by poor pay and long hours, the employees decided to strike. (The participial phrase modifies *employees*.)

Knowing what the candidates said, you can vote wisely.
(The participial phrase modifies *you*. The noun clause *what the candidates said* is the object of the participle *Knowing*.)

Diagraming. The participle and the participial phrase are diagramed as follows:

Purring softly, the kitten lay down.

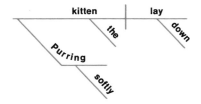

---

* See also Section 1.13.

Sailing his boat brilliantly, Jeff won the race.

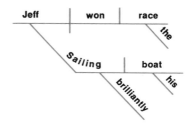

Exercise A: Find the participial phrases. Tell the word each phrase modifies. Do not overlook phrases made from past participles and present participles.

1. Arriving in Philadelphia, Franklin looked for a job.
2. Having finished her required work, Cara began an investigation of her own.
3. Lincoln entered the capital at night, disguised in strange clothing.
4. Alarmed by the condition of the troops, the general ordered a retreat.
5. Appearing before the committee, the accountant admitted her guilt.
6. Both pros, wilting under the hot sun, played a slow game.
7. The girls came into the house, carrying a mysterious package.
8. Woodrow Wilson went to bed, convinced of his defeat.
9. Having studied the chapter thoroughly, I was ready for the test.
10. Lynn limped out onto the court, determined to finish the game.

Exercise B: Follow the same directions as for Exercise A.

1. Panting heavily, Kris dove across the finish line.
2. The people driving the tractors have a dangerous job.
3. The woman riding the ten-speed bicycle is my biology teacher.
4. Two nurses, having finished their work, left the ward.
5. The audience grew restless, waiting for the show to begin.
6. Best known for her novels, Willa Cather also wrote short stories.

7. Movies intended for a general audience are rated G.

8. The player scoring the most points loses the game.

9. The notice posted on the bulletin board gives the examination schedule.

10. Seared by the drought, the farms looked lifeless.

2.15   The Gerund Phrase*

The **gerund phrase** consists of the gerund, which always ends in -*ing*, and the modifiers and complements of the gerund. The modifiers themselves may be phrases. The gerund phrase is always used as a noun.

> *Finding an apartment* is a difficult job. (The gerund phrase is the subject of the verb *is.*)
>
> We liked *picnicking on the island.* (The gerund phrase is the object of *liked.*)
>
> After *training intensively*, the team was ready for opening day. (The gerund phrase is the object of the preposition *After.*)

Diagraming. The gerund and the gerund phrase are diagramed as follows:

Hiking is her favorite sport.

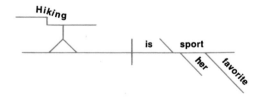

* See also Section 1.12.

Fine passing won the game.

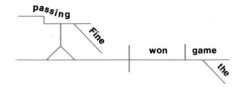

We disliked taking the test.

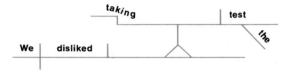

After trudging through the snow, we relaxed.

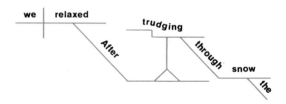

Exercise A: Find the gerund or gerund phrase in each of the following sentences.

1. Cooking is a hobby of many famous men and women.
2. Several football coaches enjoy painting in their spare hours.
3. By shopping carefully you can make your money go farther.
4. Courteous driving saves lives.
5. After studying, Mike took a long walk.
6. We enjoyed hearing your speech.
7. Getting there is half the fun.
8. Don't blame Sarah for losing the game.
9. Before going to bed, Mr. Harris turned on the radio.

10. Sleeping late on Saturdays is a great luxury.
11. Turn off the water before closing the camp.
12. Most of the class have stopped reading comic books.
13. Concentration is most important in playing chess.
14. Climbing the fence is forbidden.
15. Watching the clock is hard work.

Exercise B: Identify the verbals (see Sections 1.10–1.13).

1. Sitting on our roof, we watched the strange light in the sky.
2. Wounded by English ships, the Armada sailed north to its destruction.
3. Anyone can learn to fly a plane by taking lessons.
4. Lost in his thoughts, Perry stepped right over a wallet lying on the sidewalk.
5. Eric stayed behind, hoping to talk to his teacher.
6. Oil companies have started to mine the oil and minerals off the coast of Louisiana.
7. We are hoping to see many old friends at the reunion.
8. After landing in Richmond, we had to wait two hours for the next plane.
9. Finding new sources of water is essential if our cities are to survive.
10. Paul expected to pay his expenses by working after school.

2.16　The Appositive Phrase

An appositive is a word placed after another word to explain or identify it.

The police chief, *Carolyn Vance,* spoke to the youth group.
John Keats, *the English poet,* wrote "Ode on a Grecian Urn."

The appositive always appears after the word it explains or identifies. It is always a noun or pronoun. The word that it explains is also always a noun or pronoun.

An **appositive phrase** consists of the appositive and its modifiers, which themselves may be phrases.

> Gina's cat, *a streetwise old tiger,* is missing. (The appositive phrase identifies *cat.* The adjectives *streetwise* and *old* modify the appositive, *tiger.*)

> The Donnellys bought the house, *a split-level ranch model with a swimming pool.* (The italicized words are the appositive phrase, identifying *house.* The adjectives *split-level* and *ranch* modify the appositive, *model,* as does the adjective phrase *with a swimming pool.*)

Diagraming. The appositive is diagramed as follows:

Mary Alvarez, the new secretary, comes from El Paso.

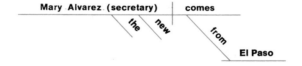

2.17 Diagraming the Simple Sentence

Meaning is conveyed in English by word-groups arranged in definite order in the sentence. Diagraming will help you see which words go together and how they are arranged.

The simple sentence is composed of subject-verb-complement. These words are placed on the base line of the diagram. The indirect object is placed below the verb.

The introductory word *There* or *Here* is placed above the base line. Also note the slant line after the linking verb.

There
Subject | Linking Verb \ Predicate Word

The subject of an imperative sentence, *you* (understood), is placed in parentheses.

(You) | Verb | Direct Object

A single-word modifier is placed on a slant line below the word it modifies. An adverb modifying an adjective or adverb is placed as shown below.

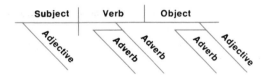

The prepositional phrase is attached to the word it modifies, as follows:

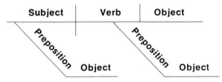

The participial phrase is shown as follows:

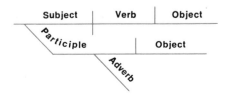

The gerund phrase is placed above the base line unless it is the object of a preposition.

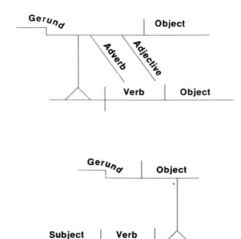

The infinitive phrase is shown in this way:

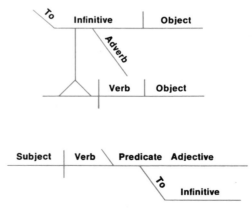

2.18 The Basic Sentence Patterns

If we examine English sentences, looking at the different orders in which words occur, we find that English sentences are based on a few ways of putting words together. We call these different word orders the **basic sentence patterns.** In this section we will discuss the most important of these patterns.

Pattern One

N	V	(ADVERB OR PREPOSITIONAL PHRASE)
The fans	cheered.	
Casey	struck	out.
Vinnie	is going	by bus.
They	should hurry.	
That movie	ended	strangely.

Pattern One sentences consist most simply of a noun (N) followed by a verb (V). Frequently, the pattern is completed by an adverb or a prepositional phrase. Verbs that occur in Pattern One sentences are *intransitive verbs.*

Note: Remember, pronouns are words used in place of nouns. They can therefore be substituted for nouns in any of these patterns.

Pattern Two

N	V	N
The choir	sang	several selections.
The pitcher	hit	a home run.
Someone	has given	the money.
Carelessness	causes	accidents.
We	should win	every game.

The noun following the verb in a Pattern Two sentence is a *direct object*. The verbs that occur in this pattern are *transitive verbs*.

Most of the thousands of transitive verbs in English occur only in Pattern Two sentences. However, some transitive verbs may occur in sentences that have two nouns following the verb. Such sentences are Pattern Three sentences.

Pattern Three

N	V	N	N
Mother	got	Sybil	that job.
Valerie	gave	us	the keys.
He	wrote	each aunt	a postcard.
Jimmy	should tell	his parents	our plans.

In Pattern Three the first noun following the verb is the *indirect object*; the second noun is the *direct object*.

Pattern Four

N	LV	N
My aunt	is	a doctor.
Both books	have become	best sellers.
Luther	remained	my friend.
They	are	exchange students.

Be, become, and *remain* are the verbs that usually appear in Pattern Four sentences. They are *linking verbs* (LV). The noun following the linking verb in a Pattern Four sentence is a *predicate noun*. The linking verbs that occur in this pattern produce sentences in which two nouns refer to the *same* person or thing.

In Pattern Two (N-V-N), the transitive verbs produce sentences in which the two nouns in each sentence refer to *different* persons or things.

In each pair of sentences below, notice how the relationship between the nouns changes when we replace a linking verb with a transitive verb:

> His sister became a doctor. **(N-LV-N)**
> His sister needed a doctor. **(N-V-N)**
>
> Fran was my friend. **(N-LV-N)**
> Fran snubbed my friend. **(N-V-N)**

Pattern Five

N	LV	ADJ
Those rocks	are	treacherous.
My overcoat	has become	quite shabby.
His mother	seems	very young.
He	remained	calm.
Her story	sounded	true.

Verbs that occur in Patterns Four and Five are *linking verbs*. There are thousands of intransitive verbs in English, but only a few words are regularly used as linking verbs. The most important are *be* (and its various forms), *become, seem,* and *remain.* The word following the linking verb is a *predicate adjective* (*ADJ*).

English sentences are seldom as simple as the basic sentences listed above. In order to convey meaning adequately, we usually need to expand the basic patterns by adding modifiers and more complicated constructions. No matter how complicated or how long a sentence becomes, however, it will always have one of the basic patterns as a foundation.

Exercise A: Identify the sentence pattern in each sentence below.

1. Our school has a rugby team.
2. Barbara smiled radiantly.
3. Ms. Tortina told the class a funny story.
4. My friends are considerate.
5. Salem is the state capital.
6. The bleachers are full now.
7. Julia mailed her parents a postcard from camp.
8. Someone must have taken my watch!
9. The spark quickly became a blaze.
10. The store detective raced onto the elevator.

Exercise B: Follow the same directions as for Exercise A.

1. The gym floor seems slippery.
2. Carole writes in a diary.
3. Juan reads rapidly.
4. Rembrandt is a famous painter.
5. That cake looks spectacular.
6. The teacher gave us a special project assignment.
7. Selina made her brother a bookcase.
8. The high school has become a familiar place.
9. The editor-in-chief wrote a controversial editorial.
10. Archaeologists find the remains of past civilizations.

Exercise C: Write three different sentences that follow each of the sentence patterns listed below.

1. Noun   Verb
2. Noun   Verb   Noun
3. Noun   Verb   Noun   Noun
4. Noun   Linking Verb   Noun
5. Noun   Linking Verb   Adjective

REVIEW: THE PARTS OF A SENTENCE This exercise is a review of Section 2. Make six columns. Head them *Subject, Verb, Direct Object, Indirect Object, Predicate Word,* and *Prepositional Phrase.* Place those parts of the following sentences in the proper columns. Some of the sentence parts may be compound.

1. Our class wrote and produced a musical.
2. My aunt in Mexico sent me a piñata and a sombrero.
3. A heavy snowfall stopped trains and buses in the city.
4. During the trial, the defendant admitted his guilt.
5. Four-person bobsledding is one event in the Olympics.
6. The magician showed Willy several card tricks.
7. The Latin class wore togas for a Roman banquet.
8. The babysitter gave the children crackers and cheese.
9. My helicopter ride was much too short.
10. Pigs and cattle were loaded onto railroad cars.
11. This cave seems eerie and hazardous.
12. A gust of wind scattered Jason's homework around the parking lot.
13. Three airplanes performed stunts for the crowd.
14. The gymnastics coach spotted Kendra during her backflip.
15. R. L. Jeffries is the supervisor at the glassworks.
16. Billie Holiday was a famous blues singer.
17. Cindy asked the veterinarian some questions about proper pet care.
18. Dad taught us a new dive.
19. Cassie seems confused about the algebra assignment.
20. Whom did their class elect for president?

3.0 Sentence and Clause

We have seen (Section 2.2) that sentences can be classified according to the purpose of the speaker: *declarative, imperative, interrogative,* and *exclamatory.* This classification is helpful in problems of punctuation.

For help in writing better sentences, there is another classification. This is the classification by form. There are three basic forms of sentences: the *simple sentence,* the *compound sentence,* and the *complex sentence.* A fourth kind, the *compound-complex sentence,* is a combination of basic forms.

3.1 The Simple Sentence

A simple sentence contains only one subject and predicate. Both the subject and the predicate may be compound.

You will recall that *compound* means having two or more similar parts.

> COMPOUND SUBJECT: The *producer* and the *playwright* argued about script changes. (The producer argued; the playwright argued.)

> COMPOUND VERB: Shakespeare *wrote* and *produced* his own plays. (Shakespeare wrote; Shakespeare produced.)

COMPOUND PREDICATE: Terry *fished all day* and *caught nothing.* (Terry fished; Terry caught.)

COMPOUND SUBJECT AND COMPOUND PREDICATE: Both *Mayor Flynn* and the *city council attended the hearings* and *defended the proposals.* (Mayor Flynn and the city council attended; Mayor Flynn and the city council defended.)

All of the preceding sentences are simple sentences. In these sentences both parts of a compound subject go with the same verb. Or both parts of a compound verb have the same subject. In each of these sentences there is only one subject-verb connection.

In the following sentence the first subject goes with the first verb, but the second subject goes with the second verb. There are two subject-verb connections. This is not a simple sentence:

The *visitors played* tennis; their *host took* a nap.

The Compound Predicate. The compound predicate is useful in writing clear, smooth sentences.

The compound predicate consists of two verbs having the same subject. At least one of the verbs has a complement.

The heavy snowfall *stalled buses* and *grounded planes.*
My uncle *bought* some *land* and *farmed it.*
The champion *waved* and *boarded* the *jet.*
The actors *bowed* and *left* the *stage.*

Exercise A: Identify the compound parts in the following sentences. Look for compound subjects, compound verbs, and compound predicates.

1. Both the manager and his assistant were injured in the crash.
2. We left the house early and walked to school.
3. The committee will hire an orchestra and arrange for decorations.

4. The stage crew designed and painted the sets.

5. Strawberries and asparagus are in season now.

6. The logs spark and sputter in the fireplace.

7. Claire read several books about Marie Curie and wrote a report about the famous chemist.

8. The attendant filled the gas tank and checked the oil.

9. The guitarist and the bass player rehearsed for the concert.

10. Hamilton and Washington wrote the Farewell Address together.

Exercise B: Follow the same directions as for Exercise A.

1. Experts examined the old paintings and declared them priceless.

2. Under the fence raced a rabbit and a dog.

3. For the parade the children decorated their bikes and wore costumes.

4. Will you and Evan do the dishes?

5. All calculators add, subtract, multiply, and divide.

6. Before recycling cans, Carolyn removes the ends and flattens the metal.

7. The general suddenly looked up and gave an order to one of the aides.

8. Bells, sirens, and whistles joined in a deafening welcome.

9. The bus skidded and whined to a stop, inches from the huge hole.

10. Thomas Jefferson mounted his horse and rode through the snow alone to his beloved home at Monticello.

3.2 The Compound Sentence

The compound sentence consists of two or more simple sentences put together.

The parts of a compound sentence are put together: (1) with a comma and a coordinating conjunction (*and, but, or, for, nor*); (2) with a semicolon.

Chris likes all outdoor sports, *but* she enjoys backpacking the most.

The Revolutionary War had been won, *but* the thirteen states were still far from united.

You can take five hours by bus, *or* you can get there in an hour by plane.

He had known the Governor well, *for* he had been her campaign manager.

Charlie could not play the guitar, *nor* could he sing.

Sally missed Prince terribly; he had been her first pet.

George watched the line intently; he expected the tuna to strike.

Conjunctive adverbs (*then, however, moreover, hence, consequently, therefore,* etc.) are also used to join the parts of a compound sentence. The conjunctive adverb is preceded by a semicolon.

They went to the stadium; *however,* the game had been rained out.

She qualified in the Olympic trials; *then* she won a gold medal.

Jamie's sweater was too small; *therefore,* he gave it away.

Diagraming. The compound sentence is diagramed on two parallel base lines as follows:

The game was close, but we finally won.

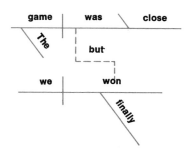

Leslie grilled the steaks; Jesse made the salad.

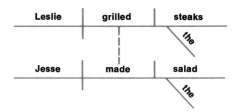

Compound Sentences and Compound Predicates. In the compound predicate, every verb has the same subject. In the compound sentence, each verb has a different subject. This difference can be seen readily in diagrams.

SIMPLE SENTENCE WITH COMPOUND PREDICATE:

Anne completed three applications and mailed them.

COMPOUND SENTENCE:

Anne completed three applications, and her brother mailed them.

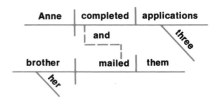

Exercise A: Decide which of these sentences are compound and which are simple. In the simple sentences, identify all compound predicates.

1. The house was small, but the grounds were spacious.
2. You can start French this year or wait until next year.
3. The huge rocket left the launching pad and vanished into the upper sky.
4. Leonardo painted only a few pictures, but they are all masterpieces.
5. Our library is small; however, it has a good collection of reference books.
6. We can take a train tonight or fly to Detroit in the morning.
7. Peter ate all of his food but complained about every bite.
8. The unemployment rate dropped in May, but it rose in June.
9. The class visited the Museum of Modern Art and spent hours studying the new paintings.
10. Stephanie was happy as a successful businessperson; her work was interesting and challenging.

Exercise B: Follow the same directions as for Exercise A.

1. The moon turns on its axis every 28 days and therefore always presents the same face to the earth.
2. Two small moons circle the planet Mars; they are thought to be hollow.
3. Does Amtrak run between Chicago and St. Louis, or was that line discontinued?
4. Several astronauts are being considered for the crew of the next space flight, but probably only one woman will be chosen.
5. New machines used in industry not only reduce back-breaking labor but also increase production.
6. There are probably rich mineral deposits at the South Pole, but they lie under hundreds of feet of ice.
7. Thousands of students attend college but do not stay to graduate.
8. After the death of a football player, Centerville dropped its program and did not start it again until last year.

9. The hotel room was luxurious, but we couldn't open the windows or turn off the lights.

10. Expecting a long-distance call, Lou sat by the telephone all evening and drove everyone else away.

3.3 The Clause

A clause is a group of words containing a verb and its subject.

According to this definition, a simple sentence is a clause. Indeed, the simple sentence is sometimes defined as consisting of one main clause. However, we shall find it simpler to use the word *clause* to name a *part* of a sentence.

Each part of a compound sentence has its own verb and subject. These parts are therefore called clauses.

Each clause in a compound sentence can be lifted out and written separately as a simple sentence.

A clause that can stand by itself as a sentence is a main clause.

We have defined a compound sentence as consisting of two or more simple sentences put together. We can now also define it as consisting of two main clauses.

A clause that cannot stand by itself as a sentence is a subordinate clause.

> s.   v.
> When he asked me . . . (What happened?)

> s.   v.
> If you don't vote . . . (Then what?)

> s.   v.
> While you were away . . . (What?)

Phrase or Clause? A clause has a subject and a verb. A phrase does not.

She saw Jack *playing in the band.* (phrase)

She met Jack *when he was playing in the band.* (clause)
　　　　　　　s.　　v.

The box *of jewels* had been stolen. (phrase)

The box *that contained the jewels* had been stolen. (clause)
　　　　　s.　　v.

Exercise: Are the italicized words in each sentence a phrase or a clause?

1. *To photograph the ocean bottom,* two women descended in a metal sphere.
2. It was hard to believe *that we would not see the coach again.*
3. Herb started off down the road, *rolling the tire ahead of him.*
4. We had arranged *to meet at the information desk.*
5. Seven women have run *for the Presidency of the United States.*
6. *After he had broken several records,* Pete Rose became the baseball hero of the year.
7. Is this the prize *for which you have been working so hard?*
8. Scientists are hopeful now *of finding cures for muscular dystrophy.*
9. *Ferociously barking and pawing at the window,* the dog attracted our attention.
10. We could not see *who was at the door.*
11. *After leaving high school,* Mark will go to a business school.
12. Washoe the ape, *who was trained by her owner,* communicates with sign language.
13. *Simple to learn and to use,* Esperanto was devised as an international language.
14. The men were losing weight, *for they had been too tired to eat properly.*
15. *Moving carefully under the ice,* the submarine inched its way to safety.

3.4 Complex Sentence

The complex sentence consists of one main clause and one or more subordinate clauses.

In a complex sentence, the subordinate clause is used as a modifier. The subordinate clause modifies a word in the main clause.

> *When you leave,* shut the door. (clause modifies *shut.*)

> *If he drops out of high school,* he will regret it later on. (clause modifies *will regret.*)

> This is the book *that you want.* (clause modifies *book.*)

In each example above, the main clause can stand as a sentence by itself: *Shut the door, He will regret it later on, This is the book.*

The subordinate clauses, however, cannot stand alone because their meaning is incomplete.

> When you leave . . . (What then?)
> If he drops out of high school . . . (What will happen?)
> that you want . . . (What is it?)

Exercise A: Find the subordinate clause in each sentence below.

1. This is the turn where the accident occurred.
2. Is this the book that you wanted?
3. Do you know who sent the flowers?
4. Turn off the lights before you go to bed.
5. Unless the rain stops, the game will be postponed.
6. Who knows where the Millers live?
7. Prices of farm products fell after the Erie Canal opened.
8. Mr. Bruce is the man who bought our house.
9. What will we do if the power fails?
10. When there is a heavy snowfall in the city, everything seems to stop.

Exercise B: Indicate whether each sentence below is simple, compound, or complex.

1. Stamp collecting is a fascinating hobby that may also be profitable.

2. The fight against tuberculosis is growing harder because the germs have become resistant to the new drugs.

3. Scientists searching for new medicines have found valuable drugs used by native tribes.

4. Puerto Rico is called a commonwealth, but just what is a commonwealth?

5. The young woman ordered a rose plant for her mother-in-law, but the mail-order company sent her a tractor instead.

6. During the long winter at the South Pole, the sun does not shine for six months.

7. Marysville won the toss and elected to kick.

8. On the second floor of the Philadelphia house where the Senate was meeting, Jefferson pieced together the bones of a prehistoric monster.

9. The plane taxied out into the takeoff position and started down the runway.

10. Everyone stopped talking when the doctor entered the room.

3.5 The Compound-Complex Sentence

A compound-complex sentence consists of two or more main clauses and one or more subordinate clauses.

The main clauses are joined by a coordinating conjunction (preceded by a comma), a conjunctive adverb (preceded by a semicolon), or by a semicolon alone. The subordinate clause modifies a word in one of the main clauses.

MAIN CLAUSE	MAIN CLAUSE	SUBORDINATE CLAUSE
It was night,	and we heard the cry of a loon	that nested by the lake.

MAIN CLAUSE	MAIN CLAUSE	SUBORDINATE CLAUSE
I will come,	and I will bring José	if he has the day off.

3.6 The Adjective Clause

The single-word adjective, the adjective phrase, and the adjective clause are used in the same way. They modify a noun or pronoun.

An adjective clause is a subordinate clause used to modify a noun or pronoun in the main clause.

Introductory Words. Most adjective clauses begin with an introductory word. There is a growing tendency, however, to use adjective clauses with no introductory word.

> This is the town *where Lincoln was born.* (*where* is an introductory word.)
>
> This is the time *when jonquils bloom.* (*when* is an introductory word.)
>
> There is the suit *I need.* (no introductory word)
> There is the suit *that I need.* (*that* is an introductory word.)
>
> The boat *you wanted* is out of stock. (no introductory word)
> The boat *that you wanted* is out of stock. (*that* is an introductory word.)

In the first two examples above, the introductory words *where* and *when* are both used within the subordinate clause as modifiers of the verb: *was born* **where;** *bloom* **when.**

Relative Pronouns. The pronouns *who, whose, whom, which,* and *that* are used to introduce adjective clauses. Used in this way, they refer to a word in the main clause and are used in place of that word. That word is the antecedent of the pronoun. It is also the word modified by the adjective clause.

> Eliza is the one *who got the most votes.*
> (*one* is the antecedent of *who* and is modified by the adjective clause.)

There goes the man *whose daughter is an astronaut.*
(*man* is the antecedent of *whose* and is modified
by the adjective clause.)

Relative humidity is the amount of water vapor *that the air contains.*
(*vapor* is the antecedent of *that* and is modified by
the adjective clause.)

An adjective clause introduced by a relative pronoun is some-times called a relative clause.

The relative pronoun has two functions. It introduces the clause, and it is used as a sentence-part within the clause.

Is this the book *that you want?*
(*that* is the direct object of *want.*)

Tina is the girl *whom he asked* to my party.
(*whom* is the direct object of *asked.*)

The letter *to which you refer* has been lost.
(*which* is the object of the preposition *to.*)

Jihan Sadat is a public figure *who shrugs off criticism.*
(*who* is the subject of *shrugs.*)

Diagraming. The adjective clause is joined to the word it modifies in the main clause. A dotted line leads from this word to the introductory word. Note that the relative pronoun is placed to show its use in the sentence.

The route that they took went through Washington.

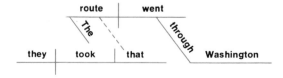

This is the spot where the plane crashed.

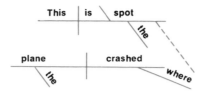

Exercise A: Find each adjective clause and the word it modifies.

1. August is the month when you can see meteors.
2. Is this the record you bought yesterday?
3. Dorothy Hamill is the American figure skater who won the gold medal.
4. This is the spot where the first state capitol stood.
5. Professor Morrison is the person to whom we wrote.
6. The aerial photographs showed buildings that no one had ever seen.
7. Many people report seeing objects that come from outer space.
8. The energy you are using came originally from the sun.
9. We need leaders who are honest and fearless.
10. What is the most embarrassing thing that ever happened to you?

Exercise B: Follow the same directions as for Exercise A.

1. Rush hour is the time when you should avoid the roads.
2. The store that sells running shoes is going out of business.
3. Scientists have invented a light that does not produce heat.
4. The trip we are planning will take us all through the West.
5. One high school, which has only 925 students, bought 10,500 paperbacks last year.
6. This is the chapter of which I was speaking.
7. Do you have everything you need for the Washington trip?
8. Here is a book of poems that you might enjoy.
9. The books that we ordered in September finally arrived.
10. The lady to whom you spoke is the director of our museum.

3.7 The Adverb Clause

The single-word adverb, the adverb phrase, and the adverb clause are all used in the same way. They are used to modify verbs, adjectives, and adverbs.

An adverb clause is a subordinate clause used to modify a verb, adjective, or adverb in the main clause.*

Adverb clauses tell *where, when, why, how, how much,* or *to what extent* about the words they modify.

ADVERB CLAUSES MODIFYING VERBS

They **put** the stop sign *where few could see it.* (where)
When the bell rings, everyone **takes** a coffee break. (when)
The Senator **talked** *as if she would run for re-election.* (how)
We **left** the beach *because we were surrounded by radios.* (why)

ADVERB CLAUSES MODIFYING ADJECTIVES

Winter seems twice as **long** *as it used to be.* (how much)

Kevin is as **funny** *as his uncle is.* (to what extent)

ADVERB CLAUSE MODIFYING AN ADVERB

Esther worked **harder** *than her sisters did.* (how much)

Subordinating Conjunctions. Every adverb clause is introduced by a subordinating conjunction. The function of this word is to show how two clauses are related. By use of the subordinating conjunction, one clause is made to tell *where, when, why, how, to what extent,* or *how much* about another.

* Some authorities suggest that an introductory adverb clause may modify an entire main clause rather than a single word in it.

When a subordinating conjunction is placed before a clause, the clause can no longer stand alone.

> Your grades are average. (*complete*)
> *If* your grades are average . . . (*incomplete*)
> *Since* your grades are average . . . (*incomplete*)
> The football season is over. (*complete*)
> *When* the football season is over . . . (*incomplete*)
> *Until* the football season is over . . . (*incomplete*)

A subordinating conjunction may be placed before either of two main clauses to tie it to the other. Which clause is subordinate depends upon the meaning the writer wants to express.

> *Although* Wade bakes delicious bread, his cakes are failures.
> *Although* Wade's cakes are failures, he bakes delicious bread.

> *Because* few people had signed up, the trip had been delayed.
> Few people had signed up, *because* the trip had been delayed.

Subordinating conjunctions can be used to show a great variety of relationships between main ideas. Choosing conjunctions carefully will enable you to express your ideas clearly and exactly.

TIME:	as, as soon as, after, before, since, until, when, whenever, while
CAUSE OR REASON:	because, since
COMPARISON:	as, as much as, than
CONDITION:	if, although, though, unless, provided
PURPOSE:	so that, in order that

Note how the meaning changes with the change of conjunctions in these sentences.

> *While* she gave the speech, she seemed confident.
> *Before* she gave the speech, she seemed confident.
> *After* she gave the speech, she seemed confident.

Elliptical Clauses. The word *elliptical* comes from *ellipsis*, which means "omission of a word." An **elliptical clause** is one from which words have been omitted.

While she is milking the cows, she sings folk songs.
While milking the cows, she sings folk songs.

When you are applying for a job, dress appropriately.
When applying for a job, dress appropriately.

Diagraming. The adverb clause is diagramed on a separate line:

When the car stopped, we lurched forward.

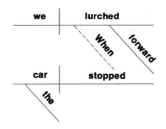

Exercise A: Find each adverb clause and the word or words it modifies.

1. When the girls returned to Paris, they sold their car.
2. As soon as the snow starts falling, the snowplows go out.
3. Whenever there is an accident, a crowd gathers.
4. While she was studying for the test, Jocelyn ate nine bags of potato chips.
5. John set the table while Martin cooked the hamburgers.
6. The stadium was hushed as Diane Pulcinski went to bat.
7. As soon as the ride started, the people were shrieking.
8. Beans grow best where the soil is sandy.
9. The people on the island are isolated until the spring thaws come.
10. Unless more funds are raised, the school will have no library.

Exercise B: Follow the same directions as for Exercise A.

1. Since this was his first meeting, Bob said very little.
2. You may return the lamp if you don't like it.
3. When the judge entered, everyone in the courtroom stood up.

4. While the car was being repaired, we walked down the road.

5. Because the snowstorm halted all buses, school was canceled.

6. Could you help me with my algebra when you have time?

7. Panamanians rejoiced when the Panama Canal treaty was signed.

8. Huckleberry Finn leaves home because his Aunt Sally wants to "civilize" him.

9. Morgan had never flown hang-gliders until he was nineteen.

10. There was no light, no sound, no movement as we approached the house.

3.8   The Noun Clause

A noun clause is a subordinate clause used as a noun.

The noun clause may be used as subject or direct object of the verb, as a predicate noun, as object of a preposition, or as an appositive.

> Officer Taylor asked *where the accident occurred.* (direct object of verb)
>
> Angela did not agree with *what José had said.* (object of preposition)
>
> Father vetoed my suggestion *that we go to the fair.* (appositive)
>
> *Who began the war* is not certain. (subject)
>
> What I'd like to know is *how this dishwasher works.* (predicate noun)

Introductory Words. As the examples above clearly show, noun clauses may be introduced by some of the same words that introduce adverb clauses: *when, where.* Used in noun clauses, these words are not regarded as subordinating conjunctions. They are merely introductory words, used as adverbs within the noun clause.

Similarly, noun clauses may be introduced by the same words used to introduce relative clauses: *who, whose, whom, which, that, when, where.* Used in noun clauses, these words are not regarded as relative pronouns, but they may serve as subjects or objects within the noun clause.

> Terry knows **where** *Henry is.* (noun clause as the direct object of *knows*)
>
> We went **where** *we could swim.* (adverb clause modifying *went*)
>
> Are you the one **who** *called me?* (adjective clause modifying *one*)
>
> **Who** *sent this package* is a mystery. (noun clause as the subject of *is*)

Many noun clauses are written without any introductory word. Every direct quotation preceded by words such as *I said, she called, Jo asked* is a noun clause without an introductory word. Every indirect quotation is a noun clause preceded by an introductory word.

> He said *that the answer was wrong.* (noun clause as the object of *said*)
>
> He said, *"The answer is wrong."* (noun clause as the object of *said*)

Diagraming. The noun clause is diagramed as shown below. Note that the use of the noun clause determines its position in the diagram.

I know that they are going.

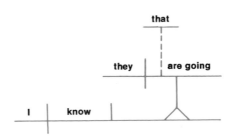

We have a job for whoever is qualified.

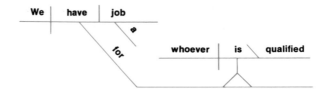

Exercise A: Identify each noun clause. Tell how it is used in the sentence.

1. Barbara would not tell us where she had been.
2. What the reporter really wanted was a mystery to us.
3. Fred was apologetic for what he had said.
4. The doctor said that Marion could get up tomorrow.
5. Do you know who invented the microscope?
6. We had no idea of what might happen.
7. The police know who wrote the threatening letters.
8. Who will win the game is anyone's guess.
9. Everyone knew that the test would be difficult.
10. We thought the day would never end.
11. What happened to the missing artist was never discovered.
12. The department will be grateful for whatever you can do.
13. You can't get what you want without hard work.
14. We did not know Jim had such powers of concentration.
15. Is your new job what you expected?

Exercise B: In each sentence below, a subordinate clause is italicized. Tell what kind of clause each is.

1. Literature *that describes future events* is called science fiction.
2. *Whoever returns the stolen wallet* will be rewarded.
3. *When the moon moves between the sun and the earth,* a solar eclipse occurs.
4. Did you ask *what time it is?*

5. One sport *that is very popular in the Midwest* is ice hockey.

6. *If the rain continues,* the baseball field will be swamped.

7. Some of the tools *that the mountain climber uses* are picks, ropes, and crampons.

8. Some students drop out of school *because they are not motivated.*

9. The gymnast felt *that her timing was off.*

10. The laborers returned to work *after the strike was over.*

11. Ms. McKillip emphasized *what she expected of her students.*

12. Mack Sennett, *who developed the Keystone Kops,* was a pioneer in film comedy.

13. Multicolored leaves drifted to the pavement *as a brisk breeze brushed the countryside.*

14. May is the month *when most tulips bloom.*

15. Mark Twain said *that cauliflower is just cabbage with a college education.*

3.9 The Sentence Redefined

We are now ready to complete the definition of a sentence that we started in Sections 2.1 and 2.3. We may begin by noting once again the differences between phrases, clauses, and sentences.

A **phrase** is a group of words used within a sentence as a single part of speech. A phrase may be used as a noun, a verb, an adjective, or an adverb. It does *not* contain a subject and a verb.

A **clause** is a group of words that contains a subject and its verb. It may be used within the sentence as a noun, an adjective, or an adverb.

PHRASE: Walking by the lake . . .

CLAUSE: When we were walking by the lake . . .

A main clause can stand by itself as a sentence. A subordinate clause cannot stand by itself.

MAIN CLAUSE   MAIN CLAUSE

The well was dry, and there was no sign of rain.

The well was dry. (*complete*)
There was no sign of rain. (*complete*)

SUBORDINATE CLAUSE   MAIN CLAUSE

Although the well was dry, there was no sign of rain.

There was no sign of rain. (*complete*)
Although the well was dry . . . (*incomplete*)

Clauses and phrases are sentence parts. The sentence itself is not part of any other grammatical construction. (The paragraph is not a grammatical construction.) Our complete definition of a sentence, then, is in three parts:

A sentence is a group of words that

1. expresses a complete thought,
2. contains a subject and verb,
3. is not part of any other grammatical construction.

REVIEW: SENTENCE AND CLAUSE This exercise is a review of Section 3. Identify each sentence as simple, compound, or complex. In addition, find each subordinate clause and tell what kind it is.

1. Blaine demonstrated how she weaves cloth on a loom.
2. The car screeched as it pulled away.
3. Black-and-white photographs can be very dramatic.
4. Are you on the swimming team, or are you playing basketball this season?
5. A pilot must consider temperature, wind, and visibility conditions.
6. Darryl dropped the bag that contained two dozen eggs.
7. The picnic will be canceled if there is rain.

8. Some shoppers hurried through the aisles, but others browsed slowly.

9. While the band members marched, they formed designs on the field.

10. Bert fed the horse oats, and then he placed a blanket on its back.

11. The audience cheered wildly when Steve Martin appeared on stage.

12. What annoys Mr. Berman most is tardiness.

13. The Chicago Fire of 1871 destroyed much of the city.

14. Unless it is threatened, an alligator usually avoids people and does not attack.

15. Joshua wants to drive a car, but he is too young.

16. While everyone slept, snow fell.

17. The man confessed to the crime, and he was jailed.

18. A cobra attacks with poison, but a python attacks with constriction.

19. The police officer stopped the boys and warned them not to hitchhike.

20. The Gutenberg Bible was the first book that was ever printed.

4.0 Complete Sentences

Uncompleted sentences are more often a problem in writing than in speaking. If you use an uncompleted sentence in speaking with someone face-to-face, he or she can interrupt and ask you what you mean. In writing, you usually do not have a second chance.

The sentence is the best means you have for getting your meaning across to someone else in writing. Through study and practice, you can learn to write effective and forceful sentences. To write effectively, however, you must learn to avoid two kinds of sentence error: (1) the sentence fragment, and (2) the run-on sentence. Both of these errors cause confusion for the reader.

4.1 Fragments Resulting from Incomplete Thought

An uncompleted sentence is called a **sentence fragment.** It is only a part, or fragment, of a sentence.

You can think much faster than you can write. Many of your sentence errors, if you make them, happen because your mind has raced on ahead of your hand. You have started to write a second thought before you have finished writing the first. Or, perhaps in haste, you have left out a key word necessary for a complete sentence. Suppose you intended to say something like this:

In 1939, Ike was a colonel. After war broke out, he soon became commander of American forces in Europe. He later led all Allied forces.

In the hurry to get on with your writing, however, what you put down was something like this:

In 1939, Ike was a colonel. After he soon became commander of American forces in Europe. He later led all Allied forces.

The second group of words is not a sentence. It causes confusion. The reader may suppose that you meant to say that Ike was a colonel after he became commander of American forces in Europe.

Exercise A: Find the sentence fragments. Add the words needed to make each fragment a sentence.

1. Then came Tom. Wearing a wide-brimmed hat and a false mustache
2. A program just like several others
3. After reaching the top of the hill
4. Most of the great books available in inexpensive paperbacks
5. Mr. Walters, one of the oldest residents in the city
6. The huge trucks rolling along the nation's highways all night
7. Finally, in a corner of the garage, the missing wrenches
8. Nothing in the newspapers about the robbery
9. There is a reward. Anyone who finds the valuable bracelet
10. After working hard all day, a little relaxation

Exercise B: Three of the following groups of words are sentences. The rest are fragments. Find the fragments and add words needed to make them sentences.

1. Ghost towns all across the country
2. Pithole, Pennsylvania, one of the most famous
3. It flourished for a brief ten years

4. For a time, 20,400 people in the town
5. Everyone left quickly when the oil wells dried up
6. Elsewhere ghost towns in timber country
7. Modern ghost towns in the iron-mining regions of Minnesota
8. The most famous of all in the mining sections of the West
9. Houses full of furniture and offices with papers in the desks
10. Wherever the resources gave out, there are ghost towns

4.2 Fragments Resulting from Incorrect Punctuation

The first word of a sentence begins with a capital letter. The sentence is closed by a punctuation mark: *period, question mark,* or *exclamation mark.* A great many sentence fragments are written simply because the writer inserts a period and a capital letter too soon. This error is called a **period fault.**

FRAGMENT: *Before accepting the invitation.* He called his wife.

SENTENCE: Before accepting the invitation, he called his wife.

FRAGMENT: The team was still in the huddle. *When time ran out.*

SENTENCE: The team was still in the huddle when time ran out.

FRAGMENT: *At the beginning of this century.* Motoring was an adventure.

SENTENCE: At the beginning of this century, motoring was an adventure.

Exercise A: Find the fragments. Correct them by changing the punctuation or by adding the words needed to make a sentence.

1. Everyone liked the banana cream pie. Except me.
2. Once again the sirens wailed. Another bad accident on the highway.

3. Glenn has been interested in music. For many years.
4. We finally arrived. Just before midnight.
5. Before signing the treaty. The President said a few words.
6. Please send your order. As soon as possible.
7. Linda joined the debate team. Hoping to improve her skills.
8. The average American teen-ager watches TV. Almost 22 hours each week.
9. The instructor taught yoga three days a week. From 9:00 to 10:30 A.M.
10. Quarterback Ken Stabler, a leader in pass completions. Plays for the Oakland Raiders.

Exercise B: Follow the same directions as for Exercise A.

1. Did you finish your project? Before the deadline?
2. Larry sold his bike. And his tape recorder.
3. The haystack caught fire. Then the barn.
4. An article rated the top ten roller coasters. Including the Tidal Wave at Great America.
5. Sixteen ushers were hired. To work during the Eagles concert.
6. Alice played the piano effortlessly. A natural talent.
7. Skiing on snow-covered mountains. A thrilling experience.
8. The plane, ready for take-off. Taxied down the runway.
9. The truck had slid into the ditch. Scattering eggs all over.
10. Katherine Graham, publisher of the *Washington Post*. A widely read newspaper.

4.3 Phrases as Fragments

You know that a phrase is a group of words that does not contain a verb and its subject. A phrase, therefore, cannot be a sentence by itself. It is a *part* of a sentence.

You are not likely to mistake a prepositional phrase for a complete sentence. If you write a long prepositional phrase or a series of phrases as a sentence, it is probably because you have punctuated incorrectly.

FRAGMENT: *In the first place.* He has had no experience
in public office.

SENTENCE: In the first place, he has had no experience
in public office.

You are more likely to mistake a verbal phrase for a complete sentence. This error occurs because verbals look like verbs and function somewhat like verbs. Like verbs, they may be modified by adverbs. They may be followed by objects or predicate words. They are not complete verbs, however, and they cannot be used as the main verb of a sentence.

The most troublesome verbals are those that end in *-ing.* All gerunds and present participles end in *-ing.* You will avoid many sentence errors if you will remember this fact:

No word ending in *-ing* can be a verb unless it is a one-syllable word like *sing, ring,* or *bring.*

If an *-ing* word is preceded by *is, are, was,* or some other form of *be,* the two words together are a verb.

PARTICIPLE	COMPLETE VERB
reading	is reading
running	had been running
studying	were studying

A long infinitive phrase may sometimes be mistaken for a complete sentence. Such a phrase sounds like a sentence since it often has everything that a sentence requires except a subject.

INCORRECT: Ray has a plan. To go to Greece.

CORRECT: Ray has a plan. His scheme is to go to Greece.

INCORRECT: Vera was overjoyed. To be one of the top
contenders for a National Merit Scholarship.

CORRECT: Vera was overjoyed to be one of the top contenders
for a National Merit Scholarship.

A noun and an appositive phrase are sometimes written incorrectly as a complete sentence. Although the combination may seem like a sentence, it lacks a verb. Look at the following example.

FRAGMENT: The rocket, *the heaviest ever launched.*

SENTENCE: The rocket, the heaviest ever launched, roared toward the moon.

SENTENCE: The rocket was the heaviest ever launched.

Exercise A: Rewrite the groups of words beside each number below to make a complete sentence. You may need to add words in some instances.

1. Margo arranged with the band leader. To play an extra hour.
2. The leader of the expedition. A scientist of wide experience.
3. Studying the ocean as a source of food and minerals.
4. We had seen the program before. A fascinating explanation of sound waves.
5. Bases loaded with Steve Garvey at bat.
6. Jane delighted with the chance to visit Hawaii.
7. The reporter asked Rep. Crane. About running for President.
8. Pete and his friends busy making plans for the hike.
9. Sally has a great ambition. To become a surgeon.
10. Was *The Thorn Birds* made into a movie? Starring Robert Redford?

Exercise B: Follow the same directions as for Exercise A.

1. The newspaper story, an unfair statement of what had happened.
2. We waited in line. To buy tickets for the Barry Manilow concert.
3. The two books, one a true story and the other a fictional account of Frémont's expedition.
4. The *Mary Deare* found drifting with no crew aboard.
5. The increasing need for more food for the world's population.
6. The boy told his story. Expecting no one to believe him.
7. The class adviser arranged for a bus. To take the group to the contest.
8. The Rose Bowl, the Gator Bowl, the Sun Bowl, the Orange Bowl, and the Cotton Bowl. Only a few of football's "bowls."
9. The unhappy motorist searching her pockets for her license.
10. The book an account of how the Spanish Armada was defeated.

4.4 Clauses as Fragments

A subordinate clause cannot stand alone as a sentence. (See Section 3.3.) A sentence may be changed into a subordinate clause by having a subordinating conjunction placed before it.

SENTENCE: We were paddling the canoes upstream.

SUBORDINATE CLAUSE: As we were paddling the canoes upstream . . .

Writers sometimes mistakenly place a period before or after a subordinate clause as though it were a sentence.

INCORRECT: When we saw the smoke. We leaped on our horses.

CORRECT: When we saw the smoke, we leaped on our horses.

INCORRECT: Richard was excited. Because he was going to Colorado.

CORRECT: Richard was excited because he was going to Colorado.

Exercise A: Rewrite the word groups below to eliminate the fragments.

1. Beth is the only one. Who knew the answers.
2. The trapper stayed in the mountains. Until the first snow fell.
3. She took the old painting. Since nobody else wanted it.
4. Although the book is unusually long. It is worth reading.
5. There will be a big celebration in Pittsburgh. When the Pirates win the pennant.
6. Linda is studying forestry. Because she likes outdoor life.
7. Preparing a report on the rock collection that we had started the year before.
8. Ruth decided to buy the red coat. Even though her mother disliked it.
9. We will be glad to see you. Whenever you can come.

10. In the camp, the explorers checked their pitons. Which are spikes used for climbing steep rock faces.

Exercise B: In this exercise you will find examples of many kinds of fragments. Change them into sentences.

1. Thomas Jefferson wrote the Declaration of Independence. At the age of thirty-three.

2. A mother rhinoceros always keeps her baby ahead of her. As she walks along.

3. India has over two hundred languages. And many religions.

4. My library at home contains many paperbacks. Also books with beautiful, gold-tooled leather covers.

5. Ernest Hemingway wrote "The Killers." One of the most famous short stories of our time.

6. In a full orchestra, there are four families of instruments. Stringed instruments, woodwinds, brasses, and percussion instruments.

7. She is one of those overly cautious people. Always raising objections.

8. Northern Canada is a vast Arctic waste. Has a few people, many caribou, and numerous fur-bearing animals.

9. The needle of a compass always points north. Because it is attracted by a center of magnetic force near the North Pole.

10. Edison's first electric light burned for forty hours. The average life of a 100-watt bulb today over 750 hours.

4.5 Run-on Sentences

A **run-on sentence** is two or more sentences written as though they were one sentence. That is, the writer fails to use a period or other end mark at the end of each sentence.

RUN-ON: Carlotta went fishing last month she caught a marlin.
CORRECT: Carlotta went fishing last month. She caught a marlin.
RUN-ON: Pedro went to the clinic he had cut his arm.
CORRECT: Pedro went to the clinic. He had cut his arm.

The most common run-on sentence error is the joining of two sentences by a comma. This error is called the **comma fault.**

COMMA FAULT:	The club held a car wash, it was a great success.
CORRECT:	The club held a car wash. It was a great success.
COMMA FAULT:	The critic read the book, she then wrote a review.
CORRECT:	The critic read the book. She then wrote a review.

In all of the foregoing examples, notice that the two sentences are closely related and that the second sentence begins with a personal pronoun: *it, he, she.* Watch for situations like these in your own writing and avoid the comma fault.

4.6 Avoiding the Run-on Sentence

There is no objection to joining two or more closely related statements into one sentence. In fact, it is often better to join them than to write them separately. There are three ways to join closely related sentences to make a compound sentence: (1) with a comma and a coordinating conjunction; (2) with a semicolon; (3) with a semicolon and a conjunctive adverb.

RUN-ON:	Neal has two choices. He can play college football, he can sign with the Yankees.
CORRECT:	Neal has two choices. He can play college football, or he can sign with the Yankees.
RUN-ON:	Churchill led England through the agonizing war years, then he was defeated in the first postwar election.
CORRECT:	Churchill led England through the agonizing war years; then he was defeated in the first postwar election.

RUN-ON: The demonstration was orderly, consequently, the
          mayor heard our plea.
CORRECT: The demonstration was orderly; consequently, the
          mayor heard our plea.

Note: When a conjunctive adverb such as *consequently, however, moreover, therefore,* or *nevertheless* introduces a second main clause, it is preceded by a semicolon. Usually, it is followed by a comma.

Exercise A: Correct each of the following run-on sentences in one of these ways: (1) by using a period and a capital letter; (2) by using a semicolon; or (3) by using a comma and *and, but,* or *or.*

1. We flew to Idaho Falls, then we took a bus to the lake.
2. Andy tries to practice the flute every day, however, he doesn't always have time.
3. Ms. Albrecht has a new car, it is a Plymouth Horizon.
4. Cooking a turkey takes several hours, it has to be started early.
5. Howard University is small, nevertheless, it has an excellent faculty.
6. The station was crowded, we nearly missed our train.
7. It isn't a new dress, I wore it to the Christmas party.
8. Pat hasn't called, he must be lost.
9. We organized a benefit dance, however, the band never showed up.
10. Mom painted the chairs, they look very nice.
11. Mark is color-blind, therefore, his wife always buys his ties.
12. You take the general course first, then you can specialize.
13. The fog was very heavy, no planes left the airport.
14. Larry started to cross the street, then the light changed.
15. Jim hesitated too long, consequently, he missed his chance.

Exercise B: The first part of a sentence is given on each line below. Add a second main clause, starting it with the word in parentheses. If the word is a conjunctive adverb, place a semicolon before it and a comma after it. If the word is a personal pronoun, use a semicolon or use a comma with a coordinating conjunction.

1. The deer started to cross the road (then)
2. The author of the article is Woody Allen (he)
3. We were not expecting you today (however)
4. The road was strewn with heavy branches (it)
5. The class had had plenty of time to study (nonetheless)
6. Jan and Sylvia were late to class (they)
7. The driver had simply been going too fast (moreover)
8. The town's population has been declining (consequently)
9. Eve will be married next summer (she)
10. Willy could scarcely lift the package (it)
11. First you send for an application blank (then)
12. We are rapidly exhausting some of our natural resources (for example)
13. Most words have more than one meaning (therefore)
14. You have seen this book before (it)
15. In the clear desert air, the mountains look very close (they)

Exercise C: Copy this paragraph, correcting the run-on sentences.

None of us could believe that Harry was guilty, he had never been known to do anything dishonest. He had always been careful to give customers the exact change, yet he was now charged with pilfering the cash register at his checkout counter. The manager himself usually picked up the extra cash twice a day, however, on Thursday he waited until the store closed. He put Harry's cash in a separate bag, then he locked it up in the safe. When he counted it the next morning, it was ten dollars short. He accused Harry of pocketing the money, however, Harry denied the charge. He thought for a while, then he asked to count the money. The manager agreed, he stood beside Harry while he counted. Harry went through each stack of bills slowly, he found the ten dollars. Two ten-dollar bills had stuck together. The manager and his assistant apologized, they even let Harry pick up the cash from the checkout counters the next week to show that they trusted him.

REVIEW: COMPLETE SENTENCES This exercise is a review of Section 4. In this exercise, you will find fragments and run-ons. Rewrite them to make complete sentences.

1. The campers pitched their tent, they had found a perfect spot.

2. They hung provisions from a tree. To prevent animals from getting the food.

3. Jeanne's favorite foods are spaghetti, steak, and ice cream. Dripping with chocolate sauce.

4. Feeling happy about his high grades in math this semester.

5. Jon practices karate, his sister is an instructor.

6. Lee has tickets to the Superbowl, it will be held in Miami.

7. The article that I read in *Rolling Stone* about Linda Ronstadt.

8. Would you like to appear on a TV talk show? Or on a game show?

9. Rosemary felt strange and lonely in her new school. Which was very large.

10. The Lindsays have built an underground home. Because it will conserve heating energy.

11. Lillian Hellman, who wrote novels and plays.

12. Drew was superstitious, he always avoided the number thirteen.

13. Chris Evert began training as a tennis player when she was very young, her father was her first coach.

14. Mr. and Mrs. Salido restore antique autos, then they display them at parades and fairs.

15. Kelp is a food source, it is plentiful and nutritious.

16. Calligraphy, the art of handwriting.

17. Several schools are closing, they have too few students.

18. During the last century. Steamboats traveled the Mississippi River.

19. Robinson Crusoe, a famous literary character. He was shipwrecked.

20. Having no permanent home. The workers followed the harvests, they lived in a bus.

5.0 Agreement of Subject and Verb

In grammar the word *agreement* means "likeness." To make two words agree is to make them alike in some respect.

A common error in American speech is the failure to make subject and verb agree (*they was* instead of *they were*). Errors of agreement in speaking are sometimes difficult to avoid. In writing, however, these errors should be easier to avoid because the writer always has the time and opportunity to revise his or her work before presenting it to a reader.

5.1 Subject-Verb Agreement in Number

There are two numbers in grammar: **singular** and **plural.** A word is singular in number if it refers to one person or thing. A word is plural if it refers to more than one person or thing.

Except for *be*, English verbs show a difference between singular and plural only in the third person and only in the present tense. The third person singular present form ends in *s*.

$$
\left.\begin{array}{l} \text{I} \\ \text{you} \\ \text{we} \\ \text{they} \end{array}\right] \text{see} \qquad \left.\begin{array}{l} \text{he} \\ \text{she} \\ \text{it} \end{array}\right] \text{sees}
$$

The verb *be* presents several special problems in agreement. First, the second person pronoun *you* is always used with the plural form of the verb: *you are, you were.* Second, the difference between singular and plural is shown in the past tense as well as in the present tense.

SINGULAR	PLURAL	PRESENT TENSE	PAST TENSE
I *was*	we *were*	I *am*	we *were*
you *were*	you *were*	you *are*	you *were*
he, she, it *was*	they *were*	he, she, it *is*	they *were*

The most common errors with *be* are *you was, we was, they was.*

A singular verb is used with a singular subject.
A plural verb is used with a plural subject.

The subject determines whether the verb is singular or plural. The verb does not agree with any other part of the sentence.

The cat (singular) *likes* liver.
The cats (plural) *like* liver.
The teacher (singular) *works* hard.
The teachers (plural) *work* hard.

Note: A verb also agrees with its subject in *person.* When there are two or more subjects that differ in person (joined by *or* or *nor*), the verb agrees with the subject nearest to it.

I *live* on a cattle ranch.
Britt *lives* in an apartment building.
Neither Fred nor I *play* chess.

5.2 Words Between Subject and Verb

The verb agrees only with its subject. Occasionally, a word with a different number from that of the subject occurs between the subject and the verb. This word usually has no effect upon the number of the verb even though it is closer to the verb than the subject is.

> The *revolution*, led by a group of guerillas, *has* been won.
> (*revolution* is the subject.)
> *One* of his classmates *is* a guide at the United Nations.
> (*One* is the subject.)
> The *Congress* of the United States *is* in session.
> (*Congress* is the subject.)
> The *pears* on that old tree *are* not edible.
> (*pears* is the subject.)

The words *with, together with, along with, as well as, in addition to,* are prepositions. The objects of these prepositions have no effect upon the number of the verb.

> The *President*, together with his aides, *was* studying the crisis.
> (*President* is the subject.)
> Your *dress*, as well as your manner, *is* important.
> (*dress* is the subject.)
> The *singer*, along with her band, *is* on tour for six months.
> (*singer* is the subject.)

Exercise: Choose the standard form of the verb for each sentence.

1. When (was, were) you at the doctor's office?
2. Is it true that one of the passengers (was, were) killed?
3. (Is, Are) the book reports due this week or next?
4. The teacher, as well as the class, (was, were) surprised by Ronny's report.
5. The pilot, in addition to the crew, (has, have) your comfort and safety in mind.
6. The age of the huge sequoias (is, are) hard to believe.
7. The high cost of repairs always (comes, come) as a surprise.
8. The lights in the store window (is, are) turned off at midnight.
9. The decision of the umpires (was, were) hotly disputed.
10. The danger of floods on the Ohio and Allegheny Rivers (has, have) been exaggerated.

11. The president of the company, along with her secretary, (plans, plan) to fly to Boston.

12. The contestants in the skateboarding contest (warms, warm) up before the start of the event.

13. Only one of these old transistor radios (works, work).

14. The scientist's report, together with the photographs, (is, are) very convincing.

15. The older members of the local school board (wants, want) to build a new school.

16. The lights in the valley down below (looks, look) like tiny jewels.

17. The co-captains of our team (has, have) a special responsibility.

18. (Was, Were) you at home all day?

19. The aim of the debates (is, are) to inform the voters.

20. The sale of the school yearbooks (has, have) been disappointing.

5.3 Indefinite Pronouns

Some indefinite pronouns are always singular. Others are always plural. Some may be either singular or plural.

SINGULAR			PLURAL
each	everyone	anyone	several
either	everybody	someone	few·
neither	no one	somebody	both
one	nobody		many

Each of the candidates *has* criticized spending.
Neither of the buses *was* full.
Everybody in the fields *was* working.
Several in this class *are* good writers.
Few in the student council *have* been re-elected.
Both of the quarterbacks *were* injured.

SINGULAR OR PLURAL

some	all	most
none	any	

Some, all, most, none, and *any* are singular when they refer to a quantity. They are plural when they refer to a number of individual items.

> *Some* of the cream *was* sour. (quantity)
> *Some* of the buildings *were* being demolished. (number)
>
> *Most* of the forest *was* saved from fire. (quantity)
> *Most* of our friends *are* going to the movie. (number)
>
> *All* of the turkey *was* eaten in two days. (quantity)
> *All* of the English classes *are* entering the writing
>   contest. (number)

Exercise: Choose the standard form of the verb for each sentence.

1. Either of these hats (suits, suit) you.
2. Most of the television programs (is, are) boring.
3. Not one of the papers (has, have) spelled my name correctly.
4. Neither of the drivers (was, were) hurt in the accident.
5. One of the violins (is, are) playing off key.
6. Each of the new cars (comes, come) equipped with safety belts.
7. (Has, Have) either of the buses left yet?
8. Obviously, one of the witnesses (was, were) not telling the truth.
9. Some of the teams (has, have) new uniforms.
10. The old houses in this block (is, are) being torn down.
11. Everyone in the stands (was, were) sure a touchdown had been scored.
12. Few in this school (knows, know) about Mr. Moore's trouble.
13. One of the boats (seems, seem) to have a leak.
14. It was reported that neither of the bridges (was, were) safe.
15. The pilot discovered that one of the engines (was, were) not working right.
16. Each of the balloons (carries, carry) scientific instruments.
17. Everyone in the pictures (is, are) grinning foolishly.
18. Neither of these patterns (is, are) what I want.
19. Several of the listeners (has, have) telephoned the studio.
20. (Has, Have) either of the candidates promised lower taxes?

5.4 Compound Subjects

Compound subjects joined by *and* are plural.*

Overloaded circuits and faulty wiring *cause* fires.

Singular words joined by *or, nor, either-or, neither-nor* to form a compound subject are singular.

Neither your grammar nor your punctuation *is* perfect.
Either Shirley or Pat *has* your baseball.
Is Joe or Olga *baby-sitting* after school?

When a singular word and a plural word are joined by *or* or *nor* to form a compound subject, the verb agrees with the subject that is nearer to it.

Neither the police nor the suspect *wants* to make a statement.
     (*suspect* is closer to the verb than *police*.)
A novel or two plays *meet* the reading requirements.
Neither the songs nor the singer *pleases* him.

Exercise A: Find the errors in subject-verb agreement in these sentences. Write the sentences correctly. Two of the sentences are correct.

1. Neither the train nor the airlines run on schedule in bad weather.
2. The chairs and the table was loaded with packages.
3. Neither the gloves nor the sweater were the right size.
4. Either Cybil or Jeff have been here.
5. The gloves and the hat is the same color.
6. Either pen or pencil is acceptable.
7. Two books and a notebook is sitting on the desk.
8. The lifeguard or the swimming coach are always on duty.
9. Neither the newspapers nor the radio have reported the story.
10. Either the meat or the potatoes is burning.

---

* If the words making up the compound subject are habitually used together to refer to a single thing, the subject may be used with a singular verb: *bread and butter, macaroni and cheese,* etc.

Exercise B: Follow the same directions as for Exercise A.

1. Have either Mr. Barnes or Ms. Brown arrived yet?
2. Neither the doctor nor her nurse were at the office.
3. Two squirrels and a jackrabbit is all we saw.
4. Both skill and constant practice go into the making of a champion.
5. Neither the French fries nor the hamburger were hot.
6. Sandwiches or soup are your only choice.
7. Was the governor or her aide interviewed?
8. Neither the guard nor the police officer were really on the job.
9. Either Jack or his sister have your books.
10. Neither the audience nor the actors was aware of the trouble backstage.

5.5 Subject Following Verb

The most difficult agreement problem in speech arises when the subject follows the verb. The speaker must think ahead to the subject in order to decide whether the verb is to be singular or plural.

This problem arises in sentences beginning with *There* and *Here*. It also arises in questions beginning with *who, why, where, what, how.*

NONSTANDARD: Here's the skis for Kay.
STANDARD: Here *are* the skis for Kay.

NONSTANDARD: There's four letters for you.
STANDARD: There *are* four letters for you.

NONSTANDARD: Who's the three boys at the door?
STANDARD: Who *are* the three boys at the door?

NONSTANDARD: What's the amendments to the constitution?
STANDARD: What *are* the amendments to the constitution?

NONSTANDARD: From out of the blue *comes* three jets.
STANDARD: From out of the blue *come* three jets.

5.6 Predicate Words

The linking verb agrees with its subject, *not* with the predicate word.

NONSTANDARD: Hamburgers *is* his favorite food.
STANDARD: Hamburgers *are* his favorite food.

NONSTANDARD: Martha's main interest *are* horses.
STANDARD: Martha's main interest *is* horses.

NONSTANDARD: Money and power *is* their only aim.
STANDARD: Money and power *are* their only aim.

5.7 *Don't* and *Doesn't*

The word *does* and the contraction *doesn't* are used with singular nouns and with the pronouns *he, she,* and *it*. The word *do* and the contraction *don't* are used with plural nouns and with the pronouns *I, we, you,* and *they*.

DOES, DOESN'T	DO, DON'T
the law does	the laws do
he doesn't	we don't
she doesn't	you don't
it doesn't	they don't

Exercise: Choose the standard form from the two in parentheses.

1. (Where's, Where are) the stack of papers I put on the desk?
2. (Doesn't, Don't) the wind sound wild tonight?
3. (Here's, Here are) the books you lent to Robin.
4. (What's, What are) the names of the mountain ranges in California?
5. It seems that there (was, were) two men named Clyde Smith.
6. Hard work and ambition (is, are) not the answer.
7. Success and fame (was, were) Wilson's goal.

8. The leader of the expedition (doesn't, don't) dare to take chances.

9. Sunny days and a beautiful beach (is, are) the town's claim to fame.

10. Up the steps (moves, move) the procession.

11. (Doesn't, Don't) the bus stop at this corner?

12. Protein and fats (is, are) the great dietary need in India.

13. (There's, There are) two good motels right outside of town.

14. Down into the cave (goes, go) Cousteau and Didi.

15. The wax on the floors (makes, make) them dangerously slippery.

16. The biggest difficulty (is, are) the inexperience and indifference of the workers.

17. Through this door (passes, pass) the lawmakers of our nation.

18. The expedition's task (was, were) to establish a base camp and to begin scientific observations.

19. (Where's, Where are) the people who are coming to help us?

20. (What's, What are) the weather predictions for this week?

5.8 Collective Nouns

A collective noun names a group of people or things: *family, choir, crew, herd, faculty.*

When the writer refers to a group acting together as one unit, the collective noun is used with a singular verb. When the writer refers to the individuals in the group acting separately, one by one, the collective noun is used with a plural verb.

> The team *was* the best in the history of the school.
>   (united action)
> The team *were* putting on their uniforms. (separate actions)
>
> The council *is* in emergency session. (united action)
> The council *were* debating the proposals. (separate actions)

Once the writer decides whether the collective noun is a unit or a group of individuals, he or she must abide by that choice. Later in the same sentence the writer may not use a verb or pronoun of different number.

NONSTANDARD: The Senate *has* (singular) changed *their* (plural) rules.

STANDARD: The Senate *has* changed *its* rules.

5.9   Nouns Plural in Form

Some nouns are plural in form but are regarded as singular in meaning. That is, they end in *s* as most plural nouns do, but they do not stand for more than one thing: *news, mumps, molasses.* Therefore, they are used with a singular verb.

There are many words ending in *-ics* that may be either singular or plural: *economics, athletics, civics, politics.* These words are singular when they are used to refer to a school subject, a science, or a general practice. When singular in meaning, they are not usually preceded by *the, his, her, some, all,* or singular modifiers.

Ethics *is* important in the study of religion and
   philosophy. (singular)
The council's ethics in this matter *are* questionable. (plural)
Politics *is* a fascinating game. (singular)
His politics *involve* only a struggle for power. (plural)

5.10   Titles and Groups of Words

The title of a book, play, story, film, musical composition, or other work of art is used with a singular verb. The name of a country is used with a singular verb. Such words, even though they may be plural in form, refer to a single thing.

The Philippines *is* made up of 7,083 islands and islets.
All the President's Men was produced by Robert Redford.
"War of the Worlds" *was* written by H. G. Wells.
The United Nations *is* discussing the problem.
Vivaldi's "The Four Seasons" *was* played at the concert.

Any group of words referring to a single thing or thought is used with a singular verb.

What we need *is* votes.
"Because I said so" is a popular phrase with many people.

5.11 Words of Amount and Time

Words or phrases that express periods of time, fractions, weights, measurements, and amounts of money are usually regarded as singular.

Ten dollars *is* too much to pay.
Two-thirds of the money *has* been raised.
Five hours *seems* a long time for that trip.
One hundred pounds of bird seed *is* ridiculous.
Ten yards of curtain material *was* not enough.

If a prepositional phrase with a plural object falls between the subject and the verb, the verb is singular if its subject is considered as a single thing or thought. The verb is plural if its subject is felt to be plural.

Five kilograms of apples *is* plenty.
Five of the bikes *are* missing.

Exercise: Choose the standard form from the two forms given in parentheses.

1. On their hours off duty, the crew (was, were) not allowed to leave the ship.
2. Making their way slowly up the cliff, the relief party (was, were) nearly at the ledge.
3. Next year, civics (is, are) to be taught in the ninth grade.

4. Politics (is, are) my aunt's hobby.

5. What we call politics (is, are) necessary in our form of government.

6. The East Indies (was, were) a source of European wealth.

7. All that we need (is, are) time and money.

8. Two-thirds of the crop (was, were) not even harvested.

9. Two-thirds of the students (wants, want) a real weekly paper.

10. Six quarts of milk (is, are) what we ordered.

11. Athletics (is, are) taking too much of Harry's time.

12. With its new plays, the team (was, were) confident of winning.

13. Economics (was, were) once known as the dismal science.

14. At its meetings, the group (sees, see) movies.

15. The United States (has, have) started explorations beneath the earth's crust.

16. Pneumatics (deals, deal) with the properties of air and other gases.

17. Two thousand dollars (is, are) a lot to pay for a used car.

18. Sixteen hours on the bus (was, were) too much for us.

19. "By the Waters of Babylon" (is, are) a thought-provoking story.

20. One of the lifeboats (has, have) sunk.

5.12 Relative Pronouns

A relative pronoun stands in place of its antecedent (the word to which it refers). If that antecedent is plural, the relative pronoun is plural. If the antecedent is singular, the relative pronoun is singular.

A relative pronoun agrees with its antecedent in number.

When a relative pronoun is used as subject of the verb in the relative clause, the number of the verb depends upon the number of the pronoun's antecedent.

They are the *candidates* (plural) who (plural) *have* been elected.

Fay is the *girl* (singular) who (singular) *manages* the store.

King is one of those *dogs* who *are* always chasing cars.
  (*dogs* are always chasing cars.)

Ms. Foss is the only *one* of the teachers who *has* a master's
  degree. (Only *one* has a master's degree.)

The problem of agreement arises in the last two sentences because there are two words, either of which *might* be the antecedent of the relative pronoun. Usually the meaning of the sentence shows which word *is* the antecedent.

Exercise A: Choose the standard form from the two forms given.

  1. Good running shoes are ones that (has, have) firm support.
  2. Those are the trees that (produces, produce) juicy apples.
  3. This is the only one of the books that (is, are) worth reading.
  4. James is the only one in the class who (has, have) climbed Mt. Washington.
  5. Anne is one of those individuals who (is, are) always finding fault.
  6. Gibson is one of the members who always (listens, listen) attentively before replying.
  7. Juan is the person in the crowd who (is, are) smiling.
  8. Mr. Marin is the only one of my teachers who (calls, call) roll.
  9. Veterans Day is one of the holidays that (falls, fall) on Saturday this year.
  10. Sarah is one of the musicians who (marches, march) in the band.

Exercise B: Follow the same directions as for Exercise A.

  1. That is the only one of her wisdom teeth that (aches, ache).
  2. Here are two fabrics of the kind that (resists, resist) moisture.
  3. He is the only one of the refugees who (speaks, speak) English fluently.
  4. Joan is the one person in the group who (has, have) a good record collection.

5. There are three members of our class who (has, have) won prizes.

6. The ivy is the only plant in these rooms that (is, are) poisonous.

7. Laura is one of the students who (has, have) straight A's.

8. He is one of the neighbors who never (fails, fail) to greet us.

9. This is the kind of jeans that (lasts, last).

10. Tim is the only one in the group who (seems, seem) confident.

REVIEW: AGREEMENT OF SUBJECT AND VERB This exercise is a review of Section 5. Choose the standard form of the verb for each sentence.

1. A pile of rocks (is, are) blocking Central Street.

2. My backpack, together with its contents, (weighs, weigh) over twenty pounds.

3. Each of these New England towns (has, have) a yearly festival.

4. Most of the new cars (uses, use) unleaded gasoline.

5. Everybody (expects, expect) to be treated fairly.

6. Fruit or fruit juice (makes, make) a nutritious snack.

7. The editors or the art director (designs, design) the magazine cover.

8. Around the barnyard (struts, strut) a colorful peacock.

9. There (is, are) many ski areas in Colorado.

10. How (does, do) artists make stained glass?

11. Hawaii (is, are) actually eight major islands.

12. Creativity and enjoyment (is, are) the aims of the crafts program.

13. Les (doesn't, don't) read any magazines except *TV Guide*.

14. The choir (sings, sing) at a special spring concert.

15. Gymnastics (requires, require) precise timing.

16. "The Muppets Show" (has, have) high viewer ratings.

17. Sixteen dollars (is, are) the price of that shirt.

18. Three-quarters of an hour (is, are) the length of each class.

19. These boots are made of material that (melts, melt) snow.

20. Laverne is one of several class officers who (is, are) meeting with the principal.

6.0 Pronoun Usage

In grammar, the term *inflection* has a special meaning. It means "a change in form to show how a word is used in a sentence." Prepositions, conjunctions, and interjections do not change their form. All other parts of speech do. Usually, the change in form is just a change in spelling.

NOUN:	girl	— girl's	— girls	— girls'
VERB:	need	— needs	— needed	— needing
ADJECTIVE:	new	— newer	— newest	
ADVERB:	near	— nearer	— nearest	

Often, however, the change involves the use of a completely new word:

VERB:	do	— did	— done
PRONOUN:	I	— me	— mine

Pronouns change their form in both ways. The changes in pronouns correspond to their use in sentences. These changes are called the **cases** of pronouns. These cases are the **nominative, possessive,** and **objective.**

You will recall that pronouns can be used in sentences in the following ways:

subject of the verb	object of a preposition
object of the verb	appositive
predicate pronoun	modifier

Nearly all pronouns change their form for different uses in the sentence. The indefinite pronouns have the least change.

They change only when used as modifiers. As modifiers, they are in the possessive case:

	POSSESSIVE
someone	— someone's
everybody	— everybody's
anybody	— anybody's

The pronouns *this, that, these, those, which,* and *what* do not change their forms to indicate case. None of these has a possessive form.

The pronoun inflections are as follows:

NOMINATIVE	POSSESSIVE	OBJECTIVE
I	my, mine	me
we	our, ours	us
you	your, yours	you
he	his	him
she	her, hers	her
it	its	it
they	their, theirs	them
who	whose	whom
whoever	whosever	whomever

6.1 The Pronoun as Subject of a Verb

The nominative form of the pronoun is used as subject of a verb.

The problem of which pronoun form to use as subject arises chiefly when the subject is compound. The compound subject may be made up of pronouns or of both nouns and pronouns.

To decide which pronoun form to use in a compound subject, *try each part of the subject by itself with the verb.*

> Hal and (I, me) went to the movies.
> (Hal went; I went, *not* me went.)
> The McCarthys and (they, them) are in the club.
> (The McCarthys are; they are, *not* them are.)

We and (they, them) tried out for the Olympics.
(We tried; they tried, *not* them tried.)
Kerry and (she, her) read *Huckleberry Finn*.
(Kerry read; she read, *not* her read.)

The plural forms *we* and *they* sound awkward in many compounds. They can be avoided by recasting the sentence.

AWKWARD: The girls and we are going.
BETTER: We and the girls are going.

AWKWARD: We and they planned to swim at dawn.
BETTER: We all planned to swim at dawn.

6.2   The Predicate Pronoun

The verb *be* is a linking verb. It links the noun, pronoun, or adjective following it to the subject. A pronoun so linked is called a **predicate pronoun.**

The nominative pronoun form is used as a predicate pronoun.*

The problem of which form to use in a predicate pronoun occurs primarily after the verb *be*. The rule applies to all verb phrases built around forms of *be: could have been, can be, should be,* etc.

It *was* **I** whom they called.
Could it *have been* **she** who won?
It *must have been* **they** in the sports car.

Sometimes the nominative form sounds awkward. The awkwardness can be avoided by recasting the sentence.

AWKWARD: The winners are she and Loretta.
BETTER: Loretta and she are the winners.

AWKWARD: It was we who found the entrance to the cave.
BETTER: We are the ones who found the entrance to the cave.

* Standard usage permits the exception in both speech and writing of *It is me*.

6.3 The Pronoun as Object of a Verb

The objective pronoun form is used as direct or indirect object.

The problem of which pronoun form to use as object of the verb arises chiefly when the object is compound. The compound object may consist of pronouns or of both nouns and pronouns.

To decide which pronoun form to use in a compound object, *try each part of the object by itself with the verb.*

DIRECT OBJECT:

The principal wanted to see George and (I, me).
   (see George; see me, *not* see I)
Jenny invited both (they, them) and (we, us) to the party.
   (invited them, *not* invited they; invited us, *not* invited we)
Did you ask (he, him) and (I, me) to dinner?
   (ask him, *not* ask he; ask me, *not* ask I)

INDIRECT OBJECT:

The counselor gave Janet and (I, me) good advice.
   (gave Janet; gave me, *not* gave I)

Exercise A: Choose the standard form from those given in parentheses.

1. Jeff and (I, me) are applying for scholarships at Northwestern.
2. The chairperson invited Mr. Dawson and (she, her) to speak to the group.
3. At the bottom of the class were Roger and (I, me).
4. How much money did Lynn and (she, her) make?
5. Give Marion and (she, her) the extra tickets.
6. Marty and (I, me) are having a party after the game.
7. The Warners and (they, them) are good friends.
8. The last on the program are Herb and (I, me).
9. The coach gave Harold and (I, me) passes to the game.
10. Was it (he, him) who answered the telephone?
11. (She, Her) and the traffic cop were having a loud argument.

12. Can you tell Beth and (I, me) where the party will be?
13. Scott and (I, me) were watching television when you called.
14. Lincoln School and (we, us) are sponsoring the play together.
15. We were sure that it was (he, him) at the door.

Exercise B: Follow the same directions as for Exercise A.

1. The bus met (he, him) and (I, me) at the station.
2. The police telephoned Gary and (they, them) right after the accident.
3. The store manager greeted (she, her) and (he, him) cordially.
4. The airlines office told (they, them) and (we, us) different stories.
5. Was it (they, them) who wrote you?
6. It might have been (we, us) in that crash.
7. The seniors scarcely noticed Betty and (I, me).
8. Why don't you let (they, them) and (we, us) take care of decorations?
9. Dad drove Casey and (I, me) into town.
10. Will you and (he, him) study together for the test?
11. It must have been (she, her) in the window.
12. If it were (he, him), I would certainly be surprised.
13. What would you do if you were (she, her)?
14. The boss gave Herb and (I, me) a difficult job.
15. We met (they, them) and their parents at the theater after the show.

6.4 The Pronoun as Object of a Preposition

The objective pronoun form is used as object of a preposition.

The problem of which pronoun form to use as object of a preposition arises only when the object is compound. The compound object may consist of pronouns or of both nouns and pronouns.

To decide which pronoun to use in a compound object of a preposition, *try each part of the object by itself with the preposition.*

Will your aunt be going with you and (I, me)?
(with you; with me, *not* with I)
We had Christmas cards from (they, them) and the Clarks.
(from them, *not* from they)
The doctor gave virus shots to both the coaches and (we, us).
(to us; *not* to we)

The preposition *between* causes especially noticeable errors in pronoun usage. Use only the objective pronoun forms after *between.*

between you and him, *not* between you and he
between him and me, *not* between he and I

6.5 The Pronoun Used with a Noun

In a construction such as *we girls* or *us boys,* the use of the noun determines the case form of the pronoun.

We girls can bring the lunch.
(girls is the subject of *can bring;* the nominative pronoun is therefore required.)
The Kiwanis Club gave the sports equipment to us girls.
(girls is the object of the preposition *to;* the objective pronoun is therefore required.)

To decide which pronoun form to use in a construction such as *we boys* or *we girls,* try the pronoun by itself with the verb or preposition.

The work was not too difficult for (we, us) girls.
(for us, *not* for we)
The police officer told (we, us) boys not to play ball in the alley.
(told us, *not* told we)
(We, Us) friends must not part.
(We must not part, *not* us must not part)

Exercise A: Choose the standard form from those given in parentheses.

1. Make out the check either to Mom or (I, me).
2. At Christmas time, we had a card from Beth and (he, him).
3. Understanding the directions was hard for Mark and (I, me).
4. There is a package for you and (she, her) at the post office.
5. Between you and (I, me), that party will never be held.
6. Stacey is going home with Grace and (he, him).
7. The law guarantees the rights of (we, us) students.
8. (We, Us) Americans can learn from other cultures.
9. The doctor recommended complete rest for Mrs. Barry and (he, him).
10. There is no quarrel between (she, her) and (I, me).
11. Will you save tickets for (they, them) and (we, us)?
12. The books have been ordered for (we, us) students.
13. (We, Us) two will have to do most of the work.
14. There were many compliments for you and (she, her).
15. There is a special practice for (we, us) flute players today.

Exercise B: Follow the same directions as for Exercise A.

1. We had a long visit with Sue and (she, her).
2. The camp counselor asked for help from Jay and (I, me).
3. To (we, us) newcomers, the coach gave special exercises.
4. Sarah, Lynn, and (she, her) are on the committee.
5. The bad news reached Ted and (I, me) just before Christmas.
6. The usher seated Terri and (he, him) way up front.
7. For Jason, Lee, and (we, us), the party was just a lot of work.
8. There are no secrets between Sally and (I, me).
9. (We, Us) baseball fans were not surprised by the Yankees' record this year.
10. After Wayne and (she, her) had spoken, there was a general discussion.
11. Only (we, us) three have been called to the office.

12. To Jack, Nancy, and (I, me), the decision was a great disappointment.

13. The principal warned (we, us) students about the new rules.

14. Just between you and (I, me), the test was really very easy.

15. The scholarship committee met with Sue and (he, him) after school.

Exercise C: Choose the standard form from those in parentheses.

1. The mechanic told Dick and (I, me) that the car needed repairs.

2. Later (she, her) and (I, me) found the book at the public library.

3. The guide showed (he, him) and (I, me) some synthetic diamonds.

4. The Clarks and (we, us) are having Thanksgiving dinner together.

5. For (we, us) girls, the lecture on job opportunities was an eye opener.

6. Mr. David had several jobs for (we, us) workers.

7. (We, Us) two had better get started.

8. The school has given (we, us) tournament winners an extra day of vacation.

9. Just between you and (I, me), our chances in this game are not good.

10. We left the selection of a class ring to (she, her) and Roger.

11. There was no mail for Jeff and (I, me).

12. Tom left ahead of Alice and (I, me).

13. (She, Her) and (he, him) used to live in Duluth.

14. The girls joined Mary and (we, us) at the bowling alley.

15. The driver called to (he, him) and (I, me) for help.

16. Unfortunately, neither (he, him) nor Brad would admit his mistake.

17. We have had no letters from Holly or (she, her).

18. The Hanleys entertained Sue and (we, us) royally.

19. Dad and (I, me) shook hands with the Governor as we left.

20. It was a long trip for (they, them) and the children.

6.6 *Who* and *Whom*

Who and *whom* are pronouns that are used either to ask questions or to introduce clauses. When they ask questions, they are called **interrogative pronouns.**

To use *who, whom,* and *whose* correctly in a sentence, you must understand how the word functions in the question.

Who is the nominative form of the pronoun. It is used as the subject of the verb or as a predicate pronoun.

Whom is the objective form of the pronoun. It is used as the direct object or as the object of a preposition.

Whose is a possessive pronoun. It can be used to modify a noun: *Whose* paper is this? However, when used alone without a noun, it may be either the subject or the direct object of the verb.

> *Who* wrote this novel? (*who* is the subject.)
>
> *Whom* will you choose? (*whom* is the direct object.)
>
> With *whom* did you dance? (*whom* is the object
> of the preposition *with.*)
>
> *Whose* is this ten-speed bike? (*whose* is the subject.)

Exercise: Choose the standard form from those given in parentheses.

1. (Who, Whom) plays the leading role?
2. (Who, Whom) will the director choose?
3. (Who, Whom) knows how to figure skate?
4. For (who, whom) does Jeff babysit?
5. Perry, (whose, whom) are those books?
6. (Who, Whom) did you speak to?
7. Of all the machines, (whose, whom) makes the least noise?
8. The attorney general is (who, whom)?
9. (Who, Whom) was your report about?
10. (Who, Whom) plays quarterback for the Rams?
11. (Who, Whom) did Paul Revere warn?

12. For (who, whom) will you vote?

13. (Who, Whom) have we forgotten?

14. (Who, Whom) called Martha Graham the founder of modern dance?

15. (Who, Whom) did we leave behind?

6.7 *Who* and *Whom* in Clauses

As explained in Sections 3.6 and 3.8, the pronouns *who*, *whose*, and *whom* are often used to begin clauses. They may introduce either adjective or noun clauses. When they are used to relate an adjective clause to the noun it modifies, they are called **relative pronouns.**

The pronouns *whoever* and *whomever*, meaning "any person that," are used in the same way as *who* and *whom*.

As a part of a clause, any of these pronouns has two jobs:

1. It introduces the clause.
2. It has a role within the clause.

Pronouns in the nominative form (*who, whoever*) can act as the subject or the predicate pronoun of the clause.

Galileo is the scientist *who invented the thermometer.* (*who* is the subject of the verb *invented* in this adjective clause.)

No one could guess *who it was.* (*who* is the predicate pronoun within this noun clause.)

The coach decided *who would play goalie.* (*who* is the subject of this noun clause.)

Pronouns in the objective form (*whom, whomever*) can act as the direct object within the clause or as the object of a preposition within the clause.

Pearl Buck is an author *whom I admire.* (*whom* is the direct object of the verb *admire* within this adjective clause.)

I will support *whomever the President appoints.* (*whomever* is the direct object in this noun clause.)

Venus was a Roman goddess *for whom a planet was named.* (*whom* is the object of the preposition *for* within this adjective clause.)

The pronoun *whose* functions as the possessive form within the clause.

This is the artist *whose painting I bought.* (*whose* is a possessive adjective modifying *painting* within this adjective clause.)

Exercise: Choose the standard form from those given in parentheses.

1. The sportscaster (whose, whom) vocabulary is famous is Howard Cosell.
2. The student (who, whom) found my watch turned it in at the office.
3. Chris is the gymnast (who, whose) specialty is the rings.
4. (Whoever, Whomever) knows how to study has an advantage.
5. The President (who, whom) initiated the New Deal was Roosevelt.
6. The people (who, whom) I resent most are cheaters.
7. Only the judges know (who, whom) the winner is.
8. Ask (whoever, whomever) you want.
9. Geologists (who, whom) study rock formations discover facts about the earth's history.
10. The police asked (who, whom) the troublemakers were.
11. (Whoever, Whomever) wants a book should get one.
12. Prisoners (who, whom) are paroled often repeat their crimes.
13. Mr. Lee is the one (who, whom) has a black belt in karate.
14. Persephone was the goddess (who, whom) Hades carried away to the underworld.
15. The letter is addressed to (whoever, whomever) lives at 123 Yellow Brick Road.

6.8 Pronouns in Comparisons

Sometimes a comparison is made by using a clause that begins with *than* or *as*.

> Fred is better at chess *than George is.*
> You have as many A's *as he has.*
> Marie likes me more *than she likes you.*

Sometimes the final clause in the comparison is left incomplete.

> Fred is better at chess than George (is).
> You have as many A's as he (has).

To decide which pronoun form to use in an incomplete comparison, complete the comparison.

> Herb plays the trumpet better than (I, me).
> (Herb plays the trumpet better than I *play.*)
> Betty wrote a better composition than (I, me).
> (Betty wrote a better composition than I *wrote.*)

6.9 Possessive Case with Gerunds

The possessive form of the pronoun is used when the pronoun immediately precedes a gerund.

All gerunds end in -*ing,* and they are all formed from verbs. The present participle also ends in -*ing,* and it, too, is formed from a verb. If the -*ing* word is used as a modifier, it is a participle. If it is used as a noun, it is a gerund.

The possessive form of the pronoun is used before a gerund. The nominative and objective forms are used before a participle.

> *His running* had improved since the last track meet.
> (*running* is a gerund, the subject of the verb *had improved.*)

> We saw *him running* toward the finish line.
> (*running* is a participle modifynig *him.*)

We disliked *their playing* the stereo at midnight.
(*playing* is a gerund, the object of the verb *disliked*.)

We heard *them playing* the stereo at midnight.
(*playing* is a participle modifying *them*.)

6.10 The Pronoun with Infinitives

The objective form of the pronoun is used as the subject, object, or predicate pronoun of an infinitive.

The officer told *me to stop*. (*me* is the subject of *to stop*.)
The official asked *them to observe* the rules. (*them* is the
subject of *to observe*.)
They took *him to be me*.
(*him* is the subject of *to be*, and *me* is the predicate
pronoun following *to be*.)
Reporters were at the airport *to question her*.
(*her* is the object of *to question*.)

6.11 The Pronoun as an Appositive

The form of a pronoun used as an appositive is determined by the use of the noun to which it is in apposition.

The delegates, *Tony and I*, want your support.
(*Tony* and *I* are in apposition to *delegates*, which is the
subject of *want*. Therefore, the nominative form of the
pronoun is required.)
For the two producers, *Margo* and *him*, the show was a success.
(*Margo* and *him* are in apposition to *producers*, which is
the object of the preposition *for*. Therefore, the objective
form of the pronoun is required.)
We gave the children, *Toby* and *her*, new tricycles.
(*Toby* and *her* are in apposition to *children*, which is the
indirect object of *gave*. Therefore, the objective form of the
pronoun is required.)

To determine which form of the pronoun to use in apposition, try the appositive by itself with the verb or preposition.

> Her friends, Jackie and (he, him), were always calling.
> (Jackie and he were, *not* Jackie and him were.)
> The flowers are from two of your friends, Sally and (I, me).
> (The flowers are from me, *not* from I.)

6.12 Compound Personal Pronouns

Compound personal pronouns are used only when their antecedents appear in the same sentence.

> STANDARD: I carried it up the stairs myself.
> STANDARD: We made lunch for ourselves.
>
> NONSTANDARD: The hat belongs to yourself.
> STANDARD: The hat belongs to you.
>
> NONSTANDARD: The cheers were meant for ourselves.
> STANDARD: The cheers were meant for us.

Exercise: Choose the standard form from those given in parentheses.

1. Bill can type much faster than (I, me).
2. Mr. Crofts was disturbed by (our, us) blowing the horn.
3. The class would rather have you for president than (he, him).
4. (Their, Them) shouting kept us awake.
5. We knew the "ghost" would turn out to be (he, him).
6. No one was more frightened than (she, her).
7. Did you hear (our, us) calling you?
8. Binnie and (I, myself) will clean up the yard.
9. We gave the soloists, Jenny and (she, her), bouquets of roses.
10. We had twice as big a squad as (they, them).
11. We kept some of the strawberry shortcake for (us, ourselves).
12. The committee gave two students, Barry and (I, me) first prizes.
13. We were expecting Ms. Kirk rather than (she, her).

14. Please return the unused cartons to Ted or (me, myself).
15. No one but (you, yourself) saw the accident.
16. I didn't like (his, him) sneaking in through the back door.
17. California played a better defensive game than (we, us).
18. We didn't expect the winner to be (he, him).
19. Write a bread-and-butter letter to your hosts, Katie and (he, him).
20. The audience was no more surprised than (they, them).

6.13 Pronouns and Antecedents

A pronoun agrees with its antecedent in number, gender, and person.

Argeement in Number. If the antecedent of a pronoun is singular, a singular pronoun is required. If the antecedent is plural, a plural pronoun is required.

The indefinite pronouns that are singular in meaning cause the greatest difficulty. The following are referred to by singular pronouns:

anybody	either	neither	somebody
anyone	everybody	nobody	someone
each	everyone	one	

Each of the boys brought *his* sleeping bag.
Everyone should make up *his or her* own mind.
Someone had left *his or her* briefcase on the bus.

Two or more singular antecedents joined by *or* or *nor* are referred to by a singular pronoun.

Either Bob or Hank will let us use *his* car.
Neither the cat nor the dog had eaten *its* meal.

Collective nouns may be referred to by either a singular or plural pronoun, depending upon the meaning intended.

The track team *has its* new coach.
The track team *have* worked out in *their* spare time.

The indefinite pronouns *all, some, any,* and *none* may be referred to by either a singular or plural pronoun, depending upon the meaning intended.

All the furniture *was* in *its* best condition.

All the students *were* taking *their* last examination.

Some of the cider *has* lost *its* tang.

None of the refugee children *have* heard from *their* parents.

Note: In all of the foregoing examples, the collective nouns and indefinite pronouns are used as subjects. The number of the verb and the number of the pronoun referring to them must be the same.

NONSTANDARD: Some of the orchestra *are* playing *its* new instruments.

STANDARD: Some of the orchestra *are* playing *their* new instruments.

NONSTANDARD: None of the singers *was* making *their* debuts.
STANDARD: None of the singers *were* making *their* debuts.
STANDARD: None of the singers *was* making *his or her* debut.

Agreement in Gender. Masculine gender is indicated by *he, his, him.* Feminine gender is indicated by *she, her, hers.* Neuter gender is indicated by *it* and *its.* These pronouns must be the same gender as the word to which they refer.

The lion had fought for *its* life. (neuter)
The actor rehearsed *his* lines. (masculine)
The queen was riding in *her* coach. (feminine)

When a singular pronoun must refer to both feminine and masculine antecedents, the phrase "his or her" is acceptable. It is, in fact, preferred by some people who wish to avoid what they consider to be sexist language.

STANDARD: Every student should have *his* ticket ready.
STANDARD: Every student should have *his or her* ticket ready.

Agreement in Person. A personal pronoun must be in the same person as its antecedent. The words *one, everyone,* and *everybody* are in the third person. They are referred to by *he, his, him, she, her, hers.*

NONSTANDARD:	*One* should always wear *your* seat belt.
STANDARD:	*One* should always wear *his or her* seat belt.
NONSTANDARD:	*I* find that the baby's crying grates on *your* nerves.
STANDARD:	*I* find that the baby's crying grates on *my* nerves.

Exercise A: Find and correct the errors in agreement in these sentences. Make sure that both the verb and the pronoun are correct. Three of the sentences are correct as they stand.

1. Someone had left their car in our driveway.
2. Each of the boys promised that they would come early.
3. Either Jane or Peggy left their scarf here.
4. Neither of the persons who complained would give their name.
5. Not one of the crew expected to see his or her home again.
6. Some of the team is wearing their new uniforms.
7. Nobody had done their homework during vacation.
8. Did either your father or grandfather change their name?
9. Neither of the witnesses admitted that they had seen the man.
10. Neither the principal nor the class adviser would give their approval to our plan.
11. None of the students were minding their own business.
12. Everyone on our street had decorated his or her house.
13. The student council has made up their mind to drop the party.
14. The majority of the class plans to buy their rings this year.
15. Everyone was doing their best to make the party a success.

Exercise B: Find and correct the errors in agreement between pronouns and antecedents in these sentences.

1. One should start early to plan your career.
2. I find that moderate exercise makes you feel better.
3. Everyone can now have your own CB radio.

4. We found that you could hear well even in the back seats.
5. You will find cooking easy if one follows the directions.
6. Everyone brought their own food to the picnic.
7. What happens if one's foot slips when you are driving?
8. Nobody in the club has their own equipment.
9. Everyone in class is busy working on their own project.
10. It is a mistake for anyone to try being your own lawyer.

6.14 Indefinite Reference

To avoid any confusion for the reader, every personal pronoun should refer clearly to a definite antecedent.

INDEFINITE:	The yearbook is good, but *they* didn't include enough pictures of the glee club.
BETTER:	The yearbook is good, but *the editors* didn't include enough pictures of the glee club.
INDEFINITE:	*It* says in the newspaper that it will rain tomorrow.
BETTER:	The newspaper says that it will rain tomorrow.
INDEFINITE:	Harry wants to run for office because *it* is exciting.
BETTER:	Harry wants to run for office because politics is exciting.
INDEFINITE:	Read what *they* say about stereo components.
BETTER:	Read what *Consumer's Guide* says about stereo components.

The pronoun *you* is sometimes used when it is not meant to refer to the person spoken to. The effect is usually confusing.

INDEFINITE:	In that course *you* have fewer exams.
BETTER:	In that course there are fewer exams.
INDEFINITE:	From a single corn kernel *you* may grow a corn plant from twelve to fourteen feet high.
BETTER:	From a single corn kernel one may grow a corn plant from twelve to fourteen feet high.

Exercise A: Revise the sentences below to remove all indefinite references of pronouns.

1. It says in the paper that the President vetoed the bill.
2. In English class you write essays.
3. He swung his racket but missed it.
4. During Prohibition, they made the sale of liquor illegal.
5. The tailor asked me to try it on.
6. They said on the radio that the mayor has resigned.
7. Andy wants to become a chef because it interests him.
8. The best show that they broadcast is "Nova."
9. In this school, they make you study a foreign language.
10. When you work in a laboratory, they expect you to be accurate.

Exercise B: Follow the same directions as for Exercise A.

1. I missed Carl's birthday, and I'm sorry about it.
2. Maureen wants to be a ski instructor because it is glamorous.
3. The exterior of the building is modern, but they ruined its interior.
4. In Hawaii, they greet you with flowers.
5. I have never told a lie, and it once paid off.
6. They never tell you the price.
7. The plumber worked hard, but it continued to leak.
8. The temperature is dropping; it may ruin the orange crop.
9. In Colonial days, they preached very long sermons.
10. They expect you to work long, hard hours at that job.

6.15 Ambiguous Reference

The word *ambiguous* means "having two or more possible meanings." The reference of a pronoun is ambiguous if the pronoun may refer to more than one word. This situation arises whenever a noun or pronoun falls between the pronoun and its true antecedent.

AMBIGUOUS:	Take the books off the shelves and dust *them*.
BETTER:	Dust the books after you take them off the shelves.
AMBIGUOUS:	The hounds chased foxes until *they* were exhausted.
BETTER:	The hounds chased foxes until the dogs were exhausted.
AMBIGUOUS:	Before they could get the rocket off the pad, *it* had to be repaired.
BETTER:	They had to repair the rocket before they could get it off the pad.
AMBIGUOUS:	Vince told Joe *he* had won the prize.
BETTER:	Vince had won the prize, he told Joe.

Exercise A: Revise the sentences below to remove all ambiguous pronoun references.

1. When I put the candle in the holder, it broke.
2. Jeff asked Mark about his assignment.
3. Sara told Tanya that she really should try out for track.
4. There's an orange in this lunch bag, but it isn't mine.
5. Alison put the plant in the wagon after she bought it.
6. Before you wash them, separate the clothes from the towels.
7. Tom explained to Fred that his car needed to be overhauled.
8. Julie told Katie that her drawing won an award.
9. I took the money out of my wallet and put it on the counter.
10. Take the tennis rackets out of the presses and dust them.

Exercise B: Follow the same directions as for Exercise A.

1. I saw the picture in a magazine, but I can't find it.
2. Joan took the belt off her dress and washed it.
3. Although I keep my books with my notebooks, I always lose them.
4. Ellen told Kay that she had made a serious mistake.
5. As the designer talked to the model, she smiled.
6. When the traffic officer spoke to Mom, she frowned.

7. We can choose a different classroom or a different schedule if we want it.

8. Take the groceries out of the bags and put them on the shelf.

9. Uncle Kevin studied acting and journalism but never pursued it.

10. We tried hanging the picture over the bookcase, but it was too big.

REVIEW: PRONOUN USAGE This exercise is a review of Section 6. Choose the standard form from those given in parentheses.

1. (They, Them) and we met at the movie theater.
2. The chef trained Britt and (he, him) as assistants.
3. That mysterious caller must be (she, her).
4. Carlotta played a joke on Jamie and (I, me).
5. (We, Us) girls defeated the other soccer team.
6. (Who, Whom) does Columbo suspect?
7. Connie runs the mile faster than (I, me).
8. Few people like (him, his) writing.
9. (Whoever, Whomever) touches the wet paint will leave fingerprints.
10. The editor encouraged (I, me) to join the newspaper staff.
11. In gym class, (they, the teachers) checked our skills.
12. The captain awarded (I, me, myself) a special trophy.
13. Everyone must provide (his or her, their) own transportation.
14. Sondra asked the ushers, Miguel and (she, her), for directions to the stage door.
15. Neither Cecilia nor Randi had learned (her, their) lines for the play.
16. The passenger in the police car was (I, me).
17. Our teacher objected to (him, his) disrupting the class.
18. Ray knitted a cowl-neck sweater for (me, myself).
19. The jury made its decision after (they, it) had deliberated for two days.
20. Anyone (who, whom) sees that horror movie is wasting (his or her, their) time.

7.0 Adjective and Adverb Usage

Some adverbs are formed by adding *-ly* to adjectives, as *rapid—rapidly*. The problem then is whether to use the modifier with or without the *-ly* ending after a verb.

7.1 Adverbs with Action Verbs

When a modifier comes just before an action verb, it is always an adverb, and no problem arises. When the modifier follows the action verb, there is a temptation to use an adjective rather than an adverb.

The problem is made more difficult by the fact that many adverbs have two forms, one with and the other without the *-ly* ending.

Come *quick!*   Drive *slow.*   Come *close.*

All of the words used above as adverbs are also used as adjectives: a *quick* response, a *slow* horse, a *close* call, and so on.

Most of the words that may be either adjectives or adverbs are words of one syllable. Adjectives of two or more syllables almost never have the same form for the adverb.

The *noisy* tenant was scolded by the landlord. (adjective)
The dishes fell *noisily* to the floor. (adverb)

The doctor received a *sudden* call. (adjective)
The doctor was called away *suddenly*. (adverb)

After an action verb use the -ly form of the modifier if the modifier has two or more syllables.

7.2 Adjectives with Linking Verbs

Linking verbs are usually followed by adjectives rather than adverbs. The adjective is a predicate adjective and modifies the subject.

There is no problem with modifiers following the form of *be*, the most common linking verb. Most of the other linking verbs, however, may also be used as action verbs. As action verbs, they may be followed by adverbs.

The groundhog *appeared suddenly*.
(*appeared* is an action verb modified by an adverb.)

The actress *appeared nervous*.
(*appeared* is a linking verb followed by a predicate adjective.)

The baby *grew quickly*.
(*grew* is an action verb modified by an adverb.)

The lake *grew dark and ominous*.
(*grew* is a linking verb followed by predicate adjectives.)

The following verbs are linking verbs. Most of them may also be used as action verbs.

look	feel	stay	become
sound	smell	remain	seem
appear	taste	grow	

To decide whether a verb is used to link or to show action, try substituting a form of *be*. If the sentence still makes sense, the verb is a linking verb.

The bride *seemed* (happy, happily).
(*The bride was happily* does not make sense. *The bride was happy* makes sense; *seemed* is a linking verb here.)

The bride *looked* (happy, happily) at the groom.
(*was* does not make sense with either modifier; *looked* is an action verb here.)

Exercise A: Choose the standard form from those given.

1. You can find the way (easy, easily) from here.
2. The man seemed (unsteady, unsteadily) on his feet.
3. Larry looked very (happy, happily) in his new job.
4. It rained (steady, steadily) all day long.
5. Jan worked at the fatiguing job as (rapid, rapidly) as possible.
6. Tony felt (uneasy, uneasily) about his mother's illness.
7. Harold found the solution to the first problem (quick, quickly) and turned to the second.
8. We thought the game was (certain, certainly) lost.
9. Your voice sounds (different, differently) over the telephone.
10. Twelve passengers in the first car were hurt (bad, badly).

Exercise B: Decide whether the italicized modifier is standard or nonstandard. If it is nonstandard, substitute the standard form.

1. You can get an office job *easier* if you can take dictation.
2. Harriet seemed *angrily* about the interruption.
3. You must drive more *careful*.
4. Dr. Sanders signs his name *differently* on every prescription.
5. Barbara felt *unhappily* about her choice.
6. The repair shop fixed the radio *perfect*.
7. Skate *cautiously* on thin ice.
8. The old cottage on the dunes smelled *damply*.
9. We thought the dog was not behaving *normal*.
10. Herb studied the letter very *careful*.

7.3 *This—These; That—Those*

This and *that* modify singular words. *These* and *those* modify plural words. The words *kind*, *sort*, and *type* require a singular modifier.

NONSTANDARD: *These* kind are the best.
STANDARD: *This* kind is the best.

NONSTANDARD: *These* sort of gloves wear well.
STANDARD: *This* sort of glove wears well.

7.4 Them—Those

Those may be either a pronoun or an adjective. *Them* is always a pronoun and never an adjective.

NONSTANDARD: How did you get *them* blisters?
STANDARD: How did you get *those* blisters? (adjective)

7.5 Bad—Badly

In standard usage, *bad* is always used after linking verbs.

I felt bad. (*not* I felt badly)
The team looked bad.
The fish tastes bad.

7.6 Good—Well

Good is used only as an adjective to modify nouns and pronouns.

Well is an adjective when it means "in good health." *Well* is used as an adverb to modify an action verb when it means that the action was performed properly or expertly.

The Vice-President looks *well*. (adjective)
The baby walks *well* now. (adverb)

7.7 Fewer—Less

Fewer is used to describe things that can be counted. *Less* refers to quantity or degree.

Patrick has *fewer* headaches than he used to have.
There has been *less* rain this year than last year.
This dishwasher will give you *less* trouble than that one.

Exercise: Decide whether the italicized words are standard or non-standard usage. Substitute a standard form for each nonstandard one.

1. There are *less* pupils studying French this year.
2. We enjoy your letters; don't stop writing *them*.
3. The milk tastes *badly* to me.
4. Be careful not to trip over *them* wires.
5. The bush grew *good* after being transplanted.
6. *Those* kind of animal belongs in a zoo.
7. Secretaries should be able to spell *good*.
8. The team felt *badly* about Lindsay's injury.
9. There are *fewer* new students in school this year.
10. *Less* voters turned out than we had expected.
11. You can't buy *those* kind of candy any more.
12. Bob has all *them* power tools in his shop.
13. Mr. Jackson has looked *badly* ever since his operation.
14. Renee gets along very *well* with her co-workers.
15. We had some of *these* kind of apples last year.
16. There have been *less* traffic deaths since we put in the new stoplight.
17. Leslie isn't singing as *good* as she did last week.
18. The boys were frightened *bad* by the runaway truck.
19. You will have *less* trouble with these new tubes.
20. The school chorus did very *good* in the regional contest.

7.8 Comparative and Superlative

The comparative form is used to compare two things; the superlative is used in comparing more than two.

STANDARD: We went to see both the Giants and the Raiders, but we liked the Giants *better*. (*not* best)

STANDARD: You can have either this dress pattern or that one, but I think you will find this one *easier* to follow. (*not* easiest)

STANDARD: Of the three speakers, the Jensen brings out the bass notes *best*. (*not* better)

7.9 The Double Comparison

The comparative form of a modifier is made either by adding *-er* or by using *more*. It is nonstandard to use both.

The superlative form of a modifier is made either by adding *-est* or by using *most*. It is nonstandard to use both.

NONSTANDARD: My boat will go much more faster than yours.
STANDARD: My boat will go much faster than yours.

NONSTANDARD: You should find it more easier to do.
STANDARD: You should find it easier to do.

NONSTANDARD: It was the most fanciest house I'd ever seen.
STANDARD: It was the fanciest house I'd ever seen.

7.10 Illogical Comparisons

The word *other*, or the word *else*, is required in comparisons of an individual member with the rest of the group.

ILLOGICAL: Sylvia has won more honors than any student.
(Sylvia is also a student.)
CLEAR: Sylvia has won more honors than any *other* student.

ILLOGICAL: George is as tall as anyone on the basketball squad.
CLEAR: George is as tall as anyone *else* on the basketball squad.

The words *than* or *as* are required in a compound comparison.

ILLOGICAL: Tim is as tall if not taller than Brad.

CLEAR BUT
AWKWARD: Tim is as tall *as*, if not taller than, Brad.

BETTER: Tim is as tall *as* Brad, if not taller.

ILLOGICAL: Sue had as many examinations to take if not more than Helen.

CLEAR: Sue had as many examinations to take *as* Helen, if not more.

ILLOGICAL: The Dodgers' chances of winning the pennant are as good if not better than the Giants'.

CLEAR: The Dodgers' chances of winning the pennant are as good *as* the Giants', if not better.

Both parts of a comparison must be stated completely if there is any chance of its being misunderstood.

CONFUSING: I miss her more than Sandra.

CLEAR: I miss her more than Sandra *does*.

CLEAR: I miss her more than *I miss* Sandra.

CONFUSING: Harvard defeated Yale worse than Dartmouth.

CLEAR: Harvard defeated Yale worse than Dartmouth *did*.

CLEAR: Harvard defeated Yale worse than *it defeated* Dartmouth.

ILLOGICAL: The population of New York is larger than London.

CLEAR: The population of New York is larger than *that of* London.

BETTER: New York has a larger population than London *has*.

Exercise A: Revise the following sentences to correct the errors in comparison.

1. Turn the radio up a little more louder.
2. Our team is more weaker this year because of minor injuries.
3. Some students can study more easier with the radio turned on.
4. Harry is the tallest of the twins.

5. This was the less expensive coat of the dozen I looked at.
6. We watched both programs, but Alistair Cooke's was the best.
7. Please open the window just a bit more wider.
8. The water is more softer now with the new filtration plant.
9. Our chances of winning are as good if not better than theirs.
10. The problem is more clearer to me now than before.

Exercise B: Follow the same directions as for Exercise A.

1. The work of a miner is more dangerous than a carpenter.
2. Joe is the smartest of that pair.
3. Joyce is as bright as any member of the committee.
4. In the 1978 World Series, the Yankees had the best team.
5. Beth chose the longest of the two books for her report.
6. Please try to come over a little more earlier than usual.
7. The coach was the better of the three speakers at the banquet.
8. I respect Betty Jean more than Chuck.
9. Our enrollment is more bigger than ever this year.
10. Eve and Janet are both good students, but Janet is the best.

7.11 The Double Negative

A double negative occurs when a negative word is added to a statement that is already negative. The double negative is nonstandard usage.

NONSTANDARD:	He did*n't* have *no* soda left.
STANDARD:	He did*n't* have *any* soda left.
NONSTANDARD:	She did*n't* know *nothing* about the Civil War.
STANDARD:	She did*n't* know *anything* about the Civil War.

Hardly or *barely*, used with a negative word, is nonstandard.

NONSTANDARD:	There was*n't* *hardly* a ticket left for the show.
STANDARD:	There was *hardly* a ticket left for the show.
NONSTANDARD:	Debby could*n't* *barely* hit the ball.
STANDARD:	Debby could *barely* hit the ball.

Exercise A: Find the nonstandard usages and change them to standard usage. Two sentences are already standard usage.

1. The bus hadn't never been so late before.
2. There hadn't been nothing said about staying out of the water.
3. We have never had any trouble with the ignition.
4. Nobody in the audience couldn't tell what had happened.
5. The doctor hasn't said nothing that should frighten you.
6. By midnight the turkey hadn't barely begun to thaw out.
7. Bob hasn't none of his brother's charm.
8. We had barely finished cleaning up, when a new crowd entered.
9. I'm sure that nobody else couldn't have done as well.
10. We haven't had no response to our letter.

Exercise B: These sentences cover many problems of adjective and adverb usage. Find the nonstandard usages and change them to standard usages. Two sentences are correct.

1. You can finish the job easy in five minutes.
2. The roads are slippery. Drive careful.
3. The papers had been stacked neat on the desks.
4. Nomads don't have no homes.
5. Kris looked sad at the empty cage.
6. You will have to speak a little more clear.
7. In every pair of shoes, the right one is the biggest.
8. The score was much more closer than in last year's game.
9. The class requested less assignments.
10. After the party there wasn't hardly any food left.
11. We had peach pie and cherry pie, but the peach was best.
12. The victim's family took the news bad.
13. In a show of great football yesterday, the best team finally won.
14. Please don't order any more of them pencils.
15. Don felt bad about forgetting his lines in the play.
16. There were less cars on the road than we had expected.
17. The patient felt more grateful to the blood donor than the doctors.

18. We stopped using those kind of helmets two years ago.
19. Be sure to clean the metal good before applying the enamel.
20. The elm is more susceptible to disease than most other trees.

REVIEW: ADJECTIVE AND ADVERB USAGE This exercise is a review of Section 7. Choose the standard form from those given in parentheses.

1. That cartoonist draws (good, well).
2. The food certainly smelled (bad, badly).
3. Would you bring me (them, those) books?
4. I've never seen (this, these) kind of shoe.
5. Diamonds are the (hardest, most hardest) natural substance.
6. Jerry hadn't (never, ever) seen a television studio.
7. Regina waited (nervous, nervously) for her audition.
8. The radio announcer sounded (serious, seriously).
9. Of all mammals, the whale is the (larger, largest).
10. Because of his cold, Eric (could, couldn't) hardly talk.
11. Most people watch (fewer, less) TV programs in summer than in winter.
12. We planted bean and tomato plants, but the bean plants grew (faster, fastest).
13. Our school library has more books than (any, any other) school library in the state.
14. My schedule doesn't allow (any, no) time for socializing.
15. Our bike club traveled (fewer, less) miles on Monday than on Tuesday.
16. Anna's scheme for the surprise party sounds (foolish, foolishly).
17. Mark types faster than (anyone, anyone else) in his class.
18. The batter (had, hadn't) barely tipped the ball.
19. Macramé seems (more easily, easier, easiest) than batik.
20. Bobby Fischer looked (intent, intently) at the chess board before making his move.

8.0 Verb Usage

Most of the several thousand verbs in our language cause no problems of usage at all. They are **regular verbs.** That is, the past tense is formed by adding *-ed* or *-d* to the present, and the past participle is the same as the past tense form:

PRESENT	PAST	PAST PARTICIPLE
talk	talk*ed*	talk*ed*
use	use*d*	use*d*
love	love*d*	love*d*

There are about sixty commonly used verbs, however, whose past forms do not follow this pattern. They are **irregular verbs.** The most commonly used verbs, *be* and *have,* not only form the past tenses irregularly but change from person to person in the present tense: *I am, you are, he is; I have, he has.*

8.1 The Past Forms

The main problem with irregular verbs is the choice between the past form and the past participle form. These are two of the **principal parts** of every verb. (See Section 1.3.) All forms of any verb are made from the principal parts. Since they are always given in the same order in dictionaries and reference books, learning them in that order will make usage choices easier.

The past tense form is used alone. The past participle form is used with forms of *be* or *have.*

> Barbara Walters *began* the interview. (past)
> The dogs *were* all *fed.* (past participle with form of *be*)
> The store *had closed.* (past participle with form of *have*)

There are five groups of irregular verbs.

Group 1. The easiest of the irregular verbs are those that have the same form in all principal parts.

PRESENT	PAST	PAST PARTICIPLE
burst	burst	burst
cost	cost	cost
hit	hit	hit
hurt	hurt	hurt
put	put	put
set	set	set
shut	shut	shut

Group 2. A second group that causes little difficulty is composed of verbs that have the same form for the past and the past participle.

PRESENT	PAST	PAST PARTICIPLE
bring	brought	brought
catch	caught	caught
dive	dived *or* dove*	dived
fight	fought	fought
flee	fled	fled
fling	flung	flung
get	got	got *or* gotten
lead	led	led
lend	lent	lent
lose	lost	lost
say	said	said
shine	shone	shone
sit	sat	sat
sting	stung	stung
swing	swung	swung

* Where two forms are given, both are standard usage, but the first is more common.

Exercise A: In the sentences below, the present form of the verb is given in parentheses. Substitute either past or past participle, whichever the sentence requires.

1. One of the teachers had (bring) a portable television set.
2. A canary (sit) on the classroom window ledge.
3. Rick (get) an invitation in the mail.
4. Ms. Allen (bring) out the fact that we need more books.
5. Two of the escaping convicts were (catch) in the swamp.
6. The two brothers, the babysitter said, had (fight) all evening.
7. Without awaiting an answer, John (flee) from the house.
8. Papers had been (fling) all over the lawn.
9. Suddenly, the lifeguard (dive) into the pool.
10. That purchase (lead) us ever deeper into debt.
11. We had (lend) the wheelbarrow to our neighbors.
12. How many games have we (lose) this year?
13. The light (shine) into my eyes so that I could hardly see.
14. The divers had been badly (sting) by jellyfish.
15. The batter (swing) at the first pitch and popped it into the stands.
16. As we passed, the men in the boat (fling) up their arms in salute.
17. Rosemary has (lead) the band for three years.
18. The sun had (shine) on only one day of our vacation.
19. The crane (swing) crazily out over the street.
20. Ned (lend) me a dollar to buy some notebook paper.

Exercise B: Choose the standard form from those in parentheses.

1. As usual, the plumber's assistant has (brung, brought) the wrong tools.
2. Running at top speed, Cal reached up and (catched, caught) the ball on his fingertips.
3. Last week the baby (hurt, hurted) herself on the sidewalk.
4. If the vampire mask had (cost, costed) less, I would have bought it.
5. Carlotta had never (dove, dived) from a diving platform.
6. When his mother suggested a bath, the child (fleed, fled).

7. Robert Graves's poem (sayed, said) that love is a universal headache.

8. With a little help from a pin, the balloon (burst, bursted).

9. Frank claimed that he had been (stang, stung) by an unidentified flying object.

10. The waiting sharks turned and (fleed, fled) as the ship approached.

11. Someone had (flang, flinged, flung) a burning cigarette from a car.

12. Gail generously (lent, lended) Greg money to buy a taco.

13. Lewis (lead, led) us up the face of the cliff.

14. George has returned the wrenches that you (lended, lent) him.

15. The travelers had (losed, lost) their way in the storm.

16. The moon (shone, shined) brightly as we started across the desert.

17. The hot liquid (stang, stung) my throat.

18. When we had finished, the car (shone, shined) like new.

19. The crane slowly (swang, swung) the steel girders into place.

20. Lars had (caught, catched) a skunk in his trap.

Group 3. Another group of irregular verbs adds *n* or *en* to the past form to make the past participle.

PRESENT	PAST	PAST PARTICIPLE
bear	bore	borne*
beat	beat	beaten
bite	bit	bitten
break	broke	broken
choose	chose	chosen
freeze	froze	frozen
speak	spoke	spoken
steal	stole	stolen
swear	swore	sworn
tear	tore	torn
wear	wore	worn

* Note that *borne* retains the final *e*

Exercise A: Choose the standard form from those in parentheses.

1. Fran has (born, beared, borne) the family burdens all alone.
2. The batter should be (beat, beaten) until it is smooth.
3. I thought I had (bit, bitten) into a piece of metal.
4. All previous heat records were (broke, broken) last summer.
5. Deirdre had already (chose, chosen) a camera for her birthday present.
6. The car door was (froze, frozen) shut.
7. At the meeting, Mr. Davis had (spoke, spoken) against driver education.
8. The stowaways had (stole, stolen) onto the ship at night.
9. The men had (swore, sworn) to hold the fort or die in the attempt.
10. Two pages had been (tore, torn) out of the index.
11. Dad has (wore, worn) the same old hat for five years.
12. The natives (beared, bore) the casket to the top of the hill.
13. The little Kansas town had (born, borne) the full fury of the tornado.
14. The Cardinals were badly (beat, beaten) in the championship game.
15. A little boy's finger was (bit, bitten) by a big dog.
16. All of our dishes were (broke, broken) when the van turned over.
17. Ramona has been (chose, chosen) to give an address at the commencement exercises.
18. With the unusually early cold, many ponds were (froze, frozen).
19. The heavy traffic has (tore, torn) up the road.
20. The rocks had been (worn, wore) down by the constant fall of the water.

Exercise B: The present form of the verb is given. Substitute past or past participle, whichever the sentence requires.

1. Betty hasn't (wear) her new suit yet.
2. The new president was (swear) into office by her father.
3. Squirrels have (steal) the food you put out for the birds.

4. I have already (speak) to the boss about a raise.
5. On the hike, Steve's ears were badly (freeze).
6. The new coach has already been (choose).
7. Hundreds of windows were (break) by the explosion.
8. When Cindy delivered papers, she was (bite) twice by that dog.
9. Jim's ankle was (break) in the first play of the game.
10. The flowers had been (beat) down by the rain.
11. The twins (bear) little resemblance to each other.
12. The wreckers (tear) down the old building in two weeks.
13. Someone has (break) the power mower.
14. Derek (swear) he had been at home all day.
15. The pond had (freeze) solid early in November.
16. The reindeer had been (steal) from the hotel's lawn.
17. The wind (tear) the door off its hinges.
18. Mr. Alvarez has never been (beat) in an election.
19. During the night we were attacked and (bite) by mosquitoes.
20. I think Hilda has (speak) for all of us.

Group 4. Another group of irregular verbs is alike in changing the middle vowel from *i* in the present, to *a* in the past, and to *u* in the past participle. Memorize these seven verbs as a unit. They are the only verbs to follow this pattern.

PRESENT	PAST	PAST PARTICIPLE
begin	began	begun
drink	drank	drunk
ring	rang	rung
sing	sang	sung
sink	sank *or* sunk	sunk
spring	sprang *or* sprung	sprung
swim	swam	swum

Exercise A: The present form is given in parentheses. Substitute the past or past participle, whichever the sentence requires.

1. Has the voting (begin) yet?
2. The three boys had (drink) a gallon of milk.

3. Sarah walked up the steps and (ring) the bell.
4. Has Alex ever (sing) before an audience?
5. The orchestra had (begin) the overture.
6. All the other swimmers floated; I (sink).
7. The shopkeeper asked if her phone had (ring).
8. The weighted line (sink) quickly to the bottom.
9. The dogs (spring) at each other in great fury.
10. A seventeen-year-old girl has (swim) across Lake Ontario.
11. The snow (begin) to fall shortly after midnight.
12. That alto (sing) off-key in my ear.
13. The toy (sink) slowly to the bottom of the pond.
14. The rescued pilot (drink) the water slowly in tiny sips.
15. East German Kornelia Ender (swim) the 200-meter freestyle in less than two minutes.
16. As the band played, the crowd (sing) the national anthem.
17. Church bells (ring) across the nation when the first transcontinental railroad was completed.
18. Our relay team had (swim) the race in record time.
19. The pipe was (sink) in the ground and anchored in concrete.
20. The volunteers had (spring) into action during the fire.

Exercise B: Follow the same directions as for Exercise A.

1. We always (sing) "Auld Lang Syne" as the New Year began.
2. By morning, we had (begin) to see our trouble in a different light.
3. The *Andrea Doria* had (sink) off the coast of Nantucket.
4. The rabbit (spring) her babies from the trap.
5. We gave a biscuit to the dog that (swim) fastest.
6. Have you ever (drink) root beer with ice cream on a hot day?
7. Someone (ring) the doorbell, left this note, and departed.
8. Has the glee club ever (sing) the "Hallelujah" chorus?
9. The ship exploded suddenly and (sink) immediately.
10. The car's right front door was (spring) in the smashup.
11. Mom (begin) classes this week at Bethel College.
12. Linda had (drink) so much grape juice that she nearly got sick.
13. Barry (spring) out of the water like a jack-in-the-box.

14. The cashier (ring) up the charge on the cash register.

15. The runner was so thirsty that she (drink) the water too quickly.

16. Ricardo had (swim) halfway across the lake before anyone noticed him.

17. Marion has (begin) to recognize the value of practice.

18. The pioneers became sick when they first (drink) the alkali waters of the Western Plains.

19. The passing bell had (ring), but we stayed in our seats, fascinated.

20. Our new boys' quartet (sing) for the school assembly.

Group 5. Another group of irregular verbs is alike in making the past participle from the present form rather than from the past form.

PRESENT	PAST	PAST PARTICIPLE
blow	blew	blown
come	came	come
do	did	done
draw	drew	drawn
drive	drove	driven
eat	ate	eaten
fall	fell	fallen
give	gave	given
go	went	gone
grow	grew	grown
know	knew	known
ride	rode	ridden
rise	rose	risen
run	ran	run
see	saw	seen
shake	shook	shaken
slay	slew	slain
take	took	taken
throw	threw	thrown
write	wrote	written

Exercise A: Choose the standard form from those in parentheses.

1. Carmen sat in the car and (blowed, blew) the horn.
2. Darla (come, came) running down the driveway.
3. By noon we had already (did, done) a day's work.
4. A police car (drawed, drew) up beside the truck.
5. Mr. Cobb had (drove, driven) off to the side of the road for a nap.
6. The birds have (ate, eaten) all the seeds we put out for them.
7. The old house has (fell, fallen) into disrepair.
8. Ms. Hanley (give, gave) her nephew a ten-year loan to cover college expenses.
9. Our neighbors have (gone, went) to Miami for the winter.
10. One of my friends (grew, growed) four inches in a year.
11. We should have (know, knowed, known) that the stores would be closed today.
12. The girls had (rode, ridden) a bus all morning to get to the capital.
13. This successful business is (ran, run) entirely by high school students.
14. Nick just (shaked, shook) his head and said nothing.
15. After twenty years in prison, the gangster was (slew, slain) on the day he got out.
16. Jeff felt that he had been (took, taken) for granted.
17. The road crews (threw, throwed) sand and salt on the icy roads.
18. It's lucky we have (wrote, written) ahead for reservations.
19. Our class has (wrote, written) a news article every week this semester.
20. Someone had (throwed, thrown) papers all along the roadside.

Exercise B: The present form is given in parentheses. Substitute the past or past participle, whichever the sentence requires.

1. The ships had been (blow) far off their course in the storm.
2. People had (come) from miles around to see the play.

3. Dad (do) his best to discourage us from buying the old car.
4. The Rose Bowl game has always (draw) a capacity crowd.
5. When the subways were on strike, we all (drive) into town.
6. Moths had (eat) holes in my winter coat.
7. Trees and telephone poles had (fall) across the road.
8. The coach's inspiring talk (give) us all a lift.
9. Two firefighters had (go) quickly into the blazing building.
10. As midnight approached, we (grow) panicky.
11. It was the worst blizzard that Rochester had ever (know).
12. The scouts had (ride) hard all night to reach the fort.
13. As we came down the hill, two deer (run) across the road.
14. By six in the evening, the Governor had (shake) hands with several hundred people.
15. Two of the convicts were (slay) trying to escape from the prison.
16. Someone has (take) down the road sign.
17. One of the passengers was (throw) from her seat when the bus stopped suddenly.
18. Has anything been (do) to improve the water supply?
19. Your Christmas package finally (come) in February.
20. No signs of the downed pilots were (see).

Exercise C: Follow the same instructions as for exercise A.

1. Fortunately, the hurricane has (blow) out to sea.
2. No one has yet (come) forward to claim the wallet.
3. Jake has (do) most of the clean-up job alone.
4. The stranger had (draw) his money out of the bank and left town.
5. The snarling tiger had been (drive) into a corner of the cage.
6. We had never (eat) a better meal.
7. Six inches of snow had (fall) during the night.
8. The clerk (give) us careful instructions on operating the projector.
9. The boys have (go) to the junkyard to look for a fender.
10. Within a year, an entire city had (grow) up near the mines.

11. Fritz has never (know) how to save money.

12. During the summer, the girls had (ride) across the state on bicycles.

13. Has Ms. Stevens ever (run) for office before?

14. The force of the blast (shake) everything for fifty miles around.

15. The local authorities have (take) every precaution for the President's safety.

16. The tractors had been (draw) up into neat lines.

17. The car had been (drive) without water.

18. The temperature has (fall) ten degrees in the last hour.

19. The judge had (give) the woman a suspended sentence.

20. A dozen communities have (grow) up just beyond the city limits.

8.2 Verbs Confused as to Meaning

Three pairs of verbs are often confused because the meanings of each pair are closely related. They are related, but they are not identical. To use these verbs correctly, keep their meanings distinct.

Lie and lay. The verb *lay* means "to put or place something." The verb *lie* has eight or nine meanings, all having in common the idea of "being in a horizontal position, or to remain, or to be situated."*

Lie is always an intransitive verb. It never has an object. *Lay* is a transitive verb. It almost always has an object. The principal parts of these verbs are as follows:

PRESENT	PAST	PAST PARTICIPLE
lay	laid	laid
lie	lay	lain

* There is a homonym meaning "to tell an untruth." The principal parts of this verb are *lie, lied, lied.*

Sit and set. The verb *sit* usually means "to rest with the legs bent and the back upright," but there are many other related meanings. The verb *set* means "to put or place something."

Sit is an intransitive verb; it never has an object. *Set* is a transitive verb; it almost always has an object. The principal parts are as follows:

PRESENT	PAST	PAST PARTICIPLE
sit	sat	sat
set	set	set

Rise and raise. The verb *rise* means "to go to a higher position." The verb *raise* means "to lift to a higher position."

Rise is intransitive; it never has an object. *Raise* is transitive; it almost always has an object. Things *rise* by themselves; they are *raised* by something else. The principal parts of these verbs are as follows:

PRESENT	PAST	PAST PARTICIPLE
rise	rose	risen
raise	raised	raised

Note: It is very difficult to make general statements about English usage that will hold without exception. There are exceptions to the statements given above about the three pairs of verbs:

> The sun *sets.* (intransitive)
> Gelatin *sets* in three hours. (intransitive)
> *Sit* the doll up. (transitive)

Exercise A: Choose the standard form from those in parentheses.

1. The necessary tools (lay, laid) in a neat row on the table.
2. The fruit had (lain, laid) too long in the sun.
3. The mayor (lay, laid) the cornerstone for the new city hall.
4. Please don't (lie, lay) your wet coats on the chairs.
5. All day, the refugees (lay, laid) hiding in the rice field.

6. The books were (lying, laying) on the floor of the closet.

7. It is impossible for Boots to (lie, lay) still.

8. The beautiful old chest had (lain, laid) in the attic for years.

9. The company is already (lying, laying) plans for further expansion.

10. The city has (lain, laid) new storm drains along the road.

11. The old dog was (lying, laying) in the middle of the road.

12. New duties have been (lain, laid) on the branch managers this year.

13. Here in the cave the wounded trapper had (lain, laid) down to die.

14. Near the beach a new tennis court has been (lain, laid) out.

15. After the earthquake, over half the city (lay, laid) in ruins.

16. We were (lying, laying) in the shade waiting for the bus to come.

17. The union has (lain, laid) plans for a huge demonstration.

18. After dinner, you must (lie, lay) down for a rest.

19. We (lay, laid) out our equipment on the rocks to dry.

20. The revolver was found (lying, laying) in twelve feet of water.

Exercise B: Choose the standard form from those in parentheses.

1. Several of the guests were (sitting, setting) on the floor.

2. Please don't (sit, set) your glass on the table.

3. The superstitious think it is bad luck to (sit, set) a hat on a bed.

4. We will be (sitting, setting) on these chairs for a long time.

5. You will find it easier to (sit, set) still as you grow older.

6. The artist (sat, set) a fresh canvas on the easel.

7. You can (sit, set) the flowers on the hall table.

8. Ms. Donovan (sat, set) two hours today for her portrait.

9. Some of the children were (sitting, setting) on the curb.

10. Leroy (sat, set) his hat carefully on the back of his head.

11. I (sat, set) the brief case on the seat and promptly forgot about it.

12. How long has the coffee pot been (sitting, setting) on this burner?

13. Extra chairs were (sat, set) on the platform.

14. (Sitting, Setting) on one's heels is called *hunkering*.

15. You can (sit, set) the bag of ice outside.

16. The family (sat, set) at the airport all night, waiting for any plane.

17. The skeleton was (sitting, setting) on a chair in the front row.

18. The empty cartons were (sat, set) in the hall outside the door.

19. A warning light had been (sat, set) in the road.

20. The students were (sitting, setting) on the steps, waiting for the library to open.

Exercise C: Choose the standard form from those in parentheses.

1. Early in the day the wind had (risen, raised).

2. The cost of living did not (rise, raise) this last year.

3. Farm prices have not (risen, raised) for several years.

4. The proposal for a new airport (rose, raised) a storm of protest.

5. When the doctor asked for volunteers, five people (rose, raised) their hands.

6. The company's business has (risen, raised) every year.

7. Tonight, the moon is (rising, raising) in the northeast.

8. The fog was (rising, raising) as we left for the airport.

9. The archaeologists (rose, raised) the heavy stone statues by ropes.

10. Will the bus fare be (risen, raised) again this year?

11. Please (rise, raise) the window a few inches more.

12. The club plans to (rise, raise) a fund to send the band to the tournament.

13. Someone was (rising, raising) a disturbance outside the hall.

14. A sigh of relief (rose, raised) from the waiting crowd.

15. It will be Bonita's duty to (rise, raise) the flag every morning.

16. The dough has not (risen, raised) yet.

17. The landlord (rose, raised) our rent again this year.

18. A month ago, no one thought to (rise, raise) those arguments.

19. During the past hour, the water has (risen, raised) three inches.

20. The flock of ducks (rose, raised) gracefully from the lake.

REVIEW: VERB USAGE This exercise is a review of Section 8. Choose the standard form of the verb from those in parentheses.

1. Jolita has (gone, went) to the library.

2. Years ago, goods (cost, costed) much less to produce.

3. A large trout (swinged, swang, swung) from the end of Jake's fishing line.

4. That blister has (hurt, hurted) for days.

5. The Bee Gees have (sang, sung) in several movies.

6. Each year Aunt Laura has (brought, brung) the pumpkin pies for Thanksgiving dinner.

7. Our dog Zap has never (bit, bitten) anyone.

8. Osaka has (broke, broken) the school record for free-style swimming.

9. A dinner bell was (rang, ringed, rung) to call the campers.

10. The candidate (shook, shaked) hands with everyone who walked past.

11. Tim (flung, flang, flinged) a dart at the target.

12. The Wildcats were (beat, beaten) in overtime.

13. Lost in the desert, Connors had (drank, drunk) no water for ten days.

14. We should have (knowed, known) that sunrise was earlier.

15. A ten-dollar bill (lay, laid) on the sidewalk.

16. A southwest wind (rose, raised) the temperature.

17. Please (lie, lay) your jacket on the couch.

18. The bricklayer (sat, set) the bricks in neat rows.

19. Ryan (sat, set) patiently in the dentist's chair.

20. Emily (rose, raised) her binoculars to view the asteroids.

9.0 The Right Word

Different words, like different clothes, are appropriate for different occasions. The word *ain't* would be just as improper in a formal paper as a bikini would be at an inaugural ball.

In preceding sections, you may have noticed the labels **standard** and **nonstandard. Standard usages** are appropriate at all times and in all places.

Nonstandard usages are not acceptable everywhere. In many cases, they mark the user as careless or untrained in the English language.

There are other levels of American English usage besides *standard* and *nonstandard. Slang, informal, dialectal, archaic,* and *poetic* are some of the other classifications of usage. These labels tell the areas in which different words are acceptable. A slang word, like *rip-off,* for instance, is suitable for casual talk but not for more formal situations.

The glossary that follows explains (a) usage items not covered in preceding pages, and (b) words commonly confused as to meaning.

This glossary does not cover every problem of usage that might arise. When in doubt, consult a good dictionary.

Distinctions of Meanings and Items of Usage

accept, except To *accept* is "to agree to something or to receive something willingly." To *except* is "to exclude or omit." As a preposition, *except* means "but" or "excluding."

Will you *accept* my invitation?
The new rule *excepts* honor students from final exams. (verb)
Everybody *except* Jean brought a lunch. (preposition)

adapt, adopt   To keep the meanings of these words straight, look at the second syllables. *Adapt* means "to make *apt* or suitable; to adjust." *Adopt*, on the other hand, means "to *opt* or choose as one's own; to accept."

The writer *adapted* the play for the screen.
She *adopted* Diane Keaton's style of dress.

advice, advise   You *advise* someone. What you give that person is *advice*.

affect, effect   *Affect* is a verb meaning either "to influence" or "to pretend." *Effect* as a verb means "to accomplish or to produce as a result." As a noun, *effect* means "result."

agree to, with, on   You agree *to* something, such as a plan of action. You agree *with* someone else. Or, something such as spinach does not agree *with* you. You agree with others *on* a course of action.

a lot   This little expression causes *a lot* of trouble. It is two words, not one. The misspelling *alot* is nonstandard.

all right   The misspelling *alright* is nonstandard usage. The two words are separate.

already, all ready   *Already* is an adverb meaning "even now" or "previously." *All ready* is an adjective phrase meaning "completely prepared."

We are *already* late.
We are *all ready* for the tournament.

altogether, all together   *Altogether* means "entirely" or "on the whole." *All together* means that all parts of a group are considered together.

This news story is *altogether* false. (entirely)
A tug of war is won by a team pulling *all together*.

among, between   *Between* expresses the joining or separation of two people or things. *Among* refers to a group of three or more.

NONSTANDARD: We shared the pie *between* the three of us.
STANDARD: We shared the pie *among* the three of us.

amount, number   *Amount* is used to indicate a total sum of things. It is usually used to refer to items that cannot be counted. *Number* is used to refer to items that can be counted.

The chef cooked the *amount* of food we ordered. (Food cannot be counted.)
The chef cooked the *number* of omelettes we ordered. (Omelettes can be counted.)

angry at, with   You are angry *with* a person and angry *at* a thing.

anywhere, nowhere, somewhere, anyway   *Anywheres, nowheres, somewheres, anyways* are nonstandard.

bad, badly   See Section 7.5.

beside, besides   *Beside* means "at the side of." *Besides* means "in addition to."

Secret Service agents stand *beside* the President.
There are other motives *besides* greed.

borrow, lend   You *borrow from* someone. You *lend to* someone.

NONSTANDARD: Will you *borrow* me your book?
STANDARD: Will you *lend* me your book?
STANDARD: May I *borrow* your book?

bring, take   *Bring* means motion toward someone or some place; *take* means motion away from someone or some place.

I will *take* you back to school. (away from here)
I hope Mom *brings* a newspaper home. (toward here)
A plane will *take* me to St. Louis. (away from here)

can, may   *Can* means "able or having the power to do something." *May* is used to ask or to grant permission. It also expresses the probability of something happening.

> *Can* you ride a horse? (ability)
> *May* I be excused? (permission)
> Eagles *may* become extinct. (probability)

Could is the past tense of *can; might* is the past tense of *may.*

differ from, with   One thing or person differs *from* another in characteristics. You differ *with* someone when you disagree with him or her.

Exercise A: Rewrite these sentences to make them follow standard usage.

1. After alot of rest the patient is feeling alright.
2. Everyone accept Monica has agreed with the new plan.
3. Did you take back the rake I borrowed you?
4. May you tell the difference among a peach and a nectarine?
5. Alligators differ with crocodiles in the shape of the snout.
6. I get angry with machines that don't return change.
7. The union members met altogether and agreed between themselves on a strike.
8. An amendment to the Constitution must be adapted by three-fourths of the states.
9. Can we go to the library?
10. A large amount of students noticed the effect of soothing music in the cafeteria.

Exercise B: Follow the same directions as for Exercise A.

1. The candidate has all ready agreed with a debate with her opponent.
2. The book I borrowed to Tom is nowheres to be found.
3. Heather adopted the story to suit the young listeners sitting besides her.

4. Now that I've accepted your advise, you're already to change your mind.

5. The weather can effect the amount of people who vote.

6. Jet takeoffs disturb alot of people who live besides the airport.

7. My counselor adviced me to take alot of math courses.

8. The two leaders disagreed among themselves on the issue of excepting the treaty.

9. Will you four girls please lift the mat altogether and take it toward me?

10. Environment effects a person's personality, but heredity also has an effect.

fewer, less   See Section 7.7.

formally, formerly   *Formally* means "in a formal manner." *Formerly* means "previously."

> Our principal was *formerly* a state senator.
> The committee *formally* ratified the proposal.

further, farther; furthest, farthest   Generally, in good usage, *farther* is used for comparisons of distance and *further* for anything else.

> Robin's punt went *farther* than Jenny's. (distance)
> Pablo has advanced *further* in his study of English. (extent)

good, well   See Section 7.6.

had of, off of   The *of* is both unnecessary and undesirable.

> NONSTANDARD: If you had of played, we would have won.
> STANDARD: If you had played, we would have won.

> NONSTANDARD: The box fell off of the shelf.
> STANDARD: The box fell off the shelf.

hanged, hung   Criminals are *hanged*. Things are *hung* on walls, hooks, or elsewhere.

> The sheriff's men *hanged* the thief.
> The children *hung* decorations on the tree.

imply, infer   A speaker or writer suggests or *implies* something. The reader, listener, or observer comes to a conclusion or *infers* something on the basis of what he or she sees and hears.

> The dealer *implied* that the jewelry was valuable.
> The class *inferred* that the teacher was pleased.

in, into   *In* means "inside something." *Into* tells of motion from the outside to the inside of something.

> NONSTANDARD: Carl dove *in* the water.
> STANDARD: Carl dove *into* the water.
> NONSTANDARD: I drove the car *in* the garage.
> STANDARD: I drove the car *into* the garage.

kind, sort, type   See Section 7.3.

kind of a, sort of a   The *a* is unnecessary.

> NONSTANDARD: What kind of a dog is Scout?
> STANDARD: What kind of dog is Scout?

lay, lie   See Section 8.2.

learn, teach   To *learn* means "to gain knowledge or instruction." To *teach* is "to provide knowledge" or "to instruct."

> The student *learns* the lessons that the tutor *teaches*.

leave, let   Leave means "to go away from." *Let* means "to permit." The principal parts are *leave, left, left*, and *let, let, let*.

> NONSTANDARD: Please *leave* the usher show you your seat.
> STANDARD: Please *let* the usher show you your seat.
> NONSTANDARD: The fisherman *left* the small fish go free.
> STANDARD: The fisherman *let* the small fish go free.
> NONSTANDARD: Don't *leave* this room get messy.
> STANDARD: Don't *let* this room get messy.

like, as, as if   While the use of *like* as a conjunction is common in speaking, its use as a conjunction is not fully established in writing. *Like* is better used as a preposition.

NOT ACCEPTED: I feel *like* Susan Anderson does about
consumers' rights.
BETTER: I feel *as* Susan Anderson does about
consumers' rights.

NOT ACCEPTED: Ralph looked *like* he had seen a ghost.
BETTER: Ralph looked *as if* he had seen a ghost

majority This word can be used only with items that can be
counted. It is incorrectly used in speaking of time or distance.

NONSTANDARD: The *majority* of the film was interesting.
STANDARD: *Most* of the film was interesting.

NONSTANDARD: The *majority* of the time was wasted.
STANDARD: *Most* of the time was wasted.
STANDARD: The *majority* of the students wasted no time.

most, almost *Almost* is an adverb meaning "nearly." *Most* is
an adjective meaning "the greater part."

NONSTANDARD: *Most* everyone attended the game.
STANDARD: *Almost* everyone attended the game.

of When *could have, might have, must have,* and similar
phrases are spoken, they usually come out as contractions:
could've, might've, must've, and so on. Because the contracted
form *'ve* sounds like *of,* some people mistakenly write *could of,
might of, must of.*

NONSTANDARD: That plant *must of* been overwatered.
STANDARD: That plant *must have* been overwatered.

raise, rise See Section 8.2.

seldom ever The *ever* is unnecessary. You may say instead
seldom, very seldom, or *hardly ever.*

AWKWARD: We *seldom ever* saw the horse unharnessed.
BETTER: We *very seldom* saw the horse unharnessed.

Exercise A: Rewrite these sentences to make them follow standard usage.

1. The delegates must of spent the majority of the hour arguing.
2. An ice rink was formally located besides the field house.
3. My parents left me choose which kind of a bike to buy.
4. Has anyone really jumped off of Niagara Falls?
5. Most all of Poe's stories keep the reader in suspense.
6. Our coach learned us how to hit an overhead smash in the corner.
7. "That upset must of been an exciting game," Randi said.
8. Most everyone felt like Liz did about the game, for there were a lot of unfair decisions.
9. Julia Child learned me how to make one kind of a cake.
10. I imply from the judge's sentence that the murderer will be hung.

Exercise B: Follow the same directions as for Exercise A.

1. I wish our math teacher had of left us leave class early.
2. Unfortunately, the first aid station was further away than we had thought.
3. Most everyone worries about falling off the catwalk, so it is seldom ever used.
4. The majority of motorcycle riders seldom ever used this sort of a helmet.
5. A farther goal of mine is to learn myself to play the guitar like James Taylor does.
6. Lavonne should of taken our advise and left her books in the car.
7. The horse looked sleek as it moved in the lead.
8. "Leave me get up!" the boy shrieked, like he had been attacked.
9. For the dance we hanged colorful decorations from the ceiling.
10. The ambassador inferred that he wanted to be formerly invited to the reception.

REVIEW: THE RIGHT WORD This exercise is a review of Section 9. Rewrite these sentences to make them follow standard usage.

1. Can I help you bring those books back to the library?
2. I wish we could of traveled somewheres in the South.
3. Will you borrow me some kind of a measuring stick?
4. Most all of the contestants looked like they might of been nervous.
5. Mr. Chang learned our class how reptiles differ from amphibians.
6. The sun is alot further from Earth than the moon is.
7. After she went in the building, Gilda hanged her coat in her locker.
8. The coach wouldn't leave us jump off of the high dive.
9. Our hockey coach, who formally played for the Blackhawks, seldom ever gives bad advice.
10. The principal has all ready agreed with a plan for changing the school's attendance policy.
11. I will except any advise that sounds alright.
12. The counselor left Alicia and her parents decide between themselves.
13. Our teams have adapted another mascot beside the bulldog.
14. The conductor became angry at the musicians because they weren't playing altogether.
15. In her speech, the commentator inferred that the majority of the legal system was corrupt.
16. Weather effects the number of crop yield that farmers get.
17. Anyways, Russia has a space program just like America does.
18. The majority of the time the Royal Family does not dress formerly.
19. The salesperson inferred that there were only a certain amount of tickets left.
20. The Senator differs from the President about the affect of inflation.

10.0 Capitalization

10.1 *A.D., B.C., I, O*

Capitalize the abbreviations *A.D.* and *B.C.*, the pronoun *I,* and the interjection *O.*

The abbreviations B.C. and A.D. occur only with the number of a year: 1001 B.C., A.D. 1492. The interjection O occurs in poetry, in the Bible, or in prayers or petitions: O Lord, O King, O Master.

O is quite different from the explosive interjection *oh,* which is capitalized only at the beginning of a sentence.

10.2 First Words

Capitalize the first word of a sentence, a direct quotation, and a line of poetry.

They handed him a bouquet of daisies.

"No one," he said, "has ever given me flowers before."

I will arise and go now, and go to Innisfree,
And a small cabin build there, of clay and wattles made;
Nine bean rows will I have there, a hive for the honey bee,
 And live alone in the bee-loud glade.*

* From "The Lake Isle of Innisfree" by William Butler Yeats, quoted by permission of the Macmillan Company.

10.3 Proper Nouns and Adjectives

A **common noun** is the name of a whole group of persons, places, or things. A **proper noun** is the name of an individual person, place, or thing. A **proper adjective** is an adjective formed from a proper noun.

COMMON NOUN	PROPER NOUN	PROPER ADJECTIVE
continent	Europe	European
playwright	Shakespeare	Shakespearean
car	Corvette	

Proper nouns and adjectives occur in many compound words. Capitalize only the parts of these words that are capitalized when they stand alone. Do not capitalize prefixes such as *pro-, un-, pre-* attached to proper nouns and adjectives.

un-American   pro-Leftist   pre-Civil War

Proper nouns occur in great variety. The following rules with their illustrations will help you solve the capitalization problems that proper nouns present.

10.4 Geographical Names

In a geographical name, capitalize the first letter of each word except articles and prepositions.

The article *the* appearing before a geographical name is not part of the geographical name and is therefore not capitalized.

CONTINENTS   North America, South America, Asia

BODIES OF WATER   the Indian Ocean, Lake Ontario, the Jordan River, Strait of Belle Isle, Cape Cod Bay, the Adriatic Sea, St. George's Channel, the Gulf of Finland

LAND FORMS   the Pyrenees, the Sinai Peninsula, the Grand Canyon, the Syrian Desert, Mount Constance, the Plains of Abraham, Raton Pass

POLITICAL UNITS   the District of Columbia, the British Isles, the Commonwealth of Pennsylvania, the State of Maine, the West Indies, San Francisco, the Republic of Texas, the First Congressional District, the Union of Soviet Socialist Republics

PUBLIC AREAS   Gettysburg National Park, Fort Niagara, the Blue Grotto, Mount Rushmore

ROADS AND HIGHWAYS   Main Street, Route 447, West Side Highway, Van Buren Avenue, the Ohio Turnpike, Strawberry Lane, Savile Row, Rue de Rivoli

10.5   Common Nouns in Names

A common noun that is part of a name is capitalized. A common noun used to define or refer to a proper noun is not capitalized.

PART OF THE NAME	REFERENCE OR DEFINITION
New York State	the state of New York*
Salt Lake City	the city of Jacksonville
the Western Plains	plains in the West
the Ohio Valley	the valley of the Ohio

10.6   Words Modified by Proper Adjectives

The word modified by a proper adjective is not capitalized unless adjective and noun together are a geographical name.

GEOGRAPHICAL NAME	MODIFIED NOUN
English Channel	English accent
the Indian Ocean	Indian customs
West Germany	German language

* In official documents, words like *city, state,* and *county* are capitalized when they are part of the name of a political unit: *the County of Westchester, the State of Mississippi, the City of Los Angeles.*

Exercise: Copy the following sentences, supplying necessary capitals.

1. How many german composers can you name?
2. The explorers skirted the gulf of mexico until they came to the mississippi river.
3. There are not many english-speaking people in the indonesian republic.
4. Many of the dutch speak german and english as well as their native tongue.
5. The republic of ghana lies on the west coast of africa.
6. The amazon river almost bisects the continent of south america.
7. In an old chest found in death valley, there was a copy of a new york newspaper.
8. The old roman walls may still be seen in the northern parts of great britain.
9. The state of minnesota is supposed to have 10,000 lakes.
10. For years, one part of the western plains was surrounded by texas and oklahoma, but it belonged to neither state.
11. You can now drive from new england to the midwest on throughways.
12. Glacier national park lies in the state of montana.
13. Some people believe there is a difference between the american language and english.
14. Several languages are spoken in the republic of the philippines.
15. The geographic south pole lies under a mass of ice in antarctica.
16. Travelers can now go directly from the jersey turnpike to the pennsylvania turnpike.
17. The ohio river forms part of the boundary of the state of ohio.
18. The bus goes down fifth avenue to washington square.
19. Several american textbooks have been translated into spanish for use in the schools of the commonwealth of puerto rico.
20. There are still many dutch ships steaming up the hudson river.

10.7 Directions and Sections

Capitalize names of sections of the country but not of directions of the compass.

> Cotton was king in the South.
> Cities in the Southwest are flourishing.
> It is just north of Paris.
> They flew east through the storm.
> She lives on the north side of the street.
> The lake is west of our cottage.
> The hurricane moved northward.

Capitalize proper adjectives derived from names of sections of the country. Do not capitalize adjectives derived from words indicating direction.

> an Eastern school   a southerly course
> a Western concept   an eastern route

Exercise: Copy the following sentences, supplying the necessary capitals. If a sentence is correct, write *C* next to the number.

1. Many factories from the north have moved into southern states.

2. The people of the southwest think of themselves as neither southern nor western.

3. Many eastern students are going to midwestern colleges.

4. The westbound flight leaves in ten minutes.

5. The southeast and the far west are the most rapidly growing sections of the country.

6. The storm is moving rapidly eastward.

7. In the Pacific there is one great current that flows eastward and another, south of it, that flows in a westerly direction.

8. The civilization of the west has much to learn from that of the east.

9. There are many points at issue in east-west relations.

10. The sunlight moves from east to west, but the prevailing winds move eastward.

11. Water shortage is becoming a serious problem in the southeast.

12. The northern papers were printing outrageous stories about the south, and southern papers retaliated in kind.

13. From Manila, Dr. Robertson will fly west to the middle east.

14. The east branch of the Delaware flows into Pennsylvania.

15. We will take the northern route on our trip to the west.

16. The western colleges are welcoming eastern students.

17. The candidate for Vice-President will probably be a westerner.

18. The birds fly south in September but return to the north in April.

19. Is it true that Atlanta lies west of New York?

20. The northern summer resorts attract many people from the south.

10.8 Languages, Races, Nationalities, and Religions

Capitalize the names of languages, races, nationalities, and religions and the adjectives formed from them.

English class	Judaism	Protestant
the Italian heritage	Episcopalian	Irish linen
Hungarian	Catholic	Peruvian

Do not capitalize the names of school subjects, except for specific course names. However, languages are always capitalized.

algebra	Algebra 2	history	Women in History
biology	Biology I	French	Earth Science II

10.9 Organizations and Institutions

Capitalize important words in the names of organizations, buildings, firms, schools, churches, and other institutions. Do not capitalize *and* or prepositions. Capitalize an article (*a, an,* or *the*) only if it appears as the first word in a name.

Pittsburgh Symphony	Carlino Tile Company
Cedars of Lebanon Hospital	Taylor Allderdice High School
Church of the Martyr	Metropolitan Museum of Art
University of Illinois	United Airlines

Note: In brand names, the common noun is not capitalized: *a Volkswagen bus; Indian River grapefruit; Crest toothpaste.*

Exercise: Copy the following sentences, supplying necessary capitals.

1. The boston choral society will appear at the university of maine.
2. The st. louis art museum has a fine collection of dutch paintings.
3. The lerner string quartet will play at the library of congress.
4. The new york public library has a fine collection of books on buddhism.
5. Ship the english books to the richmond field high school.
6. The hungarian people have an asiatic background.
7. The knights of columbus have a new office near st. mary's hospital.
8. The pennsylvania railroad runs under the hudson river into the pennsylvania station.
9. A friend of mine is teaching spanish at stanford university.
10. The anglo-african oil company is not interested in aluminum.
11. My sister bought a secondhand chevy van.
12. The summer school program offers english, chemistry, and american history.
13. Louis served us french toast with vermont maple syrup.
14. The junior chamber of commerce will campaign for a new hospital.
15. My mathematics teacher teaches geometry II as well as algebra I.
16. Where are the offices of the american red cross?
17. We bought our sunspeed power mower at the barclay hardware store.
18. Mr. Margolis works at the morgan guaranty trust company.

19. Our new offices are in the first national bank building.
20. The new teacher is a leader in the boy scouts of america.

10.10 Titles of Persons

Capitalize words that show rank, office, or profession, when they are used with a person's name.

Doctor Weber	Representative Walsh	Father Forbes
Sergeant Reilly	Rabbi Kahn	Captain Brooks
Private Harrison	Mayor Derrado	Judge Bentley

The titles of high officials are capitalized even when they are used without the official's name.

the President of the United States	the Prime Minister
the Secretary of State	the Governor

The prefix *ex-* and the suffix *-elect* are not capitalized when attached to titles: *ex-President Nixon,* the *Senator-elect.*

10.11 Family Relationships

Capitalize the name of a family relationship when it is used with a person's name.

Aunt Ruth   Uncle Bill   Cousin Joe

When words like *mother, father, dad,* and *mom* are used alone in place of a particular person's name, they are capitalized. When modified by a possessive pronoun, as in *your mother,* they are not capitalized. When these and other words of family relationship do not stand for a particular person, they are not capitalized.

My Aunt Daisy bought me this sweater.
We begged Mom to play the piano for us.
His father will meet him at the station.
I can't imagine having five sisters.

10.12 Titles of Books and Works of Art

Capitalize the first word and every important word in the titles of books, stories, articles, poems, films, works of art, and musical compositions.

The only words considered not important are conjunctions, articles (*a, an,* and *the*), and prepositions containing fewer than five letters. But even these are capitalized when used as the first word in a title.

A Tale of Two Cities	*Death of a Salesman*
Notes of a Native Son	"To Build a Fire"
"A Christmas Memory"	"Mother to Son"

Exercise: Copy each word that requires a capital in these sentences.

1. Is aunt rachel inviting dad to her camp?
2. There was a radio report of the death of ex-governor jones.
3. My aunt jenny introduced colonel hawkins as our next governor.
4. The president-elect met with the senators from his state.
5. Gershwin's most famous musical work is *rhapsody in blue.*
6. Did your father hear from cousin bert?
7. The judge asked officer swenson to testify.
8. Have you ever read the play *a raisin in the sun* by lorraine hansberry?
9. Our doctor consulted with doctor pamela payne about the diagnosis.
10. Was henry kissinger secretary of state when ex-president ford was in office?
11. The author of the article is justice laura larson.
12. We learned that the governors of these states are to meet the secretary of the interior.
13. Have mother and father met judge krantz?
14. My sister gave cousin sandra *webster's new world dictionary.*
15. You will find *art through the ages* a useful reference.
16. Heather wants a copy of *two years before the mast.*
17. Claire's favorite poem is "the first snowfall."

18. The meeting will be addressed by chief of police johnson.

19. The party consisted of colonel byrd, lieutenant wojack, and my cousin.

20. Your mother drove us out to see grandfather brown.

10.13 The Deity

Capitalize all words referring to the Deity, the Holy Family, and to religious scriptures.

God	the Holy Spirit	Jehovah	the Torah
the Father	the Virgin Mary	the Bible	the Talmud
the Son	the Lord	the Gospel	the Koran

Capitalize personal pronouns but not relative pronouns that refer to the Deity.

May God make His blessings plentiful.
Praise God from whom all mercy flows.

10.14 Days, Months, Holidays

Capitalize the names of days of the week, of months, and of holidays. Do not capitalize the names of the seasons.

Wednesday	Thanksgiving	spring
August	Easter	fall

10.15 Historical Names

Capitalize the names of historical events, documents, and periods.

World War II	the Renaissance	the Homestead Act
the Constitution	the New Deal	Bill of Rights

Exercise A: Copy the words that require capitals in these sentences.

1. Edward is reading the chaptets on the late middle ages.
2. My favorite period in american history is the age of jackson.
3. Both the declaration of independence and the emancipation proclamation are greatly admired by other nations.
4. Some authorities believe that the battle of the bulge was a decisive battle in world war II.
5. In new york, columbus day is always a holiday.
6. The prohibition era was a time of low public morals.
7. We expect to celebrate new year's eve by staying home and watching TV.
8. The convent of st. paul the apostle is the local address of the sisters of the holy ghost.
9. The romantic period began later in american literature.
10. The second continental congress lasted for five years.

Exercise B: Copy the words that require capitals in these sentences.

1. The vice-president met the french premier at national airport.
2. The social security act is administered by the department of health, education, and welfare.
3. The little group under captain siple observed christmas leave at the south pole.
4. My uncle was on an airplane carrier in the battle of midway.
5. The governor and the senator-elect exchanged cordial greetings.
6. In an address to congress, president monroe announced the monroe doctrine.
7. The settlers rode down the ohio river on their way to the west.
8. Several french communities were founded in the midwest.
9. On the eastbound flight, we were over the rocky mountains very quickly.
10. You can buy irish linen at dayton's department store on fourth street.

REVIEW: CAPITALIZATION This exercise is a review of Section 10. Copy the following sentences, supplying the necessary capitals.

1. yes, doctor caldwell advised mother to rest.
2. yellowstone national park is situated amid the rocky mountains.
3. last christmas uncle daniel gave me *roots.*
4. majorca is a spanish island resort in the mediterranean sea.
5. the orient has adopted many american customs.
6. several midwestern high schools are offering local history classes.
7. do brazilians speak spanish or portuguese?
8. the gillette company manufactures toni hair care products.
9. the gulf stream keeps winters mild along cape cod.
10. during world war II grandma worked at a munitions factory.
11. at poppin' fresh i had the dutch apple pie with swiss cheese.
12. the greyhound bus traveled north along the edens expressway.
13. in july, britain's prince charles will visit boston and hartford.
14. one reporter asked representative simms and senator pasquale for reports of their earnings.
15. great britain's prime minister visited washington, d.c., last fall.
16. at stevenson high school, advanced algebra II begins with a review of algebra I.
17. headquarters for the united nations are in new york city.
18. "who were the world rulers," ms. ellman asked, "in 100 b. c.?"
19. reciting verses from the bible, the Pilgrims celebrated the first thanksgiving day.
20. following the civil war, the reconstruction acts restored the southern states to congress.

11.0 End Marks and Commas

11.1 Periods at the Close of Sentences

Place a period at the close of every declarative sentence and of most imperative sentences.

A period is also used at the close of groups of words that are used as sentences even though they are not complete sentences.

> Don't get too near the fire.
> I'll never go back to that barber. Never.

11.2 Periods in Abbreviations

Place a period after every part of an abbreviation.

U. S. Grant	Ulysses Simpson Grant
Atty. Gen.	Attorney General
N. Dak.	North Dakota
P.M.	*post meridiem*

It has become the custom not to use periods in abbreviations of certain government agencies and of international organizations.

NATO	North Atlantic Treaty Organization
FBI	Federal Bureau of Investigation
UN	United Nations
FDA	Food and Drug Administration
IRS	Internal Revenue Service

11.3 Exclamation Points

Place an exclamation point after an exclamatory sentence and after an exclamation set off from a sentence.

Wow! What a hit!   That's enough!
Help! Help!   Look out!
Bravo!   We want Armstrong!

11.4 Question Marks

Place a question mark after an interrogative sentence or after a question that is not a complete sentence.

The word order in questions is sometimes the same as in declarative sentences. In speech, the speaker raises his or her voice at at the end of the sentence to show that it is a question. In writing, the question mark performs the same function.

Does Roger ice skate?   You call this hot?
Is this the book you want?   Who made these donuts?
The date? It's the twenty-fifth. These are yours?

Exercise A: Copy these sentences, using end marks and punctuation as required for sentences and abbreviations. Use question marks only for sentences in normal interrogative form.

1. At what time does the game begin
2. Mr. L V Costello left this office at 4:30 P M
3. I've been robbed
4. Does the plane from Omaha arrive at 4:10 A M or 4:10 P M
5. Have you ever watched "Marcus Welby, M D"
6. Gov Ella Grasso has served in Congress
7. Emily Ray, D D S, used to work for General Foods, Inc
8. Dr J A Larson, Jr will attend a conference in Washington, D C
9. The contract was arranged between Brightons, Ltd of England and Sweetways, Inc of New York
10. Who ruled the Mediterranean world from 100 B C to A D 200

Exercise B: Follow the same directions as for Exercise A.

1. Don't touch that wire
2. When the box arrives, may we open it
3. The book was written by the Reverend Thomas Powers, S J
4. Susan B Anthony was a leader in the women's suffrage movement, wasn't she
5. Help The rug is on fire
6. Brig Gen M E Clark is director of the Women's Army Corps
7. Did Dr Martin Luther King, Jr win the Nobel peace prize in 1963 or in 1964
8. Does the I R S check up on the F B I
9. The meeting was addressed by Asst Dep José Rivera
10. Professor Marilyn Barnard, D Sc was appointed to the I C C

Uses of the Comma

11.5 Introductory Words

Introductory words such as *yes, no, well, why,* and *oh* are followed by a comma.

Yes, I think I would like some soup.
Well, I haven't actually finished the assignment.
Oh, this coat belongs to you.

Adverbs such as *besides, however, anyhow, nonetheless* at the beginning of a sentence are set off by commas.

11.6 Introductory Phrases and Clauses

A participial phrase at the beginning of a sentence is followed by a comma.
A long adverbial clause at the beginning of a sentence is followed by a comma.
A succession of prepositional phrases at the beginning of a sentence is set off by a comma.

Hoping to be rescued, they treaded water all night. (participial phrase)

When the sun rose the next morning, our sleeping bags were covered with dew. (adverbial clause)

Under the rug at the top of the stairs, we found Dad's keys. (succession of prepositional phrases)

11.7 Transposed Words and Phrases

Words and phrases moved to the beginning of a sentence from their normal position are usually set off by a comma.

He is usually dressed in blue jeans. (normal order)
Usually, he is dressed in blue jeans. (transposed order)

There is obviously no exit to this cave. (normal order)
Obviously, there is no exit to this cave. (transposed order)

Call Serena for directions if necessary. (normal order)
If necessary, call Serena for directions. (transposed order)

Exercise A: Copy the following sentences, inserting commas where necessary. Two of the sentences are correct.

1. Honestly we are not justified in complaining.
2. At the start of the campaign Ms. Anson was favored to win.
3. Well no one was more surprised at the outcome than Robbie.
4. If possible make the appointment for Wednesday.
5. Wearing sunglasses gives me a headache.
6. After scoring six runs in the first inning the Mets let up.
7. To avoid excess nervous tension practice physical relaxation.
8. Counting on surprise strategy Greenville passed on the first down.
9. Exploring the wilderness requires preparation and skill.
10. Although the road was icy we made fairly good time.

Exercise B: Follow the same directions as for Exercise A. Two of the sentences are correct.

1. No there is no other way out of the valley.

2. When Mozart was six he was performing his music in the courts of Europe.

3. Concentrating intensely Lynn went over her report again.

4. Yes Amelia Earhart was the first woman to fly solo across the ocean.

5. Dropping their tools the workers scrambled for safety.

6. To save some of the money is simply good sense.

7. When the tide went out we walked along the sandy beach.

8. Keeping up the morale of the staff was Paul's hardest job.

9. Hard as she worked the younger child could not catch up to the rest of the class.

10. Why no one warned us to shut off the water.

11.8 Appositives

An appositive is set off from the rest of the sentence by commas.

Farrell, *our quarterback*, injured his shoulder.
Mother's guest, *Ms. Worthall*, was not amused.

11.9 Words of Direct Address

Words of direct address are set off by commas.

Giles, please stop humming that song.
So, *Dr. Jeffries*, what is your opinion?
Would you come here a minute, *Ms. Chilton*?

11.10 Parenthetical Expressions

Words and phrases used to explain or qualify a statement are called **parenthetical expressions.** These same words and phrases may also be used as basic parts of the sentence. It is only when they are parenthetical that they are set off by commas.

I believe our car is over there.
Our car, *I believe,* is over there. (parenthetical)

We hope that we'll get back in time for the meeting.
We'll get back, *we hope,* in time for the meeting.
(parenthetical)

Parenthetical expressions are set off by commas.

Some expressions often used parenthetically are:

of course	as a matter of fact	for example
in fact	I believe (hope, think)	on the other hand

Conjunctive adverbs (see Section 1.7) used parenthetically within the sentence are set off by commas: *therefore, moreover, nevertheless, however, consequently,* and so on.

The principal, *moreover,* was in favor of their plan.
The students, *however,* did not know this.
The rally, *consequently,* was attended by very few.

Occasionally, words like *however, therefore,* and *consequently* are used to modify a word in the sentence. As modifiers they are an essential part of the meaning of a sentence. Since they are essential, they are not set off by commas.

Pat cannot arrive on time *however* hard he tries.
The cast had performed the play the previous semester. They *therefore* needed little rehearsal.
The club's bylaws were *consequently* altered.

11.11 Dates, Addresses, Geographical Names

In dates and addresses of more than one part, set off every part after the first from the rest of the sentence.

She comes from a small town in Ohio. (one part)
I believe that East Liverpool, Ohio, is her home town. (two parts, the second set off by commas)
V-J Day was in 1945. (one part)

It was on August 14, 1945, that the fighting with Japan ended. (two parts, the second set off by commas)

All of his mail is being forwarded to 3144 Camelback Road, Phoenix, Arizona 85016, where his aunt and uncle live. (three parts, the second and third set off by commas)

Note: The day of the month and the month are one item. The name of the street and the house number are one item. The name of the state and the ZIP code are one item.

May 29   313 West Houston Street   Georgia 30312

Exercise A: Copy these sentences, inserting the necessary commas.

1. We visited the Adams Library one of the oldest in America.
2. There is no doubt my friends that we have hard times ahead of us.
3. One field of science computer technology is almost completely devoted to storing and transmitting information.
4. The damage however was less than we had expected.
5. A completely honest person I can assure you is hard to find.
6. Your second sentence for example is much too long.
7. The door was opened by the butler a tall man with brooding eyes
8. The game was played as a matter of fact exactly as we had planned it.
9. Therefore the library will be closed on Saturday.
10. The company has moved its offices to Morristown New Jersey.

Exercise B: Follow the same directions as for Exercise A.

1. Reno Nevada lies farther west than Los Angeles California.
2. Our new address is 41 East Twelfth Street New York New York 10003.
3. The treaty was signed in Geneva Switzerland on December 15 1906 but it was not ratified until March 6 1908.
4. On July 5 1835 there were snowstorms in New England.
5. Lee was born in Evanston Illinois on December 19 1965.

6. You know my colleagues we may be on the verge of a revolution in printing.

7. This house as you can see was built on a rocky ledge.

8. We will meet you at Canton Ohio on Wednesday January 10.

9. The entrapped miners decided therefore to make one more try.

10. It is up to you my friends to decide what kind of society you want to live in.

11.12   Nonrestrictive Modifiers

A clause that identifies or points out the person or thing it modifies is a **restrictive clause.** It is essential to the meaning of the sentence. It cannot be dropped without confusing the meaning or making the meaning incomplete.

> The car *that I told you about* is parked over there.
>   (The clause tells *which* car.)
> We need a car *that can seat ten.* (The clause tells
>   an essential characteristic of the car.)
> The woman *who makes her own clothes* is never shabby.
>   (Without the clause the sentence has no specific meaning.)

Restrictive clauses are not set off from the rest of the sentence by commas.

A **nonrestrictive clause** does *not* contain information essential to the meaning of the sentence. It merely presents added information. It can be dropped without confusing the meaning of the sentence.

> Lynn, *who had been accepted for admission to several colleges,*
>   was awarded a scholarship to Berkeley.
> Our cat, *who recently had kittens,* drinks a pint of milk a day.

Nonrestrictive clauses are set off by commas from the rest of the sentence.

Participial phrases that identify or point out the thing or person they modify are restrictive.

The mechanic *lying under that Ford* worked on our car.
(Without the phrase, the sentence loses its specific meaning.)
The tag *sewn into the lining* tells whose coat it is. (The phrase identifies the tag.)

Nonrestrictive participial phrases merely add meaning. They are not essential and can be dropped without making the meaning of the sentence incomplete.

Shading my eyes, I peered across the field.
Tony, *holding aloft a huge cake,* entered the room.
The pickets, *circling in front of the store,* sang freedom songs.

Nonrestrictive participial phrases are set off from the rest of the sentence by commas. Restrictive phrases are not set off by commas.

Exercise: Number your paper 1–20. Decide whether the adjective clause or the participial phrase is restrictive or nonrestrictive. After each number write *restrictive* or *nonrestrictive*. Copy and insert commas in the sentences in which commas are needed.

1. The book reviewed on the television program has had greatly increased sales.
2. Standing in the doorway Drew asked if he could come in.
3. This is the house that we expect to buy.
4. Mr. Salvatore who is a famous singer will train our class.
5. The Carlsbad Caverns which attract sightseers to New Mexico are the largest known underground caverns.
6. The train struck by the avalanche was tossed down the hillside.
7. The picture now appearing at the Tivoli stars Diane Keaton.
8. We were delighted by the report that appeared in the papers.
9. The new toll road which will be opened Friday will save us a great deal of time.
10. Mom's office which has always been dark has been redecorated.
11. The new show which was highly praised by reviewers was a disappointment to us.
12. These are the boxes that you are to return to the store.
13. We waited until the last moment hoping you would appear.
14. The person driving the car had neither insurance nor a license.

15. The hills that you see in the distance lie in New Jersey.

16. Our neighbor who is a fine mechanic helped us repair the dishwasher.

17. The horse that is pawing the ground has not been fed.

18. The coach fearing overconfidence put the team through a drill.

19. The car that you just passed is a police car.

20. The room which was too small in the first place was now overcrowded.

11.13 Compound Sentences

Place a comma before the conjunction that joins two main clauses in a compound sentence.

It snowed all night, *and* the schools were closed the next day.
Ms. Thomas must leave now, *or* she will miss her plane.
The bill may not pass this time, *but* you can be certain it will be passed soon.
Lucy did not remember where they had planned to meet, *nor* did she know Henry's phone number.

When the clauses are quite short, the comma may be omitted.

The sun rose and we awakened.
Reynolds hit a double and Lane scored a run.

11.14 Series

A **series** is a group of three or more items of the same kind.

SERIES OF NOUNS: *Clothing, books,* and *papers* were piled on top of Kent's dresser.
SERIES OF VERBS: The bus driver *honked, slammed* on the brakes, and *swerved* sharply to the left.
SERIES OF ADJECTIVES: The day that we had so long awaited was *warm, sunny,* and *cloudless.*

SERIES OF PHRASES: Groups of children were playing
behind the house, on the porch, and
in the yard.

Commas are used to separate the parts of a series.

No comma is required after the last item in a series. When the last two items of a series are joined by *and* or *or*, the comma is sometimes omitted. To avoid all possibility of misunderstanding, it is wise to use a comma before the conjunction.

Do not use a comma it all parts of the series are joined by *and, or,* or *nor: All summer the children swam and read and lolled.*

11.15   Coordinate Adjectives

Commas are placed between coordinate adjectives that modify the same noun.

The long, dull debate seemed endless.
Raging, howling winds whipped the trees.

To determine whether adjectives are coordinate, try placing an *and* between them. If it sounds natural, they are coordinate, and a comma is needed.

PROBLEM: His loud whining voice made the
audience shudder.
NATURAL: His loud *and* whining voice made the
audience shudder.
SOLUTION: His loud, whining voice made the
audience shudder.

PROBLEM: It was a dark dreary depressing day.
NATURAL: It was a dark, dreary, *and* depressing day.
SOLUTION: It was a dark, dreary, depressing day.

PROBLEM: Our house is the big white one.
NOT NATURAL: Our house is the big *and* white one.
SOLUTION: Our house is the big white one.

In general, it is safe to omit the comma after numbers and adjectives of size, shape, and age.

a big round moon   five tiny wafers

Exercise: Copy these sentences, placing commas where they are needed.

1. We asked Marion to come with us but she had another engagement.
2. The lights the movements and the presents make a pretty picture.
3. We had not intended to stay overnight but the snowfall turned into a blizzard.
4. The officer asked for Bob's license looked it over and got out her notebook.
5. The doctor must come soon or he will be too late.
6. Beethoven wrote symphonies quartets concertos and sonatas.
7. Three trucks four cars and a trailer were tangled on the icy bridge.
8. Luanne found the geology course interesting practical but difficult.
9. The boss frowned tried to look severe and finally grinned.
10. The entire roll of film was either blurred dark or out of focus.
11. Harry has his pass but he cannot leave the base until tomorrow.
12. Helen entered the room walked straight to the table and called the meeting to order.
13. Strange noises were coming from the stereo from the water pipes and from the attic.
14. I could not reach the top shelf nor could I find the stepladder.
15. You had better start now or you will miss the last bus.
16. Couples were standing in the streets sitting on telephone poles and leaning out of windows.
17. A flight attendant must be cheerful alert and always pleasant.
18. We had expected to arrive by midnight but the plane could not land.

19. All roads bridges and highways into the city have been closed by the heavy snowstorm.

20. Suddenly, the commanding officer picked up a pen reached for my papers signed them and handed them across the desk to me.

11.16 Clarity

Use a comma to separate words or phrases that might be mistakenly joined in reading.

There are three common situations in which words may be mistakenly read together. The first occurs when the conjunctions *but* and *for* are mistaken for prepositions.

CONFUSING: I liked all the speeches but one was superb.
CLEAR: I liked all the speeches, but one was superb.

CONFUSING: Rita listened for she thought she'd heard a cry.
CLEAR: Rita listened, for she thought she'd heard a cry.

A second source of confusion is a noun following a verbal phrase.

CONFUSING: Before waxing Jill swept the floor.
CLEAR: Before waxing, Jill swept the floor.

CONFUSING: To walk a cat must withdraw its nails.
CLEAR: To walk, a cat must withdraw its nails.

CONFUSING: After painting Vincent wrote his brother.
CLEAR: After painting, Vincent wrote his brother.

A third source of confusion is the word that may be either adverb, preposition, or conjunction at the beginning of the sentence.

CONFUSING: Below the earth looked like a quilt.
CLEAR: Below, the earth looked like a quilt.

CONFUSING: Outside the courtyard was in chaos.
CLEAR: Outside, the courtyard was in chaos.

11.17 Words Omitted

Use a comma when words are omitted from parallel word groups.

Anna baked a pie; Tom, some bread.
Mr. Davis makes requests; Mr. Cowan, demands.
The day became warm, and our spirits, merry.

Exercise A: Copy these sentences, placing commas where necessary to avoid confusion.

 1. Ms. Ellis sent four letters; Ms. Harris two dozen postcards.
 2. I recognized none of the group but Todd had known one of the boys in summer camp.
 3. Once before the stage curtain had stuck halfway up.
 4. After cooking Roger cleaned up the kitchen.
 5. Amy wore red socks; Melinda blue ones.
 6. Luis tasted all the pies but one was too hot.
 7. To play a stereo must have speakers.
 8. Inside the house smelled of freshly baked brownies.
 9. From calling Ben lost his voice.
 10. Beyond the residential section extends for ten miles.

Exercise B: Follow the same directions as for Exercise A.

 1. Inside the church was beautifully lighted.
 2. Above the men were dangling ropes over the cliff.
 3. Before leaving the janitor locked the windows.
 4. As he wrote the short story became very long.
 5. Underneath the boat was covered with slime.
 6. John Steinbeck wrote *Of Mice and Men*; Leonard Wibberley *The Mouse That Roared*.
 7. When a doctor is called to cure a patient is his or her aim.
 8. All the girls went to the game but Sue had to babysit.
 9. Skip set out the chairs on the porch for the guests were arriving.
 10. Outside the house looked as though no one lived there.

REVIEW: END MARKS AND COMMAS This exercise is a review of Section 11. Copy these sentences, inserting the necessary punctuation.

1. Fortunately Yoshi is much healthier now
2. Hooray Our team made the finals
3. Both of my sisters are successful salespersons but the one that sells cars is Angela
4. When the movie is over will you pick us up
5. Scanning the area the forest ranger noticed a distant cloud of smoke
6. Well leap year of course has an extra day
7. Settlers landed at Salem Massachusetts on September 6 1628
8. After calling Tina let her brother use the phone
9. J Edgar Hoover I believe was head of the FBI for many years
10. April Fool's Day a day for harmless pranks and jokes is observed on April 1
11. My uncle trying to lose weight eats a lot of salads fruit and cottage cheese
12. Ms Hansen did you travel to Paris or did you stay in London
13. The time in San Diego is 9 A M; in Baltimore 12 noon
14. The northern kit fox which is native to Canada is an endangered species
15. The East Building of the National Gallery of Art in Washington D C was designed by I M Pei
16. Traveling through outer space the astronaut radioed to Earth
17. Undoubtedly Dr. Sayner who is the team doctor will tape your ankle
18. Yes please send my T-shirt to 383 Picardy Lane Rome New York
19. Nautilus the first atomic submarine was launched on January 21 1954
20. Wow If the experts are correct Karen we will soon have computerized homes

12.0 The Semicolon, the Colon, the Dash, and Parentheses

12.1 Semicolons Between Main Clauses

A semicolon is placed between the main clauses of a compound sentence when they are not joined by a conjunction.

The clauses of a compound sentence are closely related in thought. That is the reason for joining them into one sentence rather than writing them as separate sentences.

In some sentences the semicolon is more effective in joining main clauses than one of the conjunctions. This is especially true when *and* or *but* add little meaning to the joined clauses.

> Bonita is good at set shots, *but* I am not.
> Bonita is good at set shots; I am not.
> The cyclone struck with savage fury, *and* it demolished the little coastal town.
> The cyclone struck with savage fury; it demolished the little coastal town.

12.2 Semicolons and Conjunctive Adverbs

A semicolon is used between main clauses joined by conjunctive adverbs or by phrases like *for example, in fact, for instance.*

Our treasury was nearly empty; *accordingly,* we began
considering various fund-raising projects.
Marge had studied Italian for three years; *yet,* when she
arrived in Florence, she found herself tongue-tied.
Many of their talents complemented each other; *for example,*
he played the piano and she sang.
Nick is well-liked; *in fact,* he is the most popular person
in the class.

Note that the conjunctive adverb or phrase is followed by a
comma in the examples above.

12.3 Semicolons Between Word Groups Containing Commas

A sentence containing a great many commas is difficult to read.
If commas precede the conjunction between main clauses, another comma at this point would lose its value as a guide to the
reader.

**A semicolon is used between main clauses joined by a conjunc-
tion if the clause before the conjunction contains commas.**

Jim had done research, taken notes, and made an outline; but
he didn't feel ready to begin writing.
We put out sandwiches, cider, potato chips, and donuts; and
still we wondered if there would be enough.

**A semicolon is used between a series of phrases if they contain
commas.**

Members of our class come from as far away as Leeds,
England; New Delhi, India; and San Juan, Puerto Rico.
Mabel was in charge of the scenery; Roy, the costumes; and
Charles, the directing of the play.
Eric called the children together; checked their hands, ears,
and faces; and told them to be back by five sharp.

475

Exercise: Two of the following sentences need no semicolons. For the other sentences, indicate the point at which a semicolon should replace a comma.

1. We are disappointed in the advertisement, it is too small.
2. The team went to the hospital to see Bud, he had been hurt in Saturday's game.
3. Sylvia is doing very well, in fact, she has a B+ average.
4. Dictionaries do not always agree, for instance, they differ on the pronunciation of *duty*.
5. As the game entered the last quarter, Pitt scored twice and won the game handily.
6. We have a factory in Salem, Ohio, an office in Buffalo, New York, and a mill at Andover, Massachusetts.
7. Dave Rotnam won first prize, his sister Joan, second prize, and Davina Belknap, third prize.
8. Eve was surrounded by notebooks, encyclopedias, and dictionaries, but she was reading a letter from Bill.
9. The men at the South Pole rarely got mail, but they could talk to their families by radio.
10. For Christmas, I got a radio, Mark, a typewriter, and Inez, a new suit.
11. We ought to beat Hinsdale, Elmhurst, and Bensenville, but we may lose to Oak Park.
12. The building was designed by Frank Lloyd Wright, the famous American architect, but the New York critics, in their newspaper columns, attacked it savagely.
13. The electricity was off for six hours, consequently, everything in our food locker was spoiled.
14. Ms. Novicki has been on the force for twenty-three years, she is almost ready to retire.
15. Ellen has a new camera, it was made in Germany.

12.4   Colons To Introduce Lists

The colon is used to throw the reader's attention forward to what follows. It is in some respects like an equal sign, saying that what follows is the explanation or equivalent of what has gone before.

A colon is used to introduce a list of items.

Usually, a colon is required when a list is preceded by the words *the following* or *as follows*. A colon is not used before a series of modifiers or complements immediately following the verb.

> Jim had been a member of the following groups: the Drama Club, the Debate Union, and the Archery Club. (list)
> The following nations were among those represented at the congress: Colombia, Bolivia, Panama, and Ecuador. (list)
> Sue uses cream in cereal, in coffee, and in tea. (series of modifiers)
> The candidate's characteristics were forthrightness, intelligence, and courage. (series of complements)

12.5 Colons with Formal Quotations

A colon is used to introduce a formal quotation.

> Edwin Newman's book *Strictly Speaking* begins with these words: "Will America be the death of English? I'm glad I asked me that. My well-thought-out mature judgment is that it will."

12.6 Colons Before Explanatory Statements

A colon is used between two sentences when the second explains the first. The second sentence begins with a capital letter.

> Then I knew we were in trouble: None of our boys could match the swan dive we had just seen.
> From then on we understood Ms. Gilroy: She was demanding but she was kind.

12.7 Other Uses of the Colon

A colon is used (1) after the formal salutation of a letter, (2) between hour and minute figures of clock time, (3) in Biblical references, (4) between the title and subtitle of a book, (5) between numbers referring to volume and pages of books and magazines.

> Dear Sir or Madam: Matthew 1:5
> Dear Mr. Berg: *The Raven: The Life of Sam Houston*
> 8:20 P.M.   Volume IV: pages 126–142

12.8 The Dash To Show Break in Thought

A dash is used to show an abrupt break in thought.

In dialogue, the break in thought is often caused by uncertainty or hesitancy as in the first example below.

> Photosynthesis is an action—I mean it's what happens—well,
>   it's sunlight doing something to chlorophyll.
> The movie opens with a shot of the desert—oh, you've
>   seen it.
> She told me that—oh, I really shouldn't repeat it.

12.9 The Dash with Interrupters

A dash is used to set off a long explanatory statement that interrupts the thought.

> They had searched everywhere—under the seats, in the aisles,
>   in the lobby—before Dan found the keys in his pocket.
> The meeting—between two men who had clashed violently
>   only a week before—was calm and friendly.

12.10   The Dash Before a Summary

The dash is used after a series to indicate a summarizing statement.

Insufficient heating, leaky roofs, cluttered stairways, and unsanitary corridors—for all these violations of the housing code, the landlord was hauled into court.

Yellowed song sheets, framed photographs of opera stars, programs of long-past performances—these were scattered about her room.

Exercise: Copy the following sentences, inserting semicolons, colons, or dashes where necessary.

1. Beginning next January we shall handle the following foreign cars Datsun, Volvo, Volkswagen, and Honda.

2. The candidate's main qualifications were these twelve years' experience in the Senate, a knowledge of foreign affairs, and the ability to get votes.

3. I am looking for the source of this quotation "Always do right. This will gratify some people and astonish the rest."

4. Our new text is called *Supershopper A Guide to Spending and Saving.*

5. The quotation is found in *The Oxford English Dictionary,* Vol. II page 427.

6. High school students today are more serious they expect to work hard.

7. Alice knew at least she thought she knew what was coming next.

8. It is our obligation there is no choice in the matter to pay all of Frank's expenses to the convention.

9. It's about well, it's something like I would say it's a good ten miles from here.

10. Having a lot of clothes, owning a fancy car, going to parties are these really suitable goals in life?

11. The prizes are as follows first prize, a movie camera second prize, a portable TV set third prize, a pocket-size calculator.

12. You have three jobs for today wash the car, clean up the yard, and shop for your mother.

13. The President closed with these words "With God's help, we can face the future hopefully, in full confidence that our problems can be solved."

14. Marion saw the point no one else did.

15. We shall cover the following topics in this conference planning for new products, improving customer relations, and marketing.

16. You will find the statement in *Thomas Jefferson The Man and His Times,* Volume III page 106.

17. You can take this road down but I guess the road is closed, isn't it?

18. There is a strange light a reddish light that moves very fast in the sky to the south of here.

19. All of a sudden we had already closed the door the telephone began ringing.

20. It is rather a long walk however, it is a pleasant one.

12.11 Parentheses To Enclose Supplementary or Explanatory Words

Commas, dashes, or parentheses are used to set off words that are supplementary or explanatory. Commas are used when the material set off is fairly close to the main thought of the sentence. Dashes are used to set off material more loosely connected, and parentheses are used to set off material so loosely related to the main thought that it might be made a separate sentence.

There are few occasions in high school writing when parentheses are needed. The safest course for the student is to use commas, or even dashes, to set off parenthetical matter. If the material is so distantly related as to require parentheses, the passage might better be rewritten to place the parenthetical material in a separate sentence.

COMMAS ADEQUATE: Kate's best point, *which she saved for the end,* was that every group needs leadership.

DASHES REQUIRED: Modern science no longer deals directly with the visible world—that is, it deals directly only with ions, atoms, electrons, and other particles that are too small to be seen.

PARENTHESES
APPROPRIATE: But on the whole, Arthur was a well-behaved little boy; a good pupil and obedient (except when he played with the scruffy boys in the street, whom his parents disliked).—Colin Wilson, *Religion and the Rebel*.

PARENTHESES AVOIDED: But on the whole, Arthur was a well-behaved little boy and a good pupil. He was obedient except when he played with the scruffy boys in the street, whom his parents disliked.

12.12 Punctuation Within Parentheses

Commas, semicolons, and periods are placed outside the closing parenthesis. The question mark and exclamation point are placed inside if the parenthetical material is itself a question or exclamation; otherwise, outside.

Jean (not Martha) was the dancer in the orange leotards.

Leo's speech was on disarmament; Barb's, on acting as a career (her favorite subject); Jim's, on slum clearance.

I never guessed (would you have?) that the maid did it.

Sheldon spoke of his victory over Central's debaters (*his* victory!) as if he had been a one-man team.

REVIEW: THE SEMICOLON, THE COLON, THE DASH, AND PARENTHESES This exercise is a review of Section 12. Copy the sentences, inserting necessary semicolons, colons, dashes, and parentheses.

1. Evan uses a calculator Lettie uses a slide rule.

2. Educational television has many good shows for instance, I enjoy "Once upon a Classic."

3. The horse ran, pranced, and galloped but then he needed a rest.

4. The following magazines have the highest circulation *Reader's Digest, Parade,* and *TV Guide.*

5. The librarian advised me to check Volume 4 pages 101–150.

6. Panting, the marathon runner crossed the finish line she had come in first.

7. Our school has exchange students from these countries Brazil, Kenya, Sweden, and Chile.

8. Costumes, scrapbooks, toys, and dishes we found them all in the attic.

9. I guessed the trial's outcome The accused murderer would be found guilty.

10. The water ballet routine was precisely choreographed furthermore, it was performed flawlessly.

11. My class that meets at 9 30 oh, I hope I won't be late will discuss student rights.

12. Alana is the editor-in-chief of the school newspaper Janie, the business manager and Reggie, the staff photographer.

13. The Declaration of Independence ends with these words "We mutually pledge to each other our lives, our fortunes, and our sacred honor."

14. The coach tried everything pep talks, privileges, rallies, toughness to try to improve the team's morale.

15. *Newsweek* magazine *Time*'s chief competitor features a guest essay called "My Turn."

16. Spiders, ants, fleas, roaches they're all part of my insect collection.

17. The following cities have warm winters Miami, Florida Los Angeles, California and Honolulu, Hawaii.

18. Ms. Conti, do you have *JFK The Early Years,* or has it been checked out?

19. Selina prepared for the audition She memorized her lines and practiced her dance.

20. There are many calendars for example, ancient Romans used the Julian calendar.

13.0 The Apostrophe

The apostrophe is used with nouns to show possession or ownership: *Aunt Lucy's summer cottage, Carl's goldfish, the lawyer's briefcase.* The apostrophe is also used to show the following:

CLOSE RELATIONSHIP: Amy's companion, someone's parents

SOURCE OR ORIGIN: Grace's drawings, George's ability

IDENTIFYING CHARACTERISTICS: the woman's attitude, Lee's gestures, Shelley's determination

13.1 The Possessive of Singular Nouns

The possessive form of a singular noun is usually made by adding an apostrophe and s ('s) to the noun.

dog + 's = dog's   girl + 's = girl's
Tess + 's = Tess's   town + 's = town's

Note: A few proper nouns ending in *s* may take the apostrophe only: *Jesus' Moses'.* In general, however, the correct way to make a singular noun possessive is to add an apostrophe and *s.*

13.2 The Possessive of Plural Nouns

If a plural noun does not end in s, add both apostrophe and s ('s) to form the possessive.

women + 's = women's   men + 's = men's
children + 's = children's   deer + 's = deer's

If a plural noun ends in s, add only the apostrophe to form the possessive.

animals + ' = animals'   members + ' = members'
writers + ' = writers'   soldiers + ' = soldiers'

Exercise: Number 1–20 on your paper. Write *correct* for each sentence in which the possessive form is correct. If the form is incorrect, write it correctly.

1. The girls bikes had been locked up in the basement.
2. This year the team's spirit is much better.
3. Toms' minibike was stolen.
4. The girls' friends came to her defense.
5. We found Charles's books in the back of our car.
6. The regular passengers have formed a passengers committee.
7. We have put new heaters in the salespersons' cars.
8. The ship's doctor performed the operation at sea.
9. The governors' assistants have their own meeting at the same time.
10. Stan serves at lunchtime in the teacher's lunchroom.
11. The three reporter's statements differed on important points.
12. The client's cars are ready for them.
13. Children's toys were scattered over the driveway.
14. The sailor's leaves were suddenly canceled.
15. The actor's voices were loud and harsh.
16. The watchmen's reports make no mention of a disturbance.
17. Les's garage is always open on Sunday.

18. Diplomats and soldiers alike were warmed by the Presidents' smile.
19. The alumni's contributions built the chapel.
20. Cathy has entered the womens' tennis tournament.

13.3 The Possessive of Compound Nouns

A **compound noun** is a noun composed of more than one word. Some compound nouns are written with hyphens between the parts.

Only the last part of a hyphenated noun shows possession.

jack-o'-lantern + 's = jack-o'-lantern's
sister-in-law + 's = sister-in-law's

Nouns such as *the Queen of England, the President of the United States, the Prime Minister* form the possessive by adding an apostrophe and *s* to the last word only: *the Queen of England's throne.* Often, however, an *of* phrase is less awkward.

the throne of the Queen of England
the home of the President of the United States
the husband of the Prime Minister

13.4 Joint Ownership

When the names of two or more persons are used to show joint ownership, only the name of the last person mentioned is given the possessive form. Add an apostrophe or an apostrophe and *s* in accord with the spelling of that name.

Boris and Ivan's uncle
Ed and Joanne's home
Bob and Gregory's project

The rule also applies to firm names and to names of organizations.

> Strawbridge and Clothier's location
> Cross and Hamilton Company's sales force
> the Committee on Africa's report
> Peter and Ruthie's Waffle Shop

13.5 Separate Ownership or Possession

If the names of two or more persons are used to show separate ownership, each name is given the possessive form.

> Madison's and Monroe's administrations
> Don's and Jim's grades

This construction may become awkward. It can be avoided by using an *of* phrase.

> the administrations of Madison and Monroe
> the grades of Don and Jim
> the hopes of England and France

13.6 Possessive of Indefinite Pronouns

Use an apostrophe and *s* to form the possessive of indefinite pronouns.

> everyone + 's = everyone's   one + 's = one's
> either + 's = either's   somebody + 's = somebody's

The apostrophe and *s* are added to the last word in forms like *someone else, anybody else, no one else*:

> somebody else's   no one else's

The apostrophe is not used to form the possessive of personal pronouns.

> NONSTANDARD: your's, her's, it's, our's, their's
> STANDARD: yours, hers, its, ours, theirs

13.7 Expressions of Time and Amount

When used as adjectives, words expressing time and amount are given the possessive form.

a month's time	four days' wait
a week's notice	six months' delay
a day's holiday	thirty seconds' silence
a minute's peace	ten minutes' break
a penny's worth	two centuries' tradition

Exercise: Copy the italicized words, changing them to show ownership or possession.

1. We will meet at my *sister-in-law* house.
2. *Dana* and *Paul* uniforms did not fit.
3. Who will win is *anybody* guess.
4. Ms. Blackmar has three *week* wages coming to her.
5. You can probably find the right kind of truck at *Smith and Weston* store.
6. Because of illness I have missed three *day* work.
7. *Roger and Sons* sale starts next week.
8. *Roosevelt* and *Rockefeller* backgrounds were somewhat similar.
9. Buffalo is ten *hours* ride from my town.
10. Where is the *League of Women Voters* office?
11. An *hour* wait now may save a *day* time later.
12. There is an advertisement of *Chase and Maxwell* sale in tonight's paper.
13. Dominic picked up *somebody else* books.
14. What is the *Secretary of the Treasury* salary?
15. The school is sponsoring a *mothers* and *sons* picnic.
16. Have you paid *Lord and Taylor* bill this month?
17. *Andy* and *Marge* mother is a doctor.
18. In two *month* time your leg will be as good as new.
19. *Benét* and *Twain* stories were the best-liked.
20. There is only a *moment* delay before the phone rings at the other side of the continent.

13.8 Apostrophes To Show Omissions

An apostrophe is used to show the omission of letters or figures.

the flood of '23   *1923*
the class of '84   *1984*
they're   *they are*
shouldn't   *should not*

13.9 Plurals of Letters, Words, Numbers, and Signs

An apostrophe is used to show the plurals of letters, words, numbers, and signs.

How many *r*'s are there in *embarrass?*
Her speech relies too much on *nice*'s.
I still have to dot the *i*'s and cross the *t*'s.
Frederick Lewis Allen describes the Roaring '20's in
    Only Yesterday.

Note: The plurals of letters, numbers, signs, and words used as words are always italicized in print. In manuscript and typescript they are underlined. (See Section 14.7.)

Exercise A: Copy the following sentences, inserting an apostrophe (and *s*) where needed. This exercise reviews all the uses of apostrophes.

1. There are too many *thats* in your sentence.
2. Perrys address has four 3s in it.
3. There should be great prosperity in the 1980s.
4. It was three oclock before we got started.
5. Its not likely that Mars or Venus is inhabited.
6. We dont know the answer to the question, and we cant find it.
7: It is clear now that Dads letter wont come today.
8. Jess' short story is being published in *Scholastic Magazine.*
9. Our local papers feature section gives career tips.

10. We dont yet know whos coming.

11. Is there a good mens store in town?

12. The flight attendants smiles were reassuring when the plane began to bounce.

13. The countys highway department is in charge of snow removal.

14. The waitresses hours and wages are good at Barneys Restaurant.

15. By working overtime, we earned a weeks wages in two days time.

16. You can buy womens coats in the young ladies department.

17. Ward was always too interested in everyone else business.

18. Have you ever shopped at a farmers market?

19. Charles order must have been lost in the mail.

20. The tugs whistles set up a frightful clamor in the harbor.

Exercise B: Write the possessive singular and the possessive plural of each of the following words:

1. woman	6. lady	11. day
2. man	7. fox	12. dollar
3. class	8. city	13. company
4. salesperson	9. boss	14. mouse
5. hour	10. employee	15. bus

Exercise C: The following sentences contain errors in the use of apostrophes. Copy the sentences, correcting all errors.

1. There is a new boy's camp across the lake.

2. Do you have an account at James's and Law's store?

3. Mosquitoes' find me very appealing, dont they?

4. The editor's-in-chief editorial criticized the cafeteria's food.

5. Pat's and Gladys's telephone conversation went on for hours.

6. Juanita is working at Harris' and Sons' store in Milwaukee.

7. Diana Ross's and the Supreme's records will never be equaled.

8. We are publishing a collection of the years' best sports stories.

9. The girl's locker room was built by the town's best carpenter.

10. Mr. Garvey's car wont' be ready until Friday.

11. What is your father's-in-law's business?

12. Its too late to go to Bobby Holmes' party.

13. Everyone elses boat was damaged in the storm.

14. My typewriters' keys stick on the *es*.
15. Ms. Smiths' glasses are in someones car.
16. The speakers lecture could not be heard above the audiences' coughing.
17. The Farewell Address was both Hamilton and Washington's work.
18. Ross' friend has just bought the J. C. Little's and Company building.
19. Two weeks stay here will give you a years good health.
20. Mason's and Dixon's survey settled many territorial disputes.

REVIEW: THE APOSTROPHE   This exercise is a review of Section 13. Copy the sentences, correcting all errors in the use of the apostrophe.

1. Bross and Bradys' Gourmet Shop sells pickled eel.
2. Several golfer's scores were below par.
3. Doesnt the womens locker room have a sauna?
4. It would take two weeks work to get Kellys room clean.
5. The child gleefully turned the jack's-in-the-box handle.
6. Alisons phone number has four 8s in a row.
7. This years football squad isnt strong on defense.
8. Druid and Companys' policy is never to hire teen-agers.
9. No ones jeans look as new as Terrys.
10. The treasurer of the class of 84 must collect each members' fees.
11. Youll have to borrow someone elses class notes, José.
12. A bird sheds it's feathers during molting season.
13. Katie's and Les' project demonstrates how heredity determines the color of our eyes.
14. Foxes and mink's furs are used for coats, arent they?
15. This seminar is supposed to teach the ABCs of ecology in the 1980s.
16. Their clubs skit is a parody of *The Wiz*.
17. The baseball is Adams, but the bat is her's.
18. During a speech, too many *ums* are distracting.
19. Mr. Moran and Ms. Sax's classes are visiting the space museum.
20. Cant you recognize the lilies'-of-the-valley fragrance?

14.0 Quotations

14.1 Direct and Indirect Quotations

In a direct quotation, the words of the speaker are directly quoted exactly as spoken.

> Greg said, "The streets should be cleared for our parade."
> "The town," the mayor said, "will be yours that day."

An indirect quotation reports the meaning expressed by the speaker but does not give the exact words.

> INDIRECT: Molly replied that she was always punctual.
> DIRECT: "I am always punctual," Molly replied.

Quotation marks are not used with an indirect quotation.

Exercise: Number your paper 1–10. After each number write *Direct* or *Indirect* to describe the kind of quotation in each of these sentences. Copy and correct the sentences requiring quotation marks or other punctuation.

1. The test was hard said Sam but it was fair.
2. Don replied that he had no one to blame but himself.
3. May I have a new shirt for the party asked Ken.
4. Laura said that she wanted to study advanced science.
5. The teacher asked whether anyone was ready to give his or her report.
6. No one would think to look in here said Ms. Brown.
7. Ben called out we will be home early.
8. The city is not equipped to deal with a heavy snowfall the guide explained.

9. Does anyone know asked Loretta who is to be the speaker at the assembly?

10. Well I think I left it on the bus but I may have left it in the store said Jean sadly.

14.2 Punctuation of Direct Quotations

Punctuation and capitals are used as follows in direct quotations:

1. **In dialogue, the first word of the quotation is capitalized.** The material quoted from another writer may begin in the middle of a sentence. If so, the first word is not capitalized.

> On January 1, 1863, Lincoln declared the slaves "forever free."

2. **The speaker's words are set off from the rest of the sentence.**

Note the placement of commas in these examples:

> Michael said, "Let's meet at my house next time."
> "Let's meet at my house next time," Michael said.

When the end of the quotation is also the end of the sentence, the period falls inside the quotation marks.

3. **If the quoted words are a question or an exclamation, the question mark or the exclamation point falls inside the quotation marks.**

In this situation no comma is needed.

> "May I make the poster?" Lola asked.
> "I deny everything!" the suspect cried.

4. **If the entire sentence is a question or an exclamation, the exclamation point or question mark falls outside the quotation marks.**

> Did I hear you say, "Have some cookies"?
> It's absurd to consider these thieves "responsible citizens"!

5. **The colon and the semicolon at the close of a quotation fall outside the quotation marks.**

The committee said that the following states contained "pockets of poverty": Kentucky, West Virginia, and Pennsylvania.

Read the ballad "Sir Patrick Spens"; then study its relation to Coleridge's poem "Dejection: An Ode."

6. **Both parts of a divided quotation are enclosed in quotation marks. The first word of the second part is not capitalized unless it begins a new sentence.**

"I plan," the Governor said, "to reduce taxes this year."

"Remember this," the counselor said. "Ten hours of casual work may be less effective than five of real concentration."

7. **In dialogue, a new paragraph and a new set of quotation marks show a change in speaker.**

"My working habits have no pattern," the author said. "Some writers set themselves strict schedules. I don't."

"But you've written five books in five years," the interviewer replied. "You must work very hard day after day."

"On the contrary, there are days when I spend the entire morning putting in a comma and the afternoon taking it out."

14.3 Quotations Within Quotations

Single quotation marks are used to enclose a quotation within a quotation.

Herb said, "Then she actually said to me, 'I hope I didn't keep you waiting.'"

"The announcer just said, 'More snow tonight,'" Len reported.

Ruth said, "Then Ray looked up from the ground and said, 'I don't think I'll do any more skiing.'"

14.4 Long Quotations

A quotation may be several paragraphs in length.

In long quotations, begin each paragraph with quotation marks. Place quotation marks at the end of the last paragraph only.

Exercise A: Copy the following sentences, adding the necessary punctuation marks and capital letters.

1. Molly asked does anyone remember when the book reports are due
2. We can't decide Mother said whether to paint the house or buy a new car
3. Zachary asked may I rewrite this paper
4. There is no excuse for this delay said the customer we gave you our order two months ago
5. Your Honor the defendant pleaded I beg you for another chance
6. In the Sand Creek Massacre the speaker added several hundred Indians were killed
7. Did Captain Perry's message say we have met the enemy and they are ours
8. Look out for a pass Bill shouted
9. Did you finish your homework Sarah asked
10. Do you happen to know asked Jack where we can get another tire

Exercise B: Follow the same directions as for Exercise A.

1. Are you absolutely sure Burt asked that the water has been turned off
2. What can we do now asked Beth our money is all gone
3. Dave replied I am sure the officer said to drive on through
4. You can be sure Mark promised that we will not forget your kindness
5. Is it too late to apply for a job asked Jeff
6. I am not afraid of the dark said Harold but I'm not afraid of a little light either
7. Watch out Marta yelled isn't that a snake by your foot
8. Did you hear the coach say no new plays this week
9. Do you have my pen asked Kathy I will need it
10. Did the referee say strike three Rita asked

14.5 Setting Off Titles

The title of a book, magazine, newspaper, long pamphlet, or bulletin is usually italicized in print. In your own writing, you indicate the italics by underlining.

To distinguish the title of a *part* of a book, magazine, or newspaper, quotation marks are used.

Use quotation marks to enclose the titles of chapters and other parts of books and to enclose the titles of stories, poems, essays, articles, and short musical compositions.

Faulkner's story "The Bear" has become as famous as his novels.
The subject of "Auspex" is an incident that occurred
seventy-five years before Frost wrote the poem.

14.6 Words Used in Special Ways

Words used in special ways or special senses are enclosed in quotation marks.

Writers may want to show that they are using a word as someone else has used it. Writers can make clear that they themselves do not accept this use of the word by enclosing it in quotation marks.

Slang words and phrases are also enclosed in quotation marks.

There are always a few people who consider it a shameful
waste to give aid to "inferior nations."
The agent thought Cybil's performance was "simply divine."
The reporter asked the negotiators to describe what they
meant by "a satisfactory solution."
The congressperson considered every voter his "pal."

Note: When a comma or period immediately follows the quoted word, it falls *inside* the quotation marks. A colon or semicolon falls *outside* the quotation marks. See the last example above. If the quoted word appears at the end of a question or exclamation, the question mark or exclamation point falls *outside* the quotation marks: *Is this what you mean by "cool"?*

14.7 Words Used as Words

A word referred to as a word is italicized in print. In writing, the word is underlined.

> The word *very* cannot do all the work some people require of it.
> Until then, I'd never heard the word *boondoggle*.

When a word and its definition appear in the same sentence, the word is italicized, and the definition is placed in quotation marks.

> In music, the word *pianissimo* means "very soft."

Exercise A: Copy the following sentences. Insert quotation marks where necessary. Indicate italics by underlining.

1. What does the word serendipity mean?
2. There are too many and's in your sentences.
3. Read Phyllis McGinley's poem Reflections Dental.
4. The hardest words on the vocabulary test were quay and spurn.
5. There is an interesting article entitled Swimming with Right Whales in this month's National Geographic.
6. Doris always has a hard time spelling recommend.
7. The British word for elevator is lift.
8. Rachel will lead a discussion of the story The Open Boat.
9. Epilog means a concluding part added to a literary work.
10. Helen Reddy's most popular song was I Am Woman.

Exercise B: Follow the same directions as for Exercise A.

1. In Canada the word is spelled colour.
2. Mother to Son is my favorite poem in the book Literature Lives.
3. Todd calls money bread, and Meg calls it the green stuff.
4. Read the chapter called Bacteria Are Your Friends.
5. Why are those islands called The Lesser Antilles?
6. John Denver describes nearly everything as far out.
7. Katie cringes when anyone calls her honey or sweetie.
8. What is meant by the phrase manifest destiny?

9. Would the chef call this meal a gourmet great?

10. How are you using the word break in the sentence beginning with Thieves?

REVIEW: QUOTATIONS This exercise is a review of Section 14. Copy the following sentences, inserting the necessary quotation marks, capitals, and punctuation. Indicate italics by underlining.

1. I'll be a few minutes late Johanna remarked

2. After the feast Bob asked did you get enough to eat

3. I give up said Phil what is the answer

4. Jenina complained that getting up early was a bummer

5. The consumer expert began her report commercials can make us dissatisfied

6. I did it the contest winner shouted

7. One chapter of The Martian Chronicles is called The Green Morning

8. We read O. Henry's story The Ransom of Red Chief

9. Sabrina asked did you read the poem Fifteen

10. The TV term for an added sound track of people laughing is canned laughter

11. The word madam is spelled the same forwards and backwards

12. Thanks to television Fred Allen said the next generation will have four eyes and no tongue

13. Our English teacher said that genre means a kind or type of artistic endeavor

14. Carla asked did Mr. Oldfield say class is dismissed

15. Why do TV emcees say we'll be back after this word from our sponsor

16. Who wrote the book The Long Winter Vivienne asked

17. Whoopee! the announcer shouted the Rangers have won

18. Ms. Armada, does the word subsequent mean next Sonia asked

19. The following states explained Ralph are the only ones we have ever visited: Texas, Florida, Georgia, and Arizona

20. Sherlock Holmes remarks, elementary, my dear Watson, in many of the stories, Nicole noted

15.0 Spelling

Spelling has been a problem for generations of students. However, if you want to improve your spelling, you can get plenty of first aid if you want it.

There is no simple way to teach you to spell. There is no easy way to learn. If you are concerned about the problem, however, there are several helpful suggestions:

1. **Proofread all your writing.** Even the ablest scholar may write "their" for "there" or "here" for "hear" in a first draft. Many apparent errors are not spelling errors at all. They are mistakes caused by carelessness and haste.

2. **Learn to look at the letters in a word.** Most of us have learned to read by recognizing whole words or parts of words. Spelling errors are errors in the letters that compose a word. You will find it helpful to break a word into its parts to see and to memorize the spelling of each part.

3. **Keep a list of your spelling errors.** The point is that you can spell correctly most of the words you use. Your errors fall within a narrow range. If you will concentrate on this range—provided by your list—you may show quick improvement.

4. **Practice on your own spelling problem.** There is no reason why you cannot totally eliminate spelling errors *if you want to*. One recommended procedure is to use a card pack. Print your problem words on cards in large letters. Take a card from the pack. Look at every letter and let the order of the letters sink into your mind. Pronounce each part of the word separately. Turn the card over. Write the word on a piece of paper. Turn the card over again and compare what you have written with the correct spelling.

5. Memorize and apply the few rules of spelling given below. Be sure you understand the rules, or your memory work will be wasted. Practice using the rules so that their use becomes automatic, and you can write *tapping, disappoint, receive,* and so on, quickly.

Exercise: Divide these words into syllables. Do not be concerned as to whether they conform to the dictionary division. Just make sure that every word part has a vowel sound.

1. occurrence	7. humorous	13. italicize
2. accidentally	8. specifically	14. miniature
3. accommodate	9. necessary	15. extraordinary
4. incredible	10. disappearance	16. secretarial
5. miscellaneous	11. mimeograph	17. athletic
6. maintenance	12. immediately	18. privilege

15.1 The Final Silent *e*

When a suffix beginning with a vowel is added to a word ending in a silent *e*, the *e* is usually dropped.

deceive + ing = deceiving   traverse + able = traversable
structure + al = structural   dose + age = dosage
trade + ing = trading   narrate + ion = narration
relate + ion = relation   delete + ion = deletion

When the final silent *e* is preceded by *c* or *g*, the *e* is usually retained before a suffix beginning with *a* or *o*.

trace + able = traceable   courage + ous = courageous
charge + able = chargeable   outrage + ous = outrageous

When a suffix beginning with a consonant is added to a word ending in a silent *e*, the *e* is usually retained.

grace + ful = graceful   face + less = faceless
love + ly = lovely   hope + ful = hopeful

These words are exceptions: *truly, argument, wholly, awful.*

15.2 Words Ending in y

When a suffix is added to a word ending in y preceded by a consonant, the y is usually changed to i.

There are two exceptions: (1) when -*ing* is added, the y does not change. (2) Some one-syllable words do not change the y: *dryness, shyness*.

happy + ness = happiness	marry + age = marriage
company + es = companies	marry + ing = marrying
carry + ed = carried	dally + ing = dallying

When a suffix is added to a word ending in y preceded by a vowel, the y usually does not change.

pray + ing = praying	destroy + er = destroyer
enjoy + ing = enjoying	coy + ness = coyness

Exceptions: day + ly = daily, gay + ly = gaily

Exercise A: Find the misspelled words in these sentences and spell them correctly.

1. We enjoyed sailing lazyly down the bay.
2. Mr. Howard has sent us an invitateion to meet a fameous artist.
3. She has done some architectureal work that is truly admireable.
4. The negotiators made a couragous effort to achieve a peaceable settlement.
5. There has been a noticable improvement in the safety record of our high school.
6. The caravan was moveing slowly along the icey road.
7. Creative talent can always profit from guideance.
8. Despite our arguements, the judge was immoveable.
9. The statement by the next witness was wholely false.
10. The cave was incredibely dark and terribly silent.
11. A recluse is lonly, but a hermit is lonelyer.
12. Zonkers is the crazyest dog imagineable.
13. The doctor is continueing an intenseive X-ray treatment.
14. The captain's arrival is useually prompt.

15. On the queen's sixtyeth birthday there was great merryment.
16. There was a certain hazyness about Jack's ideas.
17. The heavyer carriages were almost immoveable.
18. The earlyest Mayan writing is not easly deciphered.
19. The guide was very likeable, and her stories were exciteing.
20. We climbed clumsyly up the walls of the old fortifycations.

Exercise B: Add the suffixes as shown and write the new word.

1. mystery + ous	11. worry + ing	21. move + ment
2. relay + ing	12. carry + ed	22. change + able
3. body + ly	13. enjoy + able	23. charge + ing
4. frenzy + ed	14. create + ive	24. hurry + ing
5. appraise + ed	15. copy + ing	25. debate + able
6. waste + ful	16. educate + ion	26. hasty + ly
7. amaze + ing	17. assemble + age	27. merry + ly
8. insure + ance	18. wide + ly	28. easy + ly
9. grease + y	19. constitute + ion	29. day + ly
10. situate + ion	20. like + able	30. argue + ment

15.3 The Suffixes -*ness* and -*ly*

When the suffix -*ly* is added to a word ending in *l*, both *l*'s are retained. When -*ness* is added to a word ending in *n*, both *n*'s are retained.

real + ly = really   plain + ness = plainness
eternal + ly = eternally   mean + ness = meanness

15.4 The Addition of Prefixes

When a prefix is added to a word, the spelling of the word remains the same.

dis + approve = disapprove   dis + place = displace
mis + take = mistake   re + creation = recreation
im + balance = imbalance   trans + plant = transplant
il + legible = illegible   co + operate = cooperate

15.5 Words with the "Seed" Sound

Only one English word ends in *sede: supersede.*
Three words end in *ceed: exceed, proceed, succeed.*
All other words ending in the sound of *seed* are spelled *cede:*
secede, accede, recede, concede, precede.

Exercise A: Find the spelling errors in these sentences. Spell the words correctly. One sentence is correct.

1. Because of the thiness of the paper, the print shows through.
2. Despite hours of work on the project, Bob was disatisfied with the results.
3. Jeff peacefully admired the greeness of the countryside.
4. We usualy get a heavy snow in February.
5. Leaving the door unlocked was an iresponsible act.
6. The uneveness of the lettering ruins the whole sign.
7. The flower girl reentered and preceeded the bride down the aisle.
8. The statement is surly illogical.
9. We reccommend this restaurant; the food is extremly good.
10. Finaly, the stain dissappeared.
11. The lawyer said that the question was imaterial and irelevant.
12. Naturaly, we were dissappointed with our poor grades.
13. Several words on the ransom note were carefully misspelled.
14. The magician waved gracefuly and succeded in making a rabbit appear.
15. Samantha remained imobile while her sister cooly removed the splinter.
16. Cheating on taxes is not only ilegal but also imoral.
17. Alice proceded to pack the rest of the dishes more carefully.
18. Actualy, the tests are always preceeded by a review.
19. It is unecessary to excede the speed limit.
20. The doctor conceeded that eventualy an operation would be needed.

Exercise B: Add the suffixes and prefixes as indicated. Write the new word.

1. thin + ness	6. co + operate	11. confidential + ly
2. mis + state	7. incidental + ly	12. re + examine
3. ir + relevant	8. im + mobilize	13. dis + appear
4. im + moderate	9. uneven + ness	14. cordial + ly
5. dis + satisfied	10. im + moral	15. dis + agree

15.6 Words with *ie* and *ei*

When the sound is long *e* (ē), the word is spelled *ie* except after *c*.

I BEFORE E

retrieve	pier	chief
belief	shield	field
piece	brief	niece

EXCEPT AFTER C

receive	ceiling	deceive
perceive	conceit	receipt

Exceptions: *either, neither, financier, weird, species, seize, leisure.* You can remember these words by combining them into such a sentence as: *Neither financier seized either weird species of leisure.*

Exercise A: Correct the spelling errors in these sentences.

1. The peice in the newspaper about our play was very breif.
2. The preist sheilded the child from the attacking dog.
3. My niece is sitting in the first teir of seats.
4. The sentenced prisoner received a repreive.
5. The cheif carried a handsome sheild.
6. We do not beleive that the crop yeild will be good this year.
7. The banker gave her neice a reciept for the money.

8. You can just barely percieve the spot on the cieling.

9. The naturalist spotted a rare species of bird in the feild.

10. Niether of my parents has much liesure.

11. Conceit causes nearly as much trouble as deciet.

12. The caretaker weilded the mop like a baseball bat.

13. It is hard to beleive that the merchant's grief is real.

14. We were releived when the cornered thief yielded the gun to the police.

15. You could not concieve of a setting more wierd.

16. A chilling shreik peirced the silence.

17. The old lady waved a breif farewell with her handkercheif.

18. The cheif engineer has a peice of iron ore on her desk.

19. On a leisurely stroll to the peir, we retreived our lost paddle.

20. We percieved that some mischief was afoot.

Exercise B: Copy the words below, filling the blank spaces with *ie* or *ei*.

1. perc__ve	6. f__rce	11. gr__vance
2. n__ther	7. n__ce	12. hyg__ne
3. c__ling	8. sh__ld	13. p__r
4. rec__pt	9. s__ze	14. th__f
5. ch__f	10. p__ce	15. l__sure

15.7 Doubling the Final Consonant

Words of one syllable, ending in one consonant preceded by one vowel, double the final consonant before adding a suffix beginning with a vowel.

1. Words of one syllable ending in one consonant preceded by one vowel:

grab   dig   drug   slim

These words are the kind to which the rule applies.

These words double the final consonant if the suffix begins with a vowel.

grab + ing = grabbing   drug + ist = druggist
dig + er = digger   slim + est = slimmest

2. Words of one syllable ending in one consonant preceded by *two* vowels:

treat   feel   loot   clean

The rule does not apply to these one-syllable words because two vowels precede the final consonant.

3. The final consonant is doubled in words of more than one syllable:
When they end in one consonant preceded by one vowel.
When they are accented on the last syllable.

re·gret′   per·mit′   de·ter′

The same syllable is accented in the new word formed by adding the suffix:

re·gret′ + ed = re·gret′ted
per·mit′ + ing = per·mit′ting
de·ter′ + ence = de·ter′rence

If the newly formed word is accented on a different syllable, the final consonant is not doubled.

re·fer′ + ence = ref′er·ence
pre·fer′ + ence = pref′er·ence

Exercise A: Copy these words, indicating with an accent mark (′) where each word is accented.

1. control	6. regret	11. forget	16. differ
2. excel	7. allot	12. murmur	17. infer
3. limit	8. impel	13. defer	18. propel
4. resist	9. travel	14. benefit	19. submit
5. omit	10. distill	15. admit	20. begin

Exercise B: Add the ending indicated, and write the new word.

1. control + ing
2. bat + ed
3. compel + ed
4. bed + ing
5. differ + ence
6. limit + ed
7. commit + ed
8. book + ed
9. fur + y
10. disappear + ed
11. put + ing
12. get + ing
13. plan + ing
14. prefer + ed
15. sit + ing
16. remit + ance
17. transfer + ing
18. nod + ing
19. begin + ing
20. expel + ed
21. admit + ance
22. let + ing
23. pad + ed
24. murmur + ing
25. repel + ed
26. omit + ed
27. commit + ed
28. ton + age
29. allot + ed
30. defer + ed

15.8   Words Often Confused

capital means most important.
capitol is a building in which a state legislature meets.
the Capitol is the building in Washington, D.C., in which the United States Congress meets.

des'ert means a wilderness or dry, sandy region with sparse, scrubby vegetation.
de·sert means to abandon.
dessert (note the change in spelling) is a sweet such as cake or pie served at the end of a meal.

hear means to listen to, or take notice of.
here means in this place.

its is a word that indicates ownership.
it's is a contraction for *it is* or *it has*.

lose means to mislay or suffer the loss of something.
loose means free or not fastened.

principal describes something of chief or central importance. It also refers to the head of an elementary or high school.
principle is a basic truth, standard, or rule of behavior.

stationary means fixed or unmoving.
stationery refers to paper and envelopes used for writing letters.

there means in that place.
their means belonging to them.
they're is a contraction for *they are*.

to means toward, or in the direction of.
too means also or very.
two is the number 2.

weather refers to atmospheric conditions such as temperature or cloudiness.
whether helps express choice or alternative.

whose is the possessive form of *who*.
who's is a contraction for *who is* or *who has*.

your is the possessive form of *you*.
you're is a contraction for *you are*.

Exercise: Choose the right word from the words in parentheses.

1. For (desert, dessert) we had strawberry shortcake.
2. The Cubs' loyal fans refuse to (desert, dessert) them.
3. The cat arched (it's, its) back.
4. (It's, Its) too hot to play tennis today.
5. I was (there, their) on time.
6. They said (they're, their) names were Sam and Tamara.
7. (Their, They're) always first in line.
8. I am going (weather, whether) you go or not.
9. The (weather, whether) in August is hot and humid.
10. (Whose, Who's) got the tickets?
11. (Whose, Who's) dollar is this?
12. It's (your, you're) fault as much as mine.
13. Call me by ten if (your, you're) not going.
14. I hope the Hawks don't (lose, loose) tonight's game.
15. Somehow the puppies got (loose, lose).

16. Telling a lie is against my (principals, principles).
17. Ms. Happ is (principal, principle) at Brent High School.
18. We rode our bikes (too, to) the park.
19. The soup was (too, two, to) salty.
20. The North Star is almost (stationery, stationary).

A List of Commonly Misspelled Words

abbreviate	ab-bre-vi-ate	argument	ar-gu-ment
absence	ab-sence	arising	a-ris-ing
accidentally	ac-ci-den-tal-ly	arrangement	ar-range-ment
accommodate	ac-com-mo-date	ascend	as-cend
accompanying	ac-com-pa-ny-ing	assassinate	as-sas-si-nate
achievement	a-chieve-ment	associate	as-so-ci-ate
acknowledge	ac-know-ledge	attendance	at-tend-ance
acquaintance	ac-quaint-ance	audience	au-di-ence
across	a-cross	auxiliary	aux-il-ia-ry
address	ad-dress	awkward	awk-ward
all right	all right	bachelor	bach-e-lor
altogether	al-to-geth-er	balance	bal-ance
always	al-ways	bargain	bar-gain
amateur	am-a-teur	becoming	be-com-ing
analyze	an-a-lyze	beginning	be-gin-ning
annihilate	an-ni-hi-late	believe	be-lieve
anonymous	a-non-y-mous	benefited	ben-e-fit-ed
answer	an-swer	bicycle	bi-cy-cle
apologize	a-pol-o-gize	biscuit	bis-cuit
appearance	ap-pear-ance	bookkeeper	book-keep-er
appreciate	ap-pre-ci-ate	bulletin	bul-le-tin
appropriate	ap-pro-pri-ate	bureau	bu-reau
arctic	arc-tic	business	busi-ness

cafeteria	caf-e-te-ri-a	definitely	def-i-nite-ly
calendar	cal-en-dar	despair	de-spair
campaign	cam-paign	desperate	des-per-ate
candidate	can-di-date	dictionary	dic-tion-ar-y
cellophane	cel-lo-phane	dependent	de-pend-ent
cemetery	cem-e-ter-y	descent	de-scent
certain	cer-tain	description	de-scrip-tion
changeable	change-a-ble	desirable	de-sir-a-ble
characteristic	char-ac-ter-is-tic	different	dif-fer-ent
colonel	colo-nel	dining	din-ing
colossal	co-los-sal	diphtheria	diph-the-ri-a
column	col-umn	disagree	dis-a-gree
commission	com-mis-sion	disappear	dis-ap-pear
committed	com-mit-ted	disappoint	dis-ap-point
committee	com-mit-tee	discipline	dis-ci-pline
comparative	com-par-a-tive	dissatisfied	dis-sat-is-fied
compel	com-pel	economical	e-co-nom-i-cal
competitive	com-pet-i-tive	efficient	ef-fi-cient
complexion	com-plex-ion	eighth	eighth
compulsory	com-pul-so-ry	eligible	el-i-gi-ble
conscience	con-science	eliminate	e-lim-i-nate
conscientious	con-sci-en-tious	embarrass	em-bar-rass
conscious	con-scious	eminent	em-i-nent
consensus	con-sen-sus	emphasize	em-pha-size
contemptible	con-tempt-i-ble	environment	en-vi-ron-ment
convenience	con-ven-ience	enthusiastic	en-thu-si-as-tic
corps	corps	equipped	e-quipped
correspondence	cor-re-spond-ence	especially	es-pe-cial-ly
courageous	cou-ra-geous	etiquette	et-i-quette
courteous	cour-te-ous	exaggerate	ex-ag-ger-ate
criticism	crit-i-cism	excellent	ex-cel-lent
criticize	crit-i-cize	exceptional	ex-cep-tion-al
curiosity	cu-ri-os-i-ty	exhaust	ex-haust
cylinder	cyl-in-der	exhilarate	ex-hil-a-rate
dealt	dealt	existence	ex-ist-ence
decision	de-ci-sion	expense	ex-pense

experience	ex-pe-ri-ence	irrelevant	ir-rel-e-vant
familiar	fa-mil-iar	irresistible	ir-re-sist-i-ble
fascinating	fas-ci-nat-ing	knowledge	knowl-edge
fatigue	fa-tigue	laboratory	lab-o-ra-to-ry
February	Feb-ru-ar-y	legitimate	le-git-i-mate
feminine	fem-i-nine	leisure	lei-sure
financial	fi-nan-cial	lieutenant	lieu-ten-ant
foreign	for-eign	lightning	light-ning
forfeit	for-feit	literacy	lit-er-a-cy
fourth	fourth	literature	lit-er-a-ture
fragile	frag-ile	loneliness	lone-li-ness
generally	gen-er-al-ly	luxurious	lux-u-ri-ous
genius	gen-ius	maintenance	main-te-nance
government	gov-ern-ment	maneuver	ma-neu-ver
grammar	gram-mar	marriage	mar-riage
guarantee	guar-an-tee	mathematics	math-e-mat-ics
guard	guard	matinee	mat-i-nee
gymnasium	gym-na-si-um	medicine	med-i-cine
handkerchief	hand-ker-chief	medieval	me-di-e-val
height	height	microphone	mi-cro-phone
hindrance	hin-drance	miniature	min-i-a-ture
horizon	ho-ri-zon	minimum	min-i-mum
humorous	hu-mor-ous	mischievous	mis-chie-vous
imaginary	im-ag-i-nar-y	missile	mis-sile
immediately	im-me-di-ate-ly	misspell	mis-spell
incidentally	in-ci-den-tal-ly	mortgage	mort-gage
inconvenience	in-con-ven-ience	municipal	mu-nic-i-pal
incredible	in-cred-i-ble	necessary	nec-es-sar-y
indefinitely	in-def-i-nite-ly	nickel	nick-el
indispensable	in-dis-pen-sa-ble	ninety	nine-ty
inevitable	in-ev-i-ta-ble	noticeable	no-tice-a-ble
infinite	in-fi-nite	nuclear	nu-cle-ar
influence	in-flu-ence	nuisance	nui-sance
inoculation	in-oc-u-la-tion	obstacle	ob-sta-cle
intelligence	in-tel-li-gence	occasionally	oc-ca-sion-al-ly
interesting	in-ter-est-ing	occur	oc-cur

occurrence	oc-cur-rence	realize	re-al-ize
opinion	o-pin-ion	recognize	rec-og-nize
opportunity	op-por-tu-ni-ty	recommend	rec-om-mend
optimistic	op-ti-mis-tic	reference	ref-er-ence
original	o-rig-i-nal	referred	re-ferred
outrageous	out-ra-geous	rehearse	re-hearse
pamphlet	pam-phlet	reign	reign
parallel	par-al-lel	repetition	rep-e-ti-tion
parliament	par-lia-ment	representative	rep-re-sent-a-tive
particularly	par-tic-u-lar-ly	restaurant	res-tau-rant
pastime	pas-time	rhythm	rhythm
permanent	per-ma-nent	ridiculous	ri-dic-u-lous
permissible	per-mis-si-ble	sandwich	sand-wich
perseverance	per-se-ver-ance	schedule	sched-ule
perspiration	per-spi-ra-tion	scissors	scis-sors
persuade	per-suade	secretary	sec-re-tar-y
picnicking	pic-nick-ing	separate	sep-a-rate
pleasant	pleas-ant	sergeant	ser-geant
pneumonia	pneu-mo-ni-a	similar	sim-i-lar
politics	pol-i-tics	sincerely	sin-cere-ly
possess	pos-sess	sophomore	soph-o-more
possibility	pos-si-bil-i-ty	souvenir	sou-ve-nir
practice	prac-tice	specifically	spe-cif-i-cal-ly
preference	pref-er-ence	specimen	spec-i-men
prejudice	prej-u-dice	strategy	strat-e-gy
preparation	prep-a-ra-tion	strictly	strict-ly
privilege	priv-i-lege	subtle	sub-tle
probably	prob-a-bly	success	suc-cess
professor	pro-fes-sor	sufficient	suf-fi-cient
pronunciation	pro-nun-ci-a-tion	surprise	sur-prise
propeller	pro-pel-ler	syllable	syl-la-ble
prophecy	proph-e-cy	sympathy	sym-pa-thy
psychology	psy-chol-o-gy	symptom	symp-tom
pursue	pur-sue	tariff	tar-iff
quantity	quan-ti-ty	temperament	tem-per-a-ment
questionnaire	ques-tion-naire	temperature	tem-per-a-ture

thorough	thor-ough	unanimous	u-nan-i-mous
throughout	through-out	undoubtedly	un-doubt-ed-ly
together	to-geth-er	unnecessary	un-nec-es-sar-y
tomorrow	to-mor-row	vacuum	vac-u-um
traffic	traf-fic	vengeance	venge-ance
tragedy	trag-e-dy	vicinity	vi-cin-i-ty
transferred	trans-ferred	village	vil-lage
truly	tru-ly	villain	vil-lain
Tuesday	Tues-day	weird	weird
tyranny	tyr-an-ny	wholly	whol-ly
twelfth	twelfth	writing	writ-ing

REVIEW: SPELLING   This exercise is a review of Section 15. Correct the spelling errors in these sentences. One sentence is correct.

1. Peter checked the feild carfully for broken glass.
2. Rakeing leaves, I beleive, is Evie's chore.
3. The firefighter's actions were truely couragous.
4. Writeing precisly, Jeff copied the outline from the blackboard.
5. Mother usualy dissapproves of sugared snacks.
6. The caravan proceded on it's journey through the dessert.
7. The crowd claped and cheered as the two winners appearred.
8. Roger exceled at drawing inferrences in a logical way.
9. If these aren't you're books, then who's are they?
10. The pilot landed at one of the busyest airports.
11. Tyrone is enjoying a suspensful novel about ilegal spying.
12. One principle of friendship is openness of communication.
13. "The same wierd dream recured," Kim answerred.
14. The lookout percieved a stationery ship in the distance.
15. Lobbyists are generaly employed by companys and organizations.
16. Cecilia asked weather or not Dorothy Hamill would be skating in the ice show.
17. Donna happyly and gracfully accepted the award.
18. An arguement is innappropriate hear.
19. For desert I'd like a peice of cake and some creammy pudding to.
20. Trish's good cordination shows in the eveness of her gymnastics.

16.0 The Plurals of Nouns

16.1 Regular Formation of Plurals

The plural of most nouns is formed by adding s.

building + s = buildings   ground + s = grounds
yard + s = yards   carrot + s = carrots

16.2 Plurals Formed with *es*

The plural of nouns ending in *s*, *sh*, *ch*, *x*, and *z* is formed by adding *es*.

rash + es = rashes   crutch + es = crutches
bus + es = buses   box + es = boxes

16.3 Plurals of Nouns Ending in *y*

When a noun ends in *y* preceded by a consonant, the plural is formed by changing the *y* to *i* and adding *es*.

duty   duti + es = duties
party   parti + es = parties
pantry   pantri + es = pantries

When a noun ends in *y* preceded by a vowel, the plural is formed by adding *s*.

tray + s = trays   envoy + s = envoys
day + s = days   boy + s = boys
pulley + s = pulleys   foray + s = forays

16.4 Plurals of Nouns Ending in *o*

The plural of nouns ending in *o*, preceded by a vowel, is formed by adding *s*.

studio + s = studios	radio + s = radios
rodeo + s = rodeos	ratio + s = ratios
cameo + s = cameos	duo + s = duos

The plural of most nouns ending in *o*, preceded by a consonant, is formed by adding *s*, but for some nouns of this class the plural is formed by adding *es*.

piano + s = pianos	auto + s = autos
solo + s = solos	silo + s = silos
credo + s = credos	banjo + s = banjos
tomato + es = tomatoes	echo + es = echoes
potato + es = potatoes	hero + es = heroes

There are some words ending in -o with a preceding consonant that may form the plural with either *s* or *es*: *motto, zero, mosquito*. The safest thing to do is to memorize the few words that add *-es* and to consult the dictionary when in doubt about others.

16.5 Plurals of Nouns Ending in *f* or *ff*

The plural of most nouns ending in *f* or *ff* is formed regularly by adding *s*.

roof + s = roofs	dwarf + s = dwarfs
belief + s = beliefs	handkerchief + s = handkerchiefs
gulf + s = gulfs	staff + s = staffs

The plural of some nouns ending in *f* or *fe* is formed by changing the *f* or *fe* to *ve* and adding *s*.

calf—calves	shelf—shelves	self—selves
life—lives	knife—knives	wharf—wharves
half—halves	loaf—loaves	leaf—leaves

Since most of these words with irregular plurals are in common use, careful listening may help you to spell them correctly. If you are doubtful about spelling, however, look up the singular form of the word in a dictionary. If the plural of a word is irregularly formed, the plural will be given immediately after the singular.

16.6 Nouns with Irregular Plurals

The plural of some nouns is formed by a change of spelling.

tooth—teeth	goose—geese
man—men	mouse—mice
woman—women	ox—oxen
child—children	basis—bases
datum—data	phenomenon—phenomena
crisis—crises	hypothesis—hypotheses

The plural and singular forms are the same for a few nouns.

sheep	corps	Japanese
deer	moose	Swiss

16.7 The Plurals of Names

The plural of a name is formed by adding s or es.

Albert Steele—the Steeles	Jack Amos—the Amoses
Judy Lyons—the Lyonses	Bob Sable—the Sables

16.8 The Plurals of Compound Nouns

When a compound noun is written without a hyphen, the plural is formed at the end of the word.

armful + s = armfuls	teaspoonful + s = teaspoonfuls
cupful + s = cupfuls	skateboard + s = skateboards

When a compound noun is made up of a noun plus a modifier, the plural is added to the noun.

mothers-in-law (the phrase *in law* is a modifier.)
editors-in-chief (the phrase *in chief* is a modifier.)
attorneys-general (*general* modifies *attorneys.*)
notaries public (*public* modifies *notaries.*)
passers-by (*by* modifies *passers.*)
bills of sale (the phrase *of sale* modifies *bills.*)

The following are exceptions: *drive-ins, stand-bys, lean-tos.*

Exercise A: Form the plural of each of the following words.

1. holiday	11. studio	21. tablespoonful
2. herd	12. county	22. father-in-law
3. glass	13. valley	23. drive-in
4. radio	14. belief	24. attorney-general
5. dash	15. potato	25. right of way
6. hero	16. handkerchief	26. chief of police
7. watch	17. grief	27. clerk of court
8. laboratory	18. hypothesis	28. Supreme Court Justice
9. lady	19. datum	29. bill of sale
10. cupful	20. basis	30. notary public

Exercise B: Find the errors in plural forms in the following sentences. Write the plurals correctly.

1. The economists do not have enough datums to explain what has happened.

2. There are several hypothesis to explain the twin moons of Mars.

3. We have two brother-in-laws living in Elmira.

4. Don't use more than three cupsful of flour.

5. How many leafs are missing from your book?

6. What vegetables shall we have besides potatos and tomatos?

7. There are several solos for the sopranoes.

8. There are not many home studioes big enough for two pianos.

9. After church, we stopped to chat with the March's and the Lyons's.

10. In yesterday's game, Rudi made two sensational catchs.

11. American prisoners have suffered cruelties in some foreign countrys.

12. The two mother-in-laws are great friends.

13. Not many countrys have only two major political partys.

14. There are too many autoes on the streets of our citys.

15. Even during routine dutys, the researchers discovered interesting phenomenons.

16. The Chineses have a very ancient civilization.

17. We need more than two notary publics in this big company.

18. Elena brought several armsful of wood into the house.

19. In the spring the mooses move north through the valleys.

20. The sheeps on the range are carefully protected against wolfs.

21. These heros lost their lifes in scientific research for mankind's benefit.

22. Several hanger-ons were waiting for the partys to break up.

23. There are two boxs of matchs in the kitchen cupboard.

24. The thiefs turned out to be brother-in-laws.

25. With their knifes the workers cut big gashs in the trunks of the trees.

REVIEW: THE PLURALS OF NOUNS This exercise is a review of Section 16. Form the plural of each of the following words.

1. desk	11. loaf
2. crutch	12. chef
3. paradox	13. freshman
4. convoy	14. moose
5. opportunity	15. crisis
6. tomato	16. Barnes
7. echo	17. handful
8. alto	18. bookcase
9. radio	19. sister-in-law
10. self	20. editor-in-chief

17.0 Good Manuscript Form

Readers will surely be more impressed with a paper that is neat and legible than with one that is messy and hard to read. Good manuscript form increases the impact of what a writer says. Many high schools and colleges have regular forms that students are expected to follow. Others require that students follow the manuscript form described below.

17.1 Legible Writing

Few schools require that student papers be typewritten. A typed paper, however, is easier to read than one written by hand.

If a paper is written by hand, it should be written with pen, in a dark blue or black ink. An ink of any other color is not acceptable. Letters should be formed so that there is no doubt as to what they are: *a*'s and *o*'s should be distinctly different; *u*'s and *i*'s should be distinct; if *i*'s are dotted, there can be no chance of their being mistaken for *e*'s.

17.2 Margins and Spacing

Leave a margin of an inch at the top, the bottom, and the right side of each page. The left margin should be slightly wider. If a paper is typed, the left-hand margin must be carefully maintained. The right-hand margin should be approximately the same, and it should be as even as possible without an excess of hyphens to show the break in a word. It is a good rule not to permit more than two successive lines to end with a hyphen.

All typed copy should be prepared with a double space between lines. Usually five letter spaces are provided for each paragraph indention. One space separates each word; two spaces follow the end punctuation of a sentence. If material must be deleted, it can be struck out by *x*'s or capital *M*'s.

17.3 Proper Labeling

Your teacher will give you instructions on the heading for your papers. Follow these instructions exactly. Usually, you will be expected to place your name at the upper right-hand corner of the first page. On a line below your name, you will place the name or number of the course, and on a third line, you will place the date.

Number each page beginning with page two. (Do not number the first page.) The number may be placed in the upper right-hand corner. To guard against loss or misplacement, you may place your name under the page number.

17.4 Placement of the Title

The title of a paper appears only on the first page. Place the title two lines below the last line of your heading, and center it. Allow two lines between the title and the first line of your copy.

Capitalize the first word and all important words in the title. See Section 10.12. If you are typing, do not capitalize every letter but only the initial letters. Do not underline the title; do not place it in quotation marks unless it is a quotation from some other source.

If a paper is longer than three or four pages, your teacher may ask you to supply a title page. This is a separate page containing the heading in the upper right-hand corner and the title centered on the page.

17.5   Preparation of Final Copy

It is almost impossible to write a paper exactly as you want it the first time. After you have written your first draft, read it over carefully. Revise and correct it. After you have completed your revision, make a final copy. Then read over this copy.

You may find that you have left out words, or you may find errors. You can insert words neatly by writing above the line where they should appear and by using a caret (∧) to show their position. You can make corrections neatly by drawing a line through a word and writing the correction above it. If more than two or three corrections per page are necessary, recopy the page.

17.6   Numbers in Writing

Numbers that can be expressed in fewer than four words are usually spelled out; longer numbers are written in figures.

They gathered *thirty-one* bushels of apples in one day.
The piggy bank yielded *thirteen* dollars.
The tickets are selling for *eight* dollars each.
The loss amounted to $4,280.

A number beginning a sentence is spelled out.

Eight hundred were suddenly made homeless by the flood.
Twenty-five minutes passed without a word from Hugh.

17.7   Figures in Writing

Figures are used to express dates, street and room numbers, telephone numbers, page numbers, decimals, and percentages.

Shakespeare's birth date was April 23, 1564.
Carol lives at 5457 Guarino Road.
The English class is in room 312.
Is your telephone number 257-4353?
We were asked to learn the poem on page 80.
Last week the temperature reached 101 degrees.
Fred had 98 percent right in the physics test.

Note: Commas are used to separate the figures in sums of money or expressions of large quantities. They are not used in dates, serial numbers, page numbers, addresses, or telephone numbers.

RIGHT: Terry had saved $1,270 for the trip to Europe.
RIGHT: Bernie now owns more than 100,000 stamps.

WRONG: Washington died in 1,799.
RIGHT: Washington died in 1799.

Exercise: Copy these sentences, correcting any errors in the writing of figures. Some sentences are correct.

1. There are now two hundred thousand volumes in the library.
2. 7 of the students in my class worked on the float for the parade.
3. When we arrived in Duluth, it was twenty degrees below zero.
4. The cost of the land alone is $7,500.
5. Nearly sixty percent of high school graduates now go on to college.
6. The offices are now located at 1,741 Broadway.
7. The satellite whirled about the earth every four and three-tenths minutes.
8. New Orleans then had a population of 125,000.
9. Our room number is four twenty-six.
10. We have had 2,275 replies to our letter.
11. The telephone number here is 275–4,000.
12. The date on the flyleaf was eighteen hundred ninety seven.
13. Helen's new address is two hundred twenty East End Avenue.
14. We have room for only 700 students in the college.
15. More than 500 students are singing in the all-state chorus.

17.8 Abbreviations in Writing

Abbreviations may be used for most titles before and after proper names, for names of government agencies, and in dates.

BEFORE PROPER NAMES: Dr., Mr., Mrs., Ms., Messrs., Rev., Hon., Gov., Sgt.

AFTER PROPER NAMES:	Jr., Sr., M.D., Ph.D.
GOVERNMENT AGENCIES:	CIA, FCC, FDA
DATES AND TIME:	A.D., B.C., A.M., P.M.

There are no periods after abbreviations of government agencies. The abbreviations of titles are acceptable only when used as part of a name. It is not acceptable to write *The pres. of the club is a dr.* The titles *Honorable* and *Reverend* are not abbreviated when preceded by *the*: *The Honorable Lois Tate.* They appear with the person's full name, not just the last name. Abbreviations are not appropriate for the President and Vice-President of the United States.

In ordinary writing, abbreviations are not acceptable for names of countries and states, months and days of the week, nor for words that are part of addresses or firm names.

UNACCEPTABLE:	We spent a month in Ariz.
BETTER:	We spent a month in Arizona.
UNACCEPTABLE:	I have never been to Toronto, Ont.
BETTER:	I have never been to Toronto, Ontario.
UNACCEPTABLE:	Miller's play opened on Thurs., Jan. 23.
BETTER:	Miller's play opened on Thursday, January 23.
UNACCEPTABLE:	Pay your bill to the Bell Tel. Co.
BETTER:	Pay your bill to the Bell Telephone Company.

In ordinary writing, abbreviations are not acceptable for the following: names of school courses, *page*, *chapter*, *Christmas*, and words standing for measurements such as *km., mi., ml., hr., lb.*

17.9 The Hyphen

At the end of a line, use a hyphen to divide a word between syllables.

Tracy Austin has charmed and aston-
ished fans with a lively brand of tennis.

Note: Each line should have at least two letters of the hyphenated word.

Use a hyphen in any compound word that requires one. Check a dictionary for correct hyphenation.

trade-in	T-shirt	sister-in-law	show-off
play-off	vice-president	ten-year-old	close-up

Words used together as an adjective before a noun are usually hyphenated.

hard-working student	middle-income salary
good-looking bike	two-career family
long-distance call	real-life story
well-balanced meal	quick-drying fabric

However, when the same words are used after the noun, they often are not hyphenated.

CORRECT: We found a well-informed source.
CORRECT: The source was well informed.

Compound numbers between twenty-one and ninety-nine are hyphenated, as are fractions, such as *two-thirds* and *one one-hundredth.*

Some proper nouns with prefixes and suffixes attached to them require a hyphen.

ex-Governor   all-American   Cosby-like

Exercise: Correct the errors in the following sentences.

1. The Rev. Carol Anderson, D. D., is one of the speakers.
2. Your reservation is on Am. Airlines for next Saturday.
3. Twelve year old Pam is the youngest student at Mather H. S.
4. The Hershey Co. is located in Hershey, Pa.
5. For twenty three days during Aug. Anita will be traveling in Ire.
6. Mr. Walsh and Jas. Perrin are at a convention in Denver, Colo.
7. Bob has an appointment with Dr. Kim at 4:00 P M on Fri.
8. Ms. Marks has just been made vice pres. of the bank.
9. The long awaited Xmas vacation will start on Dec. 21.

10. Our bio. assignment is to read pp. 46 to 62.
11. The well meaning club secy. has very little to do.
12. We used to live in Ill., but then we moved to Mich.
13. The dr. delivered a baby that weighed 7 lb. 8 oz.
14. Augustus ruled the Roman Emp. from 27 B.C. to A.D. 14.
15. In northern Minnesota, I once caught a pike 16 in. long.

17.10 Italics for Titles

The word *italics* is a printer's term. It refers to a kind of type. When a writer wants to indicate that a word is in italics, he or she underlines it in the manuscript.

Titles of complete books and plays, of newspapers, magazines, works of art, and long musical compositions are printed in italics. The names of ships, trains, and airplanes are also printed in italics.

MANUSCRIPT FORM: I never miss the ads in Seventeen.
PRINTED FORM: I never miss the ads in *Seventeen*.

MANUSCRIPT FORM: Gian Carlo Menotti's best-known opera is Amahl and the Night Visitors.
PRINTED FORM: Gian Carlo Menotti's best-known opera is *Amahl and the Night Visitors*.

MANUSCRIPT FORM: The front page of The New York Times showed the President boarding Air Force One.
PRINTED FORM: The front page of *The New York Times* showed the President boarding *Air Force One*.

17.11 Italics for Foreign Words and Phrases

Many foreign words have become so widely used that they are now part of the English language: *slalom, spaghetti, gourmet*. These naturalized words are printed in regular type. Foreign words and phrases that have not become naturalized in our language are printed in italics: *cum laude, mañana, Gesundheit.*

The only way to be sure whether a word or phrase of foreign origin should be printed in italics (underlined in manuscript) is to consult the dictionary.

17.12   Italics for Words, Letters, or Figures

Italics are used for words, letters, or figures referred to as such.

In printed works, words, letters, or figures referred to as such are in italics. In writing, they are underlined.

MANUSCRIPT FORM: In England, <u>either</u> is pronounced <u>eyether</u>.
PRINTED FORM: In England, *either* is pronounced *eyether*.

MANUSCRIPT FORM: Road signs have given <u>slow</u> the status of an adverb.
PRINTED FORM: Road signs have given *slow* the status of an adverb.

17.13   Italics for Emphasis

Italics (underlining) are used to give special emphasis to words or phrases.

The tendency in modern writing is to avoid the use of italics for emphasis. One reason is that italic type is considered harder to read than regular (roman) type, particularly if there is a great deal of it. Another reason is that modern writers are developing a direct, straightforward style which gives emphasis to important words without use of printing devices.

In high school writing, use italics for emphasis only to make meaning clear.

Woman's place *was* in the home; it certainly isn't today.
"Have you *ever* seen such a mess!" Mother exclaimed.

17.14   Correction Symbols and Revision

Both in high school and in college your teachers will make marginal notes on your themes and reports before returning them to you. These notes will indicate errors or awkward passages that require rewriting. The correction of errors will make you alert to their recurrence in your later writing. Practice in rephrasing awkward sentences will give you greater skill in turning out careful, clear writing that means what you want it to mean.

Many schools and colleges have their own system of briefly indicating writing faults. If your school has such a system of abbreviations, it will be made available to you. Your teachers may prefer to use the symbols listed below. These are symbols used by professional copyreaders who work for publishers. The manuscript bearing the marks is returned to the author, no matter how experienced or professional she or he may be, for correction and revision before the manuscript is set in type.

ab	*Abbreviation.* Either the abbreviation is not appropriate, or the abbreviation is wrong. Consult a dictionary.
agr	*Agreement.* You have made an error in agreement of subject and verb, or of pronoun and antecedent. Consult Sections 5.1 and 6.13 in your Handbook.
awk	*Awkward.* The sentence is clumsy. Rewrite it.
cap	*Capital letters.* You have omitted necessary capitals. Consult Section 10 in your Handbook.
cf	*Comma fault.* You have joined two sentences with a comma. Change the punctuation.
dang	*Dangling construction.* You have written a verbal phrase in such a way that it does not tie up to another word in the sentence. Rewrite the sentence.
frag	*Sentence fragment.* You have placed a period after a group of words that is not a sentence. Join the fragment to an existing sentence or add words to complete the thought.

ital	*Italics.* You have omitted italics that are needed.
k	*Awkward.* See *awk* above.
lc	*Lower case.* You have mistakenly used a capital letter where a small letter is required.
ms	*Manuscript form.* You have not followed the proper manuscript form. Consult Section 17 in your Handbook.
no ¶	*No paragraph.* You have started a new paragraph too soon. Join these sentences to the preceding paragraph.
¶	*Paragraph.* Begin a new paragraph at this point.
nc	*Not clear.* Your meaning is not clear. Rewrite the passage to say what you mean.
om	*Omission.* You have left out words that are needed for clarity or smoothness of style.
p	*Punctuation.* You have made an error in punctuation. Consult Section 11 in your Handbook for sentences like the one you have improperly punctuated.
ref	*Reference.* There is an error or a weakness in the reference of pronoun to antecedent. Consult Section 6 in your Handbook.
rep	*Repetition.* You have repeated a word too often, or you have repeated something you wrote in preceding sentences.
shift	*Shift.* You have shifted point of view or tense needlessly.
sp	*Spelling.* You have misspelled a word. Consult a dictionary.
t	*Tense.* You have used the wrong tense form. Consult Section 8 in your Handbook.
tr	*Transpose.* Your meaning would be more clear if a sentence or passage were placed at another point.
wd	*Wrong word.* You have confused homonyms, or you have used a word that does not fit the meaning. Consult a dictionary.

REVIEW: GOOD MANUSCRIPT FORM   This exercise is a review of Section 17. Copy the following sentences, correcting the errors in italics, abbreviation, hyphenation, and the writing of figures.

1. The play offs are between Clemente H. S. and Loyola Acad.
2. That 15 min. phone call cost $5.12, Dr. Kowinski.
3. Dial 936-1,212 for the Natl. Weather Serv. forecast.
4. A kilogram equals 2.2 lbs., and a gram equals .035 oz.
5. According to a writer in *The New York Times,* the word lifestyle is being overused.
6. 24 well qualified students were elected to Student Assoc.
7. St. Patrick's Day is celebrated on Mar. seventeenth.
8. The P.T.A. has its headquarters at seven hundred N. Rush St., Chicago, Ill.
9. The chart on page sixty of Modern Biology explains the classification of vertebrates.
10. Canada is divided into 10 provinces, just as the U.S. is divided into 50 states.
11. The largest lake in the world is the Caspian Sea with an area of 143550 sq. mi.
12. The Pres.'s appointments secy. declined three fourths of the invitations.
13. About seventy five percent of all active volcanoes are located in an area called the "Ring of Fire."
14. The ocean liner Queen Elizabeth weighed 83673 tons.
15. Birgitta has that all knowing attitude that some people call savoir-faire.
16. 60,000 people attended the all star benefit performance at Madison Sq. Garden.
17. The Osmonds are a close knit family.
18. Britishers use the word petrol when they refer to gasoline.
19. Is the St. Louis Post-Dispatch a pro Republican newspaper?
20. In all states but 4, women may marry at age 18 without consent of their parents.

18.0 Outlining

Outlining is a valuable tool. It is used for two purposes: (1) for taking notes and (2) for planning a composition. A good outline is like a road map. It helps the note-taker to see where he or she is. It helps the writer to see where he or she is going. An outline diagrams the basic course of a piece of writing or a talk.

18.1 Outlines in Note-Taking

In many situations outlined notes are helpful. You may be doing background reading to gather information for a report or paper. You may be studying for an important test. You may be listening to a lecture or a speech. In any case, outlining the information will help you to remember it, to see the author's or speaker's reasoning, and to summarize the material. You will find that you can learn more from your reading or listening if you outline.

For outlined notes, the goal is to pick out important ideas and their relation to each other. Before you begin to read an article or other written selection, look it over quickly. Note headings and titles. Such scanning can give you an idea of the organization of the piece. In a speech or lecture, listen for changes in topic and for explanations of main topics.

To write the outline, recognize and write down the main points as main headings in the outline. Outline the explanation or development of these main points as subheadings. Summarize the purpose of the talk or written piece at the top of the outline.

18.2 Outlines in Organizing Compositions

An outline is vital for organizing a good composition. Before making an outline, however, you must gather information related to the purpose of your paper. All information in the outline must directly develop the purpose of the composition. Once you have gathered enough relevant information, the outline will give you a scheme for organizing it.

First, study your purpose and your ideas for the paper. Determine which ideas are most important for developing the purpose. These will be the main topics of the outline.

Then group the remaining ideas under the main topics that they relate to. These will be the subpoints and their supporting details.

A final question is how to organize the main points and the subpoints under them. Some compositions are most logically organized in time sequence, in ascending importance, or by increasing complexity. The best order is the one that is clearest and most understandable for the topic.

Your finished outline will be the pattern for a well-organized composition.

18.3 Kinds of Outlines

An outline may be one of two kinds: (1) a **topic outline** or (2) a **sentence outline.**

The topic outline uses words or phrases instead of complete sentences. It is most appropriate for quick note-taking or for informal organizing.

An example of notes taken in topic outline form is shown on the next page.

How To Make Pottery

The purpose of the article is to explain how to make clay pottery.

I. Preparing the clay
  A. Purify the clay
  B. Mix the clay with water
  C. Knead the clay

II. Shaping the clay
  A. Hand-building
  B. Throwing it on the potter's wheel
    1. Design of wheel
    2. Technique of throwing
  C. Molding

III. Decorating the pottery
  A. Scratched designs
  B. Underglazing

IV. Firing in the kiln

V. Glazing the pottery
  A. Brushing
  B. Spraying
  C. Dipping

VI. Refiring the pottery

The sentence outline, using complete sentences, is most effective for notes that will be studied later or for formal writing purposes.

The following is an example of a sentence outline. It provides a skeleton for a composition on school activities.

Activities Rate Good Grades

Purpose: Extracurricular activities, such as participation in clubs and athletics, improve the high school experience.

I. Participation in extracurricular activities makes students happier in school.
  A. Activities of interest provide pleasure.
  B. Succeeding at activities builds pride.
  C. Enjoyable friendships grow through activities.
    1. Activities let students meet new people.
      a. Students get to know other students.
      b. Students and teachers get to know each other outside of class.
    2. Students in activities belong to a group.

II. Participation in extracurricular activities helps students to identify with the school.
  A. They get to know the school better.
  B. They feel like part of the school as a whole.
  C. Their service to the school is appreciated.

III. Participation in extracurricular activities gives students a better attitude toward learning.
  A. Students can approach schoolwork feeling refreshed.
    1. Interacting with teachers and students outside the classroom is stimulating.
    2. Activities are diversions from the regular schedule.
  B. Students have more incentive to succeed in schoolwork.
  C. Students organize their time and, therefore, learn more efficiently.
  D. Students learn about their potential in areas not always offered in the regular curriculum.
    1. Students develop new skills.
    2. New skills open doors to opportunities.

18.4 Outline Form

In general, the same form applies to both topic and sentence outlining.

1. Begin by placing the title at the top of the page. Under it, write the purpose. These are not items in the outline. The introduction and the conclusion are usually not part of the outline either.

2. Use the following arrangement of numerals and letters: Roman numerals for main topics and capital letters for subtopics, then numbers for points that develop the subtopics. Small letters are for subpoints under these points, numbers in parentheses for details developing the subpoints, and finally small letters in parentheses for subdetails. Always divide your subtopics in descending order of importance.

I.

  A.

  B.

    1.

    2.

      a.

      b.

        (1)

        (2)

          (a)

          (b)

II.

  A.

  B.

  (and so on)

3. Indent each division of the outline. Put the letter or numeral directly under the first letter in the first word of the larger heading above.

4. Do not use a single subheading. There must be at least two. For example, if there is a *1* under A, there must also be at least a *2*. An idea cannot be broken down into fewer than two parts.

5. In a topic outline, keep items of the same rank in parallel form. For instance, if A is a noun, then B and C should also be nouns. If *1* is a prepositional phrase, then 2 and 3 should also be prepositional phrases.

6. Begin each item with a capital letter. Do not use end punctuation in a topic outline.

Exercise: Below is a partial topic outline. Complete the outline by inserting the following headings in the appropriate blanks:

Poisoning	Severe bleeding
Avoiding movement of victim	Burns
Reassuring the victim	To prevent worsening
Fractures	For cuts or wounds
Frostbite	Treatment of shock
To ease pain	Symptoms of shock
Situations requiring first aid	

First Steps to First Aid

First aid techniques can provide emergency treatment until medical help arrives.

I. Goals of first aid

    A.

    B.

    C. To soothe fears

II. General techniques of first aid

    A. Staying calm

    B.

C. Examining the victim
   1. For burns
   2.
   3. For fractures
D.
E. Preventing shock
   1.
   2.
      a. Covers
      b. Hot drinks

III.

A. Animal bites
B.
C. Asphyxiation
D.
E.
F. Fainting
G. Heatstroke
H.
I.
J. Severe cuts

REVIEW: OUTLINING   Here is a review of Section 18. In this topic outline, the headings beside the Roman numerals are correct. Most of the other items are jumbled. Copy the outline and rearrange the items to make each subheading logically fit beneath its heading.

Our Noisy Earth

Noise pollution is a threat to our well-being.

I. Sources of noise pollution

    A. Loss of hearing

        1. Stricter laws

        2. Cars

        3. Mental tension

        4. Physical tension

        5. Industrial machinery

    B. Emotional tension

II. Effects of noise pollution

    A. Vehicles

    B. Increase of tension

        1. Better planning

        2. Buses

        3. Motorcycles

    C. Airplanes

III. Solutions for noise pollution

    A. Trucks

    B. Loss of energy

    C. More citizen concern

Acknowledgments

William Collins Publishers, Inc., for entries from *Webster's New World Dictionary of the American Language, Students Edition,* appearing on pages 22-23, 24, 25, 27, and 28. Theodore L. Thomas, for *Test* by Theodore L. Thomas, copyright © 1962 by Mercury Press, Inc. (reprinted by permission of the author from *The Magazine of Fantasy and Science Fiction*). Simon and Schuster, Inc., for a selection from *The Inland Island* by Josephine W. Johnson. William Morrow & Company, for a selection from *Icebergs for Sale* by Gwen Schultz, copyright © 1979 by Gwen Schultz. Penguin Books, Inc., for "The Passing" by Durango Mendoza. Random House, Inc., for a selection from "The Great Deeps," from *The Immense Journey* by Loren Eiseley, copyright 1951 by Loren Eiseley.

Editor-in-Chief: Joseph F. Littell
Editorial Director, English Programs: Joy Littell
Managing Editor: Kathleen Laya
Assistant Editors: Bonnie Dobkin, Joseph L. Page

Cover design: Sandra Gelak
Art production and handwritten art: Kenneth Izzi
Diagrams: Amy Palmer

Index

Handbook